ALL ABOUT

# Windows 11

**All About Windows 11**
Published by Black Dog Media Limited.
Registered in England & Wales No: 05311511
www.bdmpublications.com

Managing Editor: James Gale
Editorial Contributors: Russ Ware & David Hayward
Production Director: Mark Ayshford
Design: Karl Linstead

UK & European distribution: CBL Distribution Limited
www.cbldistributionltd.co.uk



Printed and bound in the United Kingdom by:
CMP (UK) Limited
www.cmp-uk.com

**ISBN: 978-1-914231-03-2**

# Chapter 1

# Windows 11 Beginner



# Chapter 2

# Windows 11 Intermediate

# Chapter 3
# Windows 11 Advanced

Chapter 1

# Windows 11 Beginner

In this chapter we will look to the basics of Windows 11. You'll discover its new features and how it all works, and you'll begin to build a solid foundation to help you throughout your Windows 11 lifetime.

From here on you will explore what makes Windows 11 great, as well as learning some valuable new technical skills.

# Updating to Windows 11

**If you're still on Windows 10, rather than tweaking with the update settings, or delving into the murky depths of the command prompt, there's a much easier way to start the ball rolling and get you up and running as soon as possible with Windows 11.**

## Before You Leap

Before we go about running the update process, it's worth checking that your system can actually run Windows 11. Many of us have already been down this route, and have discovered that we need to apply a few elements prior to installing the newest operating system from Microsoft.

## TPM 2.0

The hot story of the year, concerning Windows 11, was of course Microsoft's need for a Windows 11 computer to have a working TPM 2.0 element. Many users had their excitement of installing Windows 11 squashed when they found out that their motherboard didn't have any sign of a TPM, but what is it?

TPM stands for Trusted Platform Module, and its task is to protect data through authentication, perform platform integrity, utilise disk encryption, and store passwords and certificates. In short, it's an extra layer of hardware protection to help stop your computer from being compromised or to stop any forms of malware from infecting the core components of your computer.

Now that you know what TPM is, you can begin to understand Microsoft's insistence of it being present before even allowing Windows 11 to be installed. Windows is, by quite a margin, the most popular operating system in the world, and as such it's the main target for malware and other such unpleasant things out there in the wild. By using TPM, Microsoft is under the opinion that it's making things a little more difficult for hackers and creators of malware. It is, however, totally possible to bypass the TPM requirements.

Anyway, in general, if your computer is reasonably up to date, or roughly less than four years old, then there's a good chance that you have a TPM present in your system. For some systems, TPM comes in the form of an actual module that physically plugs into a socket on your motherboard, for most computers, though, TPM is offered via the processor.

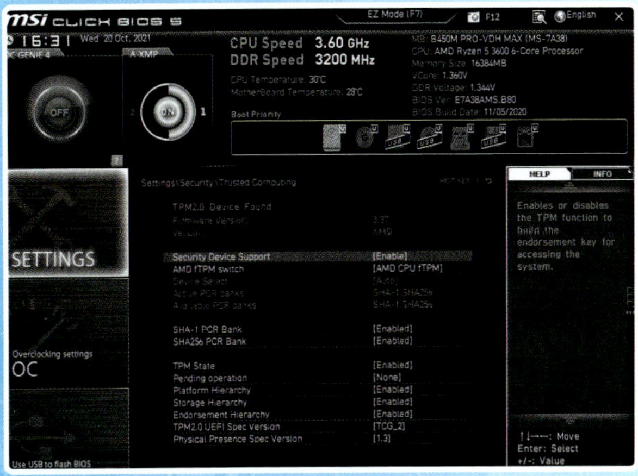


What you will need to do is drop into your BIOS, this can normally be done by tapping either the Del or F2 keys when you first power up your computer (before it starts to boot into Windows). Naturally, different motherboard manufacturers offer different keypresses, so you'll need to check with your manual.

When in the BIOS, look for Settings > Security > Trusted Computing. If you've got an AMD processor, you may also have to look for AMD CPU fTPM. Enable both, if available, save the settings and reboot the computer.

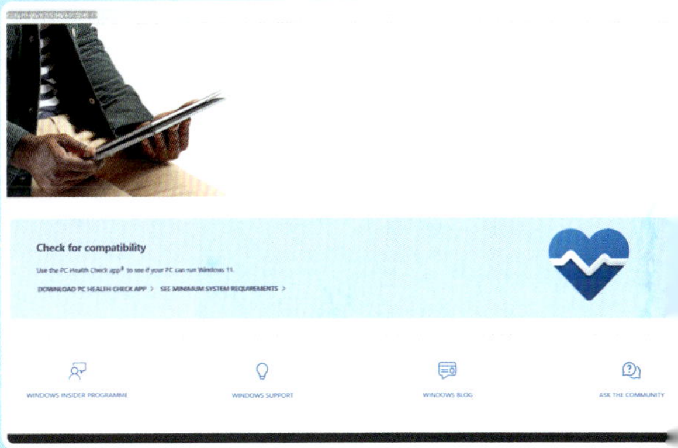


These entries will differ from one motherboard to the next, as previously mentioned. You may need to Google your motherboard make and model number, together with the words 'enable TPM', to see how to specifically enable it for you.

Once enabled, and rebooted into Windows 10, go to https://www.microsoft.com/en-gb/windows/windows-11, and scroll to the bottom of the page and click on the Download PC Health Check App button.

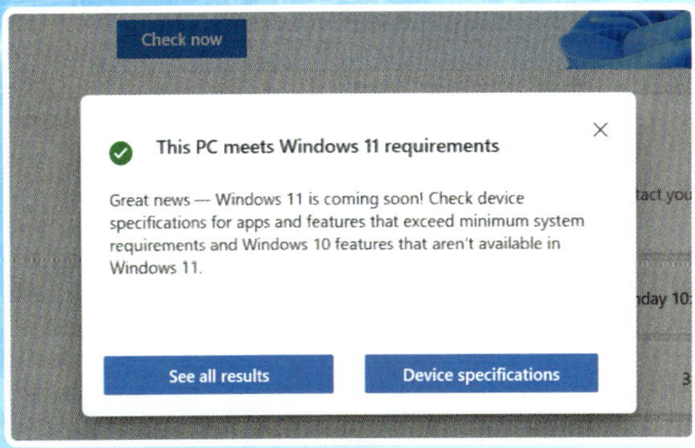


Once it's downloaded, double-click to install it. When installed, run the Health Check App, and look for the Check Now button in the Introduction Windows 11 section. Click it, and you'll be given a report as to whether your computer can run Windows 11 or not. If not, you're told where it's failed and you can look up what to do next.

# The Installation Assistant

**Microsoft has made the forced upgrade to Windows 11 very easy. If you have a Windows 10 computer, to upgrade it to Windows 11, all you'll need is the Windows Installation Assistant, and a quick check to ensure Windows 10 is the correct version.**

## Installing Windows 11

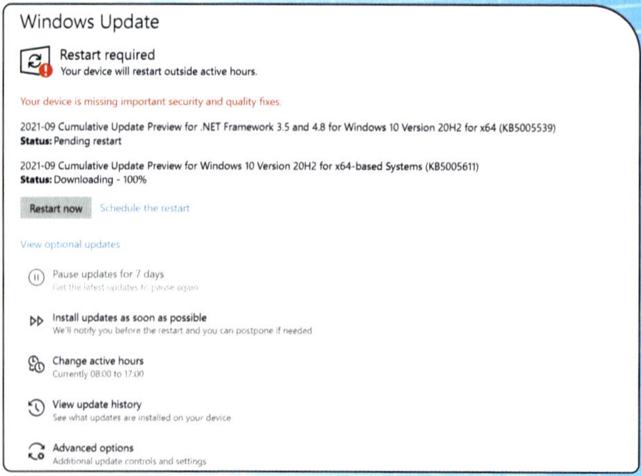


To force the update to Windows 11, providing your computer can handle it, you'll need to run the Windows 11 Installation Assistant. This is a separate app that enables Windows 10 users, who have a valid Windows license, to update their computers to the latest version of Windows 11.

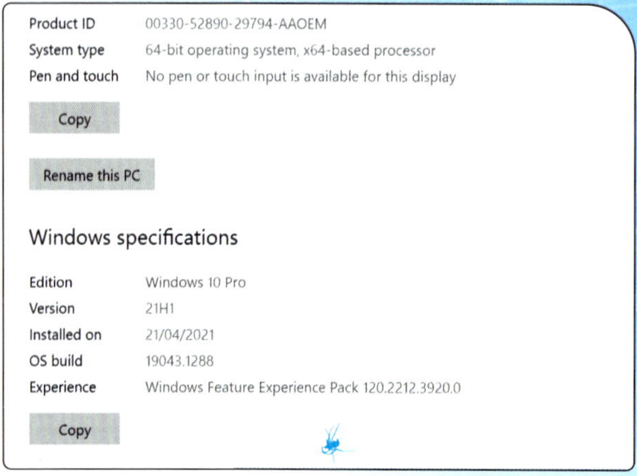


You'll need to ensure that you have at least version 2004 of Windows 10 before you begin. It will be displayed as 20H1, so anything above 20H1 is fine. It's worth going to the Windows Update section in Settings and checking for the latest updates.

## Step 1

If all is well, head on over to https://www.microsoft.com/en-us/software-download/windows11, and locate the Windows 11 Installation Assistant section. Click on the Download Now button, to save the app to your computer.

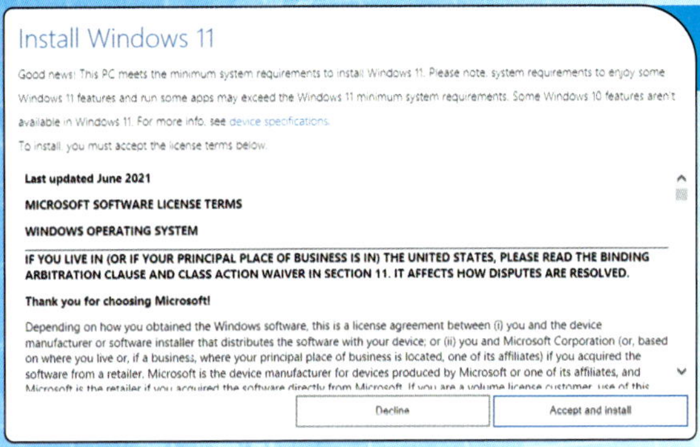


## Step 2

Locate the app on your computer, and double-click it to begin the Windows 11 installation process. If everything is as it should be, you'll be presented with an Install Windows 11 window. Click on the Accept and Install button to continue the process.

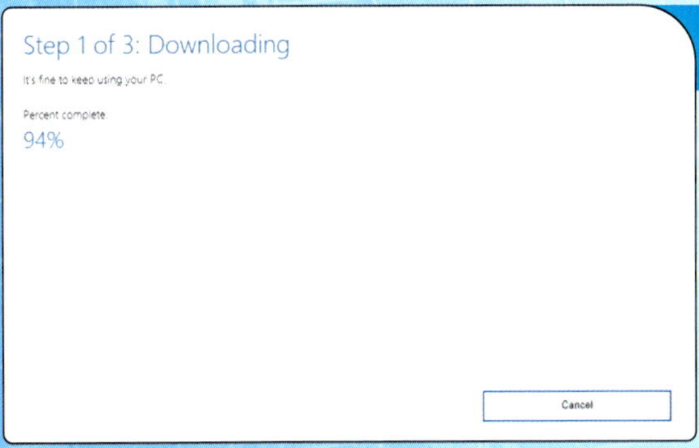


## Step 3

Next, the app will download the necessary file and perform the forced installation of Windows 11. This could be anywhere between 20 minutes to nearly an hour – depending on the speed of your computer, connection to the Internet and so on.

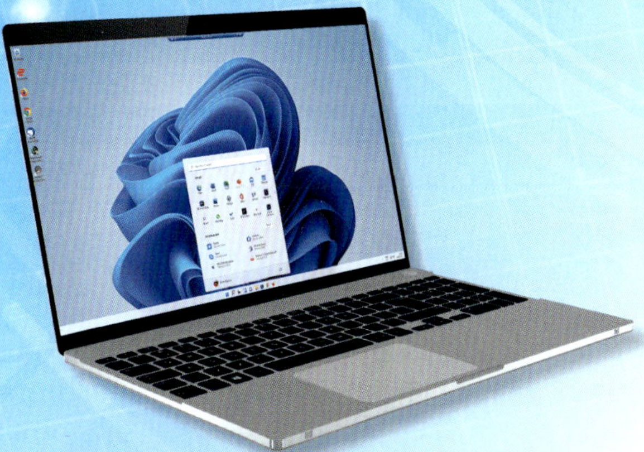

It's a three-step process, and the final step will have you reboot the computer. You'll then need to go through a Welcome process, and once that's done, the Windows 11 desktop will load; retaining all your files, desktop settings etc.

# First Time Set Up

Microsoft has greatly improved its initial Windows setup routine with intuitive guides. Where once you were simply delivered onto the desktop and left to your own devices, now Windows 11 ensures you can comfortably hit the ground running.

## Hello Windows 11

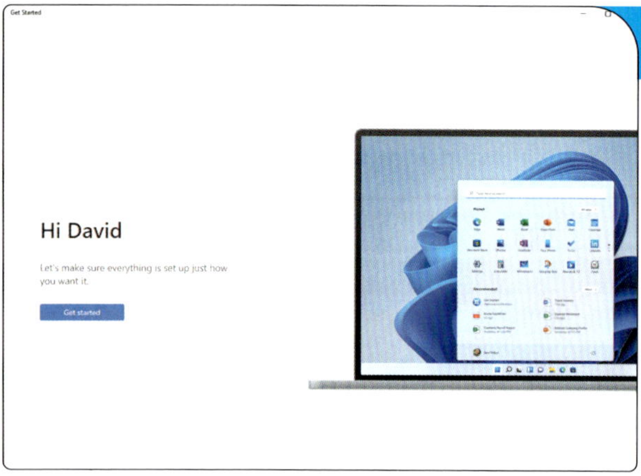


### Step 1

You'll find the Getting Started guide in the Start menu, when you click the Windows logo button on the taskbar. It's a welcome to Windows setup wizard, and makes sure you're ready to use your files, and get access to your work quickly and effectively. Once open, click the Get Started button to continue.

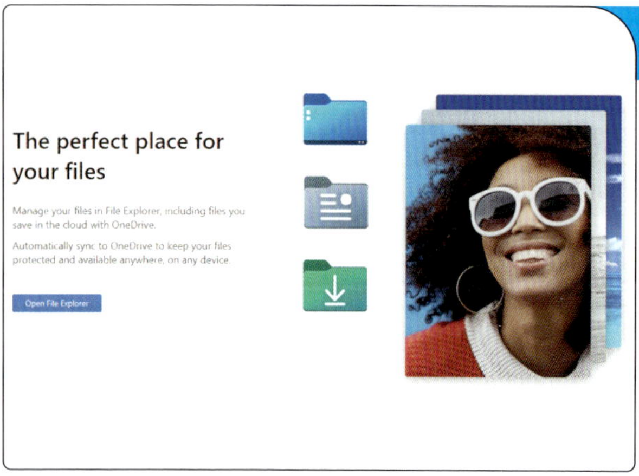


### Step 2

Microsoft's use of OneDrive for both business and personal data has become one of the cornerstones of the company's services. OneDrive offers a secure space to store your data, which will always be available no matter what happens to your computer. Click on the Open File Explorer button to begin your OneDrive setup and login.

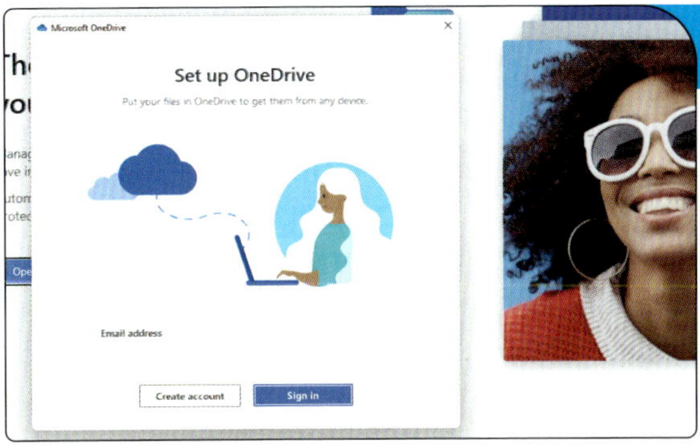


## Step 3

If you already have a OneDrive, or Microsoft, account, then click on the Sign In button to enter your details and link your OneDrive with the account on the Windows 11 PC you're currently setting up. If you don't have a OneDrive account, click the Create Account button and follow the on-screen instructions.

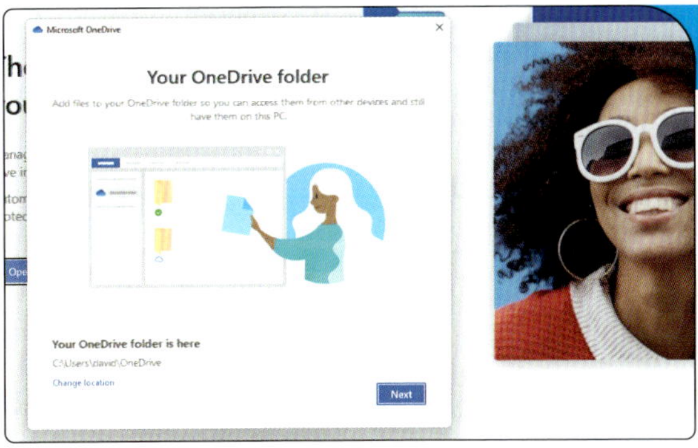


## Step 4

When you've completed the setup and logged into OneDrive, a special folder within your user account on the PC will be setup. This folder allows you to interact in real-time with the OneDrive cloud service, so any files created in the folder will be automatically uploaded to OneDrive; and vice versa.

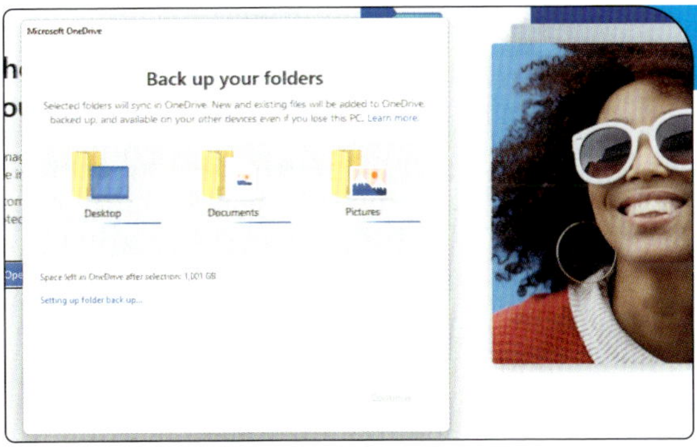


## Step 5

OneDrive will also setup an automated service that will backup any files and folders that you store on the Desktop, in your Documents folder, and in your Pictures folder. Click on the 'Setting up folder back up' link to add more folders to backup, or deselect any you don't want to.

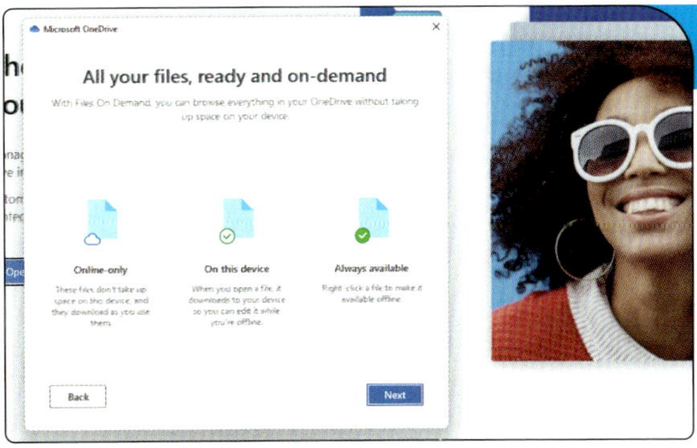


## Step 6

The service will help reduce the amount of space taken up on the PC, or other Windows 11 devices you're using, by utilising Files On Demand. This is an automatic setup that will let you view and edit files on OneDrive without downloading them locally. You can, however, opt to makes files and folder Always Available.

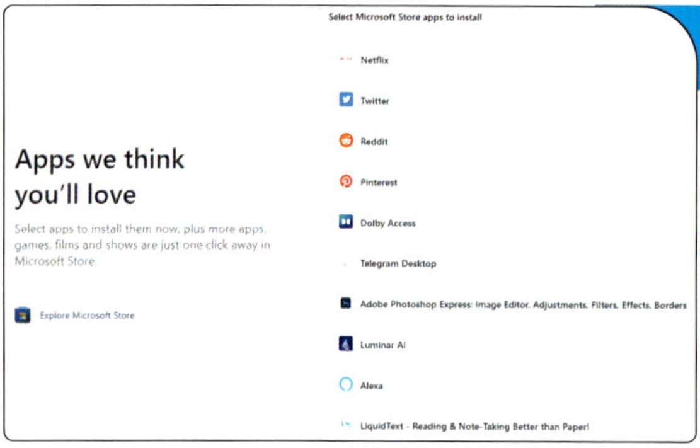


## Step 7

The next step in the Getting Started process has you viewing and selecting any of the popular apps that are currently available for Windows 11. Naturally, you can install these apps via the Windows Store at a later date, but having them to begin with can reduce the amount of time you spend setting up the computer.

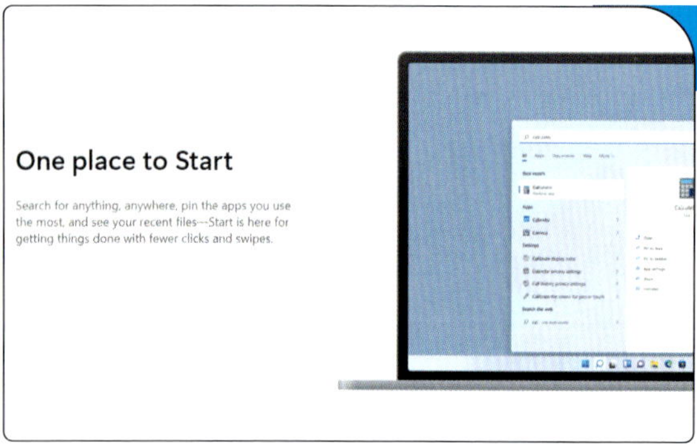


## Step 8

An interesting element to the Getting Started setup are the informational sections; such as this one. It details the new Search app that's located on the taskbar. It also highlights the new Start launch taskbar, and shows just how easy it is to use, and pin any Apps to it.

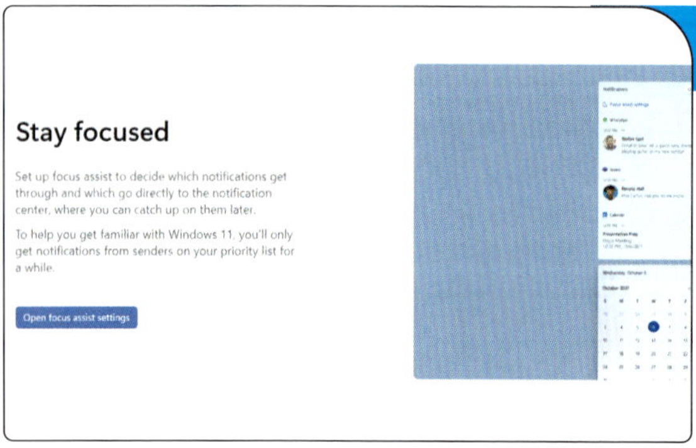


## Step 9

The Focus Assist setting is designed to help you choose the notifications you'd like to see and hear, without the distractions of those you don't. Any notification that's not set in the Priority list of apps, will be added to the Notification area without disturbing your workflow. Click the Open focus assist settings button for further information.

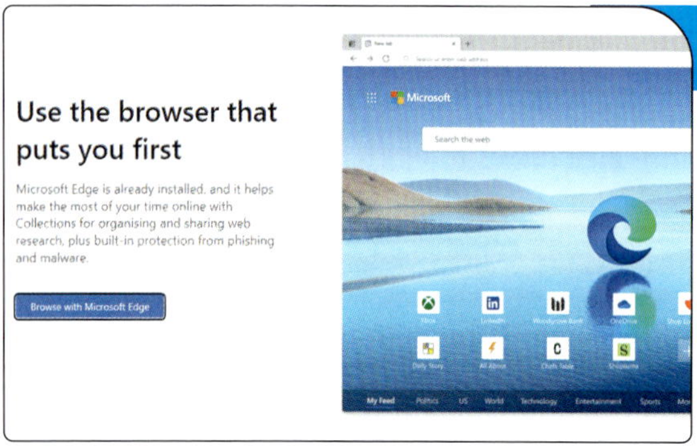


## Step 10

Microsoft Edge has seen some dramatic improvements over the years, so much so that it's now regarded as one of the most secure, and fastest browsers available. Of course, if you prefer to use Chrome, Firefox or another browser, then you're free to do so. Edge, however, is built on Chrome technologies, so it might be worth giving it a go.

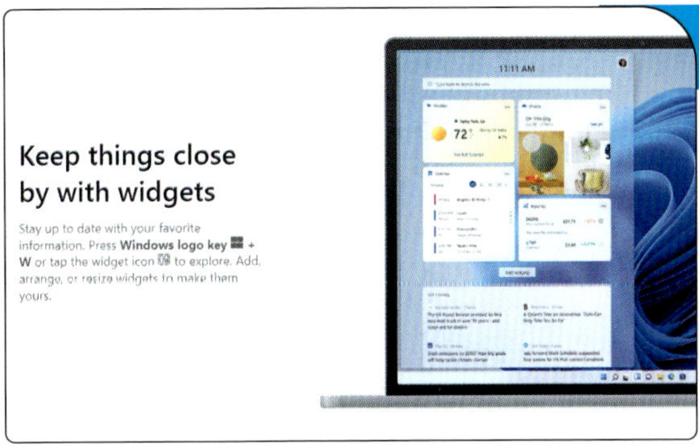


## Step 11

Widgets are a resurfacing technology from the Windows Vista days; only now they work a lot better. This panel of the Getting Started setup shows you how to access your Widgets, and how to explore what's available. The widget window scrolls in from the left of the screen, slightly raised above the taskbar.

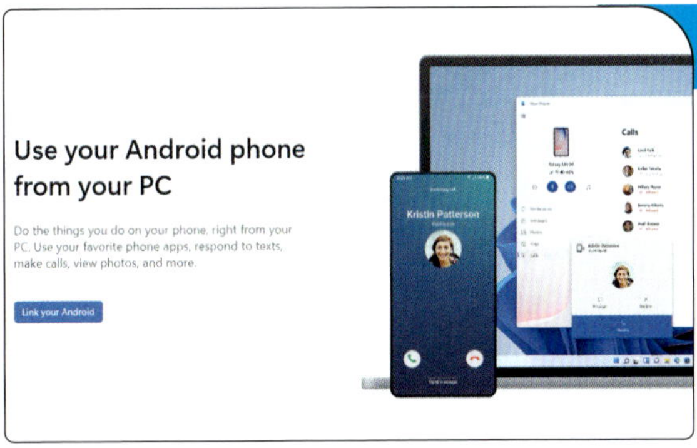


## Step 12

Linking your Android phone with Windows is a function that appeared in the early years of Windows 10. Since then it has improved significantly, and you can easily setup and configure the interface from this panel in the Getting Started guide. Simply click the, Link your Android button to begin the process.

## Step 13

The new Chat icon in the taskbar is an element of Microsoft Teams. Teams has proved its worth in gold during lockdown, and has now been included by default in Windows 11. It's cross-platform, and easy to setup and use. Just click on the Chat button in the taskbar to begin the setup process.

## Step 14

That's the Getting Started guide complete. You'll now have a fully setup and working OneDrive with active folders, sorted out your notifications, launched and begun to use the Edge browser, and connected your Android phone. You can click on the Open Tips button now, to be taken to the Microsoft page for more Windows 11 tips.

# Windows 11 Desktop

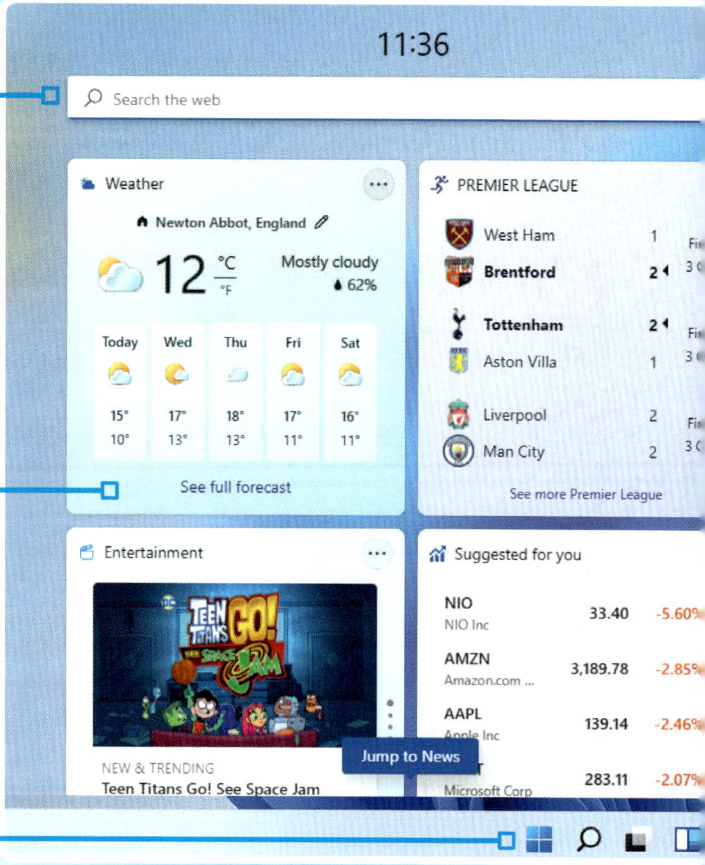


### Search for Widgets

You can use the Search field to look for more specific Widgets, and add them to your desktop for a more personalised desktop environment.

### Widgets

The Widgets snap in from the left of the desktop, and are slightly raised to avoid clashing with the taskbar; to help keep the desktop clutter-free.

### Taskbar

The new Windows 11 taskbar expands out from the centre of the desktop now. The Windows Start button still works in the same way, displaying installed apps and offering access to the OS settings.

**The latest Windows 11 desktop user interface (UI) is a radical change from what we are used to seeing with previous versions of Windows. The main differences are found within the new taskbar, Notifications and Widgets.**

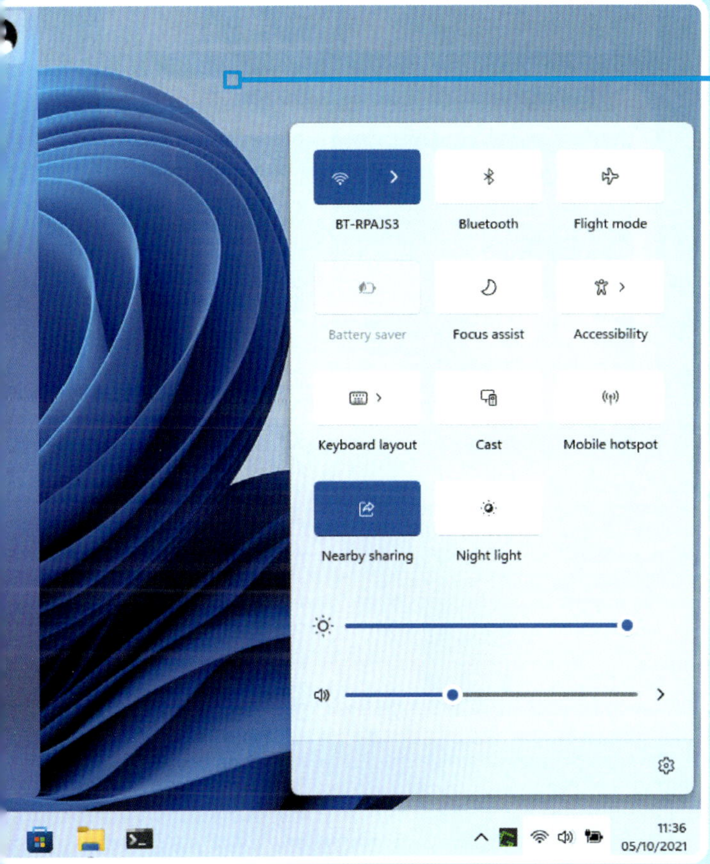


## Desktop

As with all previous versions of Windows, the Desktop can be personalised and configured how you like. Its new look is brighter, with cleaner edges and better resolution than before, to help ease eye-strain and keep you focused.

## Notifications

The Notification Centre and the taskbar are now combined. Click the set of icons that represent Wi-Fi, battery and so on, and the screen will expand upward to reveal more settings. In here you'll find access to the important elements of the computer. Notifications will be displayed next to the date; as and when they're needed. This allows you to focus more on what you're doing without unnecessary distractions.

## Search in Windows 11

The Search function within Windows 11 is greatly improved, and easier to find what you're looking for. Whether it's a document on your computer, or something online, you can find it here.

# How to Use the Start Menu

The Start menu has been given a makeover for Windows 11, simplified in some ways and expanded in others. It may look empty when compared to the Windows 10 Start menu, but it is still the main way to access your installed apps, software and games.

## Get to Grips with Start

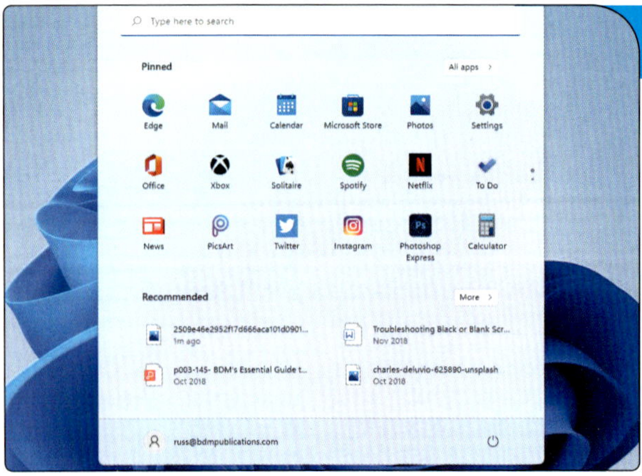


### Step 1

The completely redesigned Start menu is opened by clicking on the Windows icon in the taskbar, or by pressing the Windows Key on your keyboard. It opens above the taskbar icons, floating in the middle of the screen. It will appear over the top of any open windows.

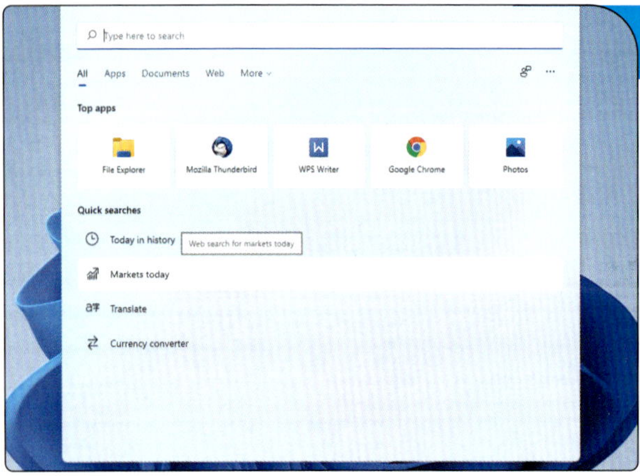


### Step 2

The Start menu is arranged in four main sections: Search, Pinned Apps, Recent or Recommended Files and Account/Power. Clicking in the Search field will switch to the dedicated Search panel, rather than letting you type your search term directly into the Start menu.

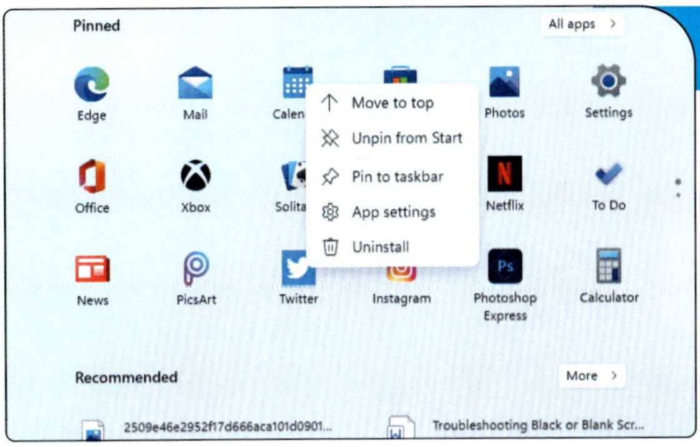


## Step 3

If the app you want to open is shown, click the icon to open it. If not, you can click the "All Apps" button to open the full, scrollable list of apps. You can change the apps that appear here by right-clicking on the icon and choosing "Unpin/Pin to Start" from the action menu.

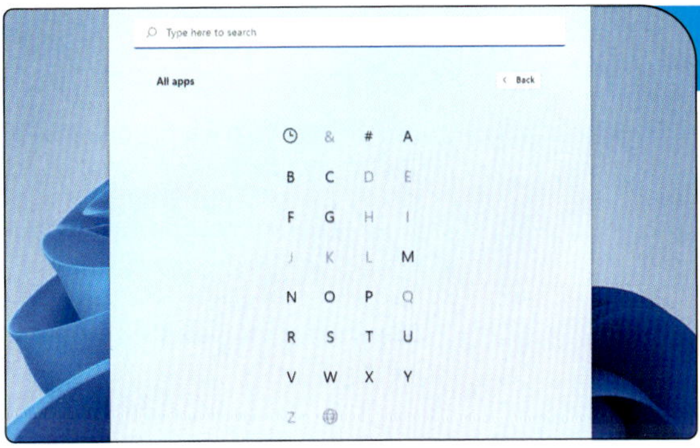


## Step 4

In the app menu, apps are sorted alphabetically, except for a Most Used section at the top. If you click the title of that section (or any other section heading), a letter grid will appear, allowing you to quickly skip to a specific section of the apps list.

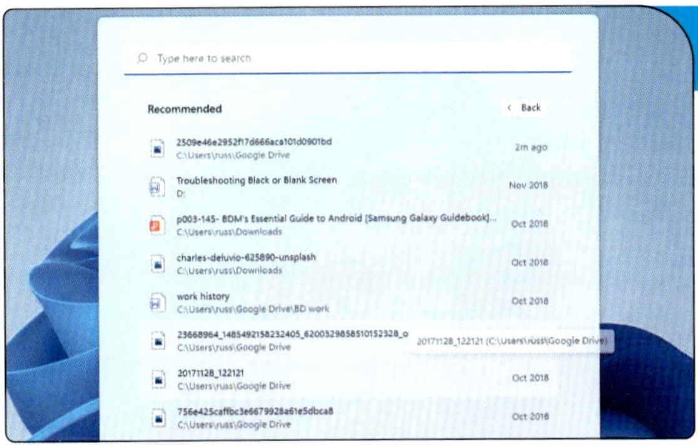


## Step 5

The Recommended section shows files that have been recently opened, or that have been opened frequently. Click on any icon to open the file in whatever app/program it is associated with. Click the "More" button to the right to open a larger list of files.

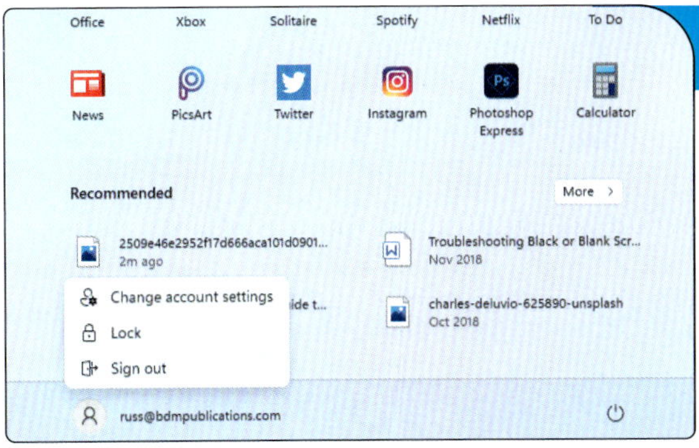


## Step 6

The bottom section contains a link to the Microsoft Account menu. Click this to change account settings, lock your computer or sign out of the current account. At the other end of the section is the power button. Click this and choose from the available power options.

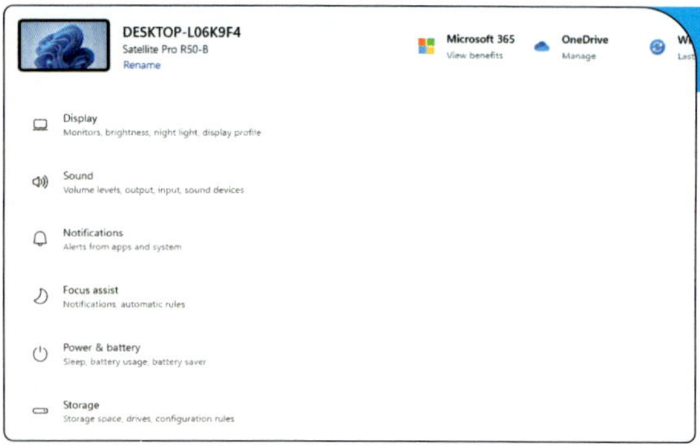


## Step 7

It is also possible to display your most used apps and a selection of folders in the Start menu. To enable these features, open the main settings menu (you should see the icon for this in the pinned apps) and click on the Personalisation section. Then choose the Start option.

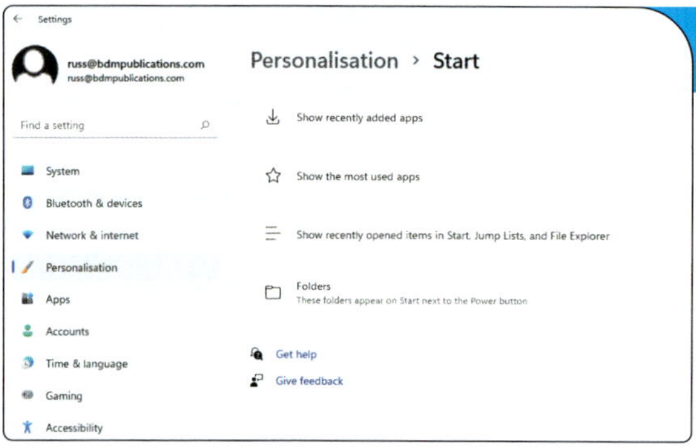


## Step 8

Use the sliders to enable or disable Start menu features you want or no longer want. To add folders to the Start menu, click the folders option in the Start settings and then use the slider switches to add any of the preset folders you want or need quick access to.

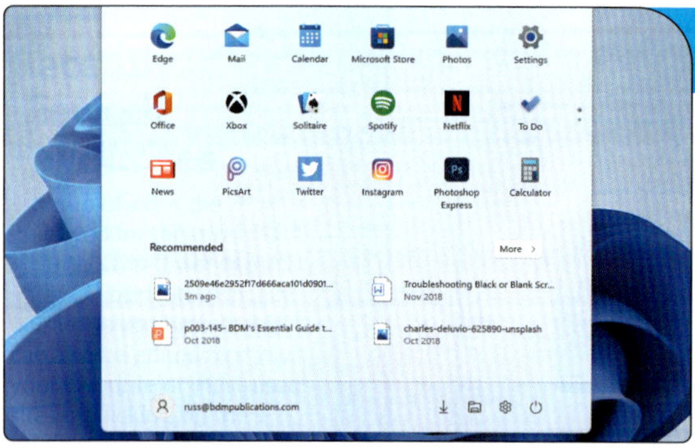


## Step 9

Open the Start menu again to see the newly added (or removed features). You may not initially notice any difference to the apps list if you have not yet used any apps repeatedly. The folders you added can be found next to the power button in the bottom section.

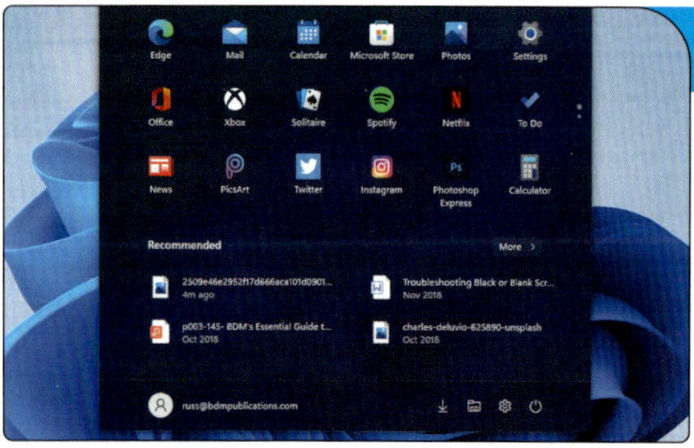


## Step 10

It is not possible to resize the Start menu, nor is it possible to change the style of it. You can change the overall colour mode (light, dark or custom), which will change the colour of the Start menu along with other main elements of the interface such as the taskbar.

# Notifications & Quick Settings

There have always been pop-up messages in Windows but now there is a centralised way in which these are viewed and interacted with. In Windows 11, this is called the Notification Center, it is designed to work more like a notifications panel on a mobile device.

## Exploring the Notification Center

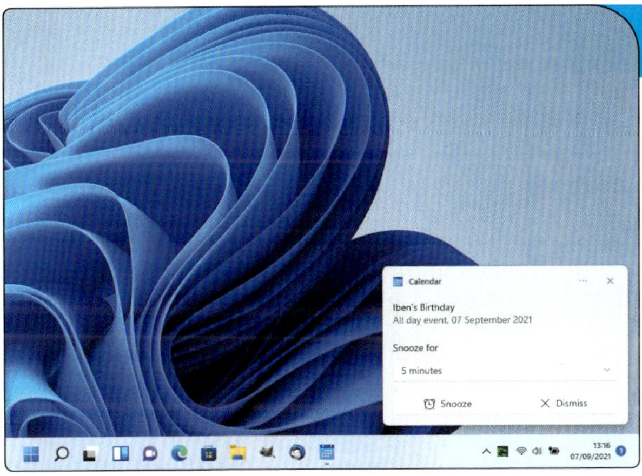


### Step 1

New notifications and alerts will pop up at the bottom-right corner of the screen (by default, but you can change the notification settings), disappearing after a few seconds. After the initial pop-up has disappeared, you can view all current notifications by clicking on the time/date in the taskbar.

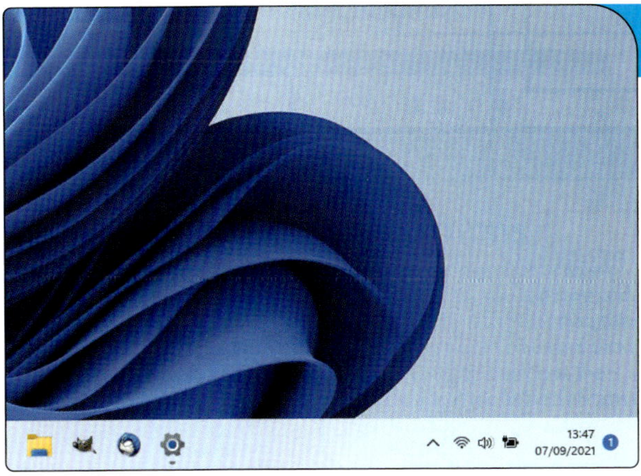


### Step 2

You can see if there are new notifications waiting to be viewed by the badge that will appear on the corner of the time/date in the taskbar. You can turn off these badges in the settings, but they are a useful and unobtrusive way to see, at a glance, if you have something requiring your attention.

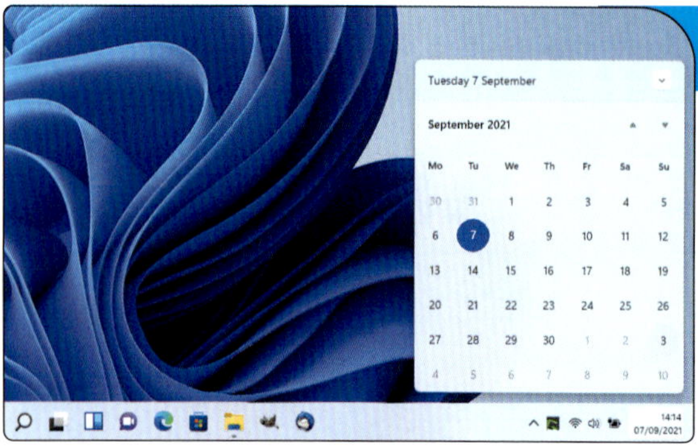


## Step 3

Unlike Windows 10, the Notification Center (which was called the Action Center previously) only contains notifications and alerts, not quick settings. It does include the calendar now, which is expanded by clicking the arrow next to the date at the bottom of the notification panel.

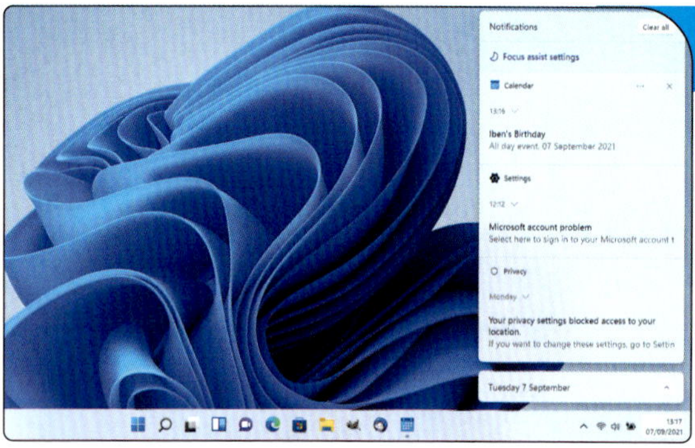


## Step 4

Above the calendar section is your notification panel. Notifications can be from the system (Windows updates for example), from your calendar, from apps and even from settings that need to be managed. Notifications are sorted into sections within the notifications panel; based on their type.

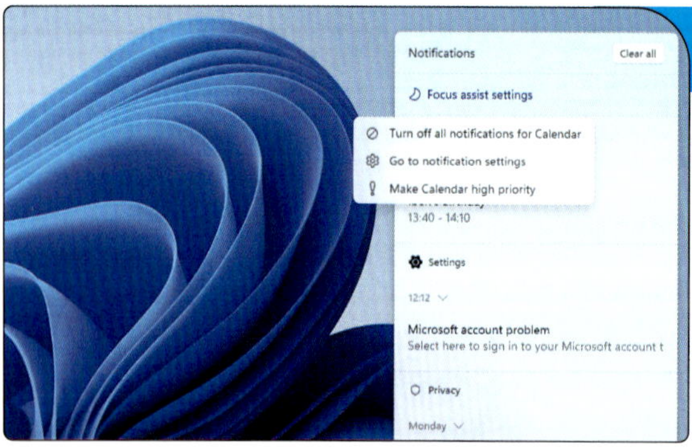


## Step 5

At the top of the Notifications panel is a button to clear all notifications. You can clear notifications individually by hovering the pointer over them and clicking the X. You can also click the menu button on each notification to see some notification settings, such as setting similar messages as a priority.

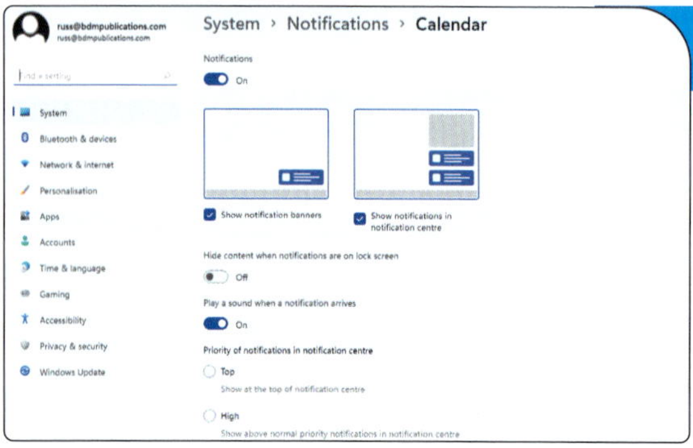


## Step 6

To manage your notification display settings, go to Settings > System > Notifications. Here you can choose the apps/features which can send you notifications, using the slider switches. Click the name of the app to see further settings, such as whether a sound is played, and the priority level.

# Quick Settings Panel

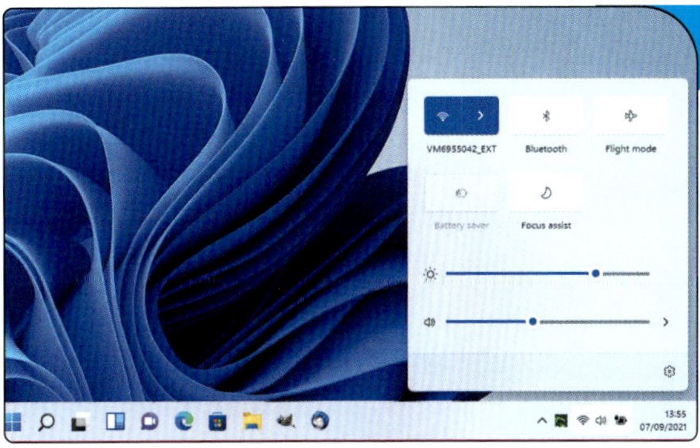


## Step 1

To access the quick settings panel in Windows 11, press Windows Key + a. The panel will appear in the same position on screen as the Notification Center. By default the panel contains buttons to quickly enable/disable Wi-Fi, Bluetooth, Flight Mode, Battery Saver (if using a laptop) and Focus Assist.

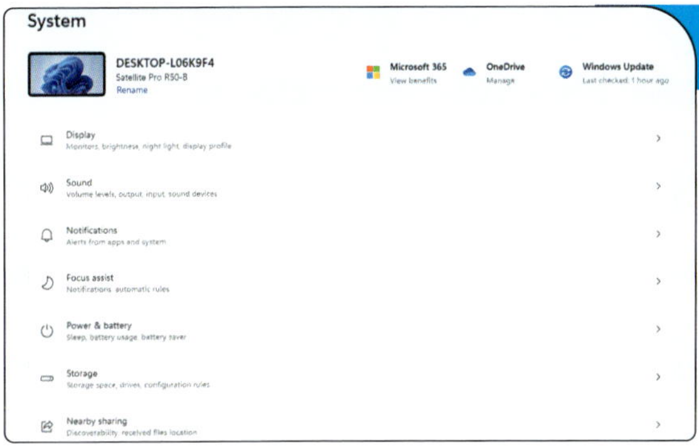


## Step 2

There are also sliders to control screen brightness and system volume. The exact settings that appear in the quick settings panel will vary, depending on if you are using a desktop or a laptop computer. At the bottom of the panel is a button to open the main Windows 11 settings app.

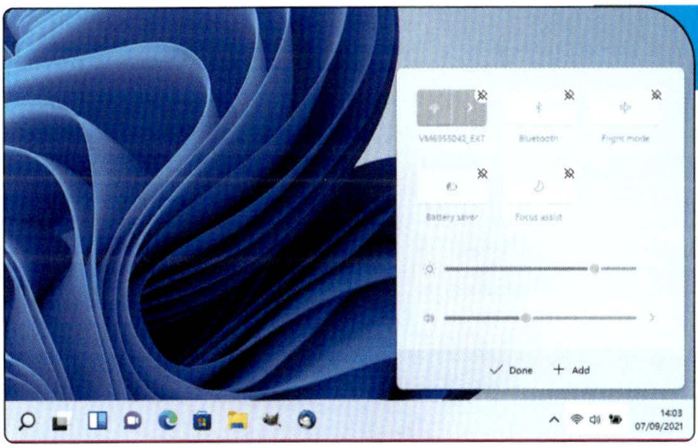


## Step 3

Right-click anywhere on the Quick Settings panel to see a link to "Edit quick settings". Click this and the buttons will be greyed out, and unpin icons will appear on each. Click these to remove a button from the panel. You can also click the + button at the bottom to add other quick settings buttons.

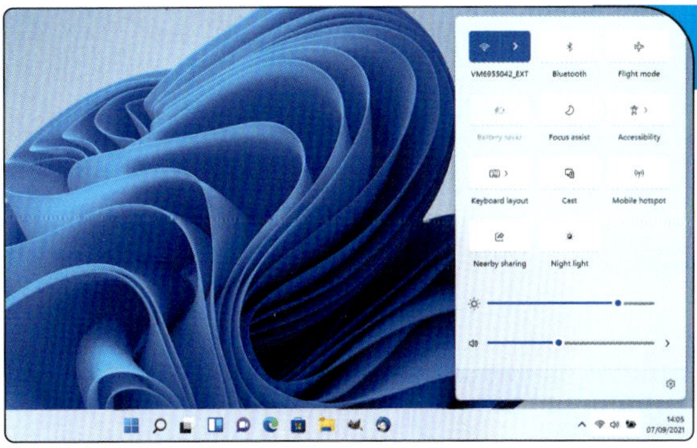


## Step 4

Some of the quick settings buttons will have an arrow on the button. Clicking these buttons will open a new panel, with further options for that particular feature. For example, the Wi-Fi button will open a list of available networks, and Keyboard Layout will open a list of the different layouts available to you.

# How to Use the Taskbar

If you're moving from Windows 10 to Windows 11, the taskbar will likely be the first change you notice. The taskbar has always been a useful tool, but in Windows 11 it becomes the focus of the desktop and contains more features and tools.

## Mastering the Windows 11 Taskbar

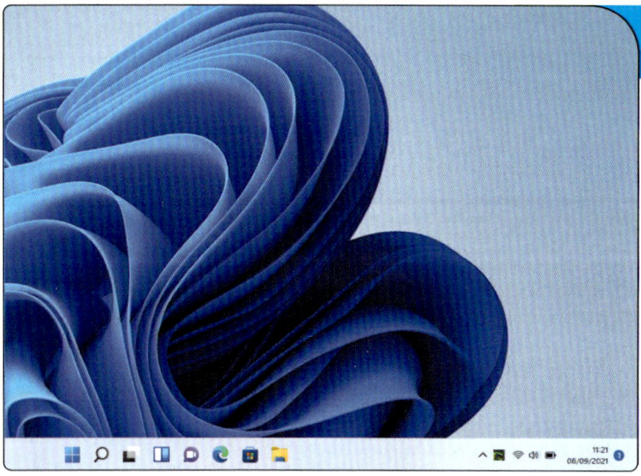

### Taskbar Layout

The taskbar runs the full length of the bottom of the screen, and is now divided into two main sections: Start Menu/Pinned App and System Tools. In Windows 11 the taskbar app icons are arranged in the centre of the taskbar (although this can be changed), with system tools on the right.

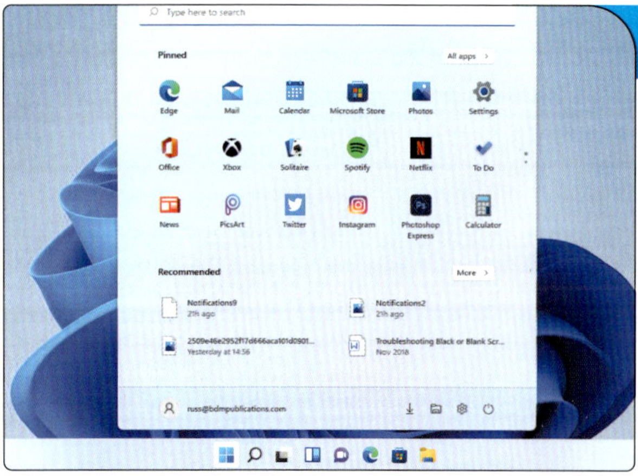


### Start Menu

The first icon in the row of taskbar icons is the Start menu button. Clicking this opens the Start menu directly above the icons. You can right-click the Start menu button to see a jump menu of additional links and tools. These include a shortcut to shut down or sign out of your computer.

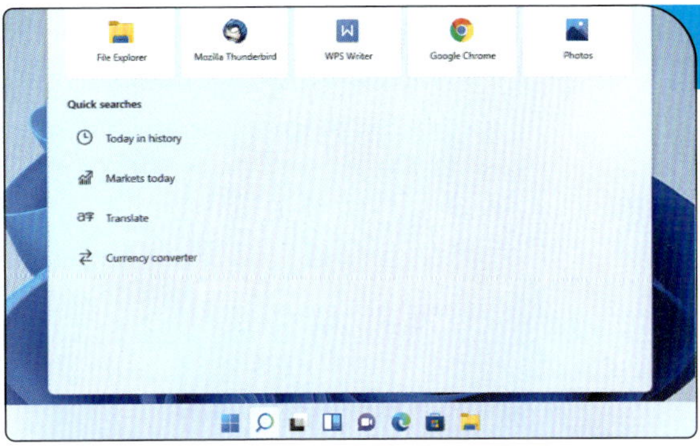


## Search Tool

The embedded search field of Windows 10 is gone, replaced by a button (magnifying glass) that opens a new system search panel. This unified search allows you to not only search for things on your computer, but also in OneDrive and for results from websites. As you begin typing, search suggestions appear.

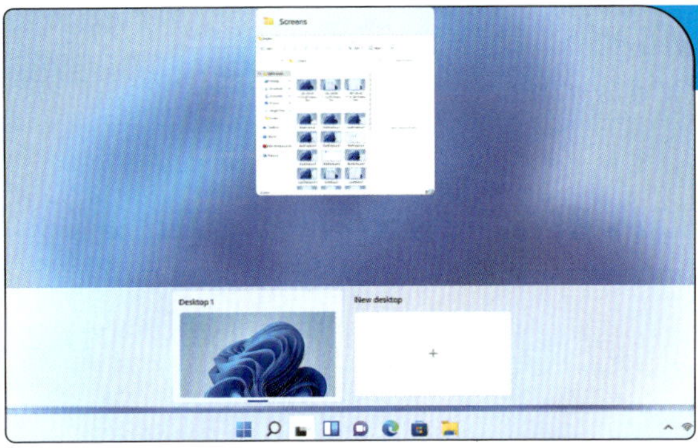


## Task View

The third button in the row of taskbar icons opens Task View. Task View is not a new feature to Windows, but it has been slightly changed and streamlined for this version. Task View allows you to quickly see every app and window you have open, switch between them and even create new desktops.

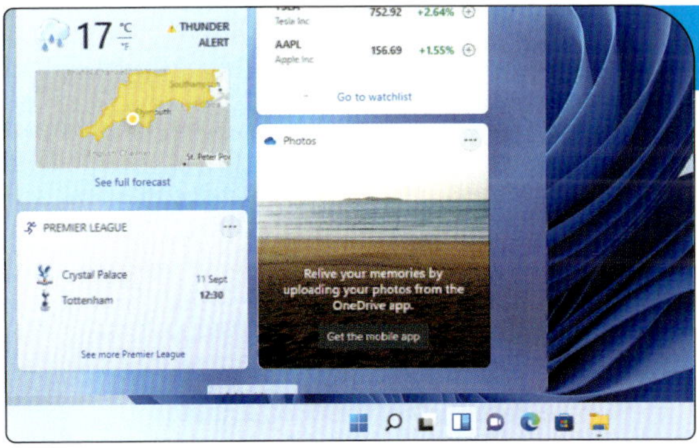


## Widgets

The fourth default button opens the Widget panel, on the left side of the screen. The widget panel can be customised to suit your needs with information such as weather, photos, stock prices, sports results and news stories. As Windows 11 develops, it is likely even more functionality will be added.

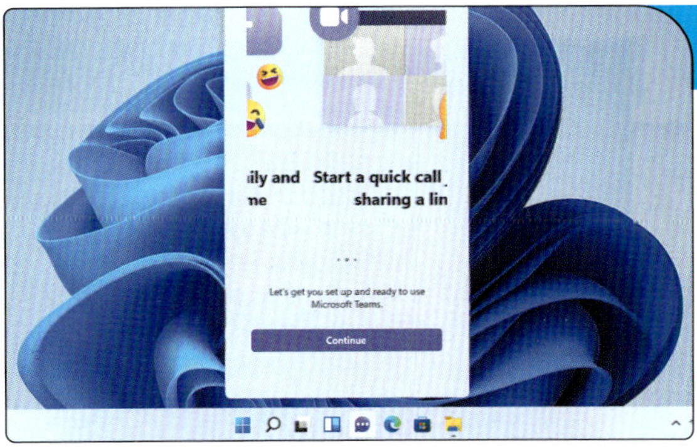


## Microsoft Teams

The huge recent rise of remote working and video meetings goes some way to explain why Microsoft have embedded Teams as part of Windows 11. Once you are set up and signed into your Teams account, clicking this button will open the start/join meeting interface.

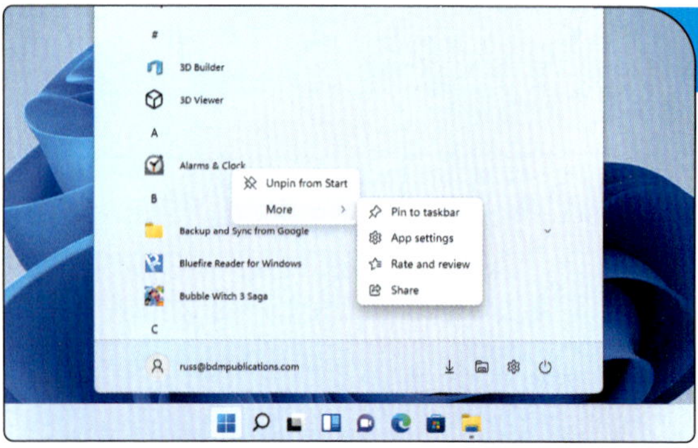


## Pinning Apps

A few other apps and other software will be pinned to the taskbar when you first use your Windows 11 PC. You can add several more as and when you choose. To pin compatible apps, right-click on the app icon anywhere you see it (Start menu for example), and then click Pin to Taskbar.

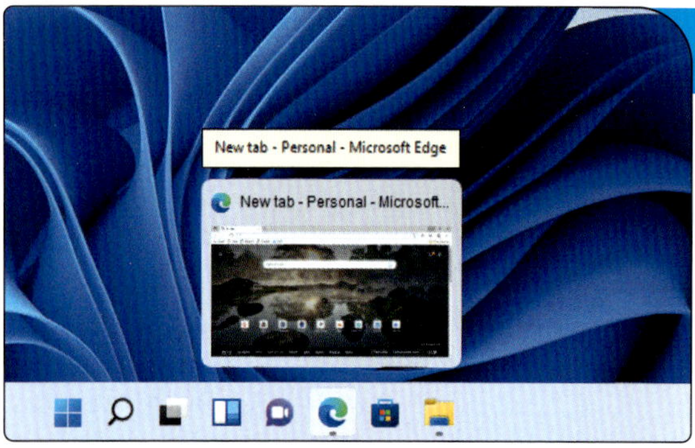


## Peek

Hovering over any open app icon in the Taskbar brings up a Peek preview of the window. If a movie is playing, you will see it playing here too. If you mouse over the preview, the actual app or window will pop up on screen. You will also see an X to close the window, without actually selecting it.

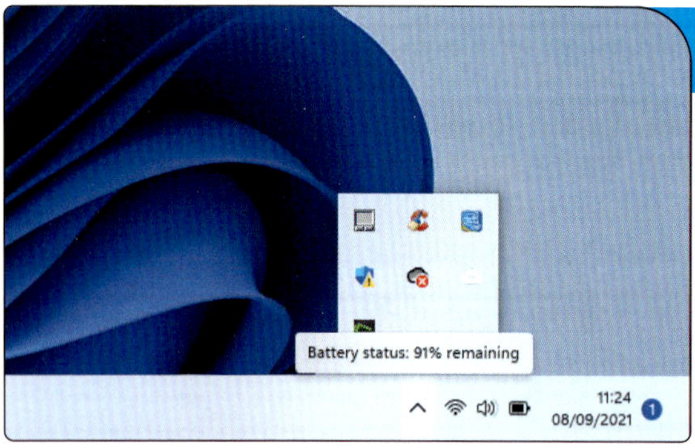


## System Tools

The right-hand side of the taskbar is reserved for the system tools, the time and date (which opens the Notification Center upon a click) and the Show Desktop button. The system tools will vary depending on your computer, but may include battery status, Wi-Fi status, Sound and OneDrive.

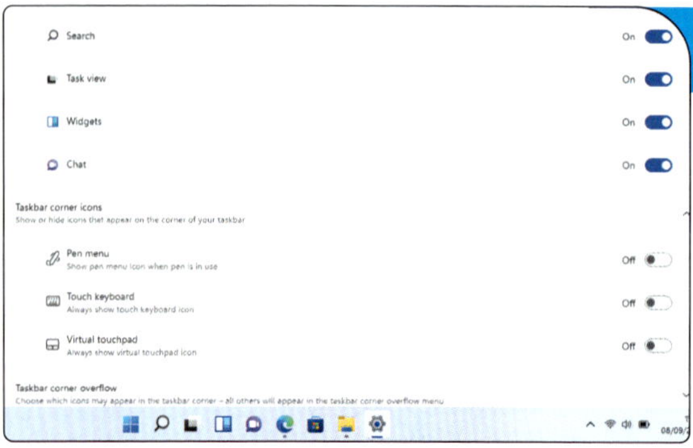


## Taskbar Settings

You have quite a lot of free reign when it comes to which apps you have showing in the taskbar. Open Settings > Personalisation > Taskbar. Here you can use the slider switches to enable or disable the default apps that appear. You can also change the alignment of the pinned apps back to the left.

# Task View and Desktops

Task View was introduced in Windows 10, as a way to make multi-tasking easier and allowing the creation of extra desktop areas. In Windows 11 it's even easier to instantly check and switch to open windows; and to create and manage multiple desktops.

## Using Task View

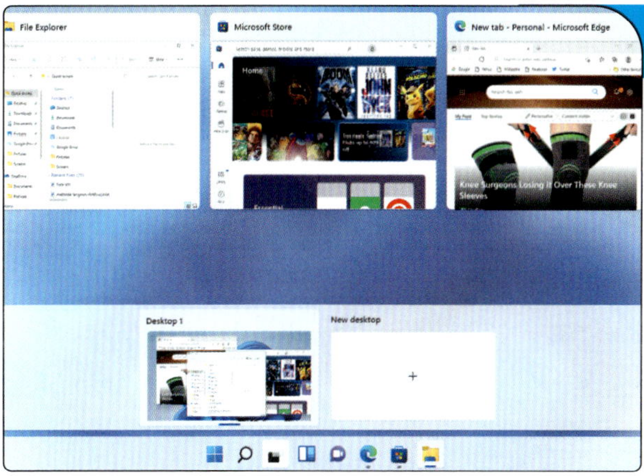


**Step 1**

Task View is accessed by clicking the third icon in the taskbar; the white square on the black square. The Task View screen is split into two sections: Open tasks and desktops. Any apps or windows you have open, even if they are currently minimised, will be displayed in the open tasks panel.

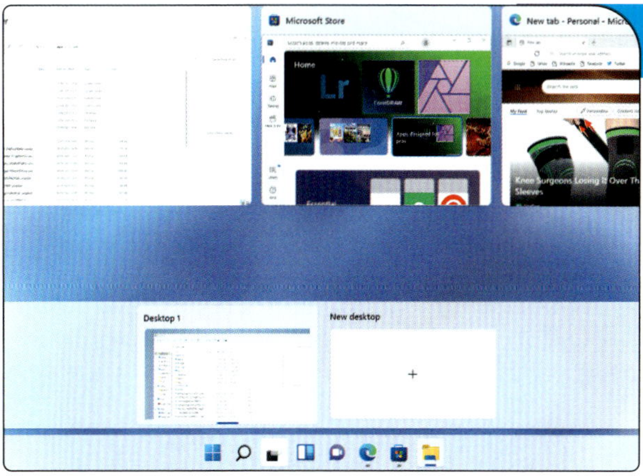


**Step 2**

The size and shape of the windows shown in Task View depend on the size and shape of the actual window. For example, if you have Microsoft Edge open at full screen, it will be displayed as a wide rectangle in Task View. If you have a lot of windows open, the open tasks panel will be scrollable.

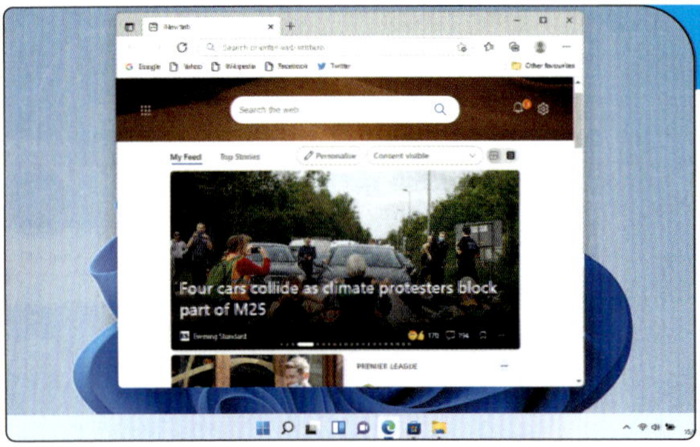


## Step 3

Click on any window or app in Task View to open it at full size on the desktop. It will appear in front of any windows you already had open and visible on the desktop. You can also close windows or apps directly from the Task view. Just hover the mouse over the window and click the X button.

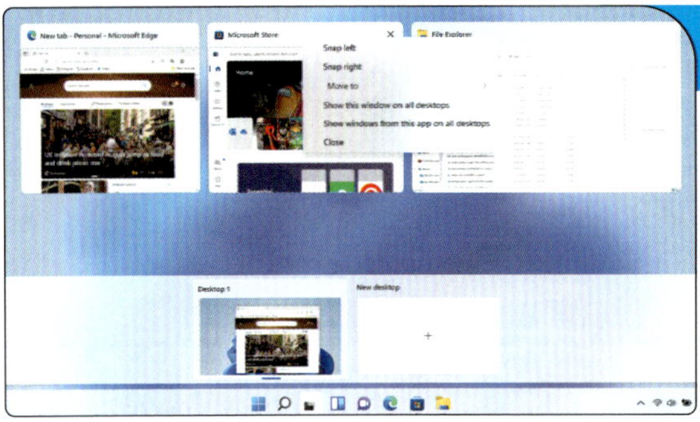


## Step 4

If you right-click on one of the windows/apps shown in Task View, you will see several more options. Snap left/right will open the selected window, but "snapped" or positioned to the left or right of the home screen. There are also several options for showing/hiding the window on new desktops.

# Using Multiple Desktops

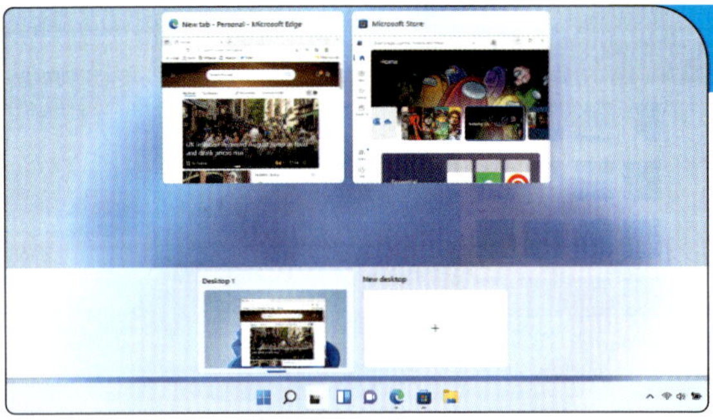


## Step 1

One of the great features in Task View is the ability to add extra desktops. Virtual desktops are essentially extra workspaces, so for example you can have one space with your email and chat windows open and another where you're working in PowerPoint without email distractions.

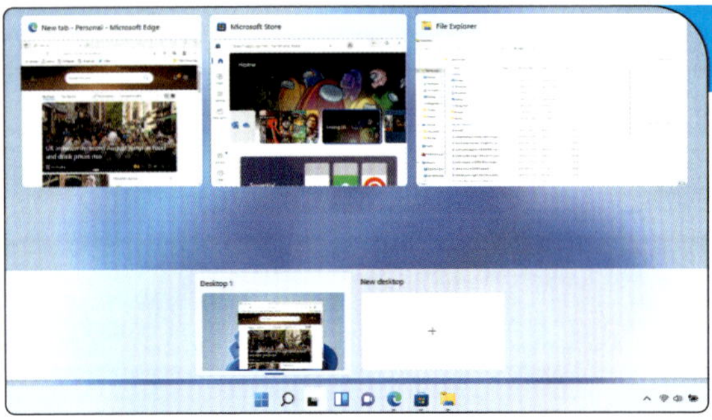


## Step 2

Click or tap the New Desktop button at the bottom of the Task View screen and you will see an entirely new and blank desktop. If you had any apps or windows open in the main desktop, they won't be open here. Don't worry, they haven't been closed, they are still open on the other desktop.

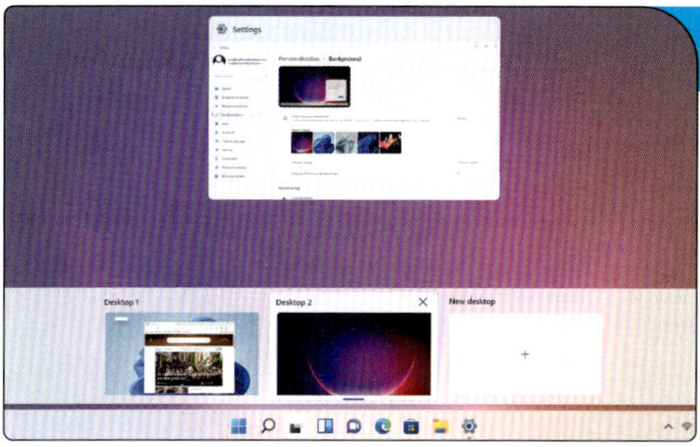


## Step 3

With Task View open, right click on one of the desktop previews at the bottom and you can choose a different background wallpaper (making identifying which desktop you are on currently easier), and also you can choose to move a desktop to the left or right, switching which one is the main desktop.

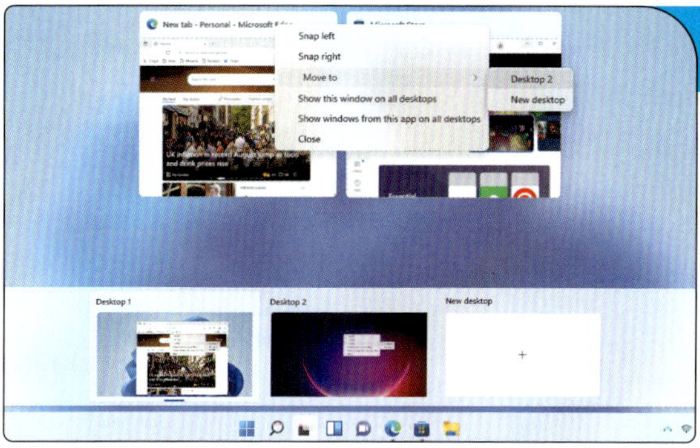


## Step 4

You can right-click the apps in Task View to send them to another desktop. You can also drag and drop windows/apps from one desktop to another. If you have an app or window open in one desktop and then try to open it in another, you will just switch to the desktop where it was already open.

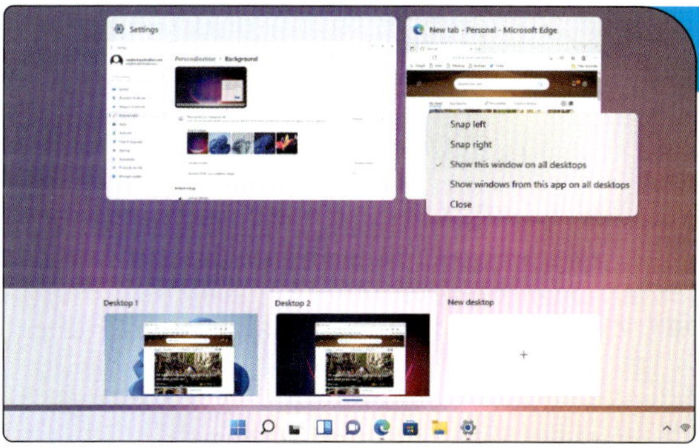


## Step 5

To get around this problem, open the Task View and right click on an app or window. From the menu, choose either "Show this window on all desktops" or "Show windows from this app on all desktops". You can also use this menu to move apps or windows between your open desktops.

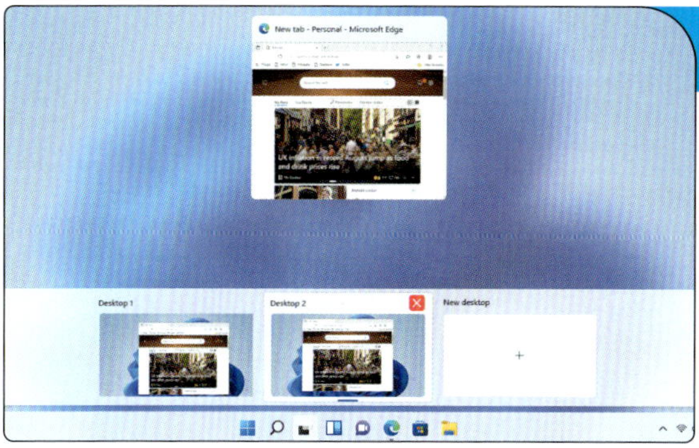


## Step 6

If you hover over the apps and windows shown in the Open Tasks panel, you will see an X appear; now you can close superfluous desktops down to save resources. Doing this doesn't close any apps down, so you don't need to manually move them. It just automatically adds them to the main desktop.

# Snap Layouts and Groups

Snap Layouts and Snap Groups, while similar to Snap Assist in Windows 10, are completely new features for Windows 11. Each is designed to make your life easier by giving you new ways to organise and retrieve apps and windows on a busy desktop.

## Using Snap Layouts

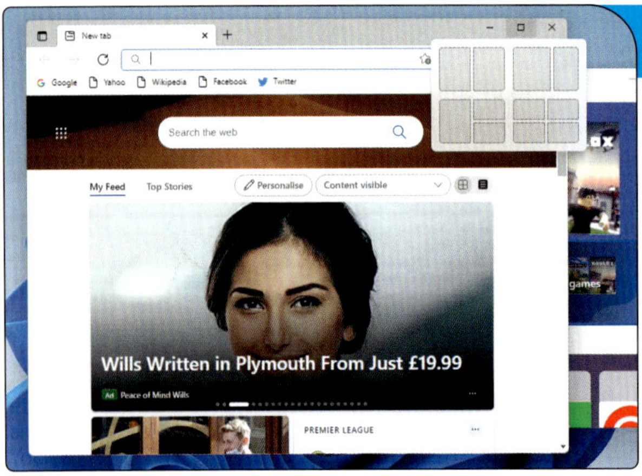


### Step 1

Snap Layouts can be created with just one open app or window, but really come into their own when several are open. Move your mouse over the Maximise button (top-right corner) of any open app or window, without clicking. After a second, a brand new menu will pop up, showing the available layouts.

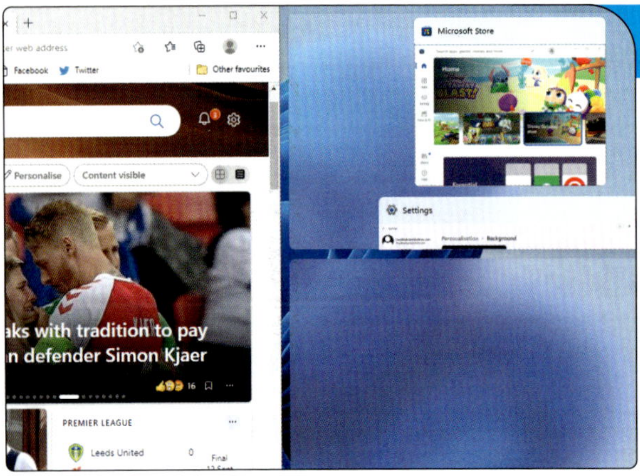


### Step 2

There are 4 preset layouts available (at present, although more may be added): 2 equal windows side-by-side, 2 unequal windows side-by-side, 3 windows and 4 equal windows. Click on whichever you want to use, and the window/app you used to open the layout will snap into one of the positions.

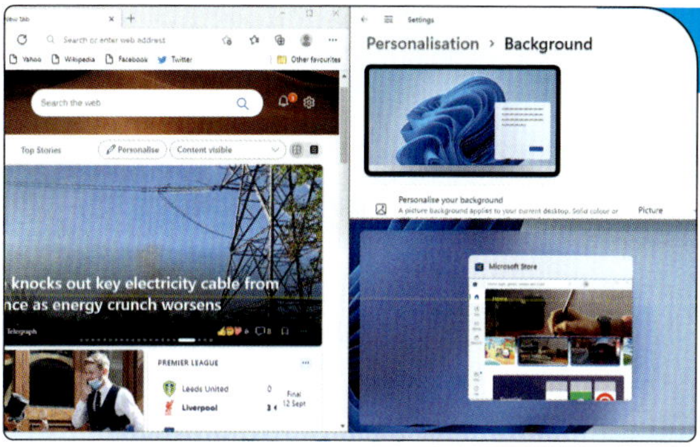


## Step 3

Your other open windows/apps will appear as previews in one of the other layout positions. Click one of them to open it in that layout position. The process is then repeated for any other open windows, if you choose a layout with more than 2 spaces. Windows are automatically resized to fit in the layout.

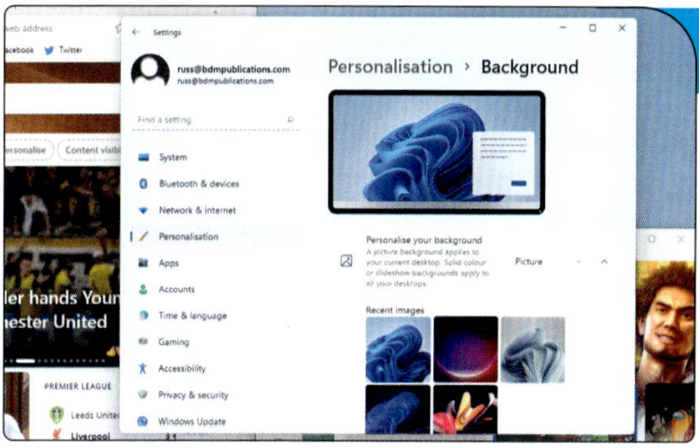


## Step 4

If you now try to move a window or app out of the layout, it will switch back to its original dimensions when it unsnaps from the grid. You can create multiple Snap Layouts, each containing different apps/ windows. These remain until the windows are closed or removed from the group.

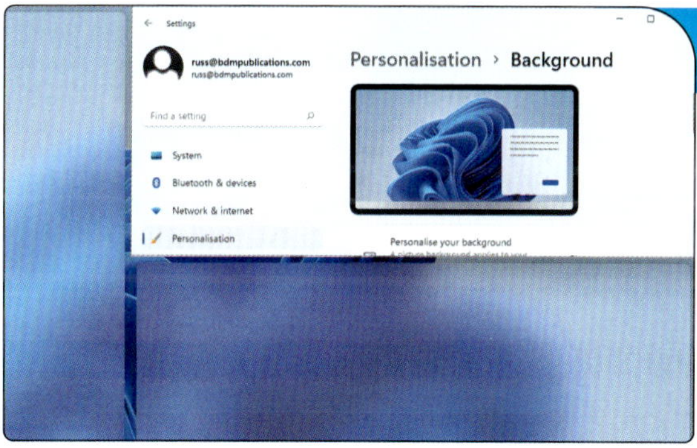


## Step 5

You can change the dimensions of the layout once you have created one. With the layout open, hover your mouse over the line where the windows meet, either horizontally or vertically. A wider bar will appear, which you can click and drag to change the horizontal or vertical dimensions of the layout.

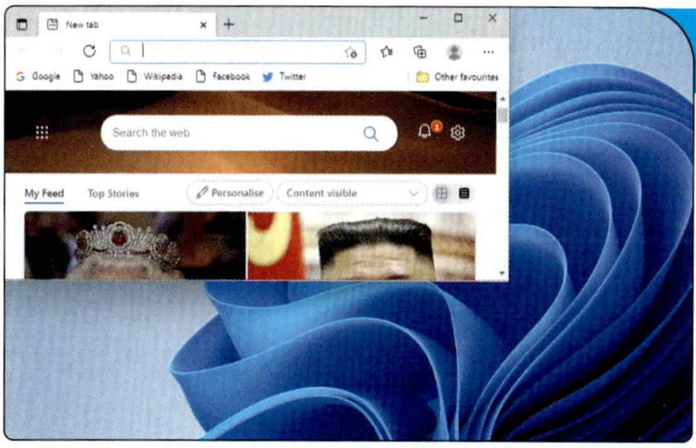


## Step 6

You can snap apps and windows into position using a keyboard shortcut as well. Highlight a window and then press Windows Key + one of the arrow keys. Depending on which direction you press, the window will snap left, right, up or down. Combine key presses to snap up and left, for example.

# Using Snap Groups

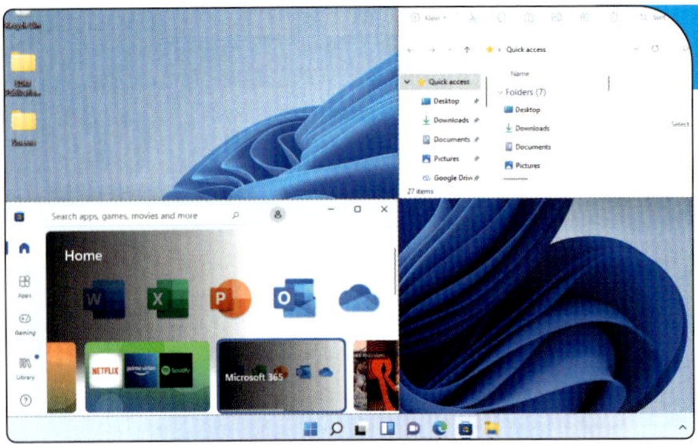


## Step 1

Once you have created a Snap Layout, or multiple layouts, you can minimise the whole thing (by clicking the Show Desktop button on the right of the taskbar) or minimise each individual app or window. As long as they are not closed, the layout persists as a Snap Group.

## Step 2

If you move your mouse over any of the Taskbar icons of apps or windows in a group, two Peek windows will pop up. One shows the app on its own, and they other shows the app in the group. To re-open the group, just click on the group preview. To open the app on its own, click that preview.

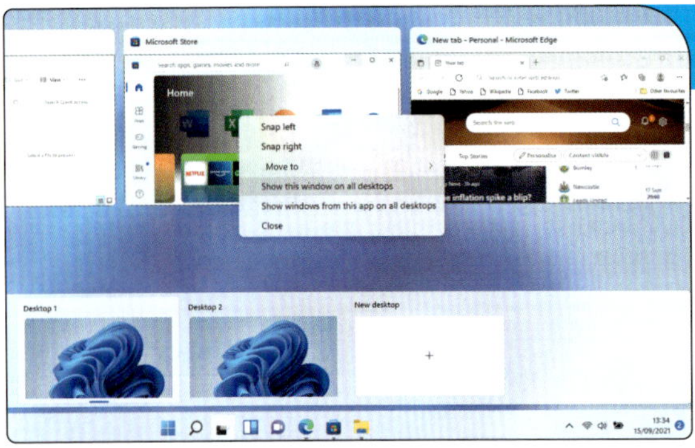


## Step 3

If you use multiple desktops, you can move Snap Groups to any of the additional desktop areas. Just open the Task View, and then right click on each of the apps or windows in the group and choose, "Show this window on all desktop". The group will automatically be recreated on the other desktop.

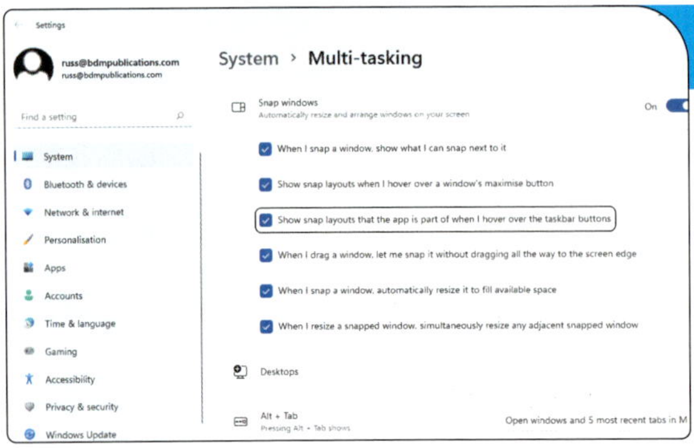


## Step 4

You can find a lot of different settings for how windows snap in the main settings > System > Multi-tasking. Click the Snap windows option and a list of different settings will open. You can also, if you wish, completely turn off window snapping here, using the slider switch.

# How to Use File Explorer

You can just use the powerful and improved search feature to find files and documents on your computer; but the new, simplified File Explorer is often a better choice, especially if you are looking for groups of files or want to preview several files to find the right one.

## What's New in File Explorer?

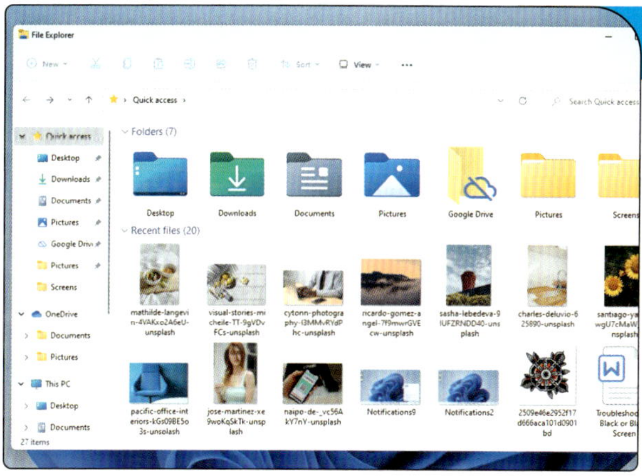


### Step 1

The way you browse files in Windows 11 is similar to previous versions of Windows, but File Explorer has been slightly simplified. The main Quick Access window shows you your most frequently used folders (after all, how many of us dip into more than five or ten folders in a day?) and also recent files.

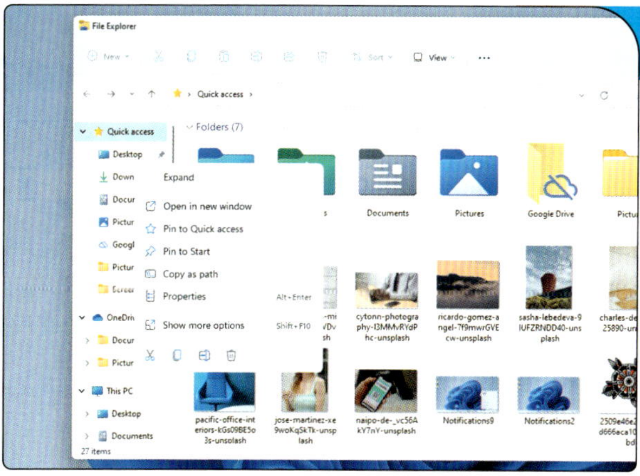


### Step 2

The sidebar also works on the same principle, and via a new Quick Access feature you can pin folders or files that you want to stick around. It will also show you Frequent folders too. You can pin things permanently onto Quick Access by right-clicking them and selecting Add to Quick Access.

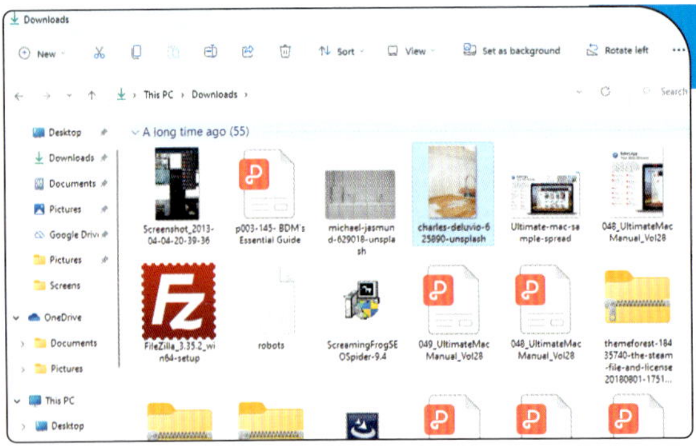


## Step 3

There are new icons across all File Explorer views. And there are a lot more file operations that you can access on the menu at the top of the window (known as the 'ribbon'), without the need to use the right-click menu. This makes it easier to use on PCs with touch screens.

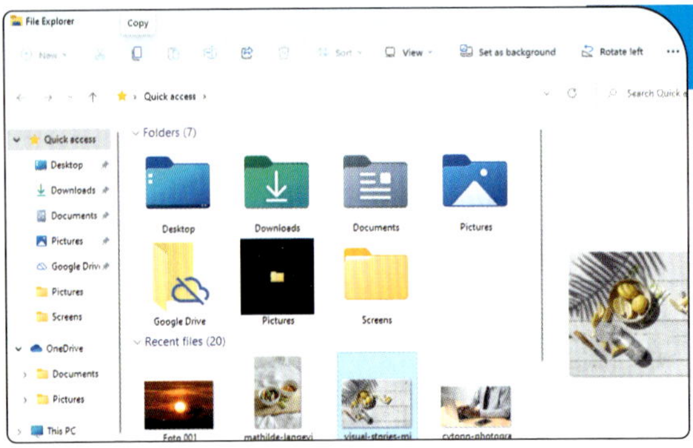


## Step 4

The new icons are all fairly self-explanatory if you have used any PC in the past. There are icons for Cut, Copy, Delete, Rename and Share, as well as folder control icons like View and Sort. If you are unsure what any icon does, just hover your pointer over one to see a label pop up.

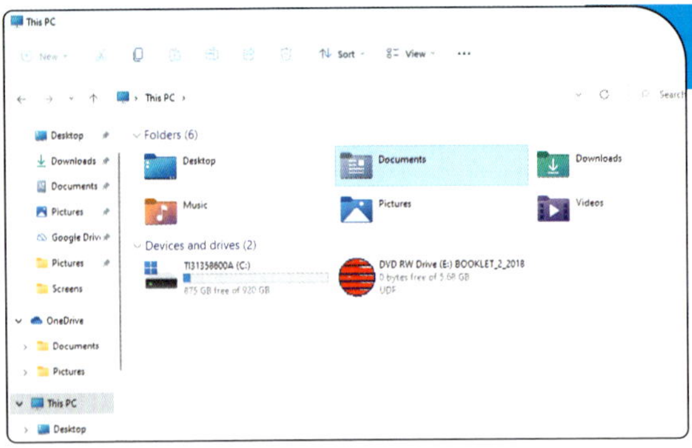


## Step 5

The simplification continues on the This PC screen. All of the controls are still there, you just need to click on the More menu (the three dots) in the top bar. This menu is contextual. For example, select a drive such as C: and then click the menu to see options such as "Map network drive" and "Burn to disc".

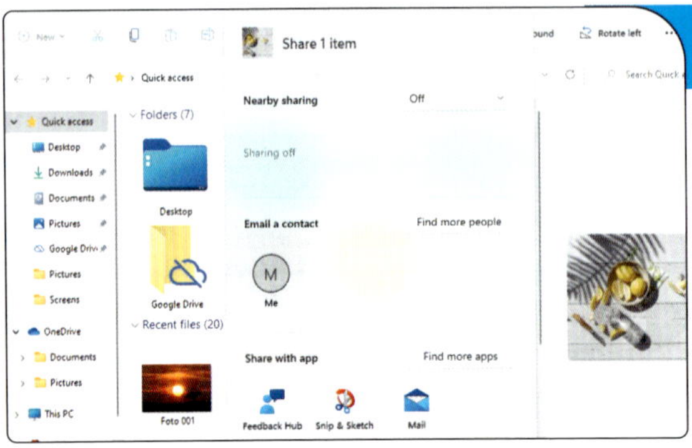


## Step 6

Sharing files in File Explorer is again similar to Windows 10. Select one or more files in the window, click the Share button and the share panel will open. The sharing options shown here will vary depending on which apps you have installed and which communication features you have set up.

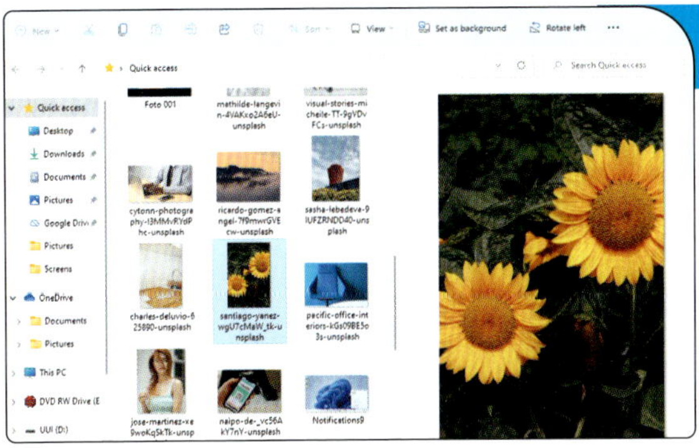

## Step 7

When viewing some files, such as photos, in File Explorer, it can be useful to see a larger preview. This feature is turned off by default, but can be enabled at any time. In any folder in File Explorer, click the View tab and then click Show. From the new menu you can choose to see a Preview pane.

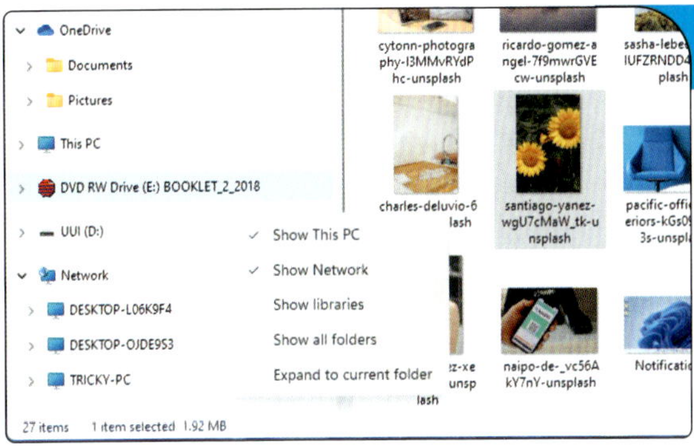


## Step 8

You can access just about every folder on your computer, both system and created folders, from the File Explorer. There are several folders in the sidebar that are always shown, including This PC, Network and OneDrive. Right click on the sidebar to add even more useful folders to this area.

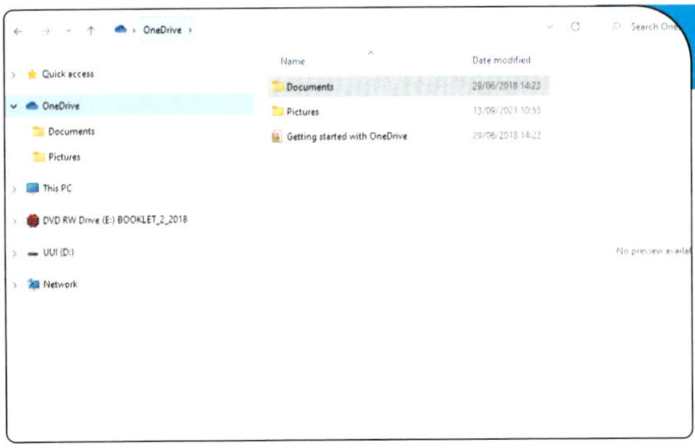

## Step 9

If you've come from an earlier version of Windows, you should be familiar with OneDrive. It's Microsoft's cloud storage application and it's available to access directly from File Explorer in Windows 11; so you can view your cloud-stored files just as if they were on your computer.

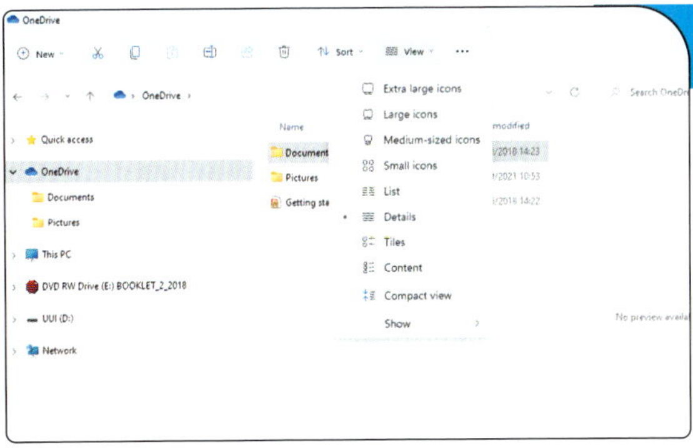


## Step 10

You can quickly change how you view files in File Explorer using the folder view buttons in the bottom-right corner (thumbnail view or detail view). There are many more folder options, including privacy and view options, accessed by clicking the More button and then choosing Options.

# Inside File Explorer

## File Explorer Toolbar

The simplified Explorer toolbar still contains all of the tools you need to manage the different files and folders you can view. Once you have selected a file or folder in the main pane, more tools become active. You can also click the "More menu" button to see additional options such as Burn to disc and Compress to Zip file.

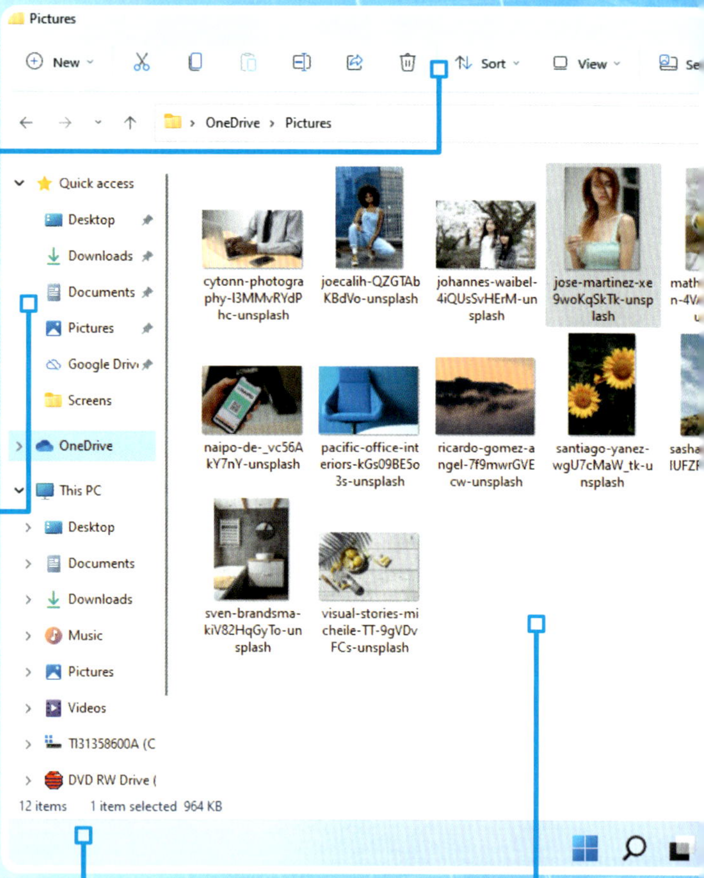


## Navigation Pane - Folders

The left-hand sidebar contains a list of different file folders on your computer. Clicking on any of the folders shown here will display the various files and folders inside; in the main pane. The list is split into sections, including Quick Access/Recent, OneDrive and This PC. If you right-click on a blank area, you can choose to show All Folders here.

## Info Bar

The thin bar along the bottom of the File Explorer displays several bits of useful information. If nothing in the main window is selected, the info bar shows the total number of items in the selected folder. Click on a file and the file size is also shown here. If you select several files, the number of items selected is shown, along with the total size of all selected items combined.

## Folder Contents Pane

When a folder is selected in the File Location sidebar, its contents are shown in the main pane. The contents of any single folder may vary, but Windows uses standard icons to show Word docs, text files, various different image formats and shortcuts to apps and software. Images will usually be displayed as a thumbnail.

**File Explorer is one of the most overlooked tools in Windows, but if you want to be able to find your accumulated photos, music files, word documents and other files, without having to use Search every time, it's definitely something you should be familiar with.**

## Window Controls

Almost every window that opens in Windows includes these controls. From left to right they are: Minimise, Maximise and Close. In Windows 11, moving the mouse over the maximise button brings up the Snap Layouts panel. Right-clicking on the control bar will show you a couple of extra controls, including Restore, Move and Size.

## Preview Pane

If the preview pane is enabled, approximately a third of the File Explorer window will be reserved for a preview of any selected files. Normally, only image, html and text files will display a preview in this pane. The preview pane can be increased or decreased in size by clicking and dragging the scroll bar to the left of it.

## Show Libraries

Your Libraries in Windows 11 are preset system folders that are the default locations for your Camera Roll, Music, Saved Pictures, Documents, Pictures and Videos. You can easily have these displayed in the File Explorer. Right-click on any free area of the Navigation Pane and from the menu, click Show Libraries. You can then expand the list of libraries by clicking the small arrow.

## Folder View

The two buttons here let you choose between viewing the contents of the folder in a thumbnail format or alternatively, as a list. When the folder items are displayed as a list, you can choose to display a varying amount of information, including date last modified, file type and file size. Items shown as a list will still display a preview in the Preview Pane when selected.

# Managing Folders

Despite all of the changes to the Window's OS, folders have remained one of the core tools for organising your files. Much more than just boxes to keep your photos or music files in, folders can really help to improve how you use Windows 11 on a day-to-day basis.

## Creating New Folders

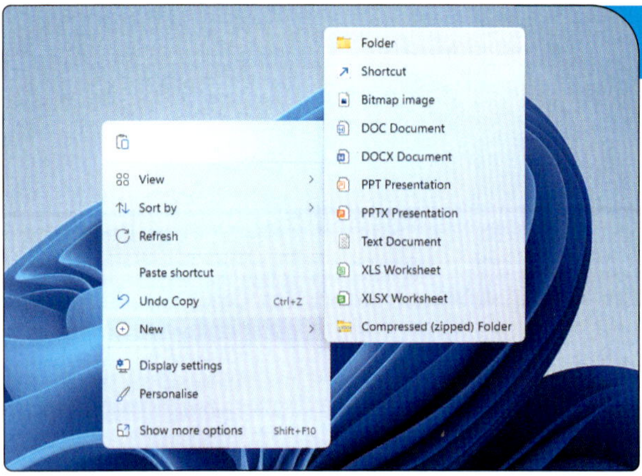


### Step 1

On the desktop, right-click and select New folder from the action menu that appears. The familiar yellow folder icon will then appear at that position on the desktop (wherever you clicked), with the name automatically set as 'New folder' but highlighted ready to change.

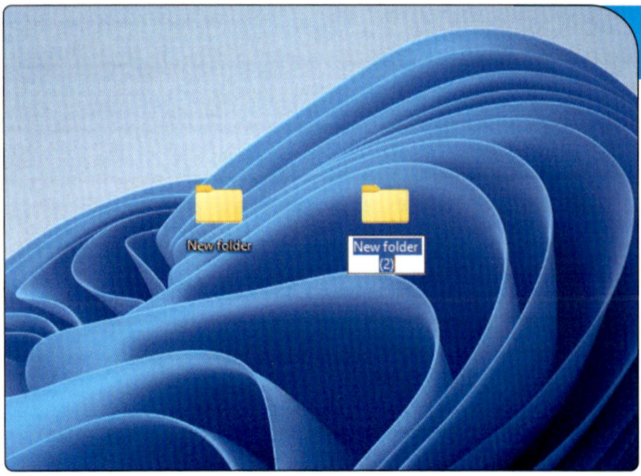


### Step 2

You can leave the name as 'New folder' if you wish. If you then create a second folder next to the first, it will automatically be named 'New folder (2)'. You can rename a folder at any time by left-clicking on the title once, or right-clicking and selecting Rename from the menu.

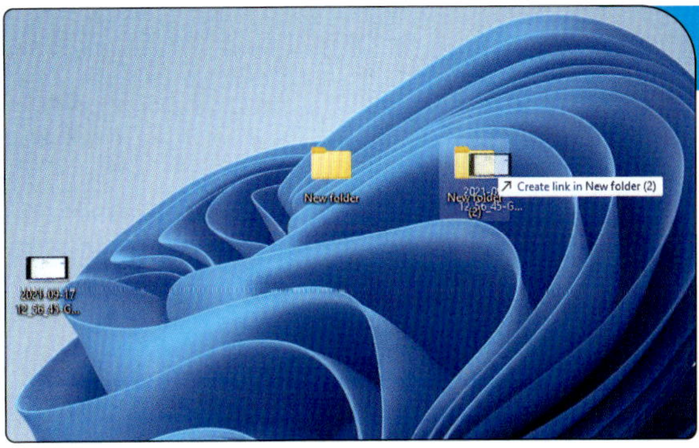


## Step 3

Double-click any folder to open it and view the contents. You can move items into a folder by selecting, dragging and dropping into an open folder or a closed one. If the folder is closed, drag the selected items over the top of it until the folder is highlighted, then release.

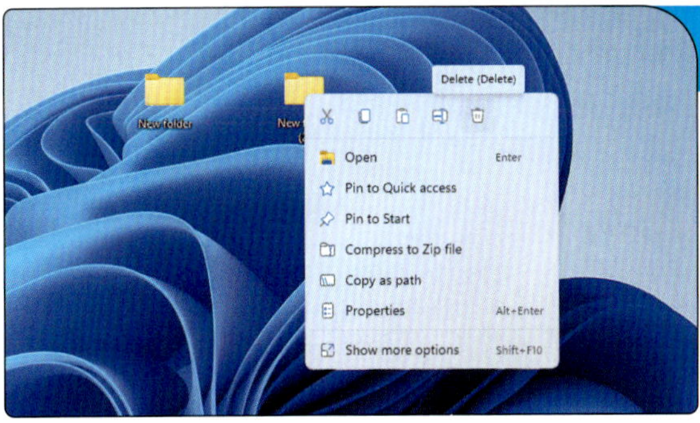


## Step 4

To delete a folder, right-click on it and select Delete from the action menu. You can also click and drag the folder to the Recycle Bin icon on your desktop. Anything in the folder will also be placed in the recycle bin. To move folders around the desktop, just click, drag and drop them.

# Managing Your Folders

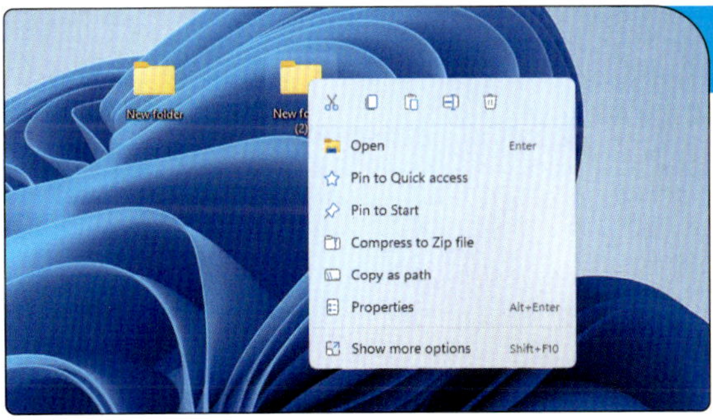


## Step 1

You can manage a folder in a number of ways, without even opening it. Right-click on any folder and the action menu appears. The exact options that appear will depend on the apps or software you have installed but can include: scan for viruses, compress, shred, zip and more.

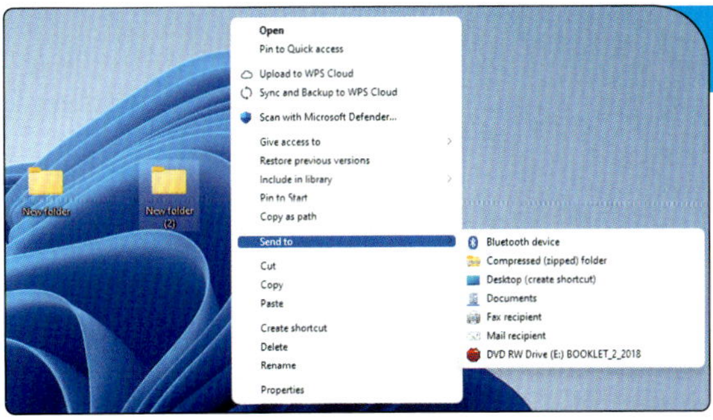


## Step 2

The standard (Windows 11) options in the folder action menu include: Pin to Quick Access, Open, Share, Pin to Start, Send To, Cut, Copy, Rename and Delete. Some of these options are shown as new icons along the top of the action menu. You can see more folder options by clicking that option.

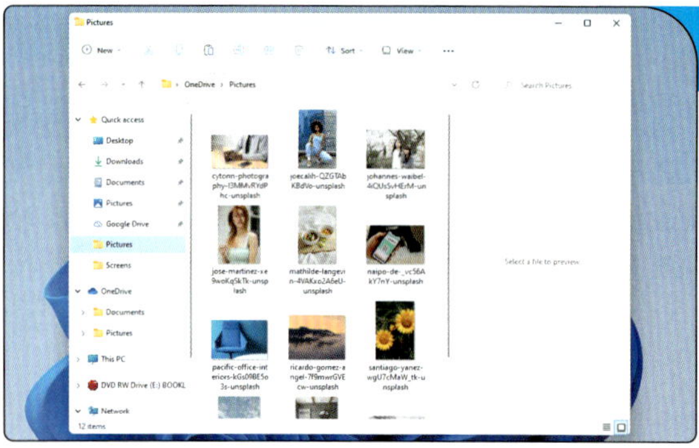

## Step 3

Open the folder and a whole range of further options are available along the top of the new window. Again, these are a mix of icons and test options. When you select something in the folder, yet more options will appear, which vary depending on the type of file you selected in the folder.

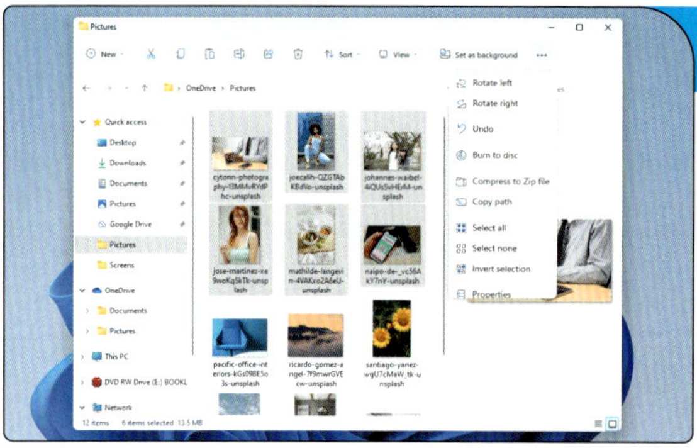

## Step 4

Most of these options are self-explanatory, such as copy, paste and select all, but some are a little more confusing. Most casual computer users won't need to use 90 per cent of the options in day-to-day use but it is worth understanding them anyway. Add a few files to the folder and experiment.

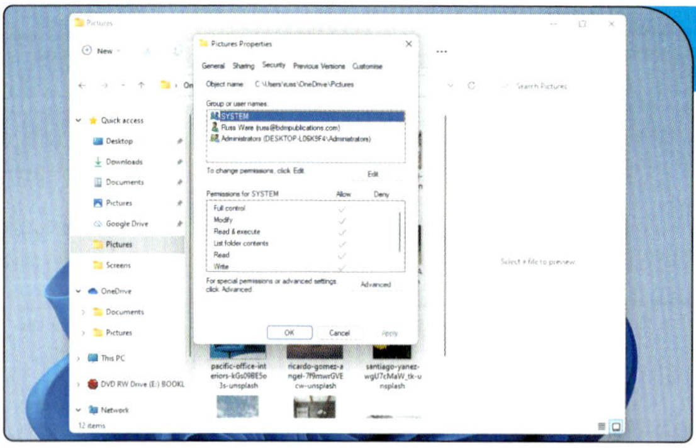

## Step 5

If you want to get really deep into managing your folders, there are even more options to explore. Open any folder and right-click anywhere inside the main window. From the action menu that appears, click Properties. Here you can manage all sorts of things; from security to icon style.

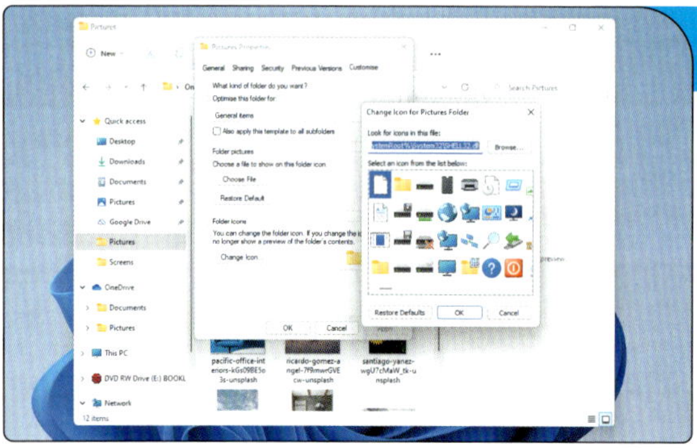

## Step 6

To change the icon style (which will change the style of all folder icons), click the customise tab and then click Change Icon at the bottom. Scroll to view all of the available icons (downloaded icons can be accessed by browsing), click on your preferred icon and click OK.

# Connecting to the Internet

Windows 11 makes joining and managing networks easier than ever before, bringing all of the relevant settings together in one convenient place, including VPN and hotspot settings; and even your Wi-Fi adaptor hardware properties.

## Connecting to Wi-Fi

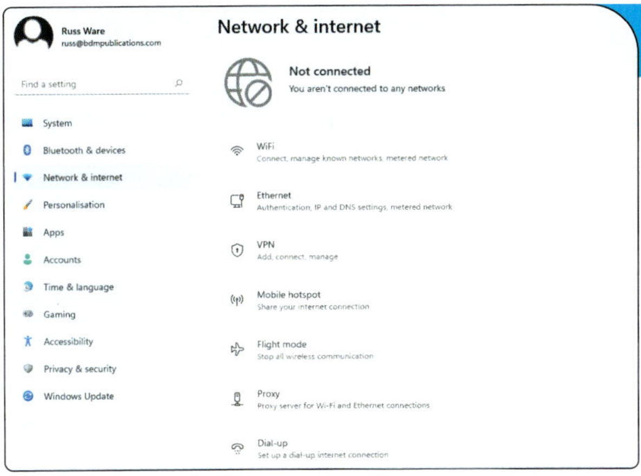


### Step 1

If your computer is not connected to the Internet, Windows will display a small globe icon on the right side of the taskbar. You can either click this and select Wi-Fi from the quick settings, or you can open the main Settings app > Network & Internet > Wi-Fi (the best route with a brand new connection).

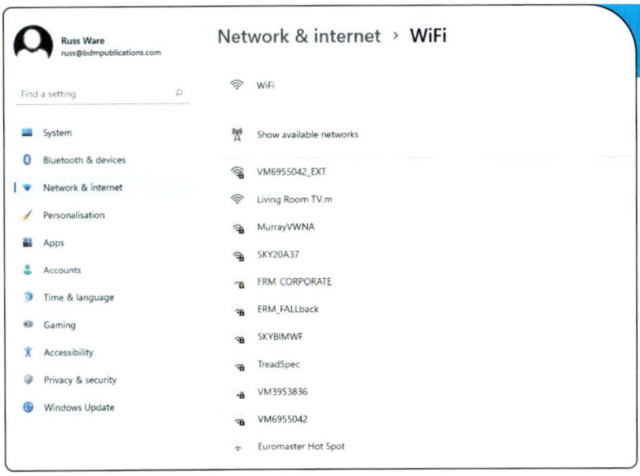


### Step 2

Use the slider switch to enable Wi-Fi on your computer. Now click "Show available networks" to see a list of the networks within range of your computer. This may take a few seconds to scan and find the networks. Hopefully you will see the Wi-Fi network you want to connect to.

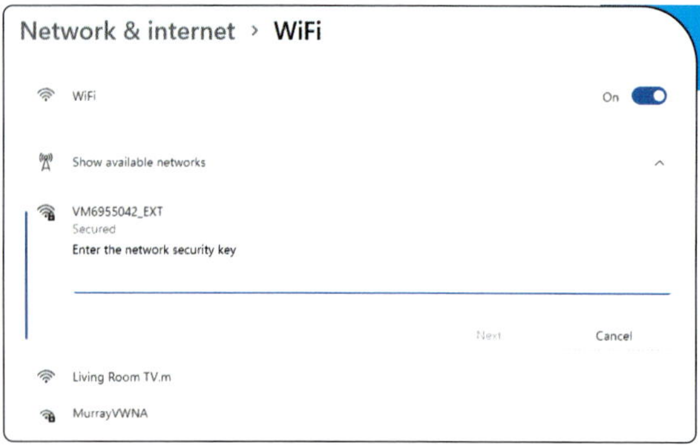


## Step 3

Click on the required network name in the list and then click "Connect". As this is probably the first time you are connecting, you will then need to enter the password (Network security key) for the network. Click "Next" and as long as the network/password is correct, you should be good to go.

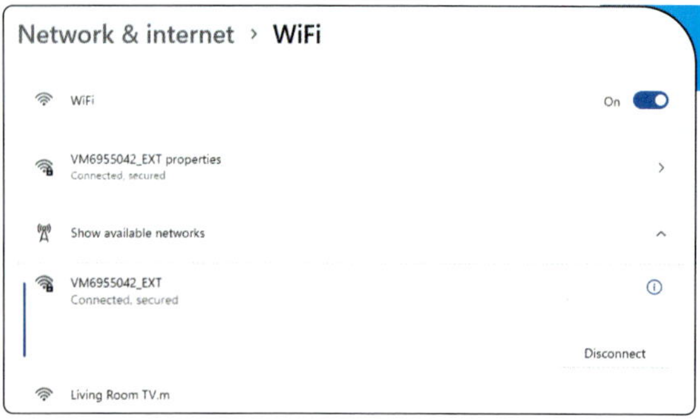


## Step 4

To disconnect from the Wi-Fi network at any time, open Settings > Network & Internet > Wi-Fi again, and click on the networks list. Click the Disconnect button. You can also choose to Forget the network (sometimes useful for troubleshooting connections), in the Manage known networks section.

# Manage Network Settings

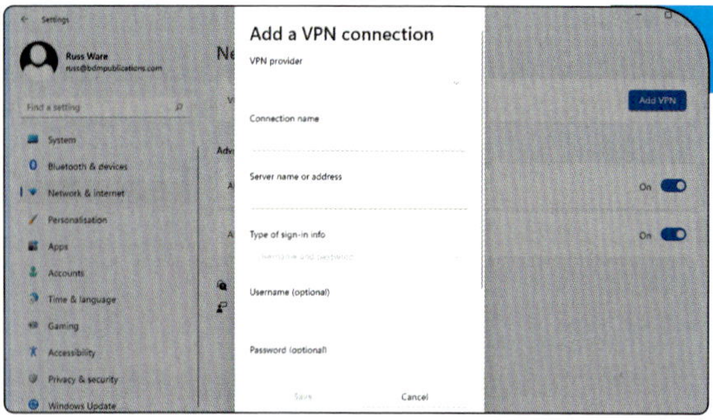


## VPN Settings

If you need to log in to a home VPN or corporate network, this is where you will need to enter the appropriate VPN settings. It's fairly easy to do but you'll need the configuration details from your IT help desk (they will have to enable your VPN access), plus your username and password.

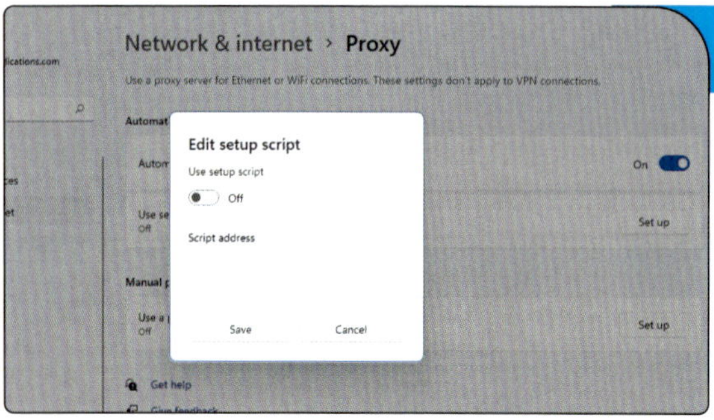


## Proxy Settings

If you use a proxy server, this is where you enter any specific settings to do with that. However, Windows 11 should automatically detect proxy settings. Note that the settings you configure here won't apply if you connect via a VPN, because a VPN essentially skips the need for a proxy.

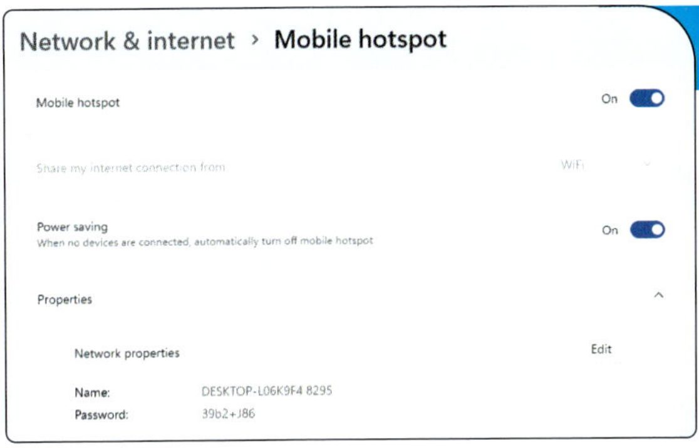


## Mobile Hotspot

You can turn your Windows 11 PC into a mobile hotspot, sharing your Internet connection with other devices over Wi-Fi. You can share Wi-Fi, ethernet or cellular data connections. Once enabled, other devices will be able to see your computer when they search for networks to connect to.

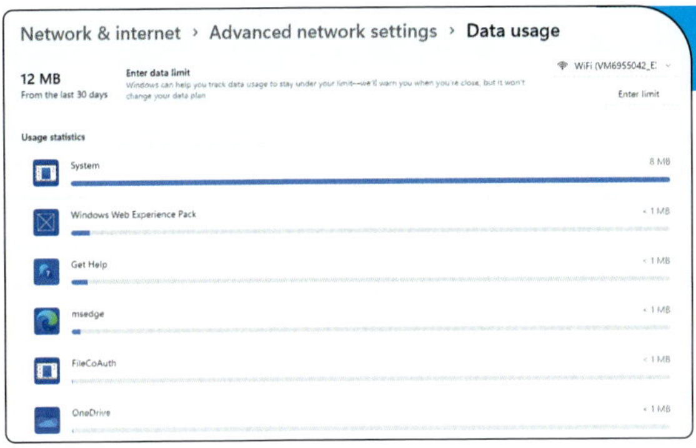


## Usage Stats

In a move designed to keep up with more mobile-based computing devices, Windows 11 includes a data usage page in Settings too. Here it splits your data between wired and wireless. We'd like to see more advanced settings than this too, so you could see how much data you used on a public wireless hotspot, for example.

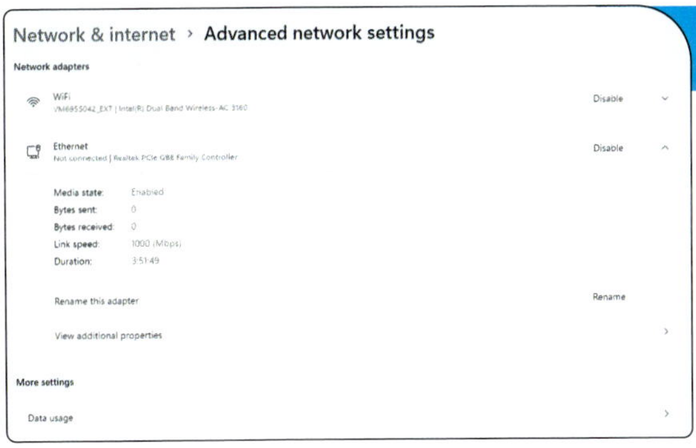


## Disable Adaptors

Another thing you can do is to disable and re-enable your network adapter (like the Wi-Fi card in your laptop). View your network connections by clicking Advanced Network Settings in Network Internet and then right-click the network connection in question. You can disable or re-enable it.

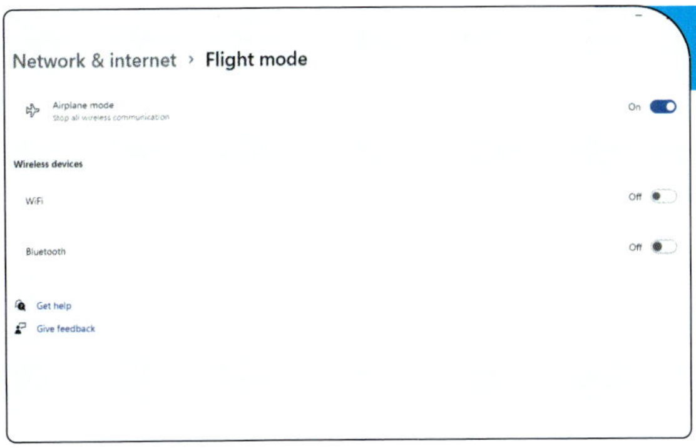


## Flight Mode

If you are using a laptop, you will also have access to Flight mode settings (this can also be accessed through the Quick settings panel from the home screen). Here you can disable Wi-Fi and Bluetooth individually, or simply use the Flight Mode slider switch to disable all wireless connections.

# Windows 11 Settings

## Account & Search

At the top-left of the settings window, you will see your Microsoft account name and email address, along with an avatar image (if you have chosen one). Clicking this will take you to the settings Accounts page. Below that is a search field, allowing you to look for specific settings within the app.

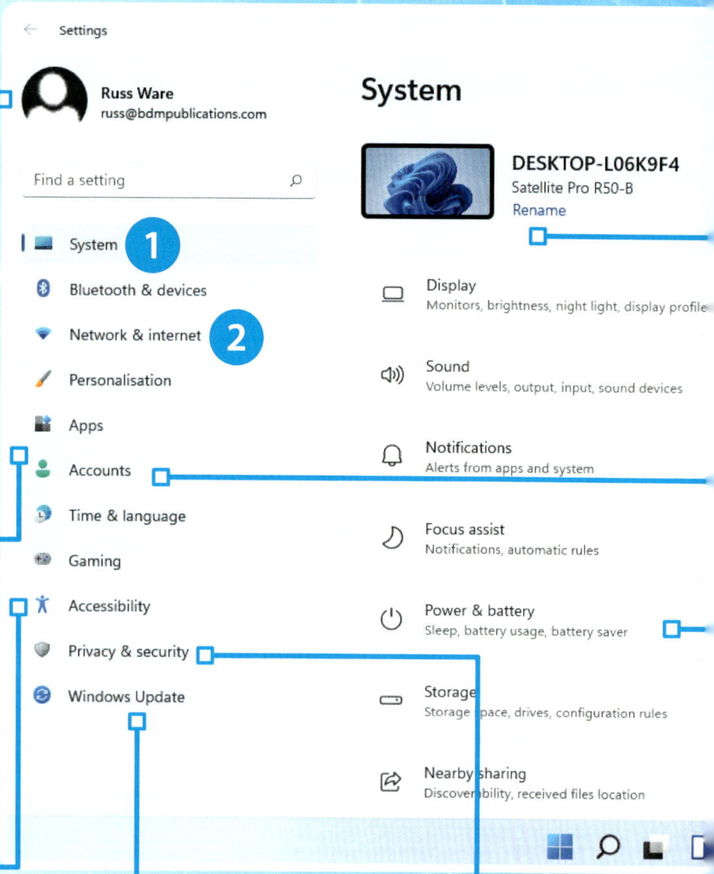


## Settings Categories

In the left sidebar are all of the main settings categories, from System settings to Windows Update settings. This sidebar remains visible no matter where you are within the settings app. Clicking each category heading will open a list of sub categories.

## Accessibility

If you have additional accessibility needs, you can find lots of settings here to make life easier. From a narrator tool and screen magnifier, to closed captioning and mouse and keyboard settings.

## Windows Update

It is important to make sure that your Windows 11 computer is up-to-date with all the latest updates and revisions. Here in Settings, you can check to see which updates are available to download and install.

## Privacy & Security

The privacy settings contains sections for all of the main areas where your privacy may be compromised, including some which might not be obvious at first.

**The main settings app in Windows 11 has been redesigned, making it much easier to find everything you need to keep your computer working the way you want. You can find the settings app in the Start menu, or open it by pressing the Windows Key + I.**

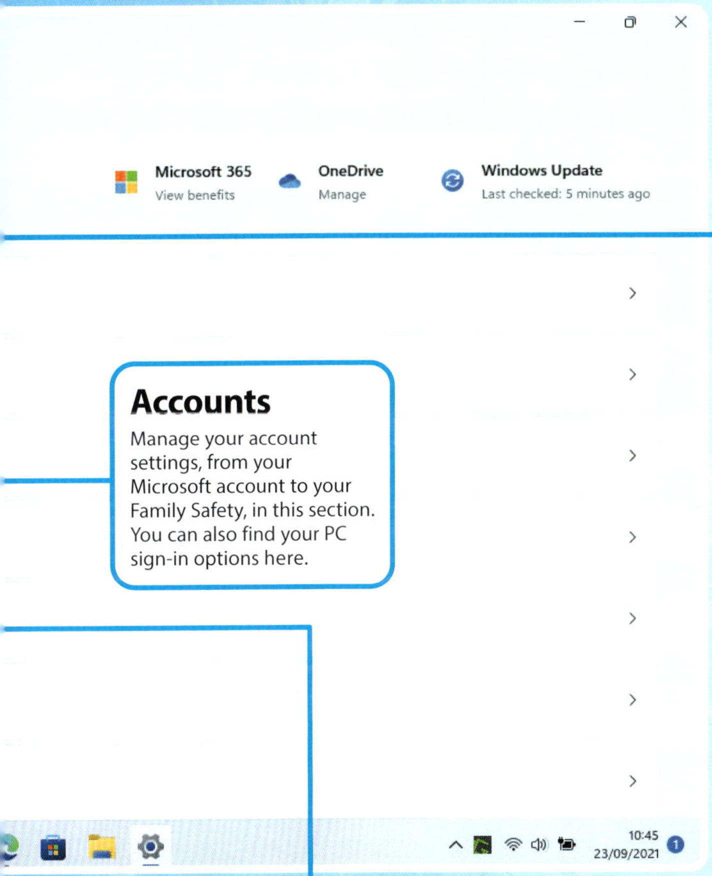


## Quick Info Panel

Along the top of several settings categories you will see relevant information about the current settings. For example, at the top of the System settings, you will see the name of the PC, Windows Update status and links to OneDrive and Office365. Then, for Network & Internet, there's currently connected network, data usage and network properties.

## Accounts

Manage your account settings, from your Microsoft account to your Family Safety, in this section. You can also find your PC sign-in options here.

## 1 System Settings

These are the core settings for your Windows computer. Things like Display, Sound, Power & Battery and Storage can be found in this settings category.

## 2 Network & Internet

View, connect to and manage your Wi-Fi, Network and other Internet settings here. You can also find a section for adding a VPN, and setting up a Mobile Hotspot.

## Settings Sub-categories

This is where you'll find the individual settings you can change. Some of the settings can be controlled using slider switches displayed in the main sub-category, but most will take you to a more detailed selection of options when clicked. Certain details about current settings may be displayed along the top of the sub-category.

# Browsing with Microsoft Edge

Edge Chromium, is a significant change to the original Edge browser; and offers a much better experience. Based on the Google Chrome browser, Edge is focused on modern web standards, privacy and security and has an impressive feature and tool list.

## Get Started with Edge

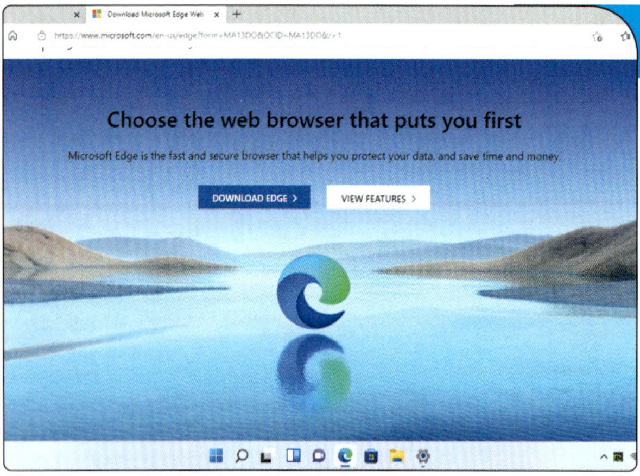


### Installing Edge

Edge comes pre-installed with Windows 11, and if you have upgraded from Windows 10 (and were using Edge previously) it should already be set up and working as normal. If you bought a PC with Windows 11 installed, or have never used Edge before, it will require a bit of setup to begin with.

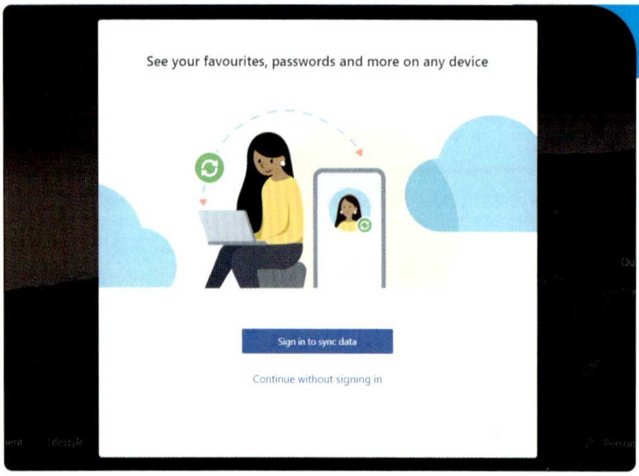


### Edge Setup

During setup, you have the option to import browser data such as bookmarks and favourites from Google Chrome, choose the initial start page layout and set up syncing across devices (other computers, your phone, etc.) Once installed, Edge opens at the start page.

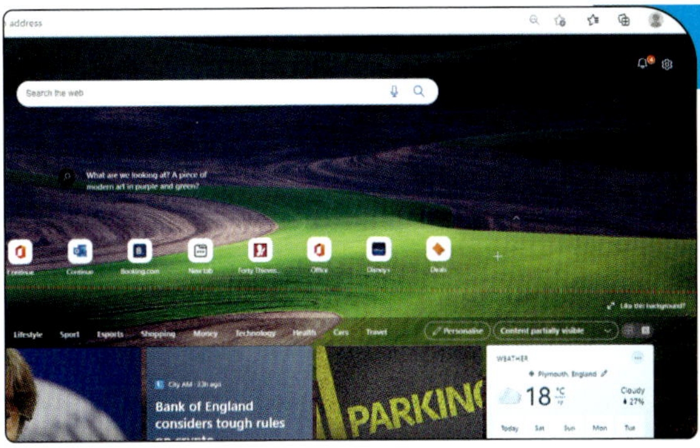


## Start Page Layout

Depending on the layout you chose during setup, the start page will either display a news feed or a cleaner page (with the news feed just a scroll away below it). You can check out the other layouts easily by clicking the Gear icon at the top right and choosing from the menu.

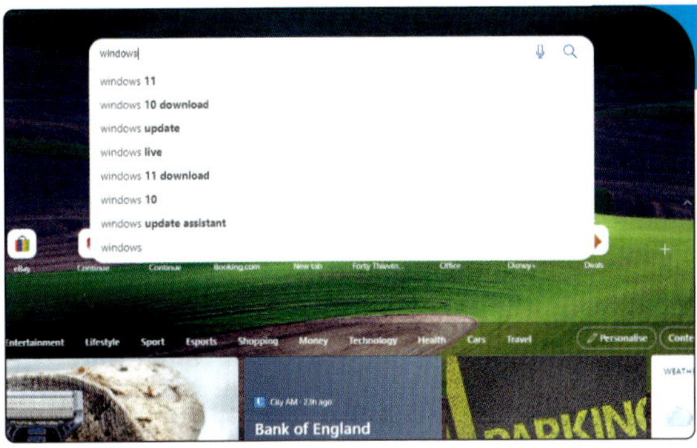


## Search in Edge

To search for a website or web page, you can type in the search field at the top (which is always there), or you can type in the search box floating on the Start page. When you type in either box, Edge shows a list of suggestions based on what it thinks you require. The default search engine is Bing.

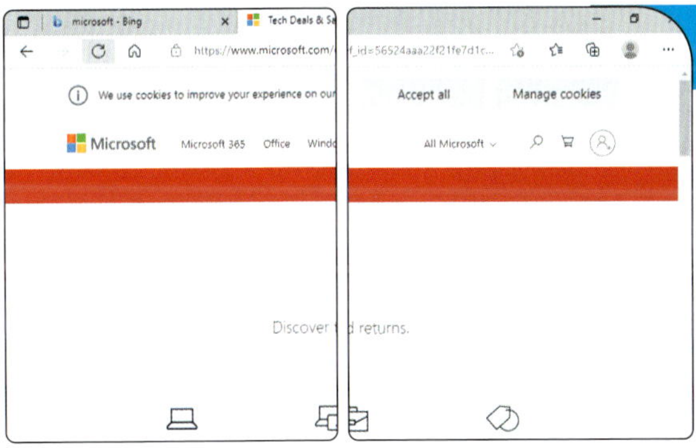


## Browser Controls

The browser controls are on the top bar. On the far left is: Back, Forwards and Refresh Page (Home button can be added in the browser settings). On the right are the zoom control, add to favourites, favourites list and collections buttons. There is also a More button to open the browser menu.

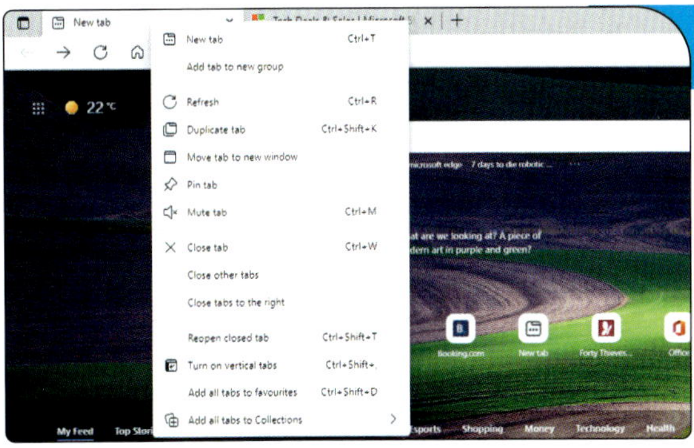


## Edge Tabs

Clicking the + opens a new tab and clicking the small, right-hand X closes the tab. To the left of the tabs is the Tab actions menu button. You can use this to move tabs to the side of the window (vertically), create tab collections and restore recently closed tabs. Right-click on any tab to see additional tab options.

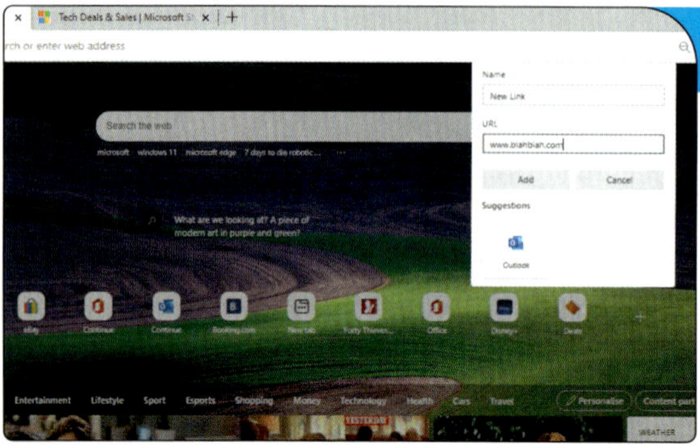


## Quick Links

Each Start page layout includes a row of quick links (website icons) below the Start page search field. These will be auto-populated if you are new to Edge, but as you use the browser, these will be replaced by your recent/often visited sites. You can add sites by clicking the + button on the right.

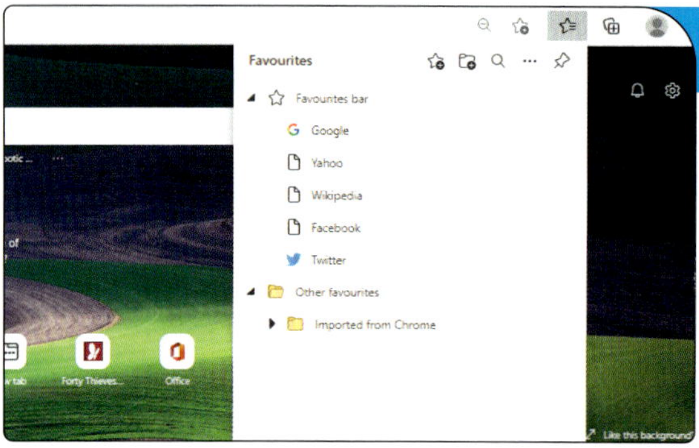


## Favourites

To access Favourites, or bookmarked sites, click the button directly to the right of the address bar (star with three lines). Clicking it opens a fly-out list, at the top of which is the option to "Manage favourites". This opens the list in a new page, where you can remove or re-order them.

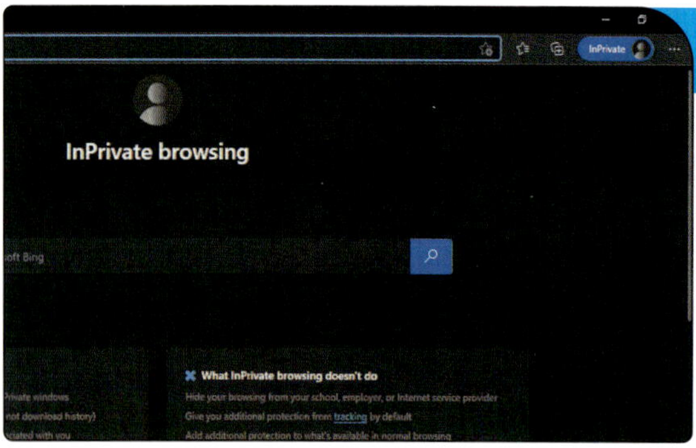


## InPrivate Window

If you want to browse in private mode when using Edge, you can do so easily. To open a new InPrivate tab, click the browser menu button at the top right and select "New InPrivate Window". You can also open a new private tab by using the keyboard shortcut Ctrl + Shift + N while Edge is active.

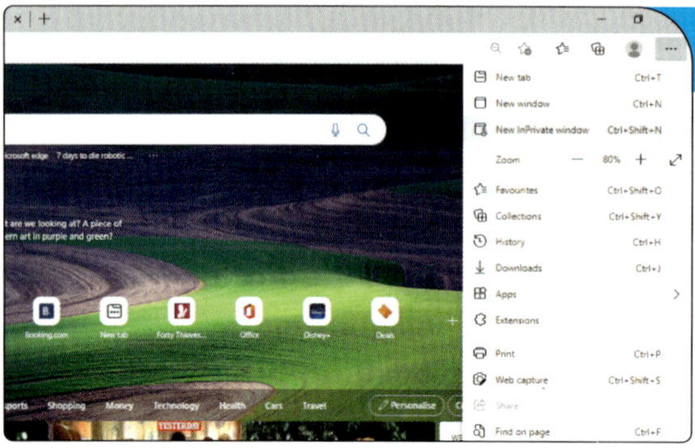


## Edge Menu

Click the Menu button (three small dots on the top right) to open the Edge menu. From this menu, you're able to access Settings, print a page and find words or phrases in the open web page. It also contains links to Favourites, Collections, History, Downloads, Apps, Extensions and much more.

# The Edge News Feed

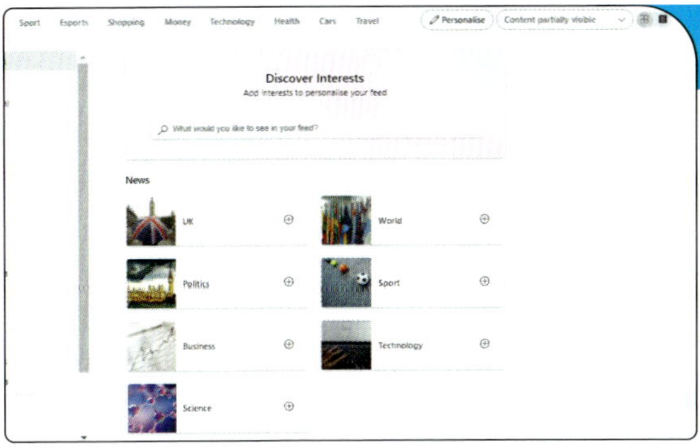


## Feed Settings

Click the Content visibility button to choose how news stories are displayed (visible, partially visible or headings only). The Personalise button lets you choose which categories are displayed, if information cards are included (weather, etc.), and which news types alert you with a notification.

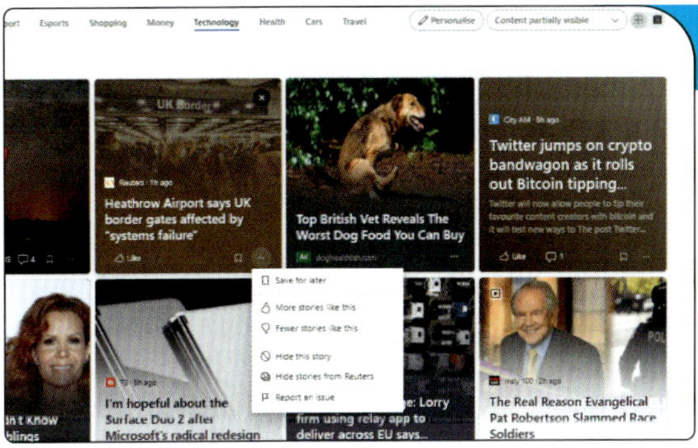


## Curating Stories

The more you use Edge, the more the stories adapt to suit your interests. You can help this process by interacting with stories. Click the X to close stories that don't interest you, click the More menu button on a story to save it, vote for more/fewer stories like this and hide stories from that source.

# Edge Privacy

**Microsoft seems to be taking users' privacy choices seriously with Edge Chromium, and you now have a much easier way to control your browsing data and history. The biggest improvement is Tracking Prevention. You can access these settings in Browser Menu > Settings > Privacy & Services.**

**You can choose three different levels of tracking prevention: Basic, Balanced and Strict. These options all block known harmful trackers, but how personalised content (such as adverts) is displayed and how well all website features work, depends on the level you choose.**

**Our advice is to switch to Strict and then see how it affects your favourite websites. If you find things are not displayed as they should be, you can always switch back to Balanced.**

**You can view sites that you have blocked from tracking you, and also allow exceptions if there are sites which you want to allow to track you.**

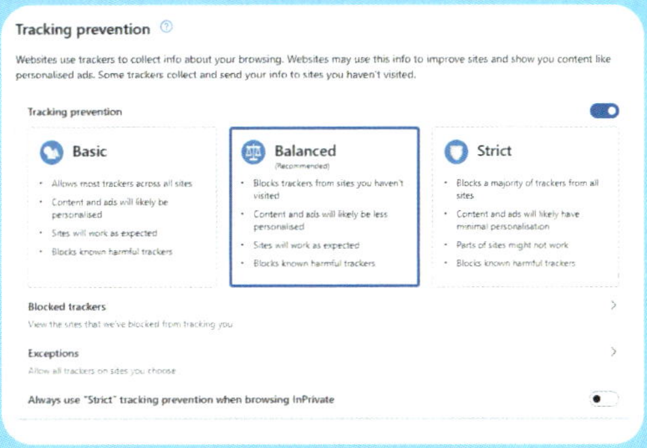

# Personalising Edge

## Light or Dark

If you have changed the system theme to light or dark, Edge should automatically be set to the same. You can, however, choose the theme for Edge separately to the system theme. Open the Edge menu > Settings, and click Appearance. Choose the light, dark or system default theme.

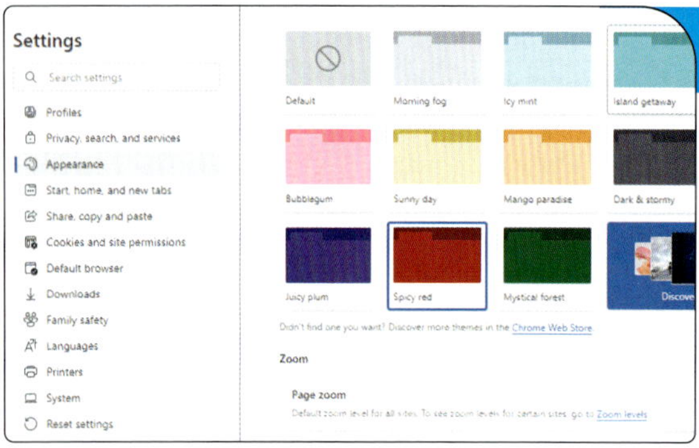


## Edge Themes

As well as light or dark, Edge lets you choose from about 15 other theme colours, from Morning Fog to Mystical Forest. Go to Edge menu > Settings > Appearance and click on the theme colour you want to apply. This will only apply colour to the top bar and tabs. It will not override the light/dark setting.

## Browser Controls

The default browser controls are Back, Forward and Refresh page. Open the menu > Settings > Appearance and you can scroll down to see more buttons to add. These include Home (including option to set the URL), Extensions, History, Downloads and strangely, a Maths Solver button.

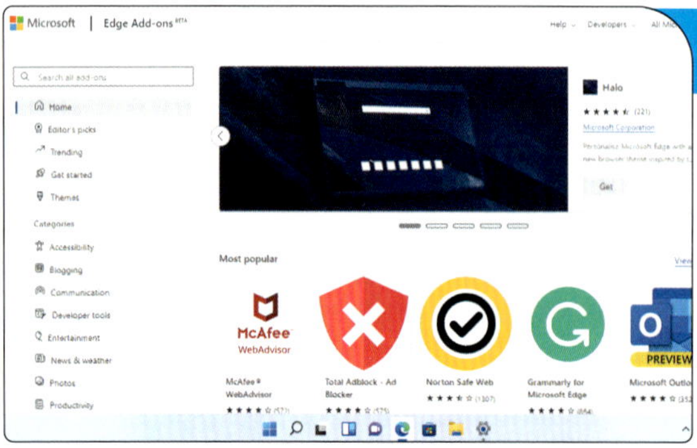


## Extensions

Just like the previous version, Edge Chromium features extensions, which are downloaded from the Microsoft Store. You can view installed extensions in the Browser Menu > Extensions. There are fewer extensions available for the new version, but this situation will improve as it matures.

# Edge Collections

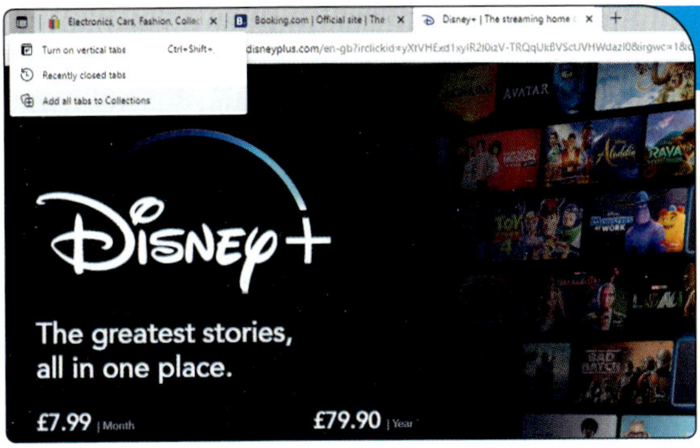


## Step 1

Open the websites that you want to save in a Collection, in separate tabs. Click the Tab Actions button (top-left) and from the menu, select "Add all tabs to Collections". A notification will appear below the Collections button in the browser tools bar, confirming the Collection was saved.

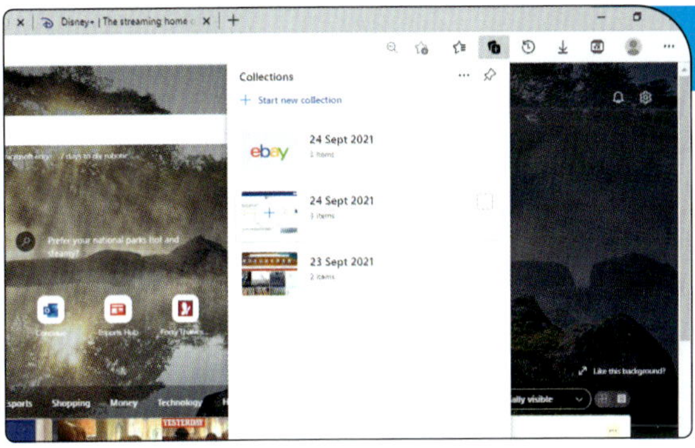


## Step 2

To open a Collection, click the Collections button, and right-click on the collection you want to open. Select "Open all [number]". You can edit the collections by clicking on them here, and adding or removing pages. You can also rename the collections by clicking on the date title at the top.

# Edge vs the Internet

**Historically speaking, Microsoft's own browser was never really one that satisfied the masses. True enough, it did the job, but the likes of Chrome, Firefox and even some of the lesser-known browsers, always managed to outperform it or be more secure.**

**However, when Microsoft released Edge, and especially since it started to build Edge on top of Chrome technology, the built-in Windows browser has, excuse the pun, had the edge over its rivals. Thanks to a facelift, and some fine-tuning under the hood, Edge can now not only compete with the leading browser names, but in some instances flat out beat them.**

**Even if you're a diehard Chrome or Firefox user, it might be worth giving Edge a try on your favourite sites. Who knows, it could become your new favourite browser of choice.**

# Exploring the Edge Browser

## Browser & Tab Controls

In the top left corner, where you would probably expect to find them, are the browser controls. These include the Home button, the Page refresh button and the Page forward/Page back buttons. Also in the top corner is the Tab control, allowing you to set the tabs vertically, or restore closed tabs. Right-click on the active tab to see additional options.

## Recently Viewed/ Favourites

A group of icons are displayed for the most recently visited websites/ pages. These automatically update as you browse, but can also be edited to show your favourite or most-used sites by clicking on the + symbol at the end of the row of icons.

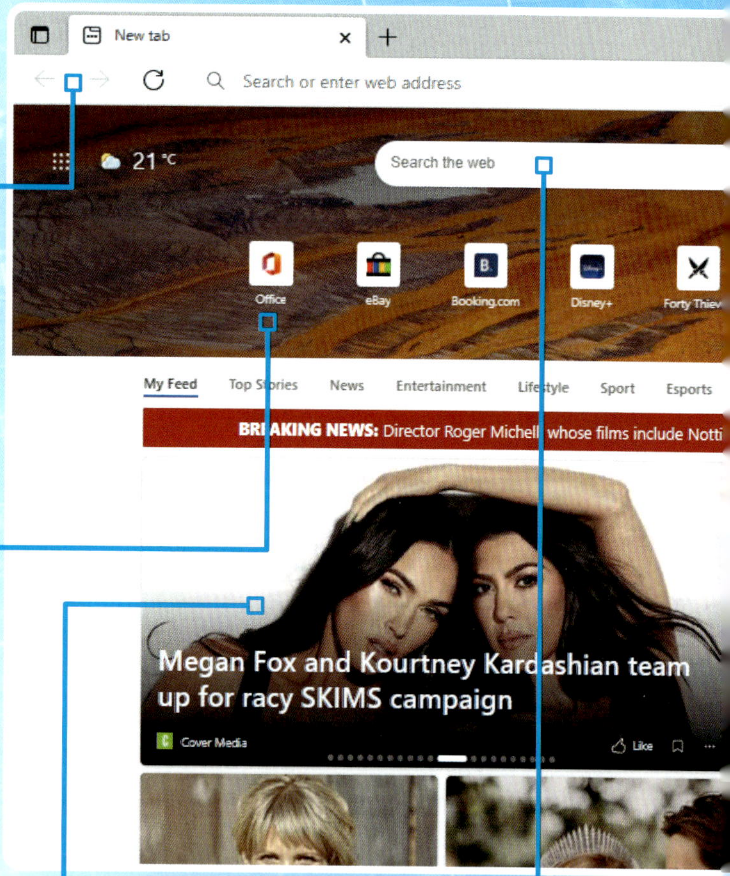


## News Feed

The Start screen of Microsoft Edge is also a news feed. The news feed is provided by MSN and is made up of news stories based on your geographical location. Either the feed is displayed at the top, or you scroll down to it; depending on the layout you choose. Click "Personalise" to filter the news types, and click "Content visible" to choose how stories are displayed.

## Search Fields

There are two search fields in Edge, one at the top (which is also the address field when viewing a website), and one which floats at the top or middle of the start page; depending on the layout you choose. Use either of these and search suggestions appear as you begin typing.

**Edge continues to get better, and the latest version in Windows 11 is no different. You should be familiar with it if you are upgrading from Windows 10, as it is basically the same version; but let's take a look at the newest and best features of Microsoft Edge.**

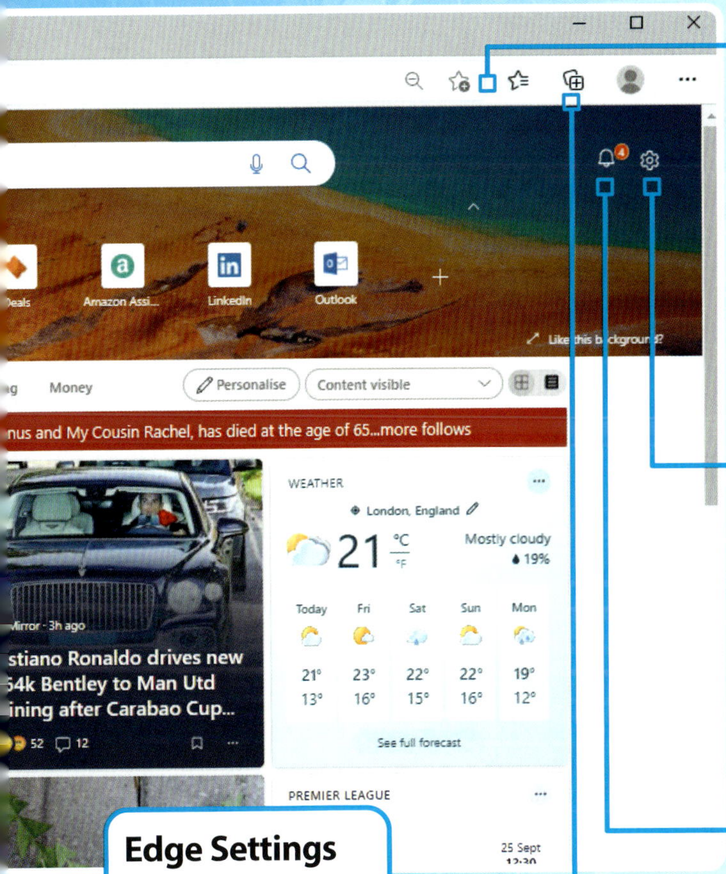


## Favourites Menu

The Hub from the old version of Edge, which contained favourites, history and a reading list has gone. Instead, you can access Favourites and Collections here. The star with a + icon in the search field is the button to add a new web page to your favourites.

## Start Page Layout

You can customise the Start screen in several ways here. There are three preset layouts: Informational, Inspirational and Focused. You can also choose a custom layout, which lets you turn on/off individual elements, such as pic of the day and the news feed.

## Notifications

The small alarm/bell icon opens a list of top news stories. A badge will appear on top of it to tell you how many new stories are waiting to be read. As you browse the news feed, Edge will learn what type of news you like to read and tailor the notifications accordingly.

## Edge Settings

Alongside options to change the style of the Edge browser, including changing to a dark theme, are several important settings. You can choose how the Edge browser opens, showing the Start page or another specified page for example. The advanced settings include options to block pop-ups and allow Flash Player.

## Collections

Collections are groups of tabs/ web pages that you can save and then instantly return to using this button. To save a Collection, click the Tab Controls button at the top-left, and choose "Add all tabs to collections".

# Exploring Windows Mail

## New Mail Button

If you are not replying to an email, but rather starting a new email, you can do so in a couple of different ways. You can either click the New Mail button at the top of the Mail Menu or you can use the Ctrl-N. Both methods open a new email in the main window, with a blank recipient field.

## Mail Menu

The left-hand menu, which can be minimised and expanded using the button at the top of the panel, contains all of your email accounts (those you have added to Windows Mail). Click on any of your email account headers and the individual folders, such as Inbox and Sent Items, are displayed here also.

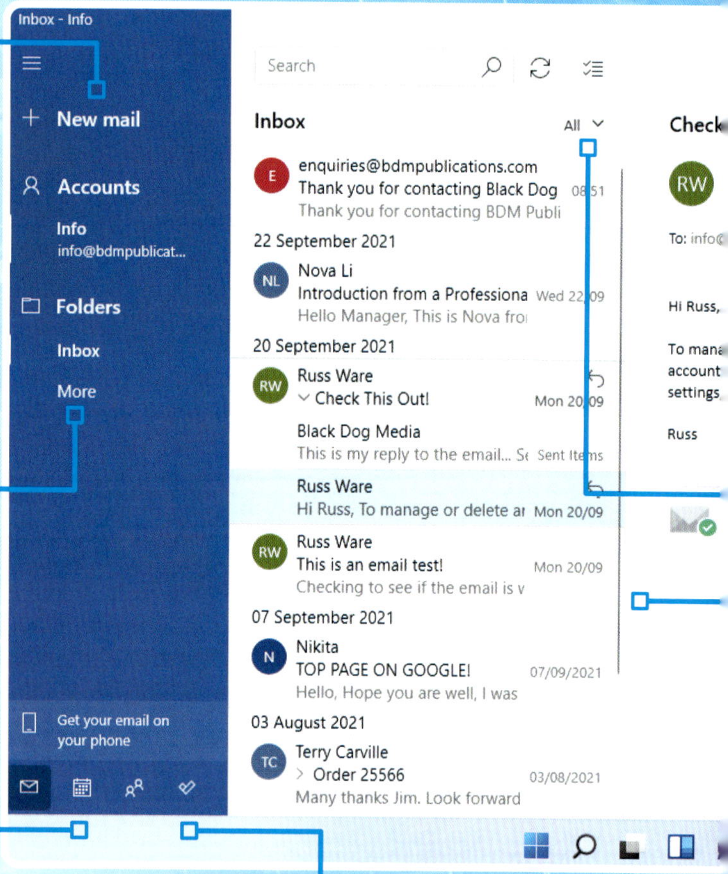


## Calendar View

You can open the Windows Calendar app directly from within the Mail app. Click the Mail app icon at the bottom of the Mail Menu panel and the calendar screen will open in a second window. If you have never used the Calendar app before, you will need to link it to an account.

## Mail Settings

The settings for the Mail app allow you to easily add accounts, change how emails are displayed when they arrive, whether outgoing emails have a signature (which can be customised) added to them, as well as how you are notified of new emails in Windows 11.

**Gone are the days of Microsoft Outlook Express being included with new releases of the OS; replaced instead by Microsoft's Mail app. This app first appeared in Windows 8, was updated in Windows 10, and has now been improved yet again for Windows 11.**

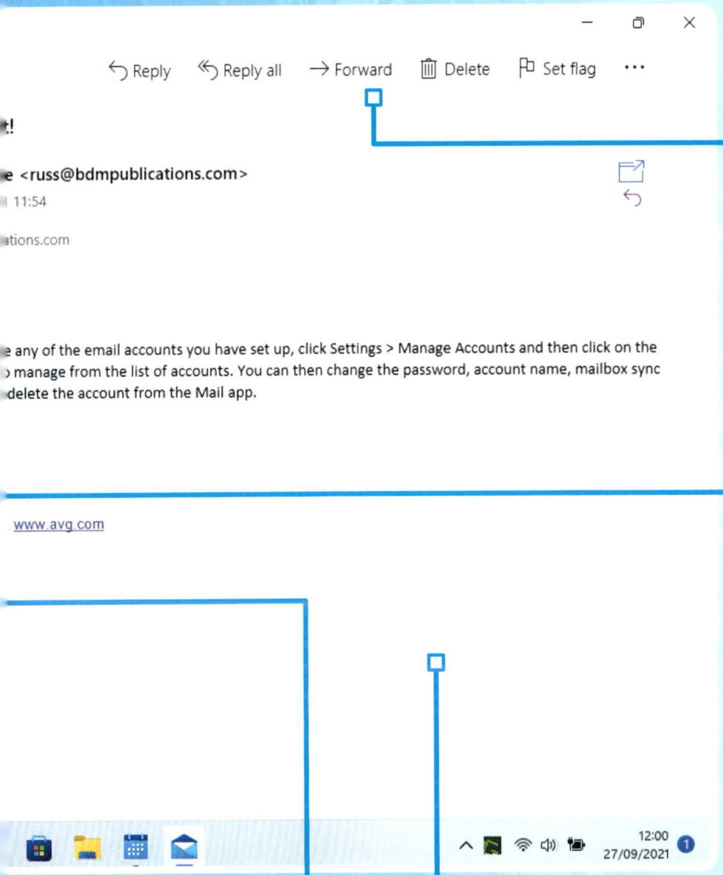


## Message Options

In a row along the top of the main message window are the message options. These include Reply, Reply All, Forward, Archive and Delete emails; more options can be seen by clicking the Menu button to the right. The message options only appear when viewing a received message.

## Message Tools

Roll over or click on any of the messages in your inbox, sent items or drafts folders and three icons will appear. These let you quickly Archive, Delete or Flag any message directly in the folder panel. Archived messages can be recovered at any time and returned to the inbox if required.

## Main Message Window

When you start a new email or select an email in one of the mail folders, it will appear in the main message window. As you would normally, you can scroll down to view all of the messages shown. You can roll over the address in the To: field, to see more contact details.

## Mail Folder

The messages in whichever email folder you have selected are shown in this panel. By default, the most recent emails are at the top of the list. You can change how the emails are viewed, so that only unread or flagged emails are displayed, using the dropdown menu at the top of the inbox.

# Using the Mail App

The Mail app in Windows 11 remains a simple and easy way to have all of your emails in one place. If you have updated from Windows 10, your email should already be up and running. But if not, here's how to set up and tailor the Mail app in Windows 11 to suit you.

## Setting Up Email Accounts

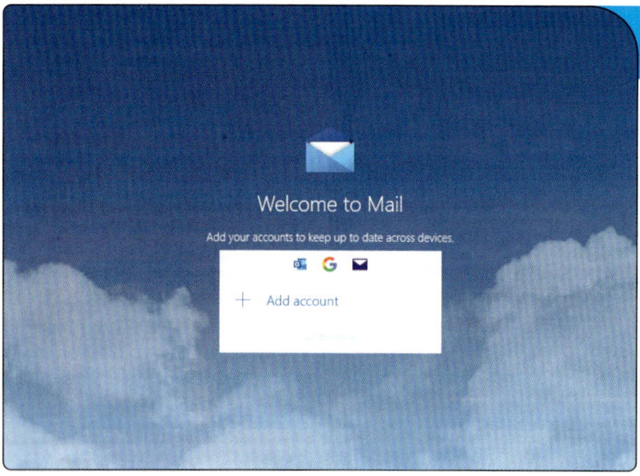


### Step 1

If opening Mail for the first time, you will be greeted by a welcome screen, containing a link to "+Add account". Click this to open the list of available account types. You will need the server, password and other information required for each email account you want to add to Mail.

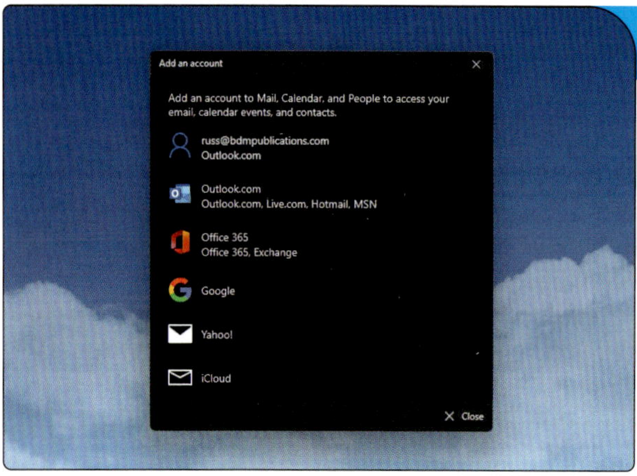


### Step 2

You can add accounts from many popular providers including Google, Yahoo! and Apple's iCloud. You can also set up other more specialist accounts if you have the details. Finally, there's also an option to add a Microsoft Exchange account, if your workplace uses that (including Office 365).

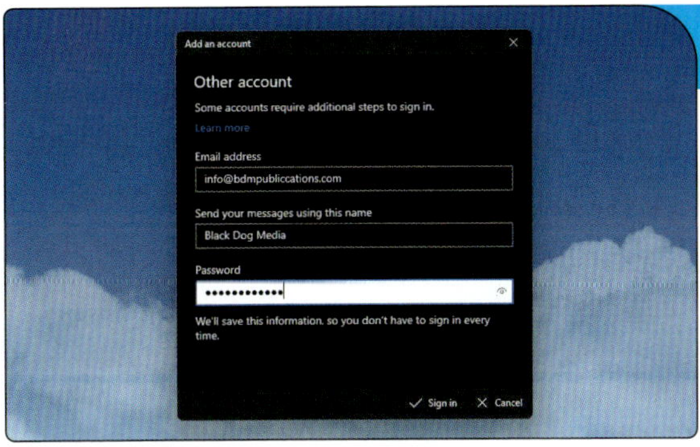


## Step 3

Click the email account type you want to set up first. We are going to start with the POP, IMAP option. Enter the email address, sender name and password for your account. You can get this info from your email service provider if you don't have it to hand. Then click "Sign in".

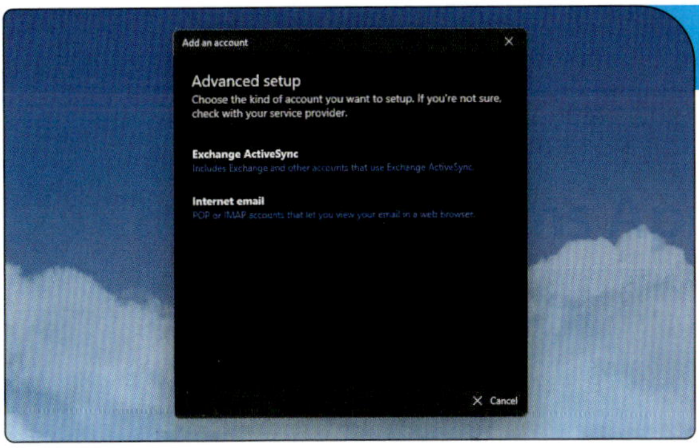


## Step 4

The app will try to look for the server settings needed to set this email account up. If it finds them, you should be finished. If not, you will need to add the settings manually. If this is the case, click "Cancel" and then select the "Advanced setup" option in the account list.

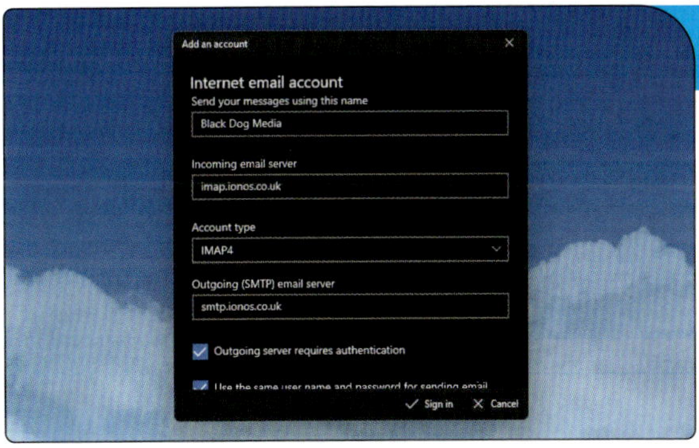


## Step 5

Choose the relevant option (in our case, this is "Internet email"), and enter all of the required information; including the incoming/outgoing mail server addresses. With all of the information added, click the Sign in button. If everything was entered correctly, that account is now set up.

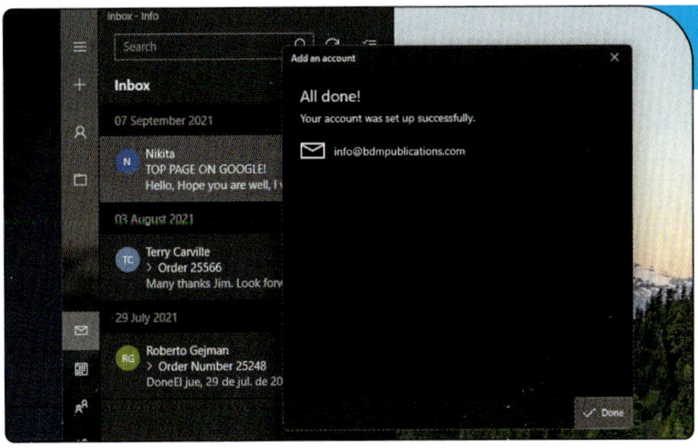


## Step 6

To add an additional account after setting up the first one, simply click the settings button in the bottom-left corner of the Mail app window, select Manage Accounts, and then +Add account. Select the account type and repeat the steps above to add the second, third or fourth account to Mail.

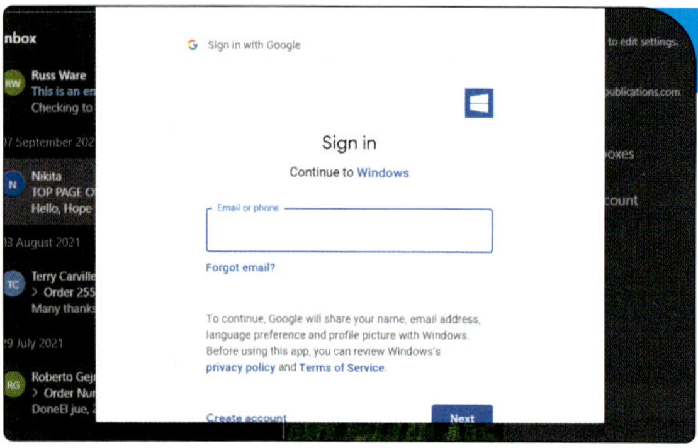


## Step 7

If you're adding a Google account, click the option in the account setup list and you'll get the familiar pop-up appearing inviting you to enter your username and password. If you have Google's two-step authentication enabled, you'll get a text message to confirm your identity before you can continue.

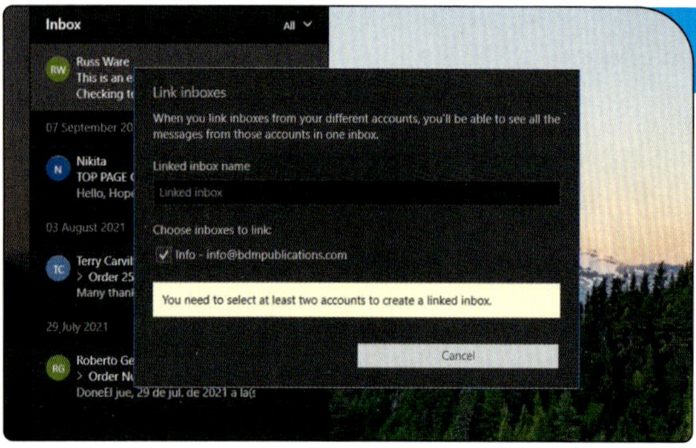


## Step 8

Having more than one email account set up in Mail can be slightly confusing. To help with this, the app allows you to Link Inboxes. This puts all of the emails from your linked accounts into one inbox. To do this, click Settings > Manage accounts > Link inboxes. Select the accounts you want to link.

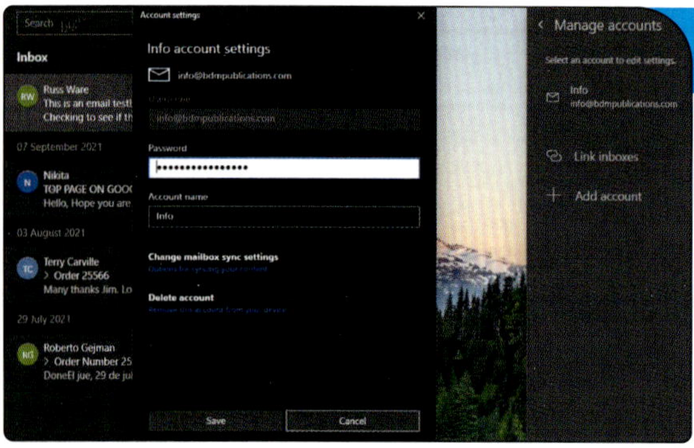


## Step 9

To manage or delete any of the email accounts you have set up, click Settings > Manage Accounts and then click on the account you want to manage from the list of accounts. You can then change the password, account name, mailbox sync settings, or delete the account from the Mail app.

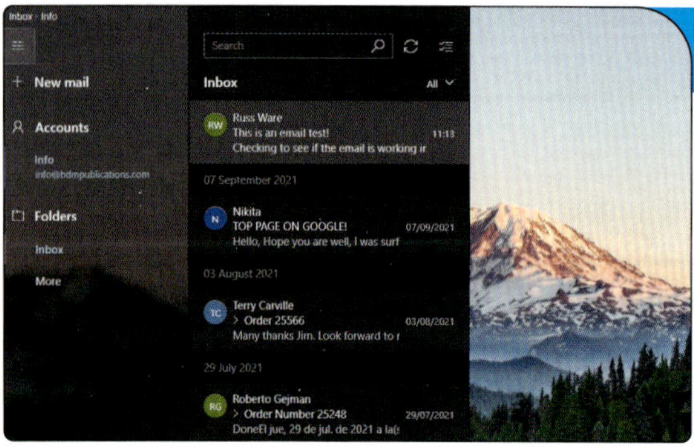


## Step 10

Your accounts are shown in the left sidebar of the mail app. Select them here to view the different folders for each account (inbox, sent mail, etc.), if you have not linked the inboxes. If you don't see the left sidebar, click the Expand button at the top-left of the Mail app window.

# Using the Mail App

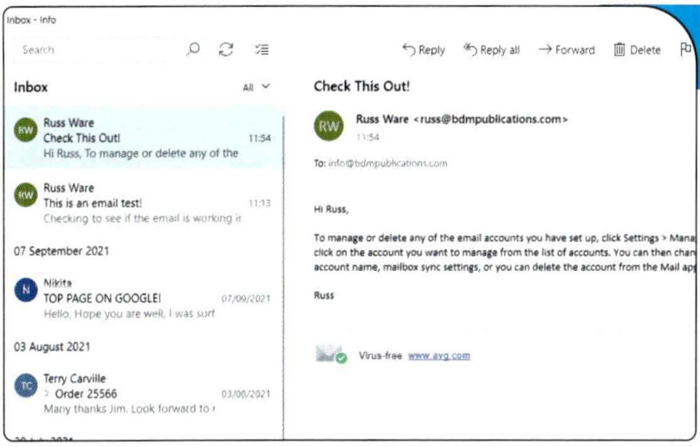


## Reading Emails

Emails will appear automatically in your inbox as and when they arrive. New emails will be displayed with a highlight in the list. Click any email in the inbox list to open It In the maln panel on the right. You can search for emails using the Mail Search field at the top of the inbox panel.

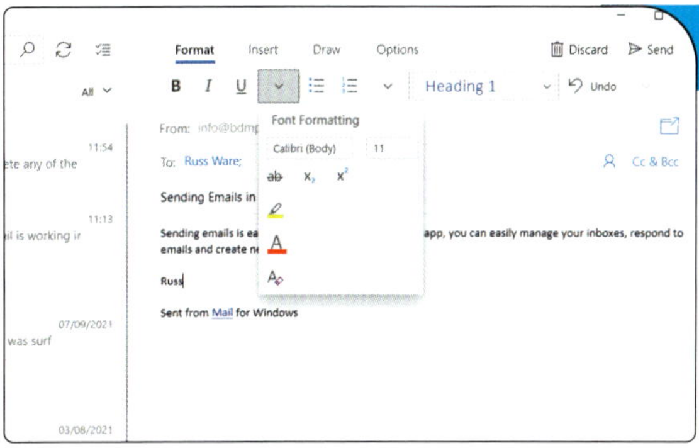


## Writing Emails

Click the New mail button in the Mail app menu (the + button if the menu is collapsed). The blank email will appear in the main panel. Enter the recipient's address, subject and then write your email text. Basic text formatting options are available at the top of the email. Click "Send" when finished.

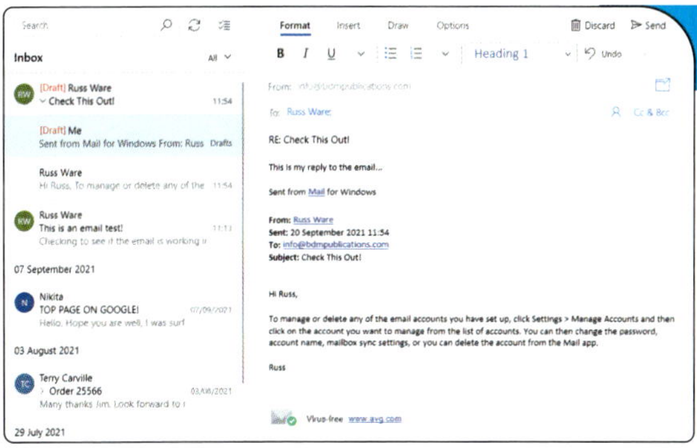


## Responding

When viewing any email in the Mail app, you will see a number of options at the top of the main panel. These include Reply, Reply All and Forward, etc., (all of the normal email options). Click reply and you can start typing your reply, with the original email text included below your reply.

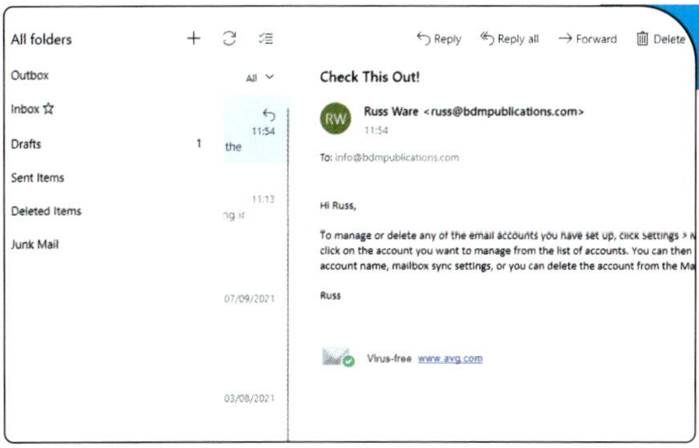


## Mail Folders

Open the Mail app menu on the left and you will see the Folders section. The inbox is listed here as well, but to see more folders, click "More". Here you can find the Outbox, Drafts, Sent items, Deleted items and Junk Mail folders. Click on any of them to see the emails in those folders.

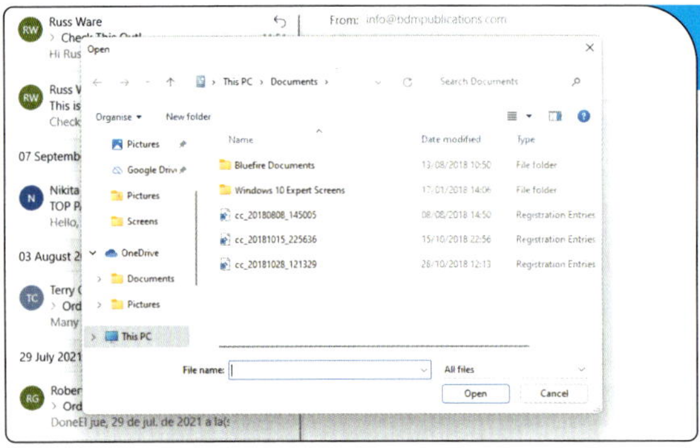


## Attachments

Adding file attachments to emails in the Mail app is easy. Write your email, and then click the Insert tab at the top. Here you can find the option for attaching files. Click the link and browse to the file you want to attach. Click "Open" and a thumbnail of the attachment will appear in the email.

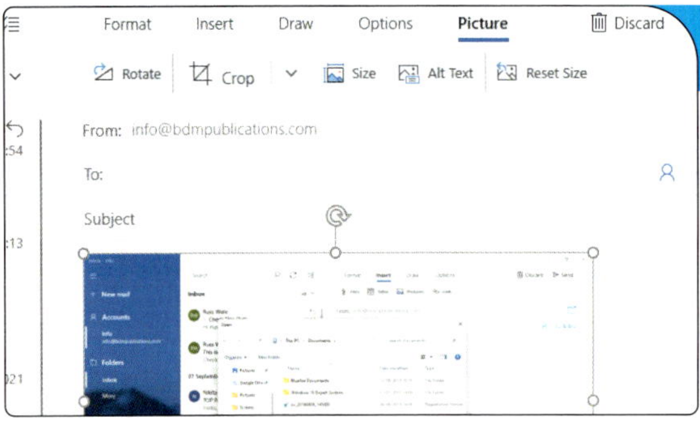


## Inserting Images

As well as the button to include attachments, the Insert tab features a Picture button so you can insert an image into your email; as opposed to just sending it as an attached file. Once inserted, you can select it with your mouse and adjust its size (drag the corners as you can see here).

# Customise the Mail App

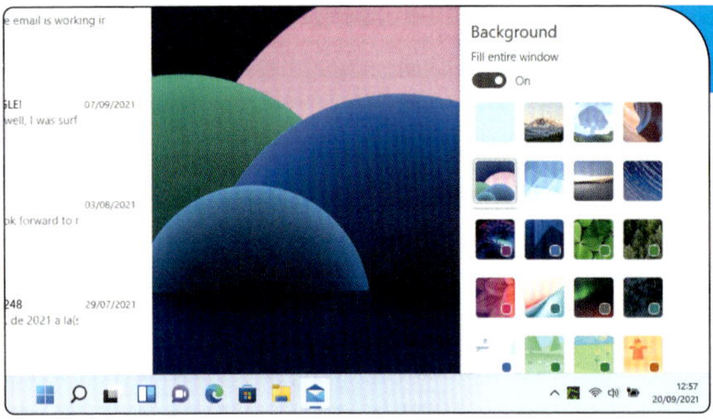


## Background

The background of the Mail app is set to an image by default. This is purely decorative, and can be changed. Open Settings > Personalisation in the Mail app, then scroll to the bottom to see the different backgrounds available. You can also add your own image by clicking the Browse button.

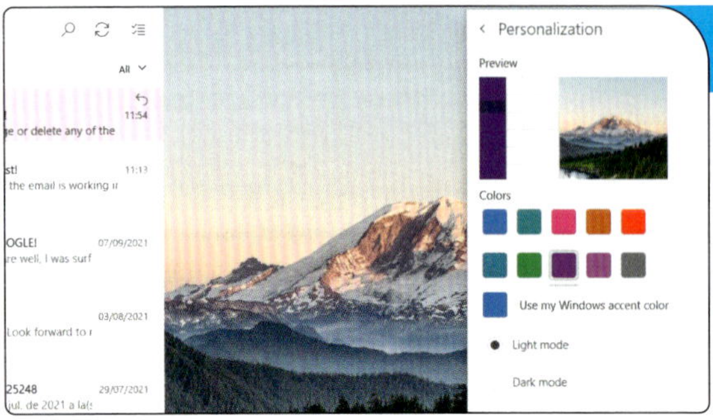


## Mail App Colour

The colour tint on the Mail app menu (on the left) and the colour of the accents such as buttons and highlights, can also be changed in the Personalisation settings. Just click a colour block to change it. You can also change the theme of the app from light to dark here, or use the Windows theme setting.

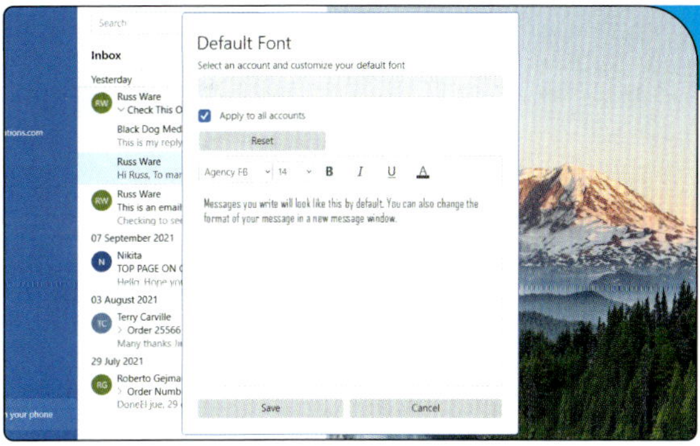


## Email Font

The default font for your emails (Calibri Body, unless you have changed the system fonts) can be changed for any and all of your email accounts. Open the Settings > Default font option, and either select an account or "Apply to all accounts", then choose your font, which is previewed in the pane.

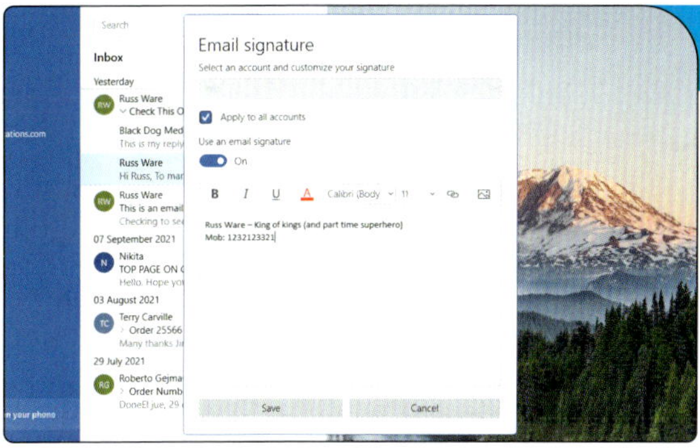


## Signature

The default signature for the Mail app is "Sent from Mail for Windows". The signature is automatically added to the end of your email message, but can be changed or turned off completely if not needed. Go to Settings > Signature, choose an account/all accounts and write your signature in the pane.

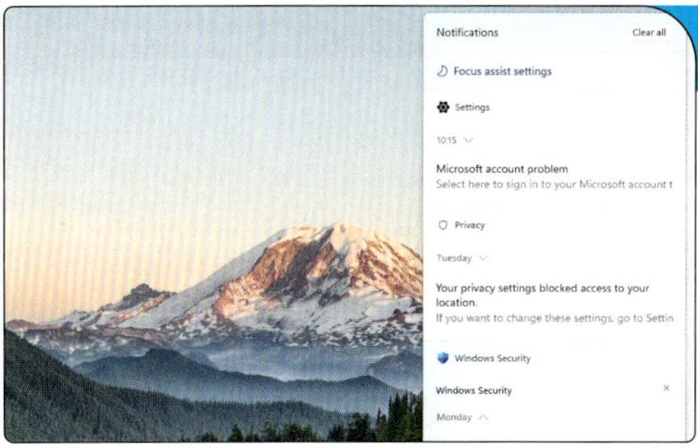


## Notifications

You can easily control how you are notified of new emails. Go to Settings > Notifications, and you can control whether notifications are shown in the Notification center (Action center), if a sound is played and if pinned folders have notifications. As with other settings, you can apply to one account or all.

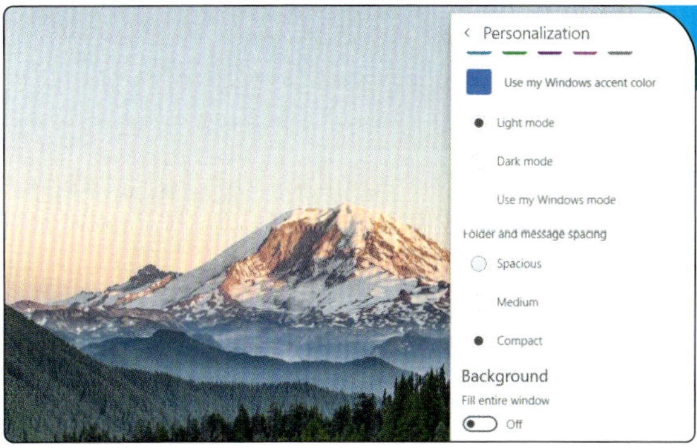


## Message Spacing

Depending on the device you are using (tablet, touchscreen, large monitor, etc.), you might want to change the spacing between messages and the folders in the Mail app (e.g. to make touch easier). To do this, go to Settings > Personalisation, and choose from Spacious, Medium and Compact.

# Inside the Calendar App

## Add New Event

There are two main ways to add a new event to your calendar. You can either click on the date in the main window or, if the date you want is not in view, you can click the New Event button here. You can then add an event name, location, and a start and end date. Give the event a short description, especially if you plan to share it with a contact. You can do that by adding people using the pane on the right of the Add Event screen.

## Monthly View

No matter which view you choose for the main Calendar pane - day, week, etc. - the month preview always shows a full month. You can use the arrows to skip to different months and clicking on a date brings that date into view on the main Calendar pane. The current day is highlighted in the Month Preview.

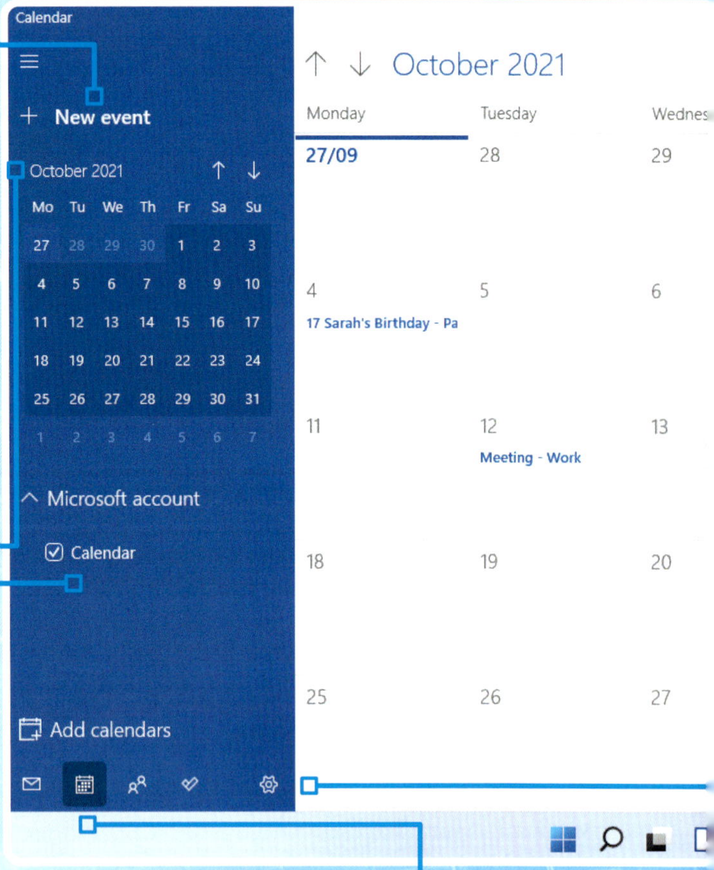


## Linked Calendars

Your calendar can be linked to your email account, which is shown here. If you are using Gmail for your email account, and have any calendars set up in Google Calendar, these are also shown here. You can use the checkboxes to select and deselect calendars from showing in the main pane; each is colour coded, so you know from which custom calendar an event comes.

## Switch Tabs

The Mail and Calendar apps are closely linked, and you can quickly switch between the two using the buttons here. Receive an email with an appointment in it, and you can quickly add it to your calendar using the tools in the Mail app. You can also quickly switch to the People app and the ToDo app using the tabs/buttons here.

**The Windows 11 Calendar app is a fully integrated planning tool that can be linked up to your email accounts and easily synced to your other Windows devices. You can add new events manually, or you can simply use it to view national and public holidays.**

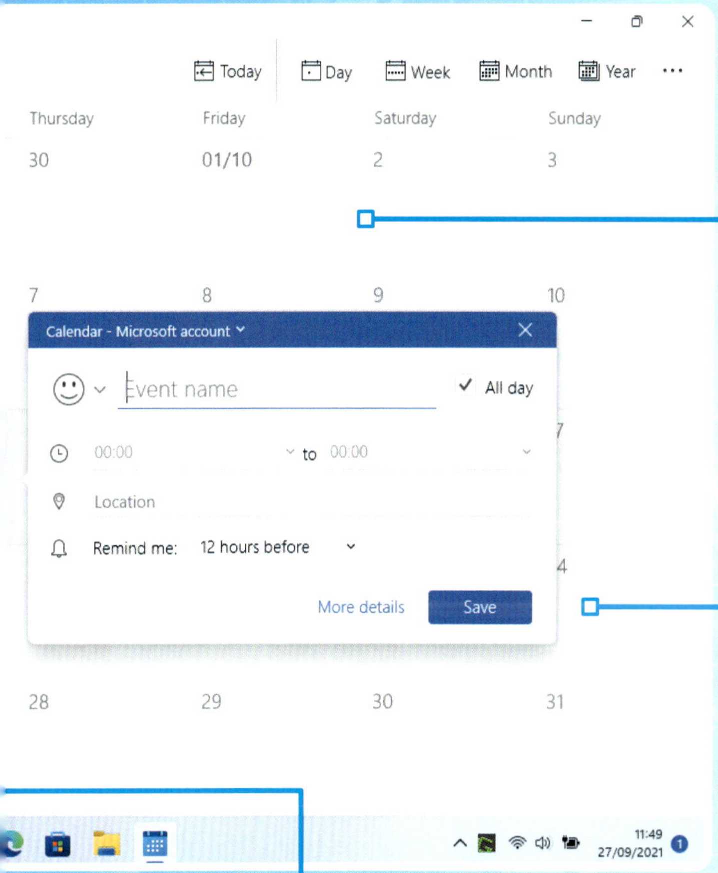


## Calendar Pane

The main Calendar pane, however you choose to view it with the View buttons, contains several different bits of useful information. Public and national holidays are automatically added, based on location. The current day is accentuated in your chosen highlight colour. Weather and temperature information is shown for the current day, along with a few days after. Clicking the weather symbol opens the Weather app.

## Add Event

Click on any day in the main pane, or any hourly slot in day view, and a mini Add Event pane opens. You can use this to add an event to your calendar quickly. The pane includes event name, time-slots and location; it also lets you choose into which custom calendar you want to add it. If you choose to add more details, click the More Details button, if not, click Done to add the event.

## Calendar Settings

Alongside various customisation settings, such as the ability to choose light and dark themes and change the default highlight colour, are settings for adding new email accounts and changing the default view. You can also add public or national holidays manually, if they have not been correctly added automatically.

# Managing Calendar

**Digital calendars are no longer the preserve of business people scheduling appointments via email. With mobile phones now our new diaries, digital calendars are being used by increasing numbers of people to organise their busy lives. Welcome to Calendar.**

## Setting Up Calendars

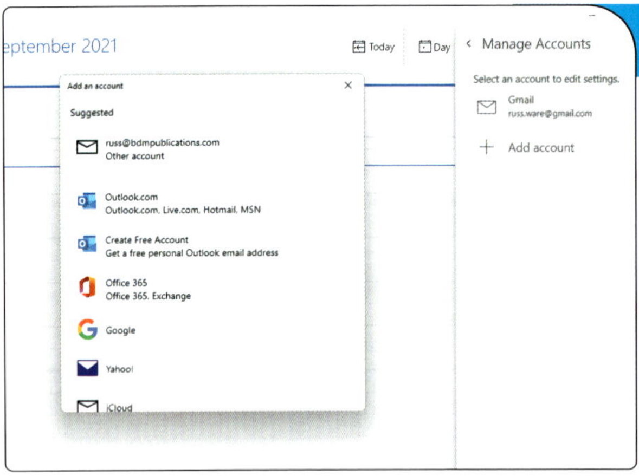


### Accounts

Like Windows 11's email app, Calendar also enables you to add multiple accounts; and from different providers too. So whether you use an Outlook calendar at work or have shared Google calendars, you can join them all together in the Calendar app. To Start click on Add Accounts.

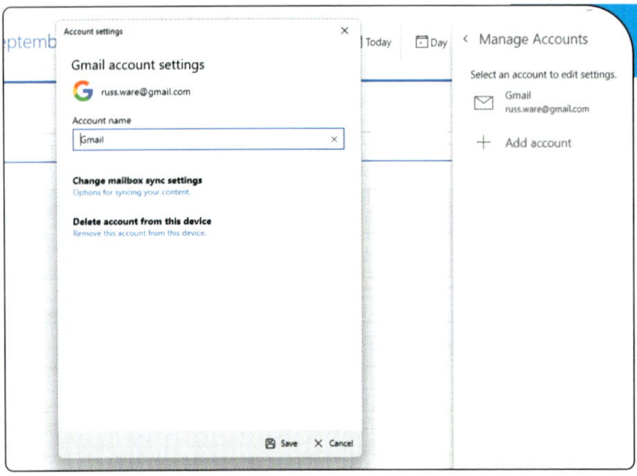


### Sign In

Now add the accounts you want to use in Calendar. You can do this at any point you choose via Settings > Accounts. From there you can easily add an Outlook.com, Exchange, Google or iCloud calendar; or enter advanced settings for any other calendars you may have from other providers.

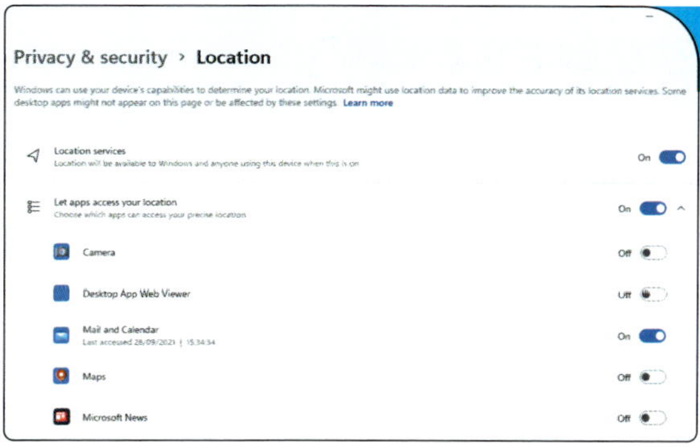


## Allow Location

You'll be asked to enable location access for Mail and Calendar. This is predominantly for one simple reason – Calendar shows you the weather for your location each day. You can always revoke access via the Settings app. Go to Location and you can turn off Calendar's access to Location.

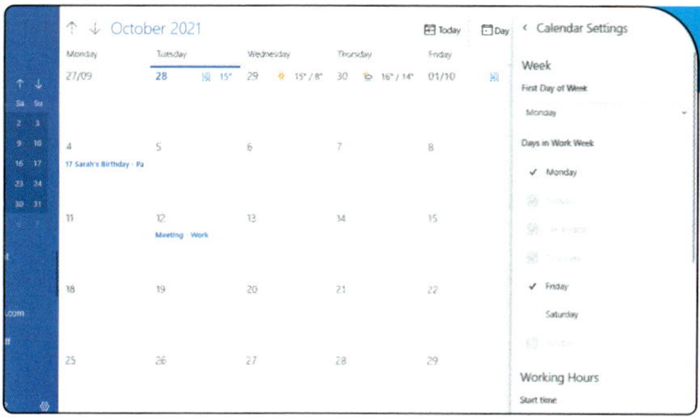


## Settings

The calendar settings are fairly basic, boiling down to adding accounts, changing the appearance and setting the weather region. The only other settings are the controls to how the calendars are displayed (First day of week, Days in work week, Week numbers on/off, etc.).

# Creating and Managing Events

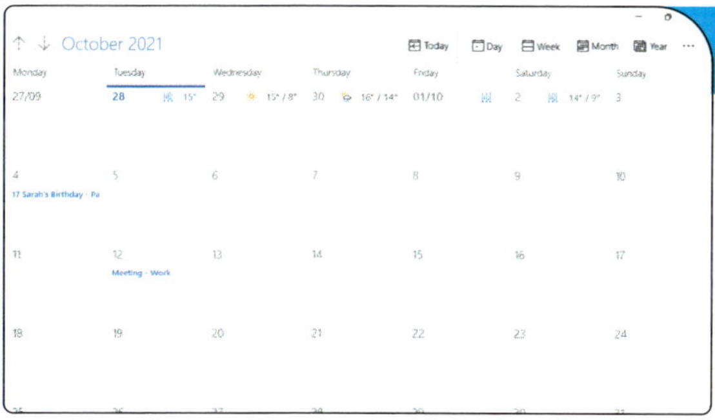


## Step 1

The default view when opening the Calendar is the month view. You can switch to the different views (Day, Week, Month and Year) using the buttons along the top of the calendar. There is also a button here to take the view back to the current day, if you have been browsing future or past months.

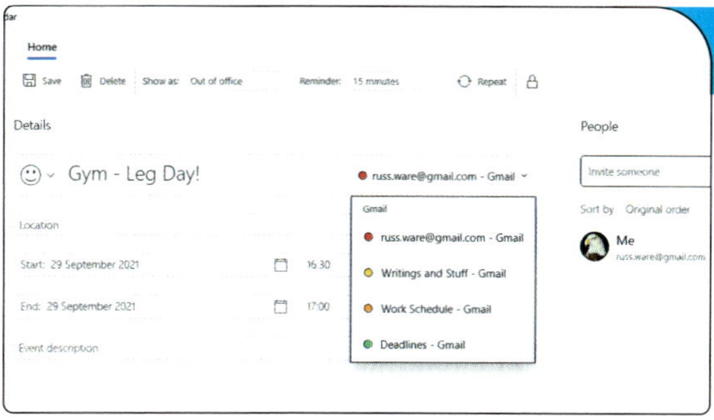


## Step 2

Click the New Event button in the top left. Add the name of the event, a location should you wish to, plus start and end dates and times. You're also able to invite people by email using the field on the right-hand side. This will then insert the event into their calendar as well.

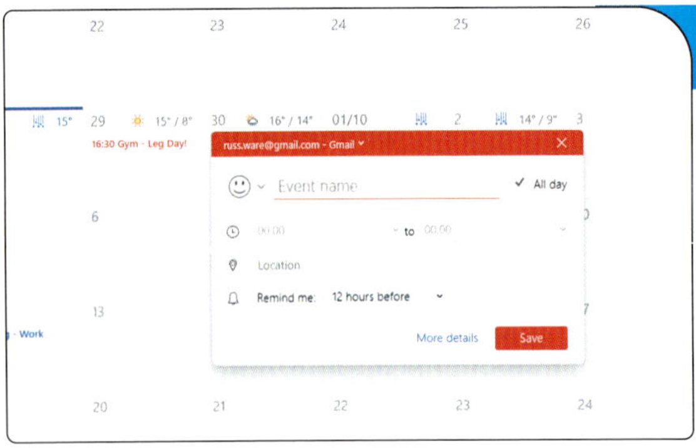


## Step 3

You can also add events by clicking on the relevant date block (or time block in Day view), and then adding the event details in the quick event pop-up box. If you want to see the full, new event screen at this point, you can click the "More details" link in the quick event box.

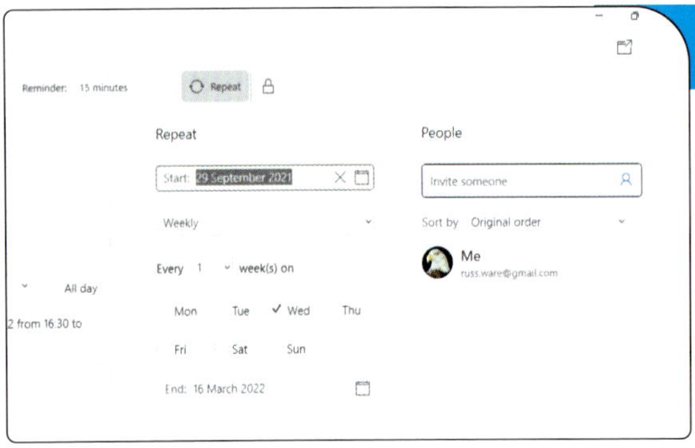

## Step 4

You can also choose to set repeat events – just click the Repeat button in the toolbar when you're creating a new event. Check the days you want. You can repeat daily, weekly, monthly or yearly, depending on what you need to do. You can even set a date when the repeated events end.

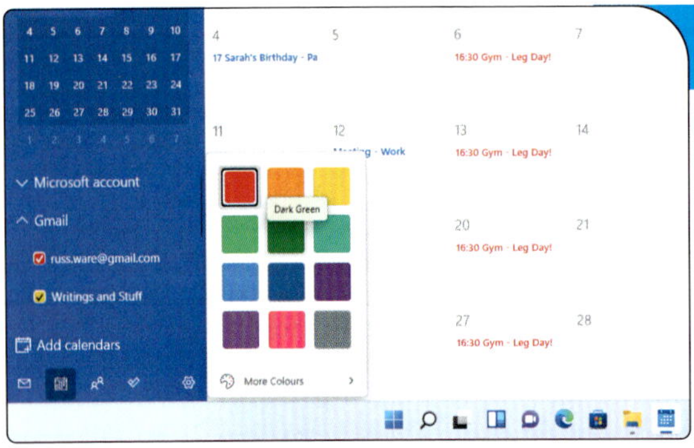

## Step 5

You're also able to assign different colours to different calendar accounts. Each calendar account you add will automatically be assigned a different colour. You can then change this assigned colour by clicking the arrow next to the calendar name and choosing from the pop out menu.

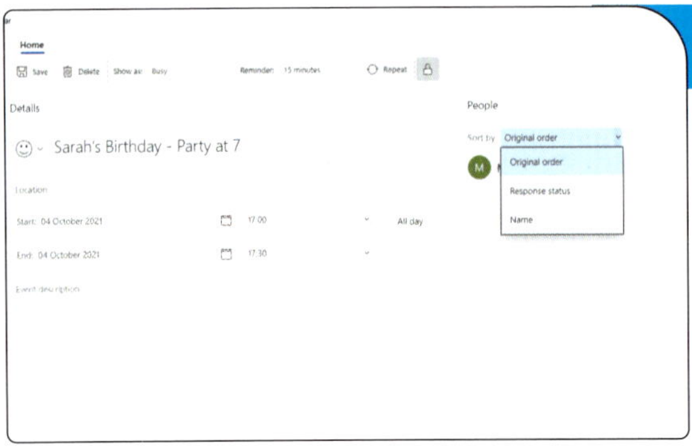

## Step 6

One of the best things about the Windows 11 Calendar app is how admirably it copes with multiple calendars. So providing they invite your account (or you invite them), you're able to easily share events with others. If you do share, you can set certain events as private, so only you see them.

# Widgets in Windows 11

Widgets are desktop app previews, allowing you to see important information from Windows apps, without needing to actually open those apps. The concept of widgets is not new, but the way they are managed and displayed in Windows 11 is new.

## Wonderful Widgets

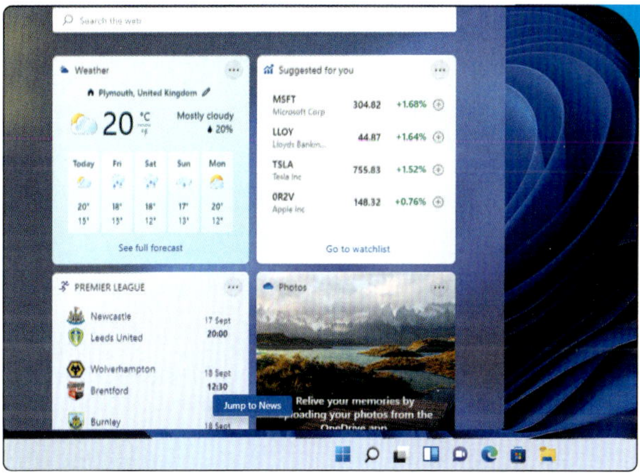


### Step 1

To open the widget panel, simply click or tap the button in the taskbar (the blue and white square icon) or press Windows key + W on your keyboard. The panel will then slide out from the left side of the screen, and will sit over the top of any other apps or windows you currently have open.

### Step 2

The widget panel is initially split up into three main sections: Search, Widgets and News stories. Scroll down the panel to see more content. At the top-right is an account icon, which opens a new panel with account information and the ability to add new widgets.

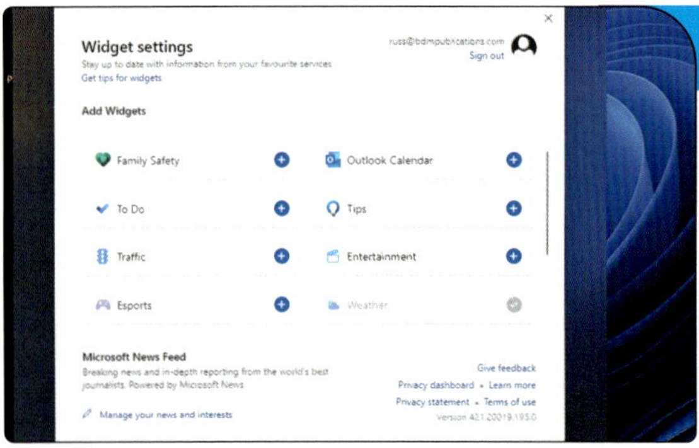


## Step 3

The exact widgets available to add will vary, depending on which apps you have installed. As Windows 11 develops, more widgets are likely to be added here, possibly from third-party developers as well as from Microsoft. To add new widgets, just click the + button on each.

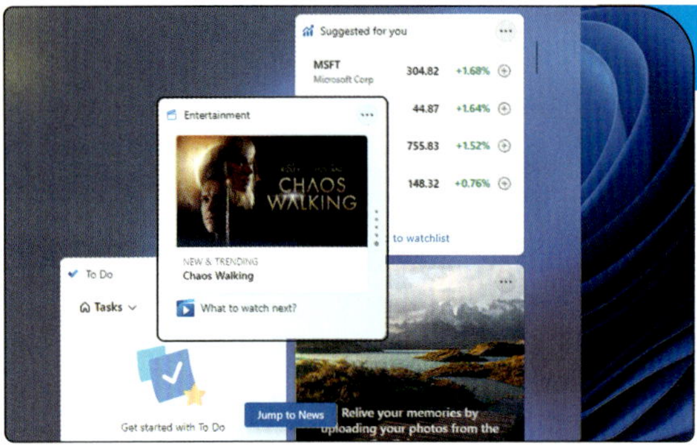


## Step 4

After adding widgets, close the account panel and you will see the added widgets in the panel. You can move widgets around in the panel by clicking on the top of the widget and dragging it to the required position. Other widgets will rearrange to fit when you do this.

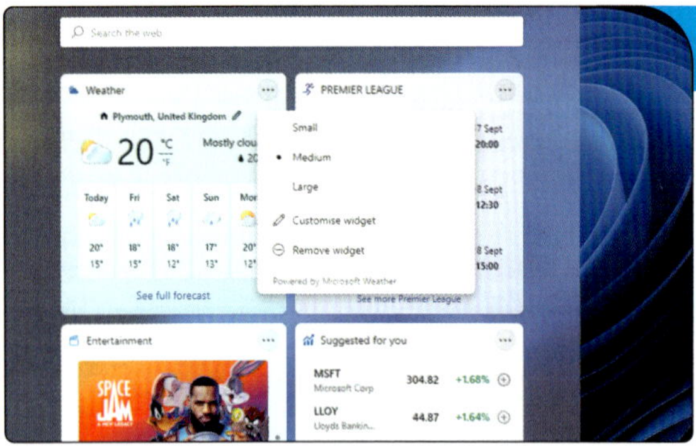


## Step 5

To remove a widget, click on the Menu button at the top-right of the widget and choose "Remove Widget" from the menu. You will also see the option to change the size of the widget in this menu. Not all of the widgets will allow all three of the sizing options.

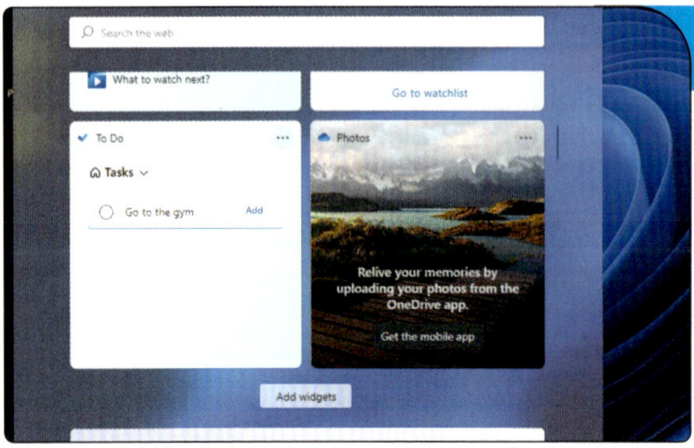


## Step 6

Some Widgets allow content editing within the widget. A good example of this is the To Do widget. You can create tasks in the widget by clicking the "Add a task" button, without having to the open the main To Do app. The task then displays instantly in the widget.

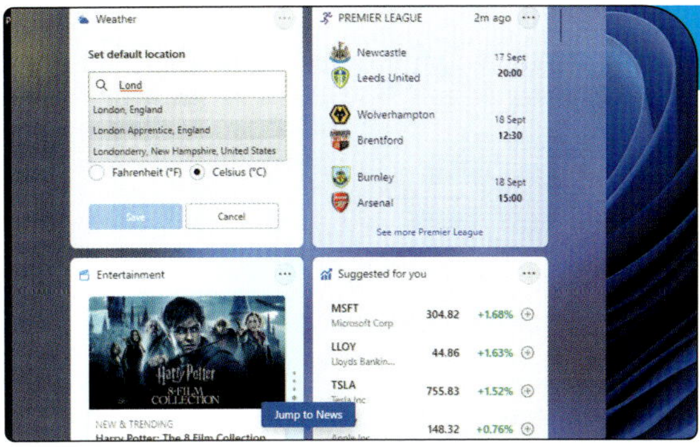


## Step 7

Some of the Widgets allow customisation through the More Menu button. The Weather widget, for example, lets you set the default location for the weather forecast that is shown. The Stocks widget lets you change which stock prices are displayed, etc.

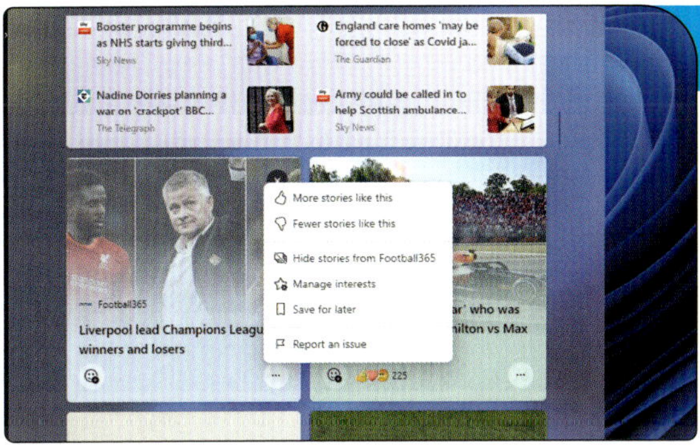


## Step 8

The news stories further down the Widgets panel also allow for some customisation. You can click the X to remove a news story, and you can click the More Menu button to choose to see "More/Fewer stories like this", or to hide all stories from that particular news source.

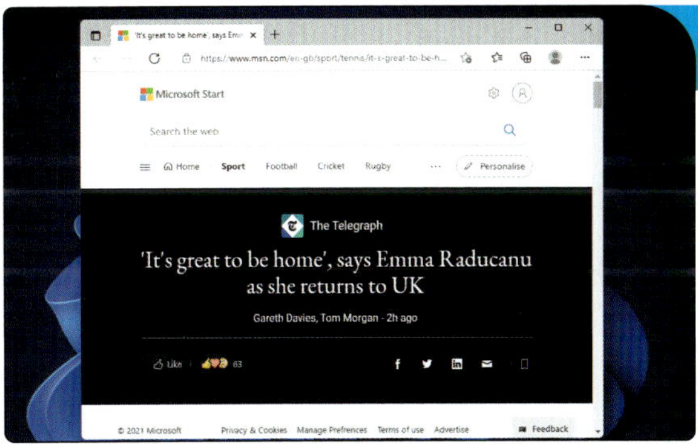


## Step 9

Clicking on a news story will take you to the webpage the story is from. At the top of the News section is a wide panel containing Top Stories. These are the top 6 news headlines. These will change as you like or dislike stories, or choose different news sources.

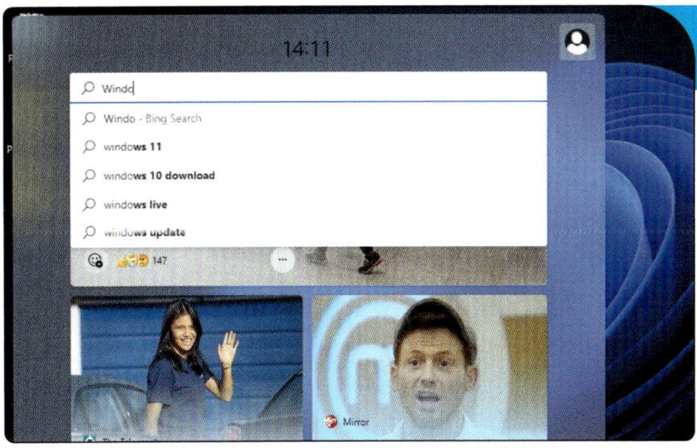


## Step 10

At the top of the Widgets panel is a clock and a search bar. You can type directly into the search bar, with any searches opening in your browser (Edge, by default). The search bar and the clock cannot be removed from the Widgets panel, nor can they be moved.

# Personalising Windows 11

As with all recent versions of Windows, you can completely change the look of Windows 11 to suit your own needs or style. From the desktop wallpaper and colour theme, to the icons, taskbar and lock screen, everything can be customised and personalised.

## Change the Desktop

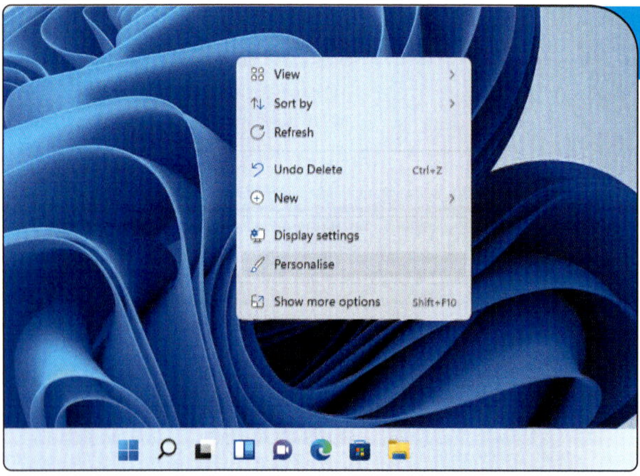


### Step 1

You can get started with personalising the Windows 11 desktop in exactly the same way you did with Windows 10. For anyone completely new to Windows, that means right-clicking anywhere on the desktop screen and selecting Personalise from the action menu that appears.

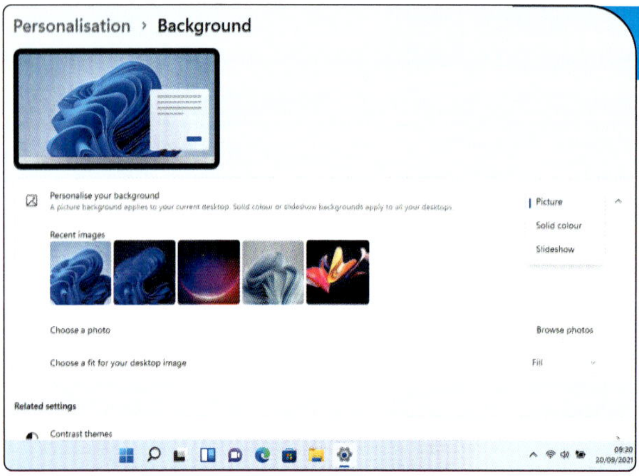


### Step 2

The Background settings will be displayed first by default. Click the first drop-down menu to select whether to use the default backgrounds, solid colours or choose to display folders of your own images. Your choices here changes what is displayed in the background settings.

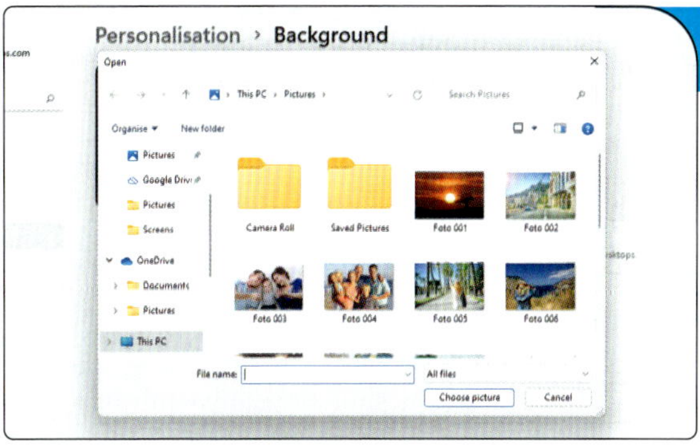


## Step 3

To select your own pictures for the background, click on Browse photos in the Choose a photo section and navigate to the folder containing the images you want to use. For best results, use pictures that have the same aspect ratio (i.e. widescreen landscape), as your monitor screen.

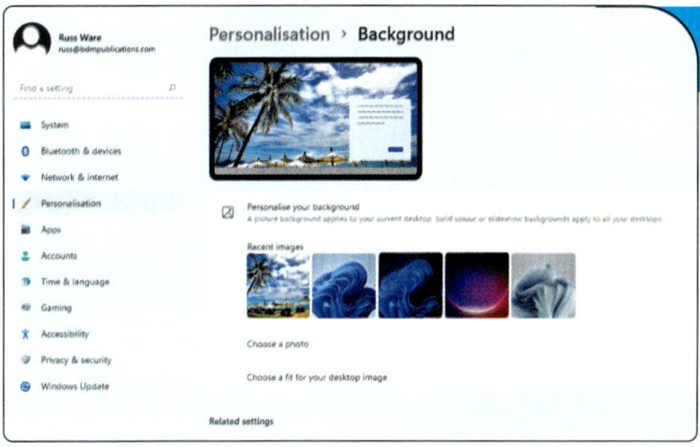


## Step 4

To set a picture as your desktop background, simply click on it. It will instantly be set as your new desktop background image (a preview will display). The screen shows you the last five images used or you can click the Browse button to choose a new one from your folders.

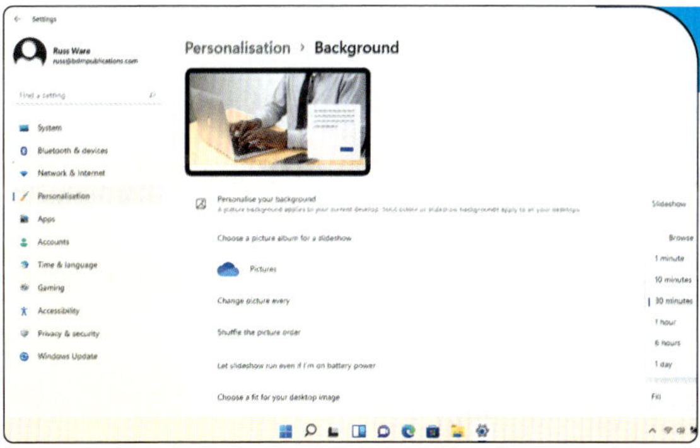


## Step 5

If you opt for Slideshow, you will see some additional options to choose from. You can set the interval for the slide show from the 'Change picture every' menu and decide how you'd like the images to fit on the screen by clicking the 'Choose a fit' menu.

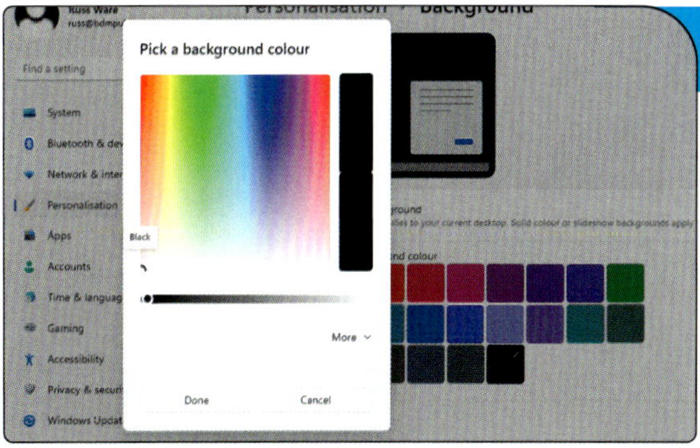


## Step 6

If you choose to set your desktop background as a solid colour, you will see a grid of about 25 colours that you can choose from. If you want to use a colour not shown in the grid, click on the View colours option and use the colour picker to select the exact colour you want to apply.

# Setting Accent Colours

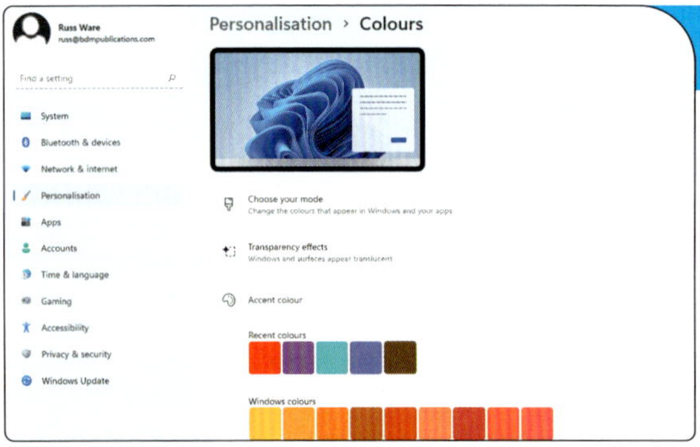


## Step 1

Aside from the desktop background, you can also change the colour of the taskbar and the Start menu and other system components. To do this, click on the Colours option in the main Settings sidebar. Here you will see several colour control options, including the option to choose light or dark mode.

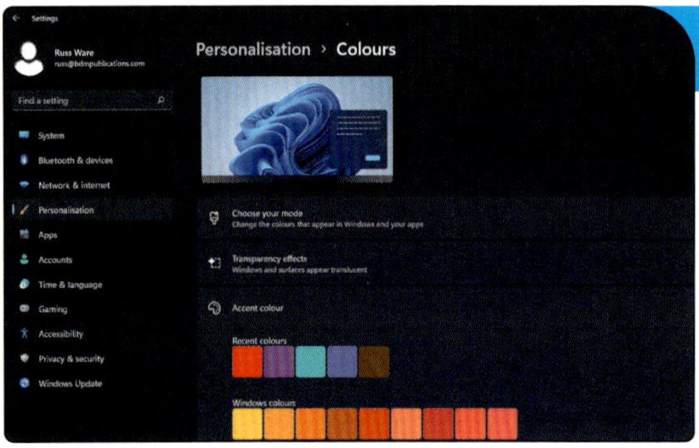


## Step 2

Light mode is the default that Windows 11 is set to when installed. Select Dark mode to see an immediate and obvious change. Dark mode affects most menus like the taskbar, Start menu and folders etc. The third option is Custom, which lets you choose light/dark modes separately for system and apps.

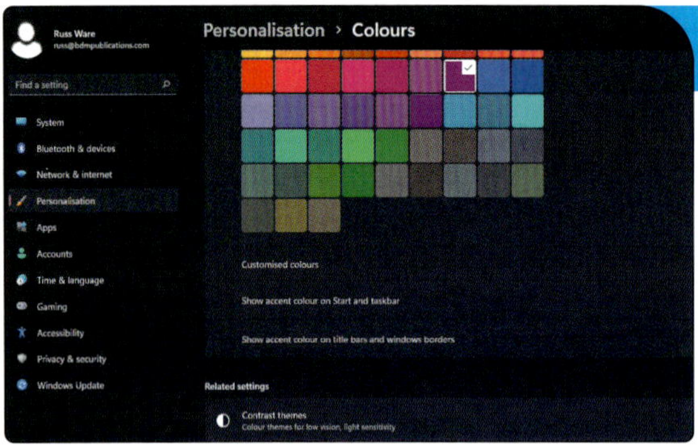


## Step 3

To apply a colour other than light or dark to the taskbar, Start menu and other accents, you need to first select Dark mode, then select a colour from the grid of colours and then select the option below that to "Show accent colour on Start and Taskbar". You can also apply it to title bars and borders.

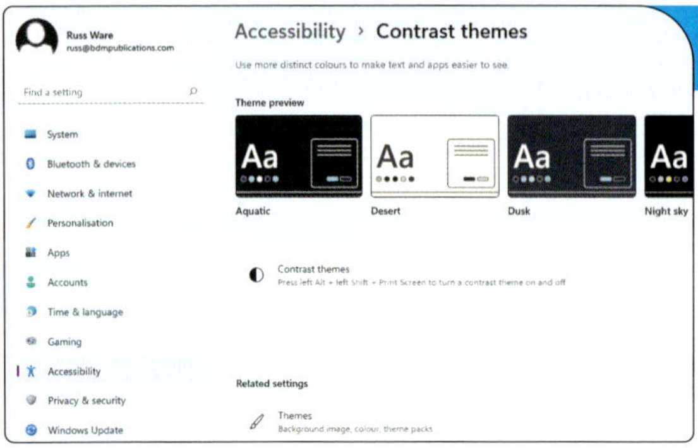


## Step 4

If you need to set the colour scheme to high contrast (if, for example, you have a vision impairment), you can access several preset colour themes from the Colours menu. You will see a preview of the different themes, and can then apply the one you like from the drop-down menu.

# Lock Screen Customisation

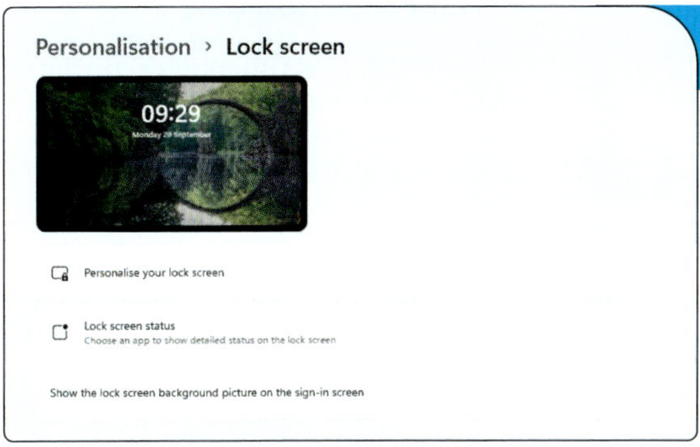


## Step 1

The lock screen is enabled by default (as it was in Windows 10) and displays an image and can also display information from one of the built-in Windows apps. To start customising the lock screen, open the main settings, click Personalisation and then Lock Screen.

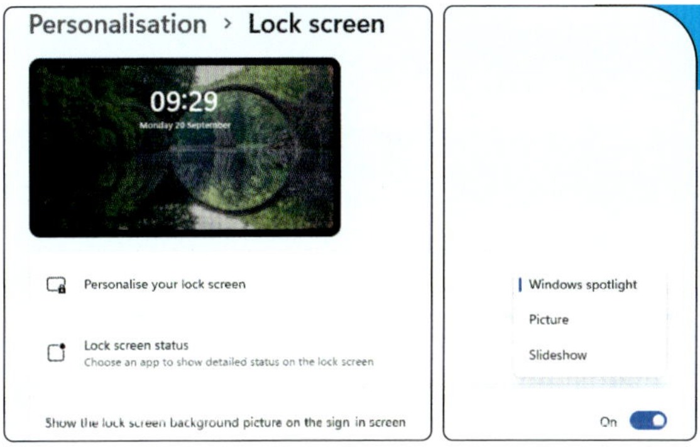


## Step 2

The first thing to choose is whether to display one of your own images, a slideshow of images or something from Windows Spotlight. If you choose either of the first two of these, more options will appear to select the images you want to use (single or multiple).

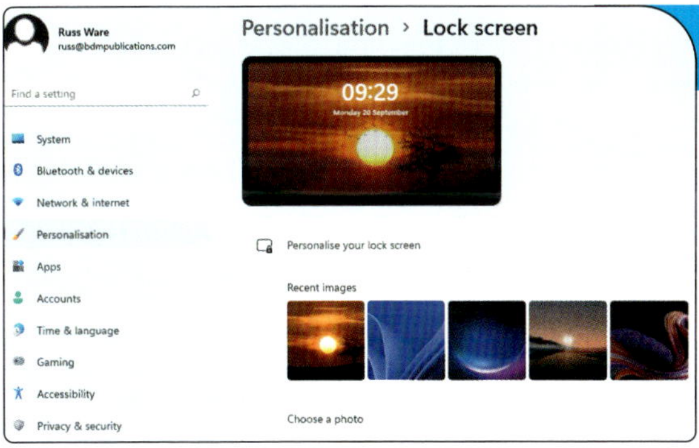


## Step 3

If you choose to apply one of your images, some recently used pictures will appear, along with a link to browse your PC for more. When you select an image, it will appear in the recently used panel. You can choose to have facts, tips and tricks displayed over the image, just like with Windows Spotlight.

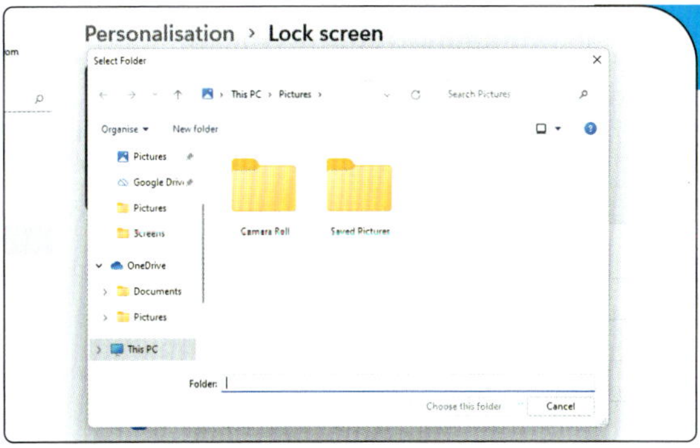


## Step 4

If you choose to set the lock screen as a slideshow, you will see the option to add a folder of images rather than just one. You can use an existing folder (such as Pictures), or you can create one. There are several advanced settings for a slideshow, including only using images that fit the screen.

## Step 5

You can add an app status to the lock screen which will show some information from the app you chose. The available apps will vary if you have removed or added some, but should include Weather, Mail, Calendar, Operator Messages and more. You can only add one app.

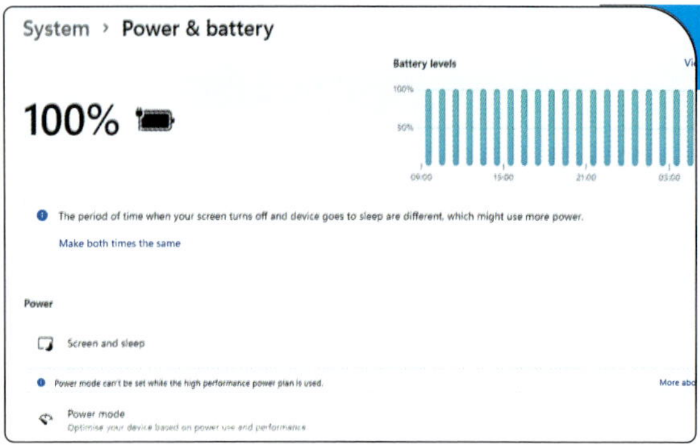


## Step 6

Also in the Lock Screen personalisation section is a Related settings section. Here you will find links to the screen timeout and screen saver settings. The settings you choose there will depend on your personal preference and also on your computer location (for security reasons).

# Disable the Lock Screen

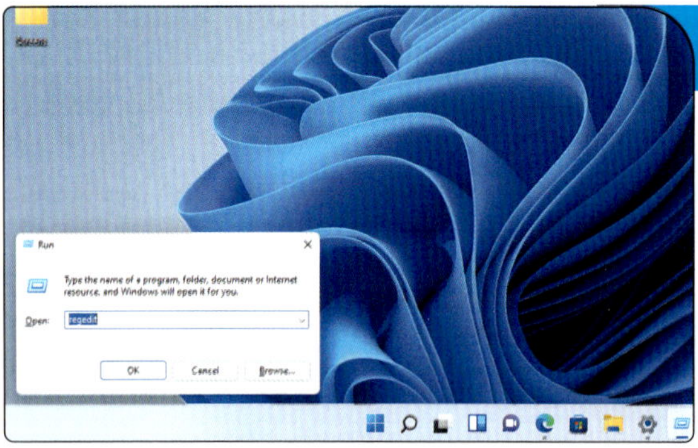


## Step 1

To access the Registry, press the Windows key + R, enter regedit, and then click OK. With the Registry open, navigate to HKEY_LOCAL_MACHINE\SOFTWARE\Policies\Microsoft\Windows\. Right-click the final Windows folder and click New > Key.

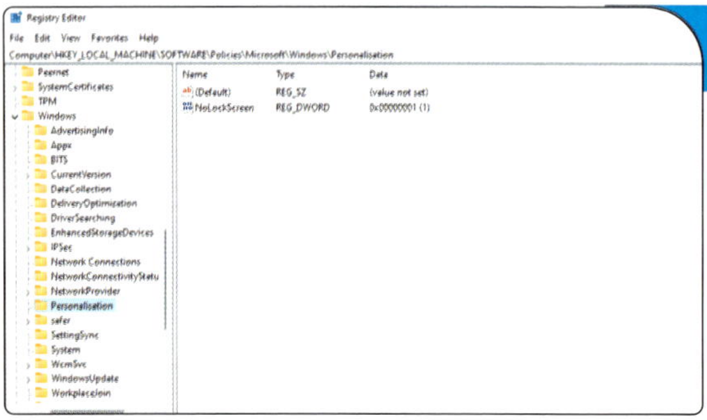


## Step 2

Name this new key "Personalisation" and then navigate inside it. Right-click inside the right-hand pane and select New > DWORD (32-bit) Value. Name it "NoLockScreen". Then double click this new value and change the Value data to 1. Then click OK and exit the Registry Editor.

# Adding New Themes

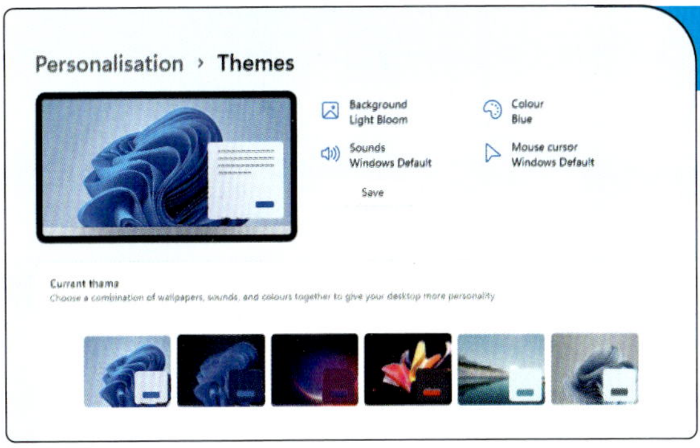


## Step 1

You can find new themes in a couple of ways: Open the Microsoft Store app and search for themes, or open the main settings app, go to Personalisation and then click on the themes option. Here you will see a link to "Get more themes…".

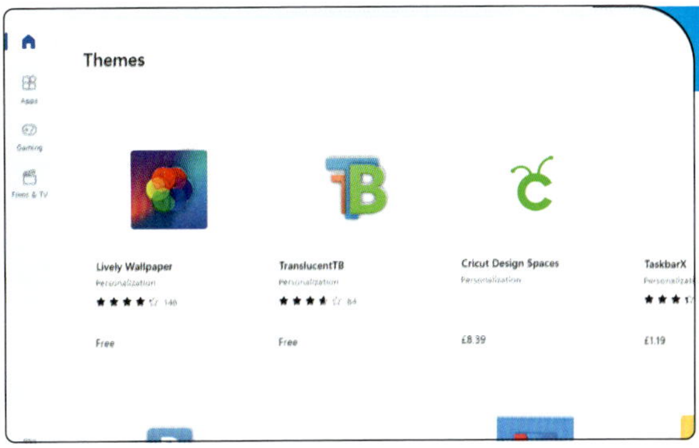


## Step 2

Both of these actions should bring you to the same themes page. All themes have now been moved into the Windows Store app, rather than on a webpage. Themes are all listed under Personalisation in the Store, so you can also search for that if your themes search doesn't bring up the expected results.

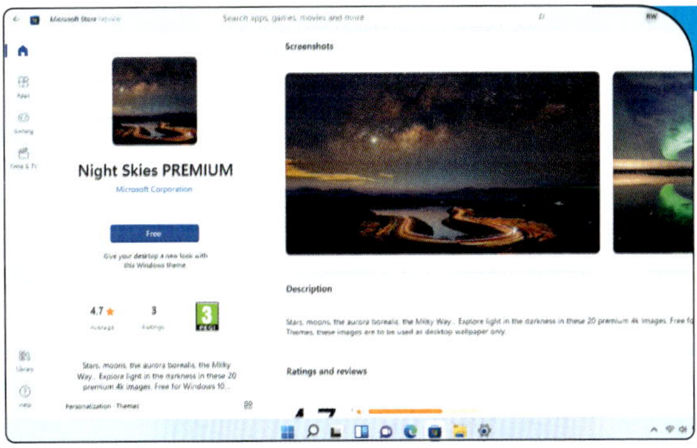


## Step 3

Each theme is displayed with a thumbnail and the number of images supplied shown. The Microsoft Store page also includes information about any other changes the theme will make, such as adding transparency effects or adding Lock Screen images. Download any you like the look of.

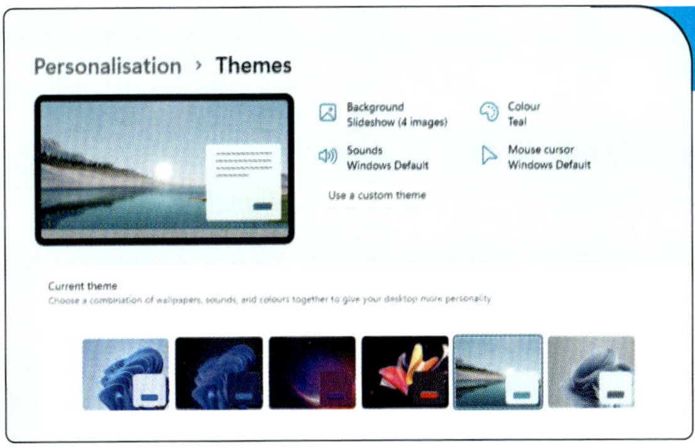


## Step 4

Each theme applied can be customised further using the options in the Themes section. You can alter the background, colour, sounds and even the mouse cursor of any theme, making it completely unique to you. When you have chosen the changes, you will need to click Save Theme.

# Modifying Themes

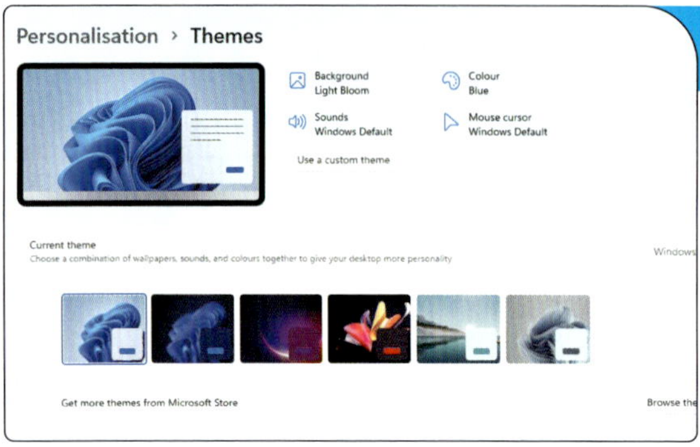


## Step 1

You can find the preset themes in Settings > Personalisation > Themes. The current theme is displayed at the top of the page, with details about background, colour, sounds and mouse cursor displayed next to it. Each of these details can be clicked to go to a section where you can edit it.

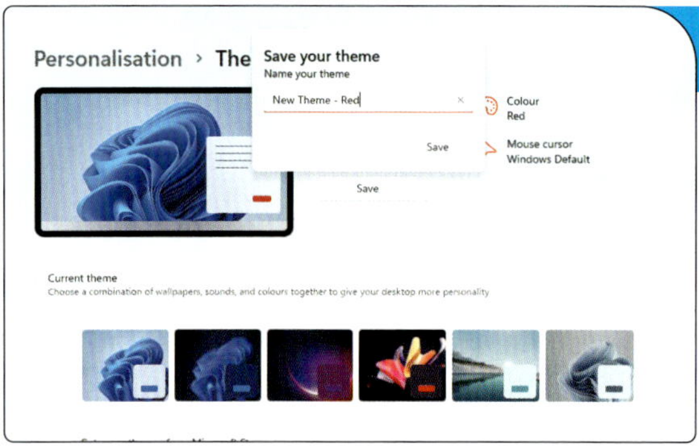


## Step 2

Each time you make a change using these links, return to the Themes section to see the changes in the preview window, or minimise the Settings app to see the desktop. When you are happy with all of the changes, click "Save" and the theme will be set and added to the other themes.

## Step 3

Further down the page are five more preset themes displayed in a panel. Simply click each one to activate it and apply the changes. Minimise the Settings app to see the changes to the background, etc. As with the default theme, the details of the new theme are displayed at the top of the page.

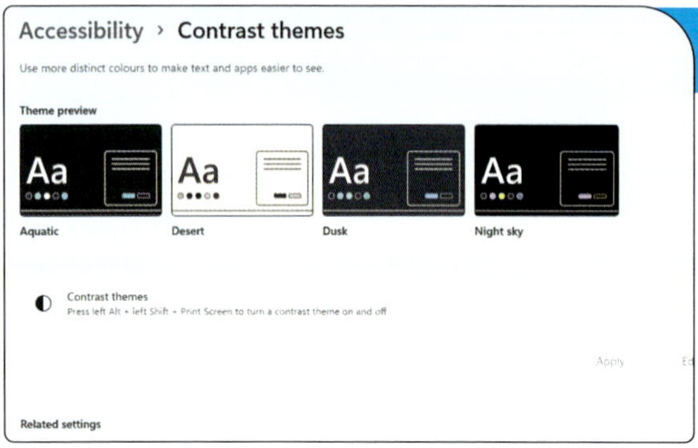


## Step 4

At the bottom of the themes settings page are a few more links, taking you directly to desktop icon settings and high/low contrast themes. Desktop icon settings are separate to the themes, so if you change these, they will remain even if you then go back and choose a new theme.

# Change Your Desktop Icons

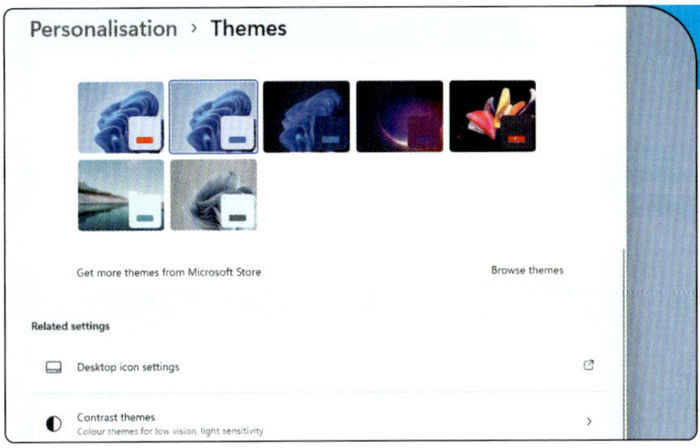


## Step 1

Open the Personalisation screen of the Settings menu and select Themes from the Sidebar menu. You now need to look for the Related Settings option. In the Related Settings section, click on the link to Desktop icon settings.

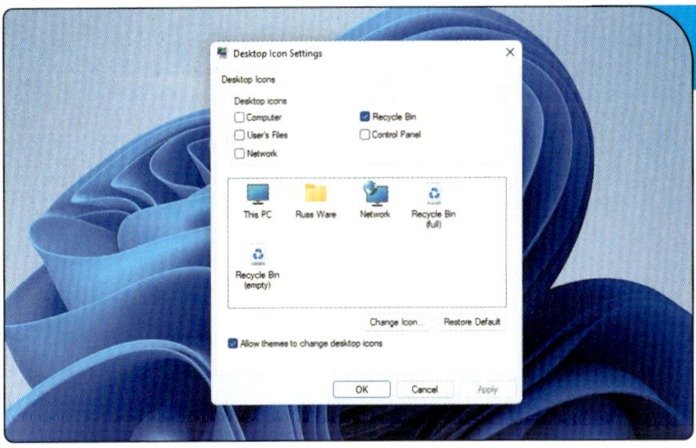


## Step 2

The window that now opens lets you choose which default icons appear on your desktop. The Recycle Bin is just about essential but the others, including Computer, Users Files, Network and Control Panel icons are optional.

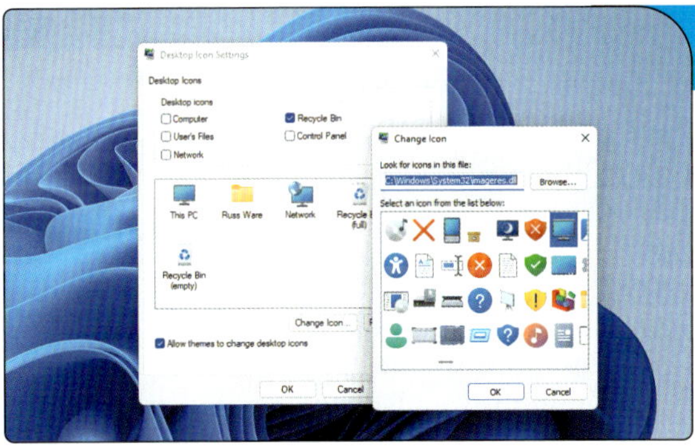


## Step 3

If you wish to do so, it is possible to choose different icons for these system tools and you can even download custom icons online. To change the appearance of the desktop icons, click on the icon you want to change and then click the Change Icon button.

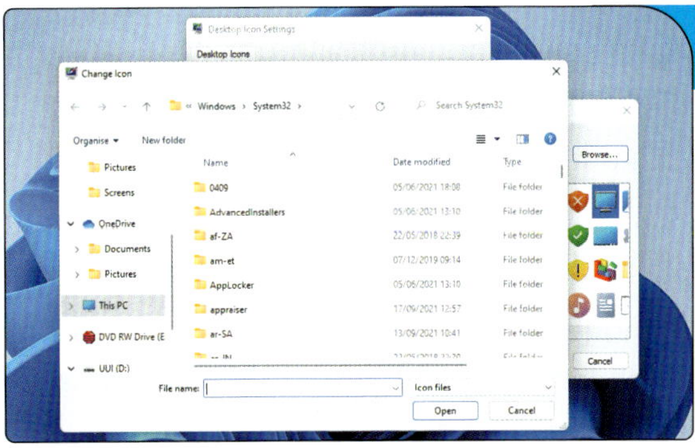


## Step 4

The icon chooser window that appears will look very familiar to veteran Windows users, since it's essentially unchanged from Windows 98. Scroll through the gallery until you find an icon you like or use the Browse button to navigate to any icon pack that you've downloaded.

# Keyboard Shortcuts

## Basic Keyboard Shortcuts

**Ctrl+C** - Copy the selected item
**Ctrl+X** - Cut the selected item
**Ctrl+V** - Paste the selected item
**Ctrl+Z** - Undo an action
**Alt+Tab** - Switch between open apps
**Alt+F4** - Close an active item, or exit an app
**Shift+Delete** - Delete item without moving to Recycle Bin
**Ctrl+Shift+Esc** - Open the Task Manager

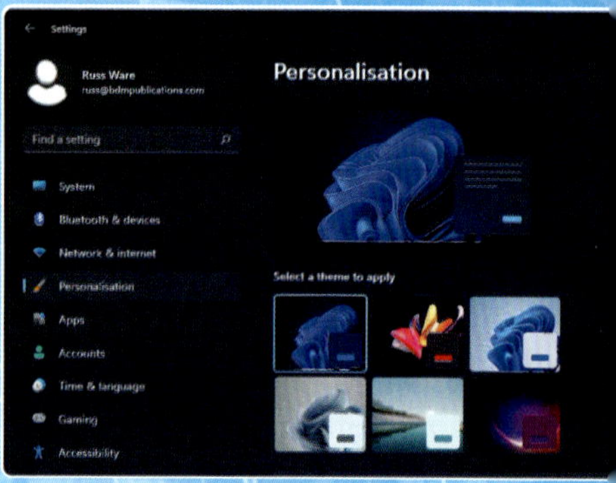


## Windows Key Shortcuts

**Windows Key** - Open Start menu
**Windows key + A** - Open Quick Settings panel
**Windows key + S** - Open Search
**Windows key + C** - Open Teams Chat
**Windows key + Tab** - Open Task view

**Windows key + I** - Open Windows 11 Settings
**Windows key + W** - Open Widgets panel
**Windows key + E** - Open File Explorer
**Windows key + R** - Open the Run app
**Windows key + V** - Open the Clipboard

**Windows key + G** - Open the Xbox Game Bar
**Windows key + N** - Open Notifications panel
**Windows key + X** - Open a system context menu
**Windows key + U** - Open Accessibility settings
**Windows key + L** - Lock your PC or switch accounts

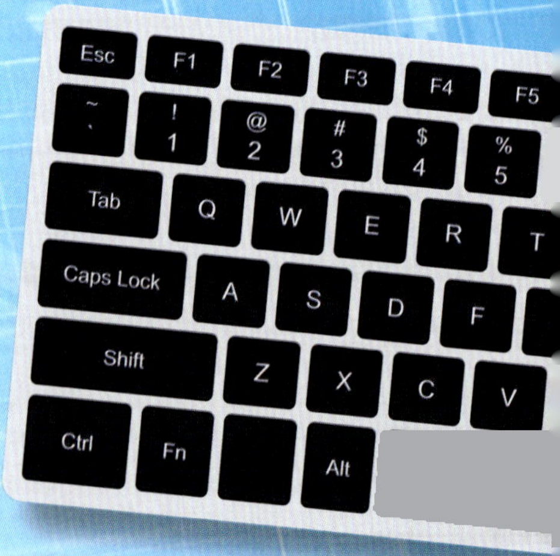


**Windows key + H** - Open Voice typing control
**Windows key + T** - Cycle through apps on the Taskbar
**Windows key + comma** - Peek at the desktop
**Windows key + D** - Display and hide the desktop
**Windows key + Ctrl + D** - Add a virtual desktop

**Windows key + Ctrl + Right Arrow** - Switch to virtual desktop on the right
**Windows key + Ctrl + Left Arrow** - Switch to virtual desktop on the left
**Windows key + Ctrl + F4** - Close the virtual desktop you're using
**Windows key + Home** - Minimise all but the active desktop window
**Windows key + Up arrow** - Stretch the desktop window to the top and bottom of the screen

**Keyboard shortcuts are a useful way to speed up navigating your way around Windows 11, especially if you are using a laptop with a touchpad. There are literally hundreds available, but here are some of the most useful keyboard shortcuts for everyday use.**

**Windows key + Down arrow** - Restore desktop windows vertically, maintaining width
**Windows key + plus or minus** - Zoom in or out using Magnifier
**Windows key + Esc** - Exit Magnifier

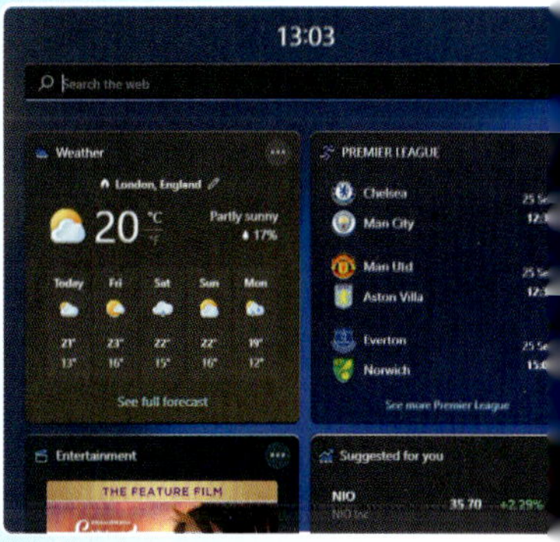


## Windows Snap Shortcuts

**Windows key + Up Arrow** - Maximise current window
**Windows key + Down Arrow** - Restores window size
**Windows key + Left Arrow** - Snaps current window to the left
**Windows key + Right Arrow** - Snaps current window to the right
**Windows key + 2 Arrow Keys** - Snaps current window into one corner

## Taskbar Shortcuts

**Shift + click a taskbar button** - Open an app or quickly open another instance of an app
**Ctrl + Shift + click a taskbar button** - Open an app as an administrator
**Shift + right-click a taskbar button** - Show the window menu for the app
**Shift + right-click a grouped taskbar button** - Show the window menu for the group
**Ctrl + click a grouped taskbar button** - Cycle through the windows of the group

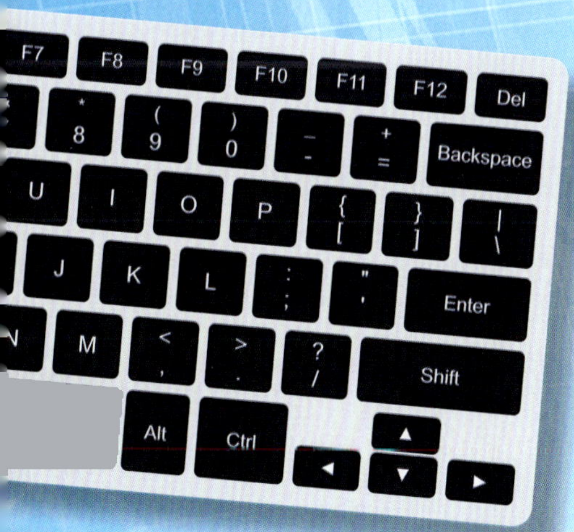


## Typing Shortcuts

**Ctrl + C** - Copy the selected item
**Ctrl + D** - Delete the selected item and move it to the Recycle Bin
**Ctrl + R** - Refresh the active window
**Ctrl + V** - Paste the selected item
**Ctrl + S** - Save document
**Ctrl + Y** - Redo an action
**Ctrl + Z** - Undo an action
**Ctrl + Right arrow** - Move the cursor to the beginning of the next word
**Ctrl + Left arrow** - Move the cursor to the beginning of the previous word
**Ctrl + Down arrow** - Move the cursor to the beginning of the next paragraph
**Ctrl + Up arrow** - Move the cursor to the beginning of the previous paragraph
**Ctrl + Shift with an arrow key** - Select a block of text

# Search in Windows 11

**Until you use it, it's difficult to explain just how much better Search is in Windows 11. Microsoft have done a lot to try to match the search functions on offer in rival operating systems such as Apple's macOS, and the results can be seen in the new search feature.**

## A Better Way to Search

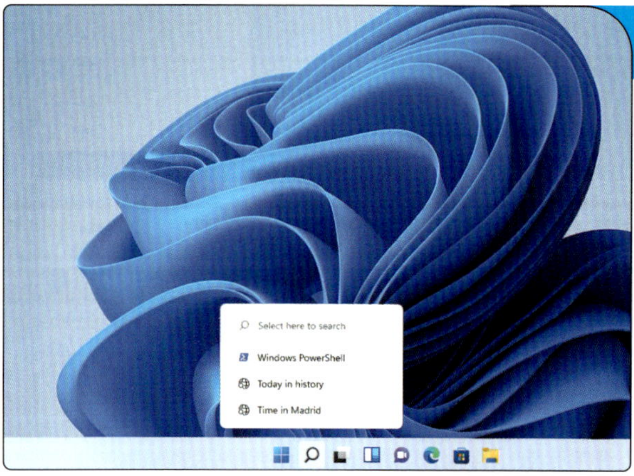


### Step 1

If you need to search for anything on your Windows 11 PC, the taskbar search tool is now the place to do it. The search field in the taskbar from Windows 10 is no longer there. You can also access search through the Start menu, or by pressing Windows key + S on your keyboard.

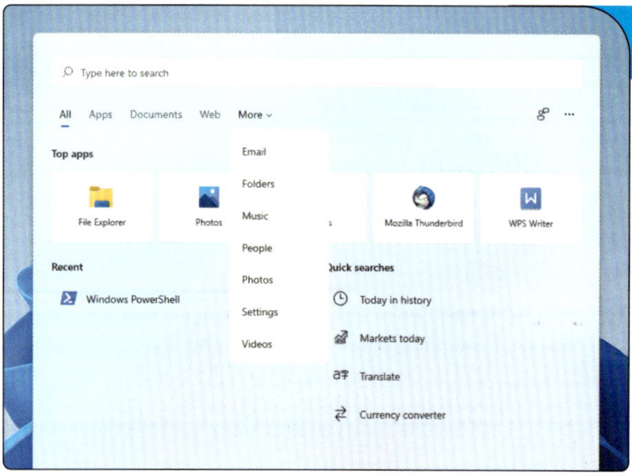


### Step 2

In addition to files and folders, you can search for web results and apps. When you first click in the search box you will see three tabs along the bottom that let you choose what to search for; but even if you don't click one of these, the search function is smart enough to return results from all.

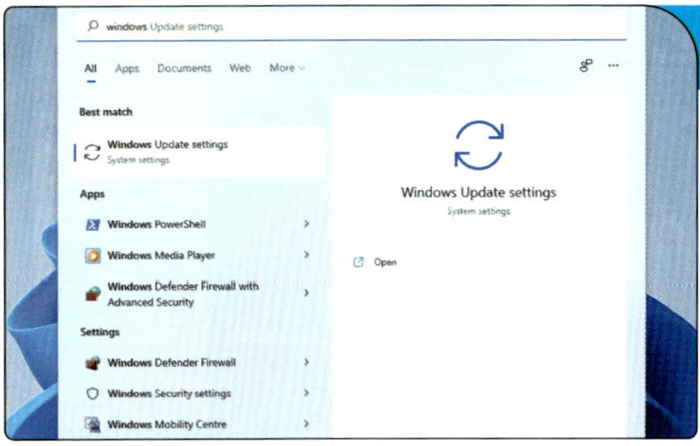


## Step 3

Search results are displayed in sections (best match, apps, folders, etc.) so that you know what you are looking at. Apps will be displayed with their icon next to them. Folders will have a folder icon and images will be shown as small thumbnails, within the search results panel.

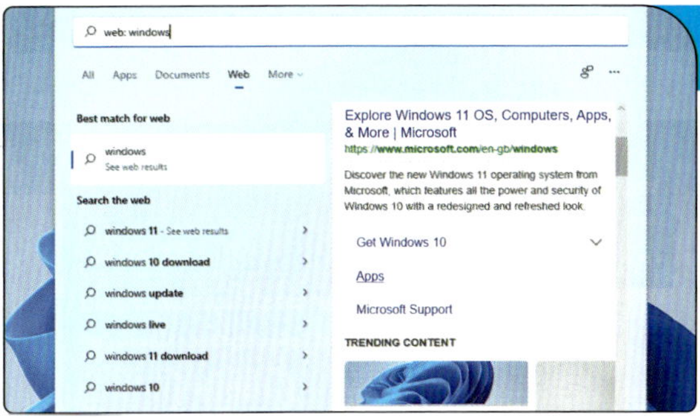


## Step 4

You can further filter the results that have appeared after you search by clicking on the titles of the results section in the panel. This lets you filter various results, even music or video. Suggested search results can be previewed by clicking the right-facing arrow next to them.

# Search Settings and Tools

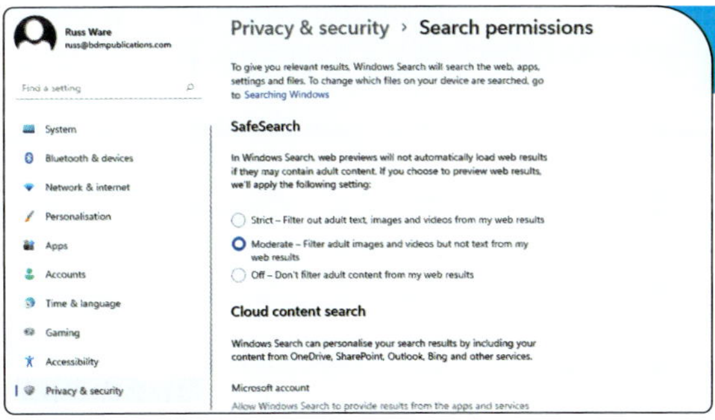


## Safe Search

Sometimes web search results may show content that is not suitable for the younger audience, which is the reason Cortana also offers search filters. Go to Settings > Cortana > Permissions and History, and under SafeSearch, select the search filter that is most appropriate for you.

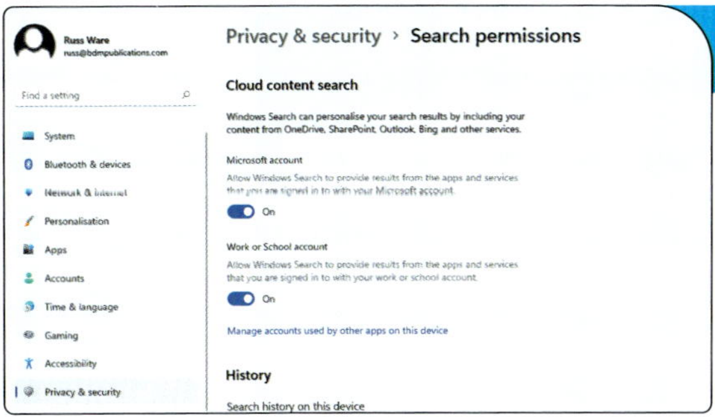


## Cloud Search

Cloud search is an option introduced in Windows 10, which allows you to suppress cloud content on search results. Under Cloud Search, you will see a toggle that says Windows Cloud Search. This option manages whether Cortana shows cloud content in Windows Search.

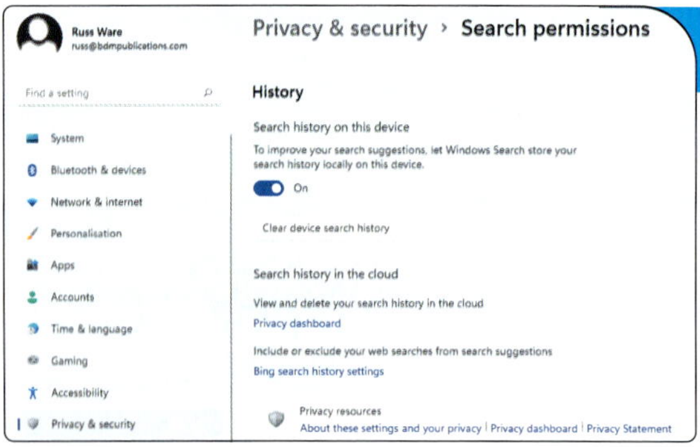


## Device History

This setting allows for the improvement of on-device search results, whether you are using an app, settings or another search from any signed in device. If you prefer that Windows does not record the on-device search history, you can switch this option off in Settings > Permissions & History.

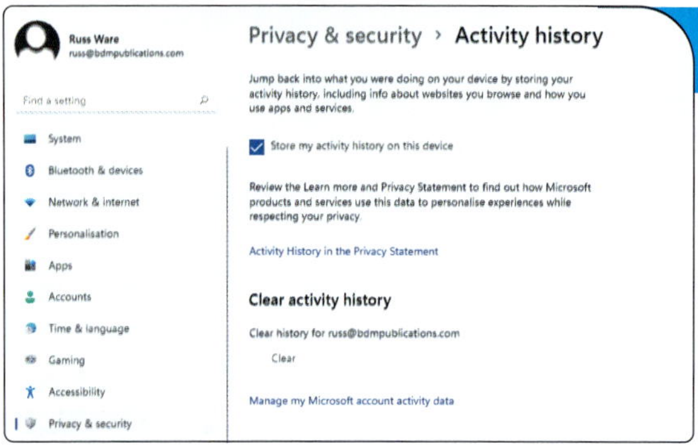


## Search History

Search History can help to provide better search results. It can also be turned off, just like the Device History. Head in to Settings > Permissions & History and use the toggle to turn it off. If you click Search History Settings a browser window opens showing the history.

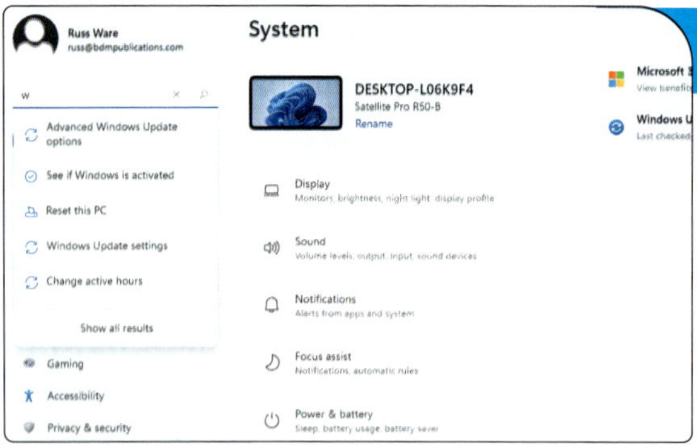


## File Explorer

You can always search for files and folders in File Explorer as you could in previous versions of Windows. With the new taskbar search you won't need to use this as often as you did, but it's still there if you need it. We don't find it as quick as the taskbar search, though.

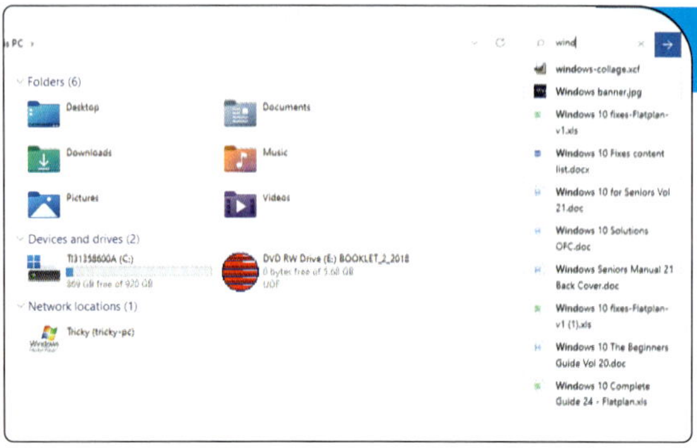


## Settings

Windows 11 allows you to search for settings from within the Settings app. Open the app and you will see the search box right at the top, underneath the window title. Possible results are displayed as you type, just like a normal search, but the results will only be from settings, nowhere else.

Chapter 2

# Windows 11 Intermediate

Do you want to do more with Windows 11 and its new features? Excellent, then this is the chapter for you.

Within the coming pages, you'll learn how to utilise Microsoft's apps to your best advantage, and how to get to grips with some of the more technical aspects of the Windows operating system.

# Explore the Microsoft Store

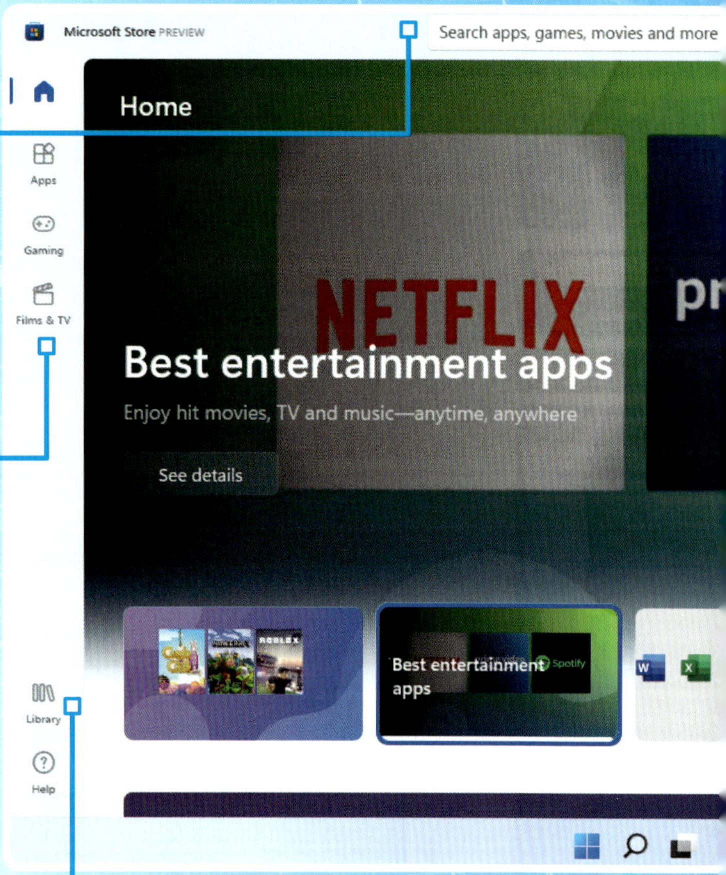


## Store Search

You can use the main search tool to search for apps, games, music and films in the Windows Store (store results will have the store icon next to them in the results list). Alternatively, you can search just inside the store by using this search bar.

## Category Tabs

Just as with other online app stores, the Microsoft Store features several different download categories. These include Apps, Gaming and Film & TV. Each category has its own Home screen, which displays collections of Most Popular, Top Free and Trending content.

## Library

If there is an update or new download available for any app you currently have installed on your computer, a notification will appear here. The number shows how many updates/app downloads are waiting. Click the button and select the required action (update, retry, etc.).

## Apps

Once you have found the app or game you want to install, click on the icon to open the app info screen. This screen displays the average app score, user reviews and similar app suggestions; as well as a list of features and updates. Click the Free, Buy or Try button to install the software.

**The new Microsoft Store has loads to help you stay in touch and get things done; plus more games and entertainment than ever before - many of them free! In Windows 11, it even contains Android apps you can use directly on your PC.**

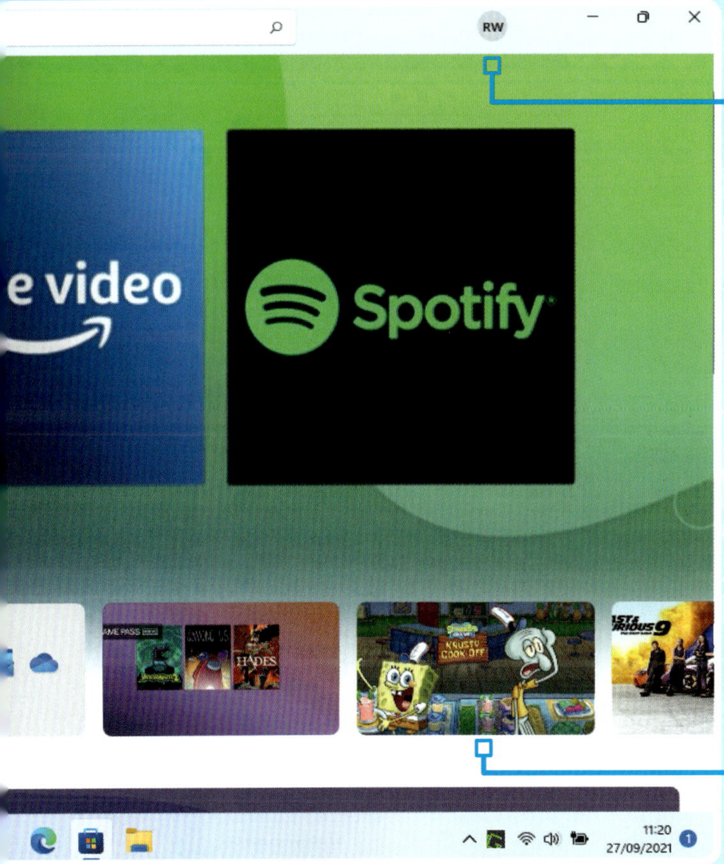


## Store Settings

Click the small Account icon here to see the store settings option. Here you will find details of the Microsoft account currently being used, along with several sliders used to control things like automatic app updates. You can also control who can install new apps on your PC.

## Store Offers

Periodically, the Windows Store will feature offers for its users. This could be a free 30 day trial, or other download offers. Click on the link to read more about the offer and then follow the instructions to take advantage of it.

## Featured Content

The Featured Apps slider will display those apps or games that are trending or have been particularly popular. This display is constantly updated, and is a good way of finding out what other Windows 11 users are using and playing.

## Apps & Games

As you scroll down the main page of the App, Game, Music or Film Home screens, you will see additional sections showing Most Popular, Top Free, etc. If you want to see all of the apps in a particular section, click the Show All button on the right.

# The Windows App Store

The Windows App Store has been updated and given a great new look, fresh for Windows 11. It's now designed to be more efficient and easier to get to the apps you want; and those that are trending or have been highlighted by Microsoft themselves.

## Go Shopping

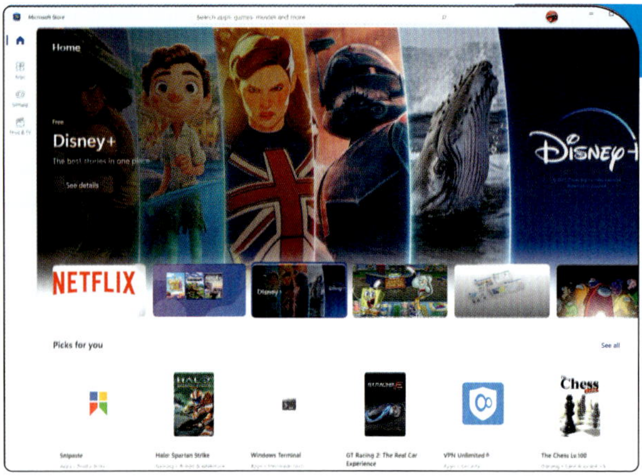


### Step 1

The Windows App Store is located, by default, within the new taskbar. It's easy to identify, it's the carrier bag icon with the Microsoft logo. Click it, and as long as you're signed into a valid Microsoft account, it will launch with the latest trending and highlighted apps displayed.

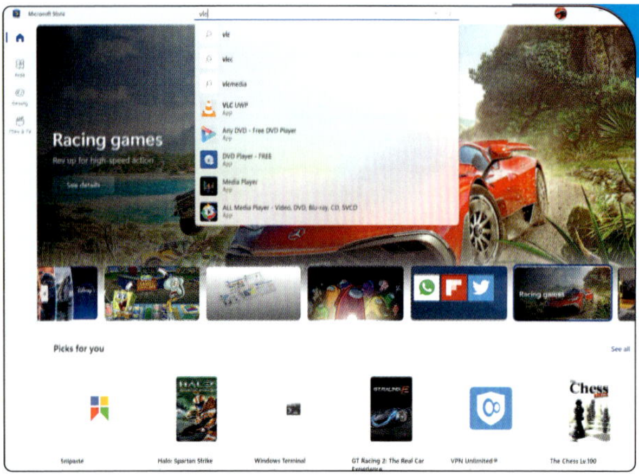


### Step 2

Let's run through locating and installing an app from the App Store. In the Search box, located at the top of the Store window, enter: VLC. In case, you're wondering, VLC is a free, cross-platform media player. In the Search bar, there will be a number of returned results, click the VLC UWP entry with the traffic cone icon.

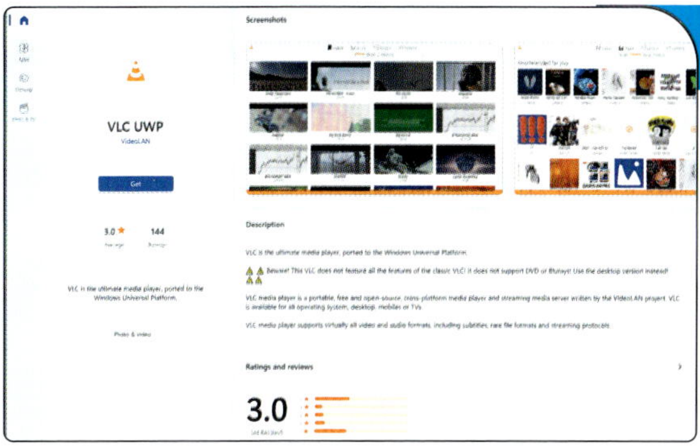


## Step 3

Every app in the App Store will behave in the same manner: there will be screen shots of the app along the top, a description, rating and reviews from other users, and in the left-hand pane there's a brief summary of the app. Also, in the left-hand pane, is a Get button. To install VLC, click on the Get button.

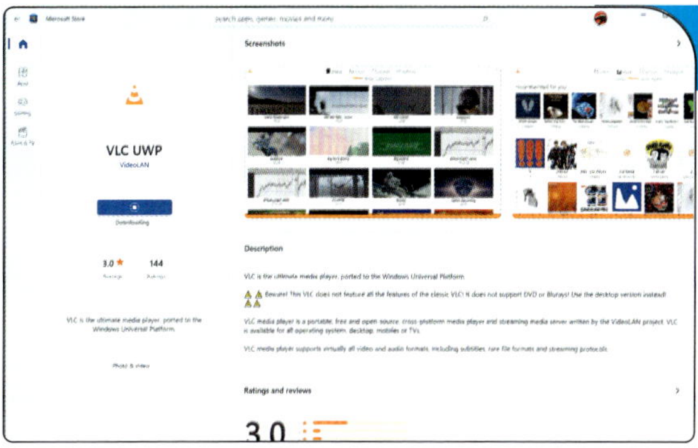


## Step 4

The information below the Get button will change, displaying the amount of time left to download through the number of megabytes (or more) remaining from the total. When it's downloaded, there'll be a brief installation display, and when that's done the button will change to read, Open.

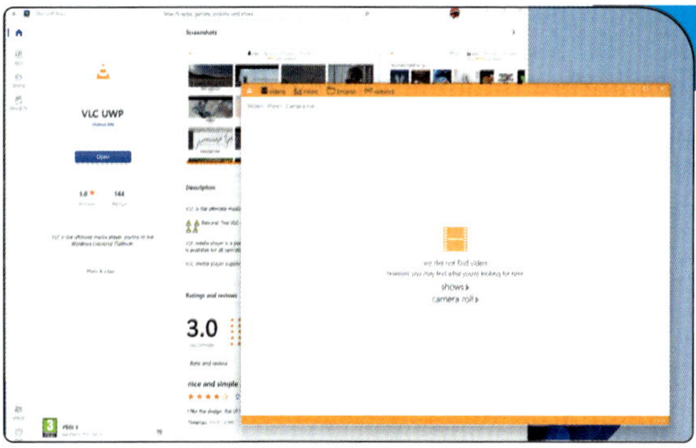


## Step 5

Click on the Open button and the app will launch. This will work for most, if not all the available apps on the App Store. Some may require further steps, such as signing into a third-party account – the Twitter app, for example, requires you to have a Twitter account.

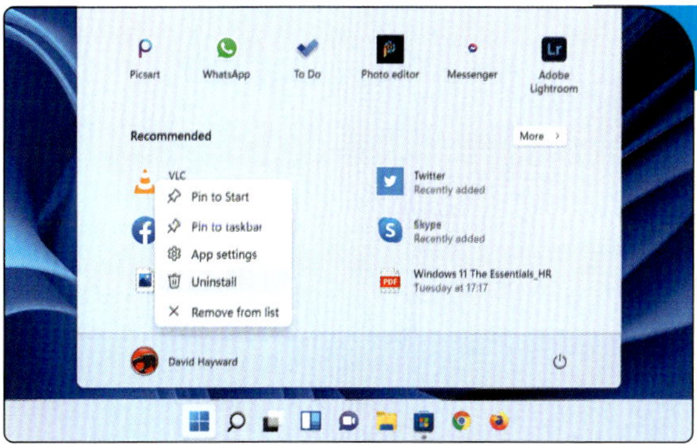


## Step 6

Sadly, you can't remove an app via the App Store. To remove an App Store installed app, locate it within the taskbar Start button, right-click the app, and select Uninstall from the list. This will remove the app, and any associated elements that were installed by the App Store. Anything you've added outside the App Store may remain, however.

## Step 7

You'll notice that down the left-hand panel of the App Store Home screen, are a number of category icons: Home, Apps, Gaming, Films & TV; and further down the screen, Library and Help. The Home button will return you to the main Home screen, click the Apps button next.

## Step 8

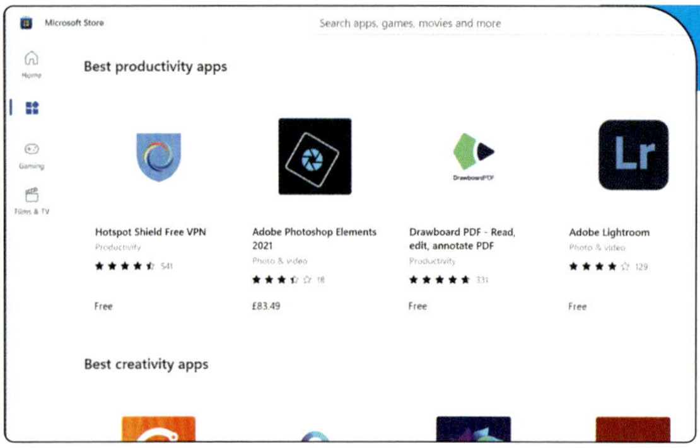


The App category simply removes the Gaming and Films & TV entries in the Home screen, to help you find what you're looking for without unnecessary content getting in the way. Scrolling down through the Apps section reveals best selling apps, collections, and specific apps such as productivity, photo and video editing and so on.

## Step 9

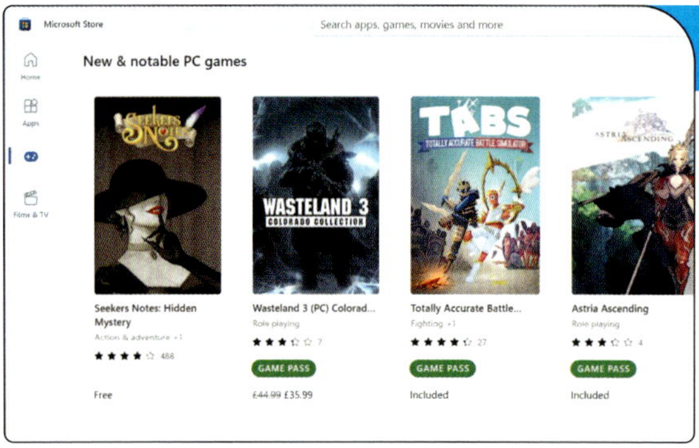


The Gaming category does the same, but removes the other apps and retains all the apps relating to games. Again, you can scroll down to reveal top free games, highest rated, top paid, and special deals that may be currently running on the App Store. Films & TV is identical in behaviour, but displays the latest titles to rent or buy.

## Step 10

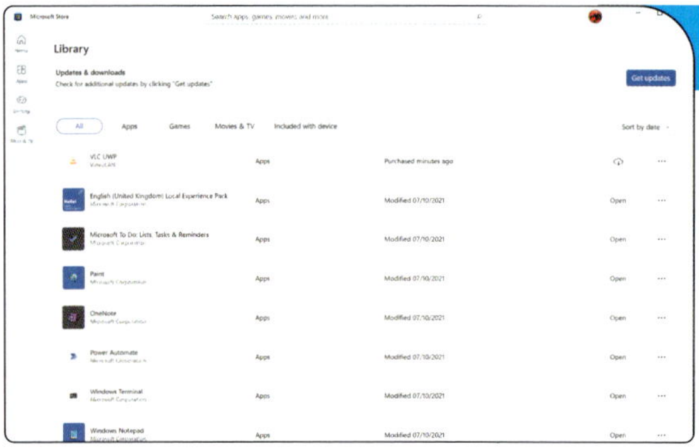


The Library section will detail all the apps you currently have installed on your Windows 11 system. These can be further broken down into Apps, Games and Movies & TV; as well as the apps that are included in Windows 11 by default. You can also check for any app updates, and Share the app across other devices.

# Using Teams Chat

Online meetings are a big thing, so Microsoft Teams in Windows 11 makes perfect sense. You'll need to have a Microsoft Teams account already set up to use the chat and video meeting tools, but once you have, remote working becomes a whole lot easier.

## Setting Up the Teams App

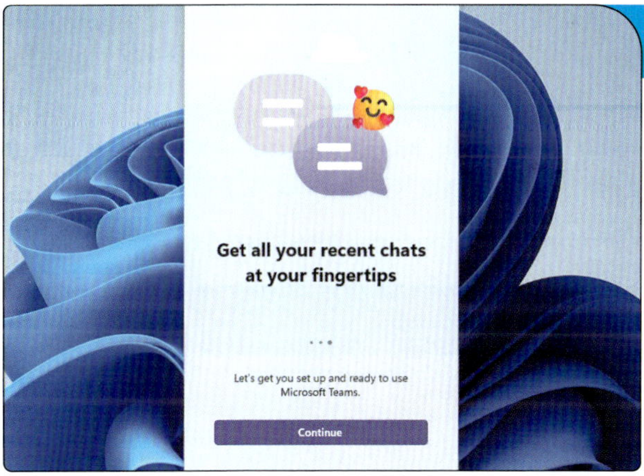


### Step 1

Click the Teams Chat icon in the taskbar, or open the Teams app in the main apps list. If your Microsoft account email matches the one you use when setting up your Teams account, the app should automatically detect it, and log you in to the app after a few moments.

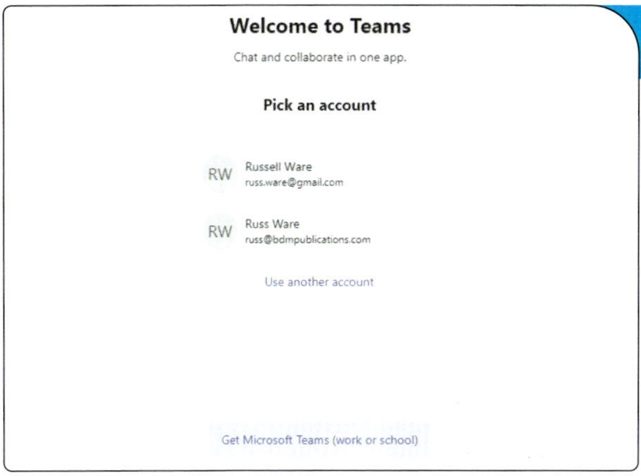


### Step 2

If the app doesn't recognise your email address, it will open the Teams login screen. Here you can choose an account to sign in to (if any are displayed), or you can pick another account. If you have yet to set up an account, you can use the link at the bottom and set one up in the browser.

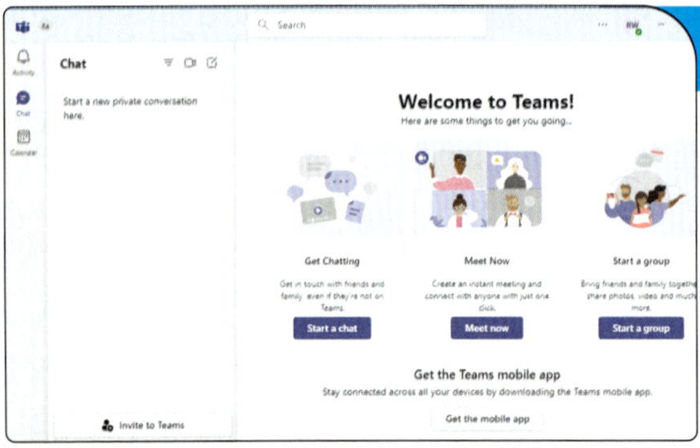


## Step 3

Once signed in to your Teams account, the main app window will open. If you automatically signed in by clicking the Chat icon (step 1), you can access the Teams app by clicking the "Open Microsoft Teams" link at the bottom of the chat pop-up window on the taskbar.

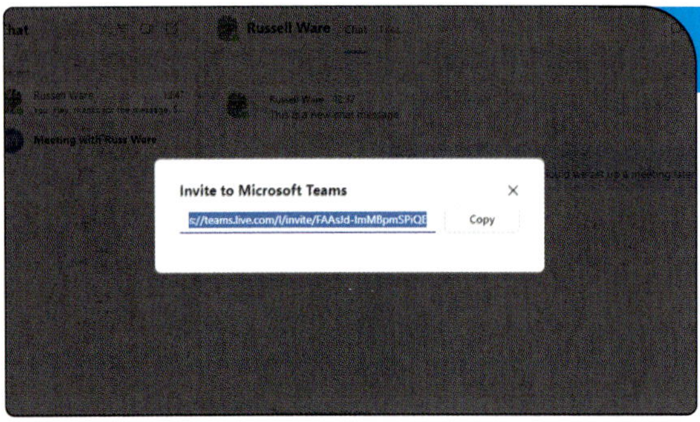


## Step 4

You can invite people to Teams using the button on the left sidebar. Clicking this will create a link that you can send to anyone you want to join Teams. You can invite people to chat by clicking the "Start a chat" button, then entering a name (if in your contacts), email address (anyone) or phone number.

# Meet and Chat in Teams

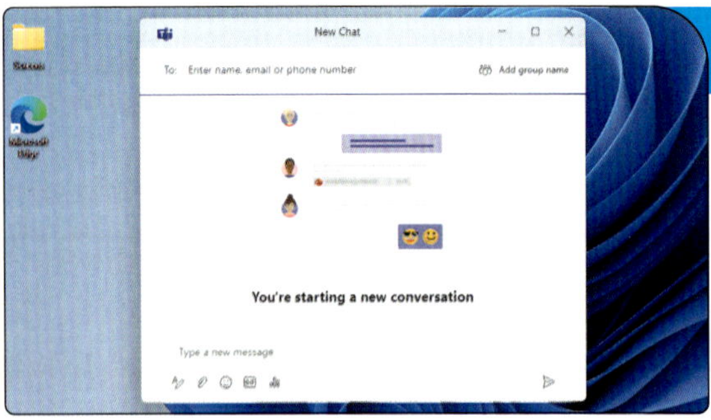


## Step 1

To begin a chat, click the Teams Chat icon in the taskbar. From the pop-up window, click on the Chat button. In the new window that opens, enter a contact name, email address or phone number. Type your message and that person will receive a notification telling them you want to start a chat.

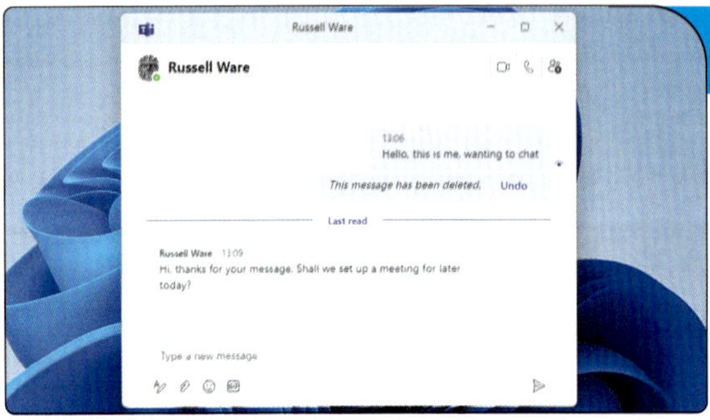


## Step 2

Your messages, and the replies, are shown in the conversation window. You can attach and send files via the chat by clicking the paper clip icon. If you want to switch from a text chat to an audio or video call, click either of the buttons at the top-right of the chat window.

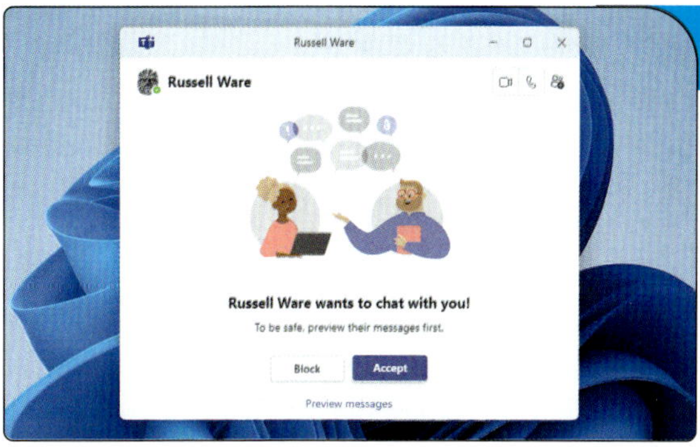


## Step 3

If you receive a chat request, you will see a notification in the main Notification center (Action center), and a badge will appear on the chat icon in the taskbar. You can choose to accept or reject the chat request. If you accept, the message will appear and you can start chatting.

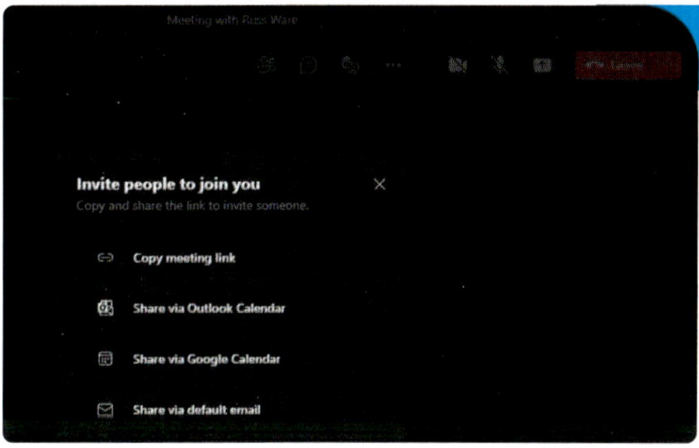


## Step 4

To start a meeting, click the Meet button. Give your meeting a name, and you will then be shown several ways to invite people. These include a link you can send, via Outlook Calendar, Google calendar or email. Once shared, you can start the meeting and wait for others to join.

## Step 5

Once you are in the meeting you have controls to enable/disable the microphone, enable/disable the camera or set a background blur, etc. To leave a meeting, you just have to click the red Hang up button. If the meeting host ends the meeting, you will automatically be hung up from everyone.

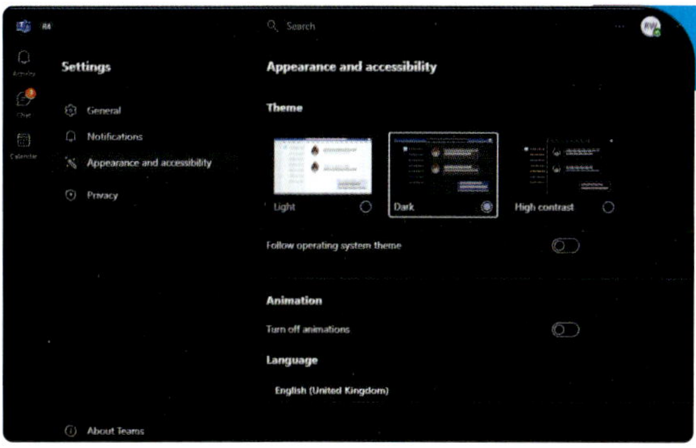


## Step 6

You can change the look of the Teams app and Teams Chat in the app settings. Under Appearance & Accessibility, choose from light, dark or high contrast themes. You can also choose to turn off animations, select the app language and change how you are notified of new chats and meetings.

# OneDrive Cloud Storage

**Microsoft's OneDrive has vastly improved over the years. Where once it was a simple backup and online storage solution, it's now a connected collaborative service, with many excellent features. All of which make it one of the best cloud services available.**

## Silver Linings

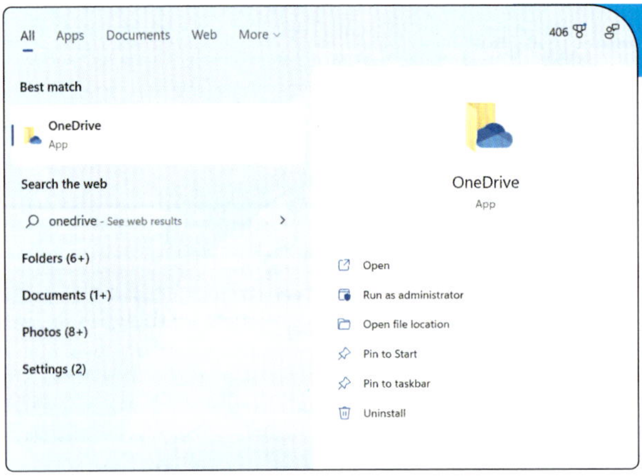


### Step 1

You can check to see if you have Microsoft's OneDrive already loaded on your Windows 11 computer by clicking in the notification area in the bottom-right of the desktop. You're looking for a cloud icon. If it's not there, simply click the Windows Start button and type 'OneDrive'. Click the OneDrive app that appears in the list.

### Step 2

You may be asked to sign in with your Microsoft account, follow the instructions, and you'll notice that the cloud icon in the notification area may have an extra icon over it to indicate it's synchronising with your computer and OneDrive. If you click it, you'll notice a flurry of activity, this is because OneDrive is automatically backing up your files.

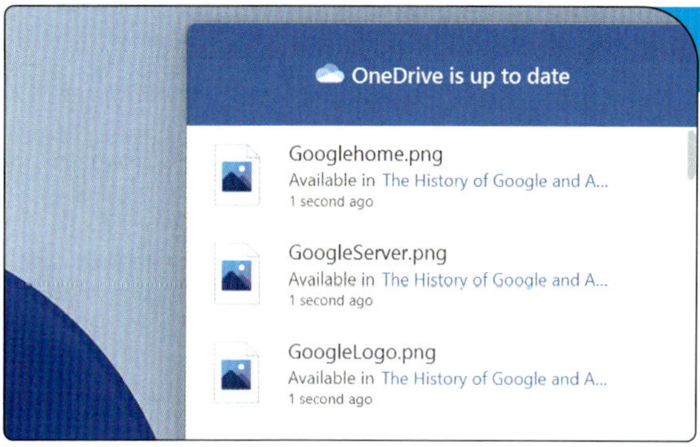


## Step 3

When your current files on your computer have been backed up, a OneDrive notification will inform you that OneDrive is up to date. This will also list the files that have been synced across from your PC to your OneDrive area in the cloud. You can scroll though the list to view the files synced.

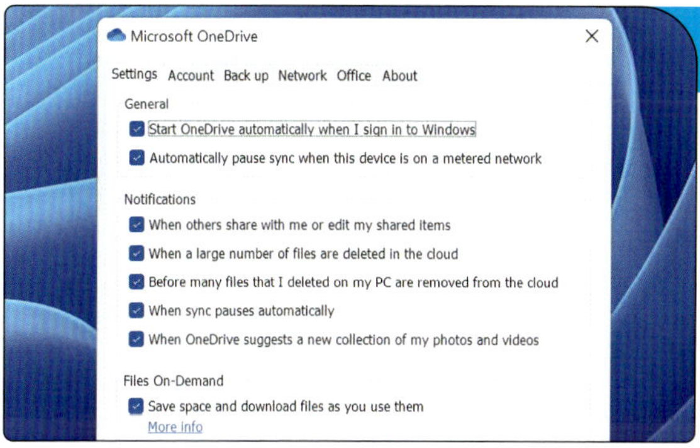


## Step 4

Right-click the OneDrive cloud icon in the notification area. Click on the Settings option within the next menu. The OneDrive Settings menu is divided into several tabs. To begin with, ensure that in the Settings tab, the first option, Start OneDrive automatically when I sign into Windows, is ticked. Otherwise, your auto-backups are pointless.

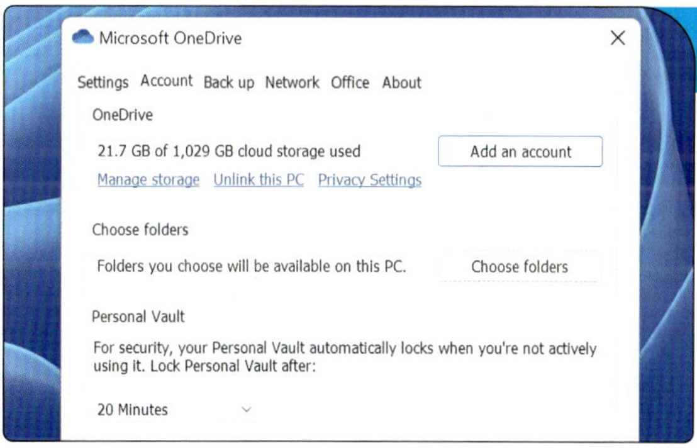


## Step 5

In the Account tab, you can choose to Unlink the PC with the OneDrive account, Add another Microsoft OneDrive account (such as your work account), and Choose which folders will be available on the PC in your personal OneDrive File Explorer area.

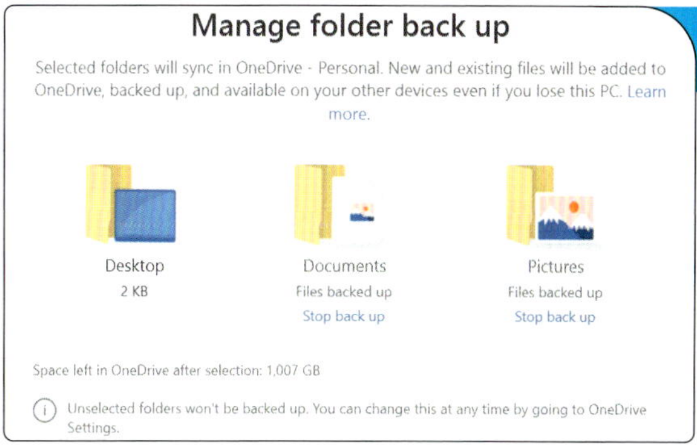


## Step 6

In the Backup Tab, click the Manage Back Up button. These are the default, important folders on your PC that will automatically be backed up by OneDrive. You can de-select these folders whenever you want, but they won't be available to other Windows or Microsoft devices when you login to them.

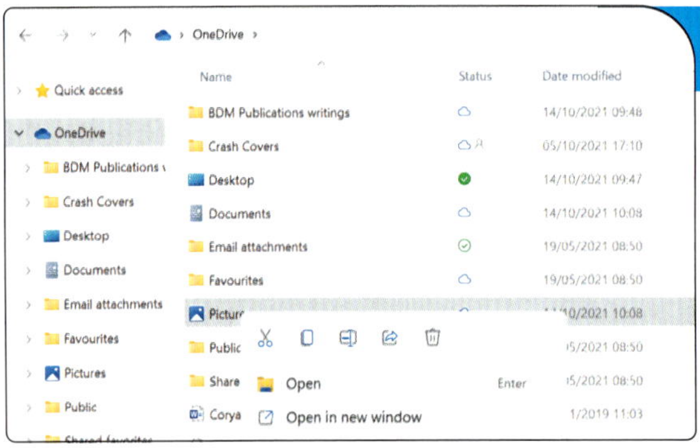


## Step 7

If you close the OneDrive Settings window, and now open File Explorer, you'll notice a new section in the left-hand pane: OneDrive. This is where you can work with your online files from your PC. They'll only be available on demand, but can be made available permanently by right-clicking and selecting Always Keep on this Device.

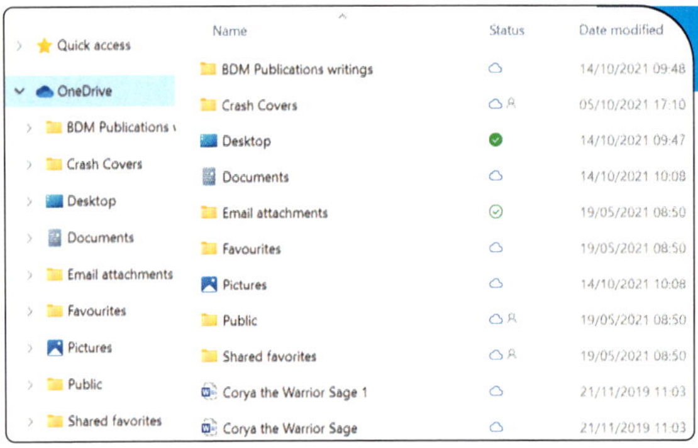


## Step 8

If you need to ensure that any file or folder is to be backed up to OneDrive, they must exist in either the main Documents, Pictures or Desktop folders within your user area, or be copied to the OneDrive folder. This will make sure they're synchronised with your online OneDrive storage area.

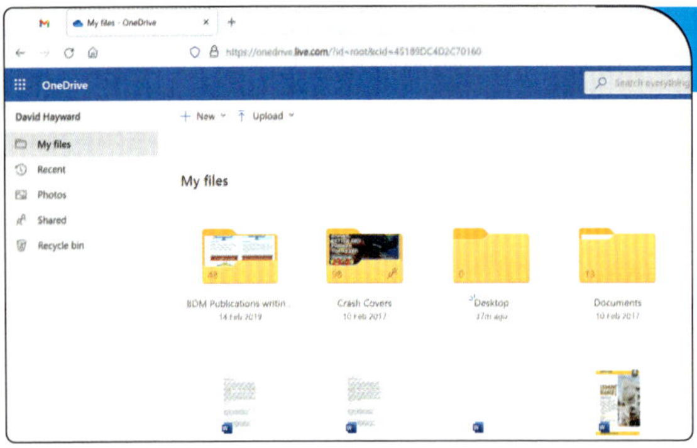


## Step 9

If you again right-click the OneDrive cloud icon in the notification area, and select the View Online option, a web browser window will open and take you directly to your OneDrive storage area in the cloud. This area is available from any device that's connected to the Internet.

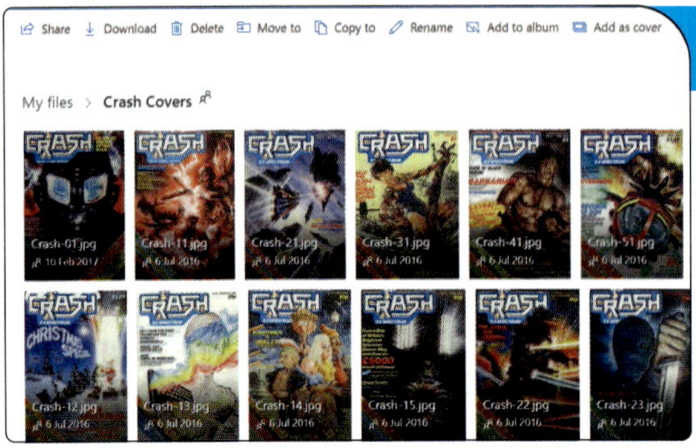


## Step 10

From within the online OneDrive view, you can create files and folders, view image galleries, move, copy, rename, upload, and most importantly, share any of the content with others. Everything can be done via the top menu bar, or by right-clicking each of the files or folders within your area.

# Connect Your Phone and PC

You can connect an Android phone to both your Microsoft account and Windows 11, allowing you to view the photos on your phone from the comfort of your desktop, and even view call and SMS details on your computer as they arrive on your phone.

## Using the Your Phone App

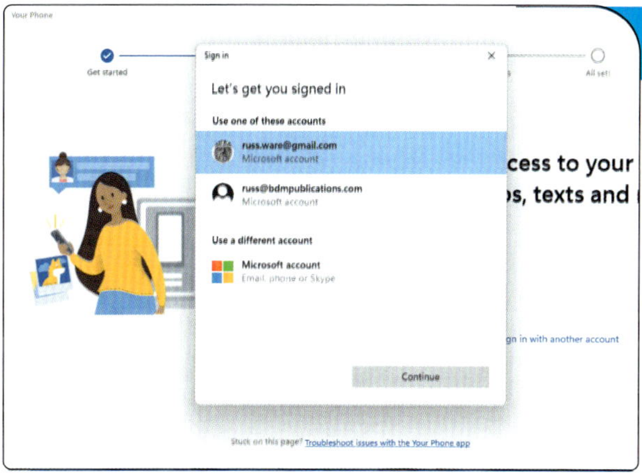


### Step 1

Open the main app list from the Start menu and look for "Your Phone". Click the app and then click the "Get Started" button on the screen that opens. You will need to sign in with the same Microsoft account on both the PC and the companion app on your phone. Select/sign in to that account next.

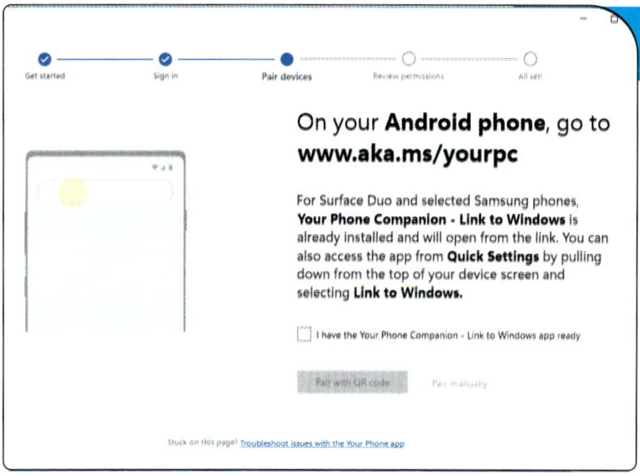


### Step 2

On your Android phone, open a browser window and go to www.aka.ms/yourpc. You may already have an app installed that can link to windows called Your Phone Companion (on Samsung, open the Quick settings and look for "Link to Windows"). If so, open the app and follow the instructions.

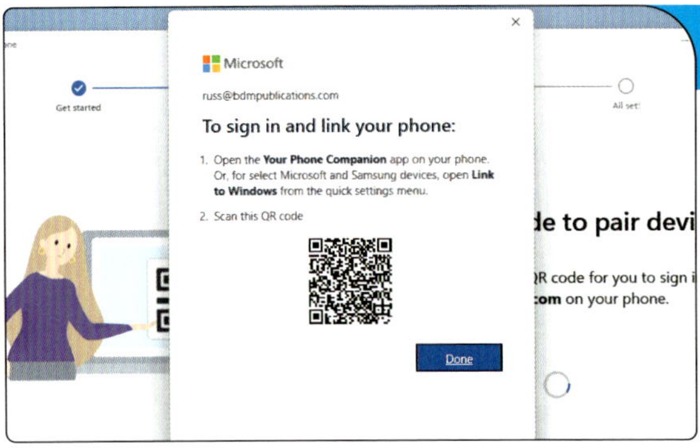


## Step 3

When you're asked, click "Pair with QR code" in the Your Phone app on your computer. A QR code will be created and appear on screen. On your phone, click Continue and a QR code reader screen will open. Use this to read the QR code on your computer screen. After a few seconds the two devices should link.

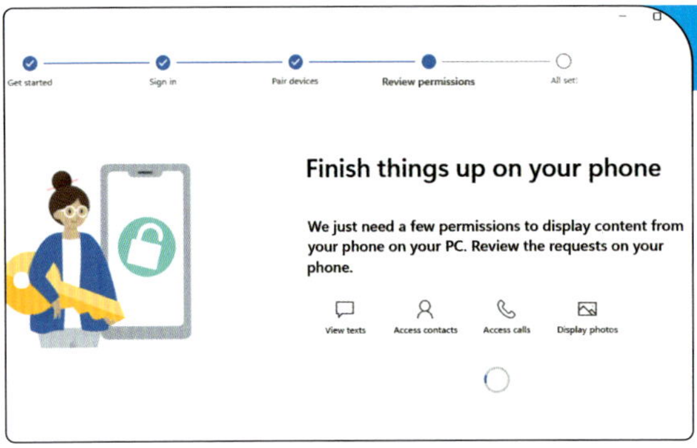


## Step 4

You will need to give the app permission to access certain things on your phone. These include contacts, calls, photos and media, and SMS messages. You can refuse any of these individual permissions and the Your Phone app will still work, just without access to that feature.

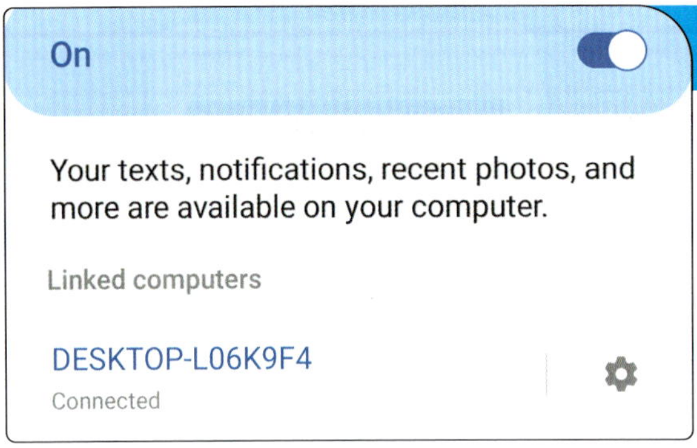


## Step 5

If all is successful, you should now see your phone displayed in the Your Phone app on your computer. There is a new screen displayed on your phone, this shows the settings for the Microsoft companion app, alongside which Windows 11 computer it is connected.

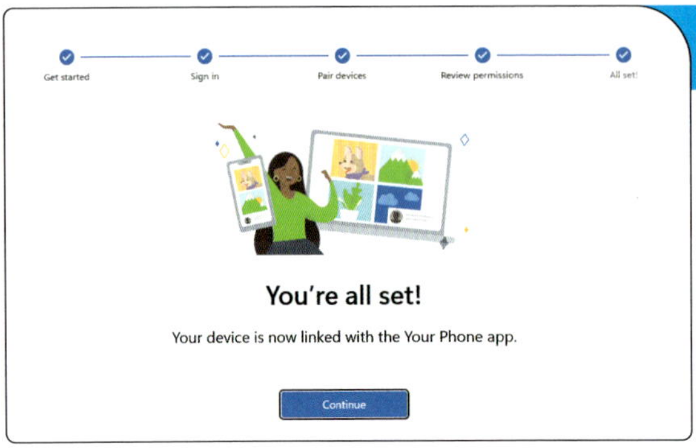


## Step 6

Now it's time to start using the Your Mobile app. In the left-hand sidebar are several different sections. These include Photos, Messages, Notifications and Apps. Some of these need to be set up further to begin using them, follow the on-screen instructions to do so.

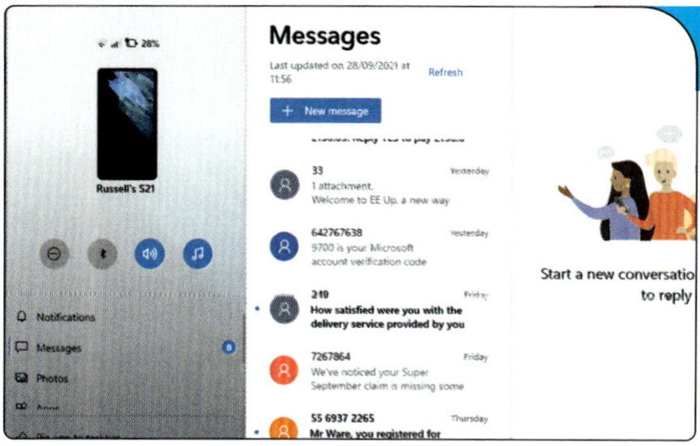


## Step 7

Click on Messages first. When asked, send a notification to your phone to ask permission to access messages (if already given, this opens the messages list). Your phone messages are now displayed, and you can click on any to read and reply. You can also create new messages from your PC.

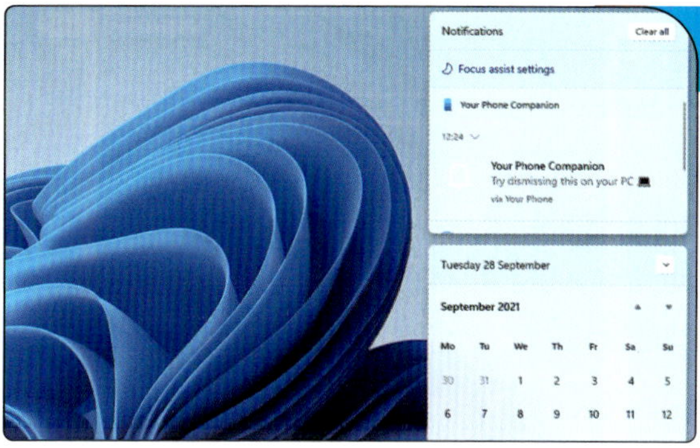


## Step 8

If you want to be able to see notifications from your phone on your PC screen, you need to click on Notifications and then click "Get Started". Again, you need to allow this on your phone settings. Phone notifications will pop up on your PC screen in the same place as other notifications.

## Step 9

To view photos stored on your phone from the comfort of your PC, click the Photos section. Allow access as before, and then wait while the view refreshes. You can open them in the Photos app by clicking on them. You can now also delete photos on your phone from the PC app.

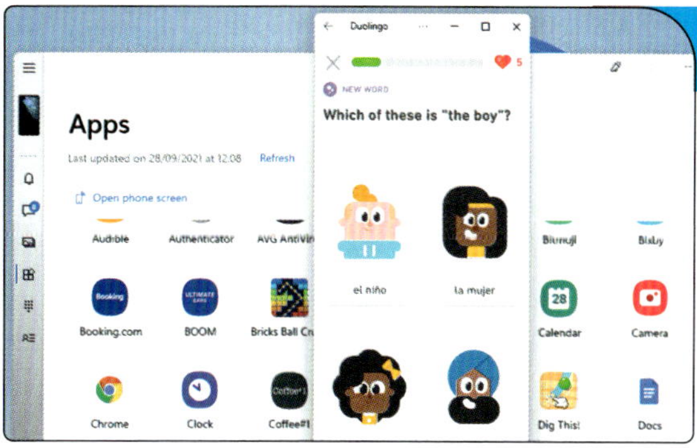


## Step 10

You can open apps that are on your phone, on your computer. Click the apps section, then click on an app icon in the list. You will need to give permission on your phone to cast to the Windows app, but once done, the app will open on your computer screen in a phone screen shaped window.

# The Focus Assist Tool

Focus Assist allows you to create distraction-free periods by blocking alerts, notifications and other sounds. Turn on Focus Assist to stop distractions like social media or alternatively set it to turn on automatically at certain times during the day.

## Blocking Notifications

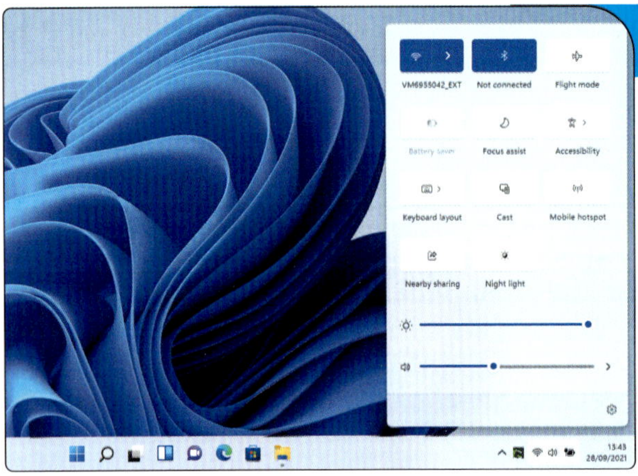


### Step 1

You can easily activate Focus Assist using the quick actions panel in the Action Center. The default setting is Off. Click the Quick action button once to allow priority notifications only, click it a second time to allow alarms only. Click the button a third time to turn Focus Assist off again.

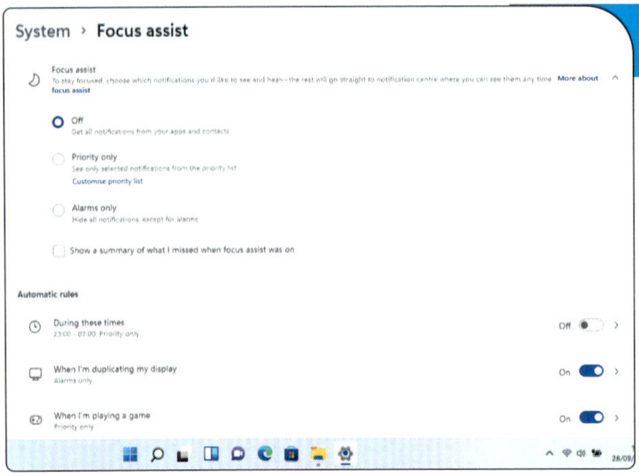


### Step 2

You can also turn Focus Assist on or off in the main settings (settings > system > focus assist). Once there, you can also set up your automatic rules and customise your priority list. You can set automatic rules based on times, when you are duplicating your display or when playing a game.

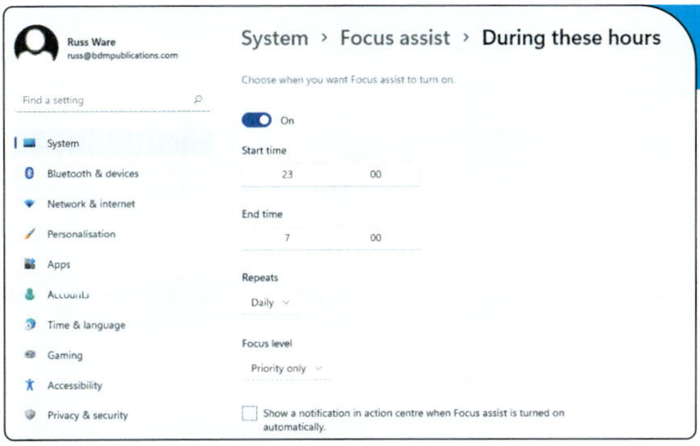


## Step 3

To set an automatic rule by time, click on the option and then click the slider to On. You will now see menus to set start time, end time and whether to repeat the rule daily, just on weekdays or just on weekends. The focus level lets you choose if this applies to priority notifications or alarms.

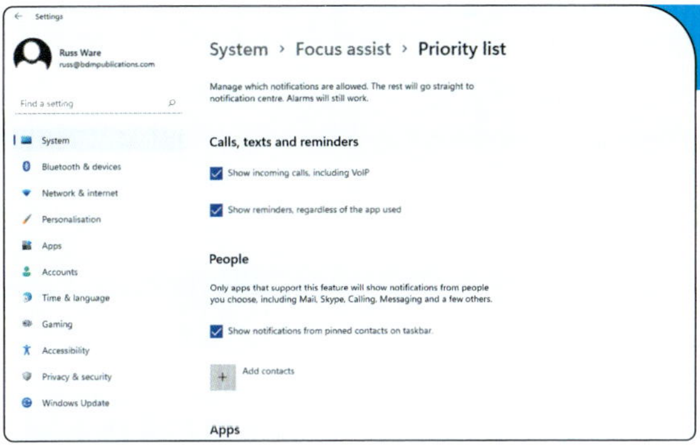


## Step 4

If setting Focus Assist to priority, you can set a priority list by clicking 'Customise your list'. Here you can add or remove specific apps, people or Windows 11 features that notify you. When you turn off Focus Assist (manually or automatically), a summary of missed notifications can be shown.

# Get Focused

**Focus Assist started life back in an early update for Windows 10 (then called Quiet Hours), and the idea has proved to be one of the more popular functions for the modern operating system. Do not disturb and Focus Mode are used throughout Apple devices, Linux, Android and even some of the more esoteric operating systems you'll find dotted around the Internet.**

**The all work very well, but it's a shame we have to use them in the first place. There are simply too many distractions these days when working on a modern OS – news feeds, notifications from social media, contacts popping up with something on their minds.**

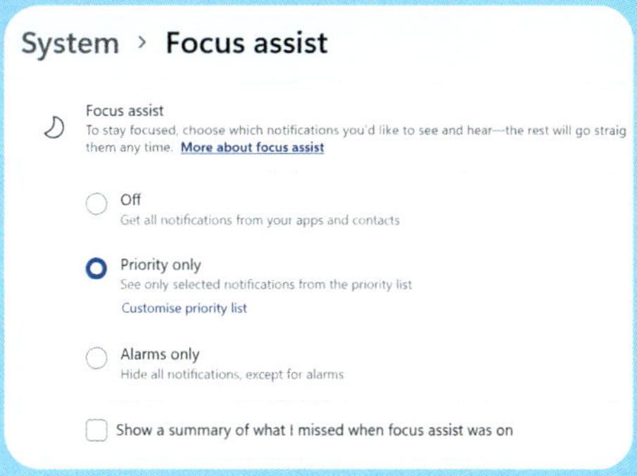


**As the legendary Douglas Adams once said, "in the old days, writers used to sit in front of a typewriter and stare out of the window. Nowadays, because of the marvels of convergent technology, the thing you type on and the window you stare out of are now the same thing." Focus Assist can hopefully help you find the right balance.**

# Sharing to Nearby Devices

Nearby Sharing lets you share your videos, photos, documents and websites with people and devices close by, over Bluetooth or Wi-Fi. Useful if, for example, you're in a meeting with colleagues and need to quickly send them a report you're looking at on your screen.

## Nearby Sharing

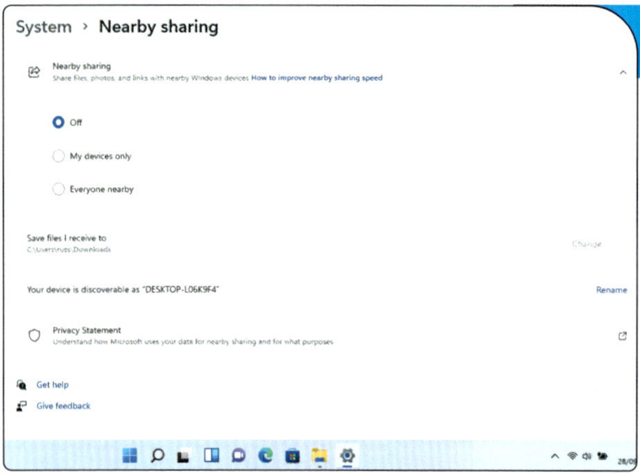


### Step 1

To enable Nearby Sharing, open Settings and click on System. Now click on Shared experiences and turn on the Nearby Sharing option. You may be asked to sign in, or confirm sign in, if you have several accounts associated with your computer (Microsoft account, email account, etc.).

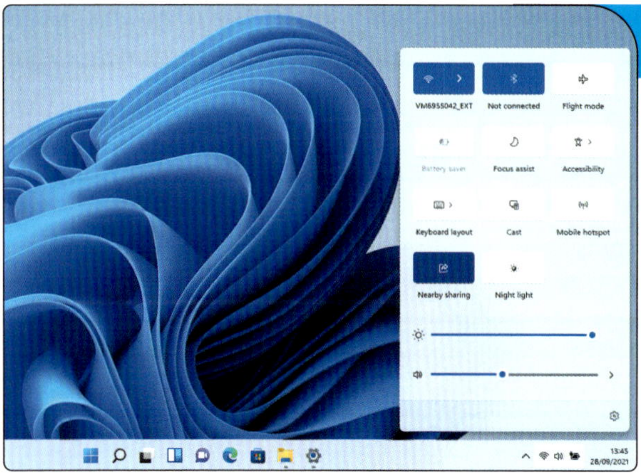


### Step 2

You can also activate Nearby Sharing from the quick actions menu in the Action Center. You can send any video, photo, document or webpage viewed on Microsoft Edge to people or devices nearby by clicking on the share icon in the top right corner of the app or right-clicking to view the share menu.

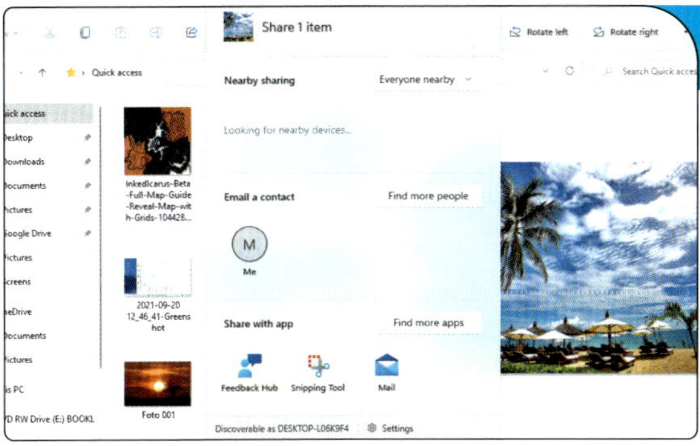


## Step 3

If there is a nearby device available, it will be shown in the share menu that pops up. You will need to know the name of the device you want to share to. Once you select the device, the other user will see a notification asking them to accept the transfer. This will time out in a few seconds if not accepted.

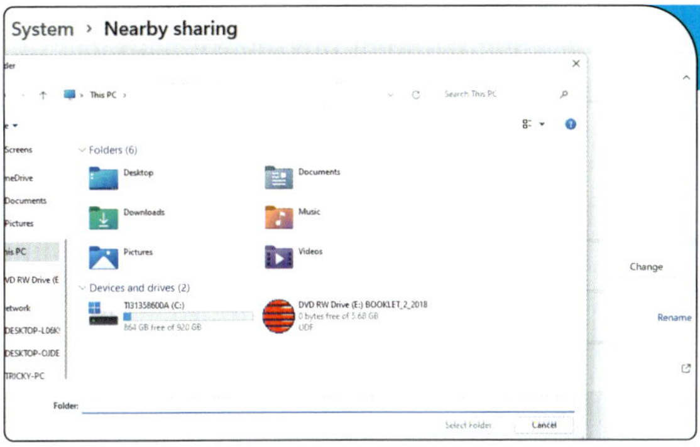


## Step 4

By default, transfers will be stored in the Downloads folder but you can specify another folder or another drive very easily. Open settings and click on system > shared experiences. Under 'Nearby Sharing', look for the 'Save files I receive to' option and click the Change button.

# Share and Share Alike

**Quick sharing between available devices over Bluetooth and Wi-Fi isn't a new technology; it's been around for as long as we've been able to send an image from one phone to another. However, it's one that in recent years has really gathered pace in the desktop operating system market.**

**Nearby Sharing probably has Apple to thank for the technology used. Apple's AirDrop protocol really pushed the boundaries of sharing tech, so much so that you'll be hard-pressed to find a modern operating system that doesn't feature some form of near device sharing – even Linux has Snapdrop available.**

**Nearby Sharing is one of the most secure protocols for locally connected file and folder sharing, because the user needs to authorise the transfer. Other file sharing protocols rely on having access privileges to a drive or folder, which can easily be circumvented, and malware dropped in place. So where possible, consider using Nearby Sharing more in future.**

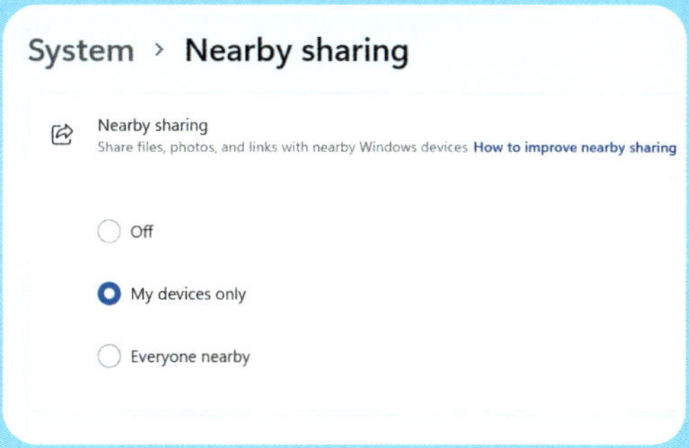

# Importing Photos

Importing photos from a digital camera, or phone, is a fairly simple task; but you can encounter problems. Here we take a look at importing photos from your phone, tablet or camera; using different methods and tools already included in Windows 11.

## Importing to a Folder

### Step 1

The first thing you need to do to import photos directly from a phone or camera is to connect the relevant cable to your PC. In almost all cases, this will be a USB cable of some sort. You will have been supplied a transfer cable with the device you are using. Plug this into a free USB port.

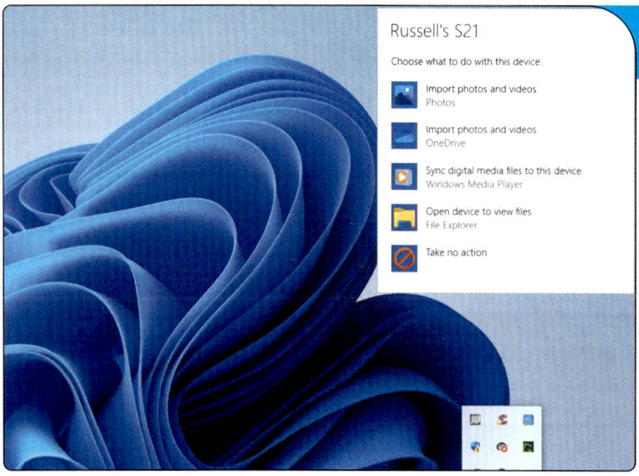


### Step 2

Normally, when you first plug a device in to your computer which contains storage of some sort, Windows will ask how you want to handle the files in that storage. Scroll down the list to see 'Open in a Folder'. In some cases, Explorer will open showing the connected device.

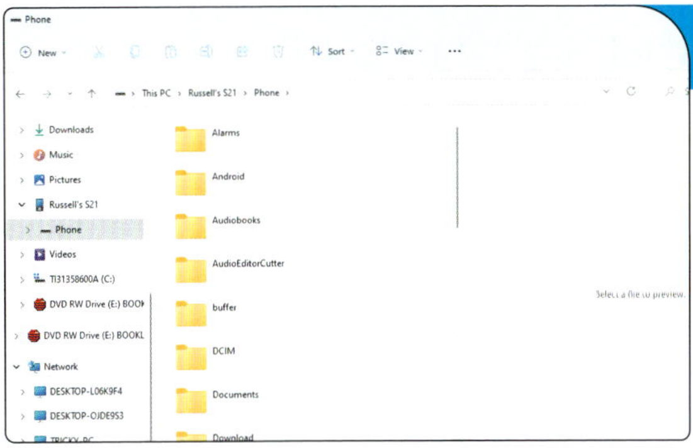


## Step 3

Now click on the device storage, this may be Phone and Card on a smartphone, and navigate to where the photos are stored. This will normally be in a folder called DCIM on your phone or camera. You can now simply cut and paste, or drag and drop, images to a new folder on your PC.

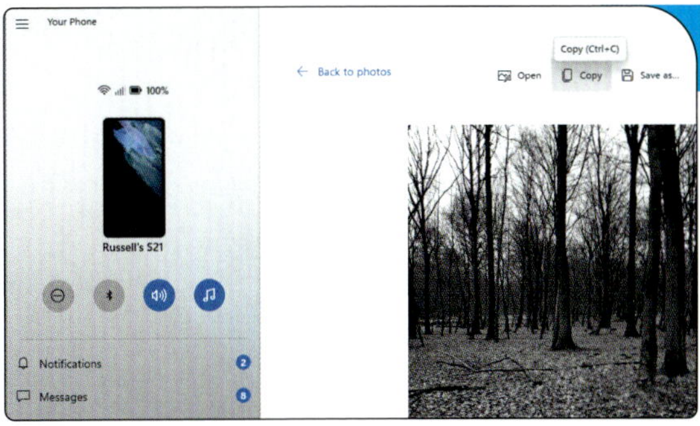


## Step 4

If you have connected your phone and PC using the Your Phone app, you can import images from your phone wirelessly. Simply open the app, click on the Photos tab and then browse to the photos you want to import. You can then choose Save as…, or copy and paste to a folder.

# Importing to the Photos App

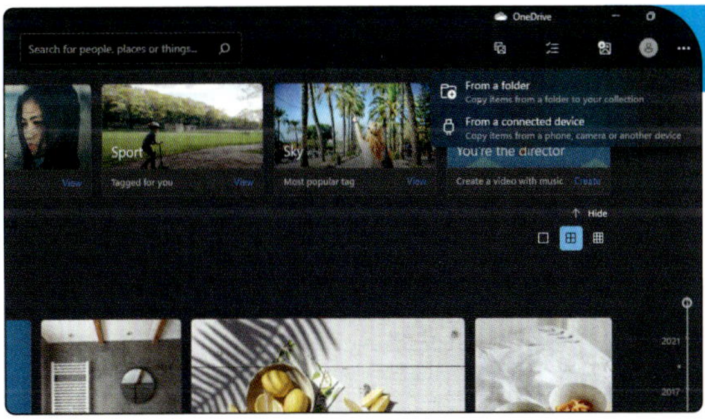


## Step 1

Open the Photos app on your Windows 11 PC. Now connect your phone or camera to your computer using the relevant USB cable. If you see the pop-up menu asking how you want to deal with the storage media you just connected, ignore it or click it closed.

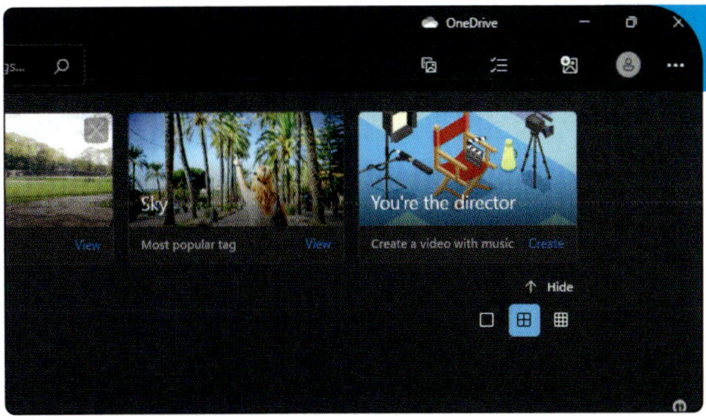


## Step 2

The Photos app should have opened up with the Collections screen showing. If not, click the tab at the top to open it now. Along the top of the Collections tab are your controls: Refresh, Select, Slideshow and Import. Import is the only one you need to click at this point.

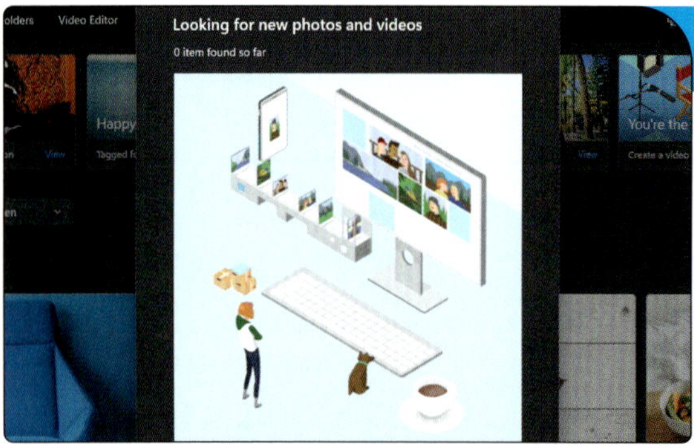


## Step 3

The Photos app will now search for photos available to be imported. If your device is not connected properly, or the correct USB drivers are not installed, it will fail to find anything at this point. If you are transferring from a phone or tablet, you may also have to unlock the screen to continue.

## Step 4

By default, every image detected on your device will be selected for importing. If you want to import everything, click Continue. If not, you can use the check boxes on the images to select those you want to import; use the Clear All and Select All buttons as required.

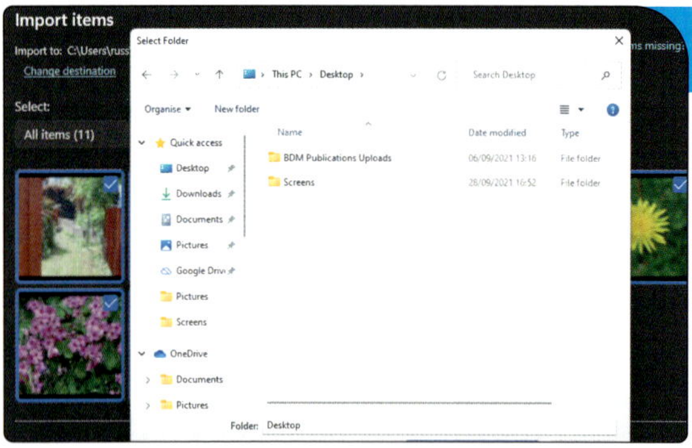


## Step 5

You can now choose where the imported photos will be saved. By default, this will probably be somewhere like C:\Users\YourName\Pictures. Click the 'Change where they're imported' link to do just that. You can also choose to import into folders arranged by month or day.

## Step 6

Click Import. Your image will now begin to appear in the Photos app window, within the Collections section. An album will also be created called Last Import. Click on one of the images shown to begin editing or enhancing it with the tools Photos offers.

# Manage & Edit Your Photos

**The Photos app was first introduced in Windows 8, but it wasn't the best experience compared to most third party apps. In Windows 11 it has been improved, with better ways to browse photos and a lot more editing options to make the most of your images.**

## Managing Your Images

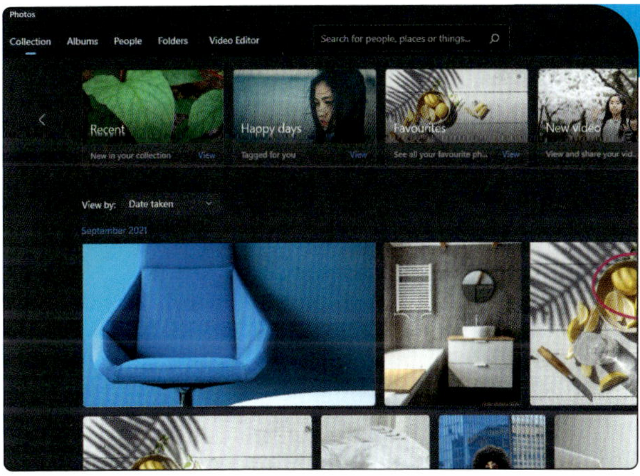


### Step 1

Photos shows all of your images in a scrolling timeline of images, called the Collection, with some automatically created collections at the top (this can be hidden using the Hide button). You can click on any image to get a full-window view, with a quick-select bar of images shown along the bottom.

### Step 2

Along the top of the full image view is a toolbar. This contains zoom and rotate buttons, an edit image button and draw button, as well as delete, add to favourites, file information, save as, resize and several more. You can click the Back arrow in the top left corner to return to the main image list.

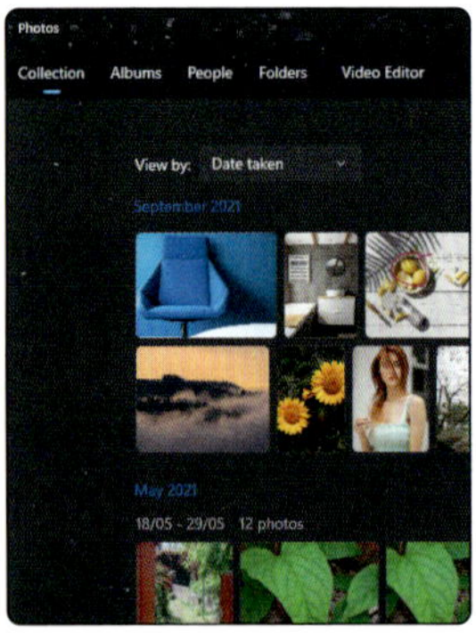


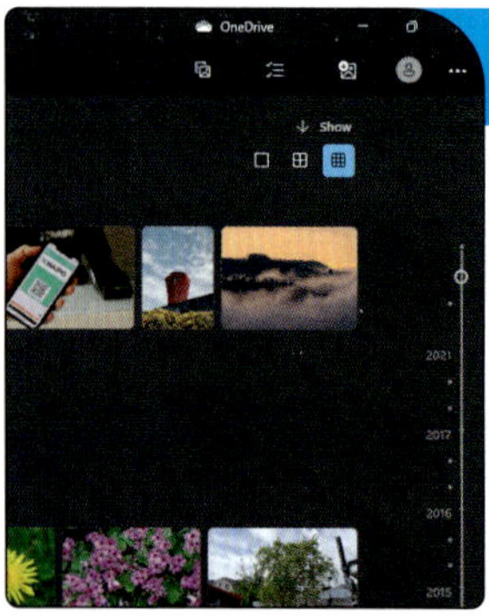


## Step 3

You can manage the main image view (Collection) in several ways. The View by menu lets you switch between sorting images by date taken or recently added. On the opposite side of the screen are the view controls, changing between large view, medium view and small thumbnail view.

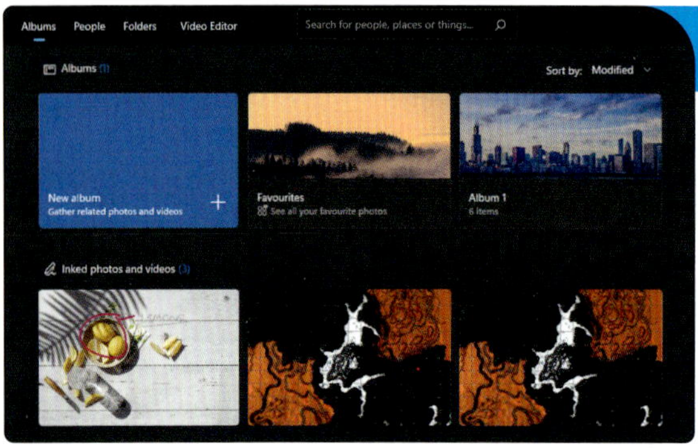


## Step 4

Albums, accessed by clicking the tab at the top of the main window, is a partially automated feature that creates groups of photos based on several different criteria. For example, images that have been drawn on with Windows Ink, or images that have been tagged as favourites.

## Step 5

You can create your own albums by clicking the "New Album" button. You can then select any images in the Photos app you want to add. With all of the images you want selected, click the Create button and the album will be shown with a slideshow. You can then rename the album.

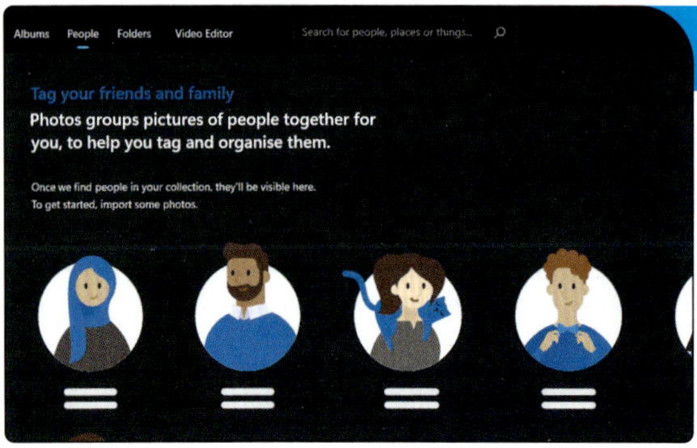


## Step 6

The People option is another automatically-created section, that builds collections of images based on facial recognition. As you begin to add photos of people, it will initially pull in any images that include faces, and then begin to sort those images by different people that are recognised.

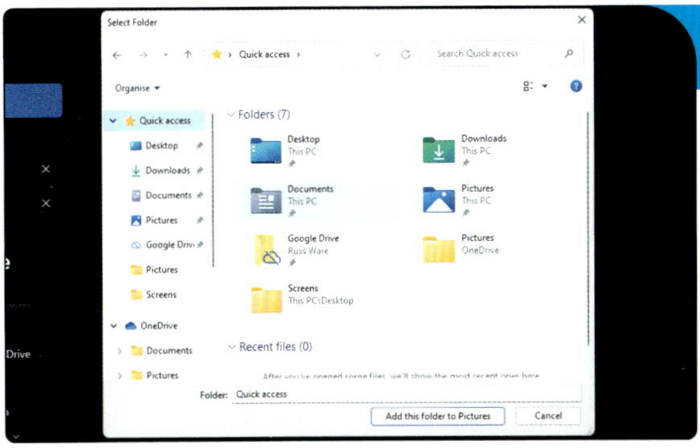


## Step 7

You can choose where Photos should look for images in the app Settings. Your own Pictures folder, plus the OneDrive Pictures folder, are automatically included (if you have OneDrive set up), but you can change this if you store your images somewhere else; perhaps on an external hard drive.

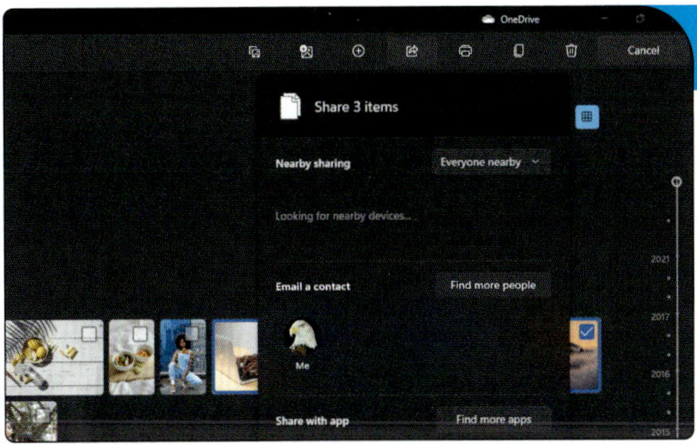


## Step 8

The Select feature, found in the menu at the top right, enables you to select individual or multiple images. You'll see the top menu bar changes, and each image has a tick box appear on it. Click them to choose the images you want. You can then use the tools at the top (share, copy, add to and delete, etc.).

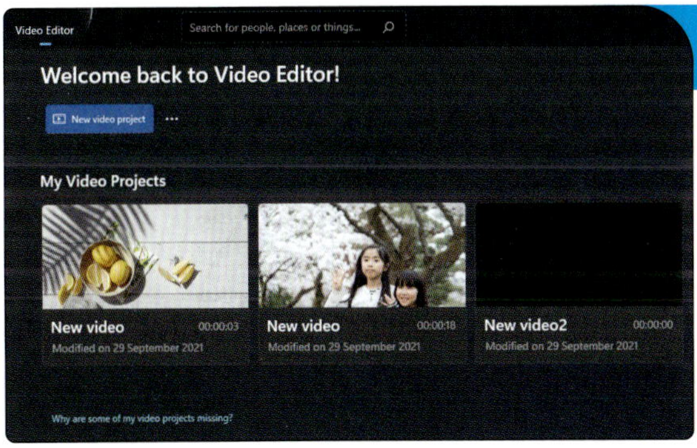


## Step 9

The final option on the Photos home screen is the Video Editor. This allows you to make videos made up of multiple images or video clips in your collections. It isn't the most powerful video editing tool, but it does allow you to create simple videos with music, effects and text overlays.

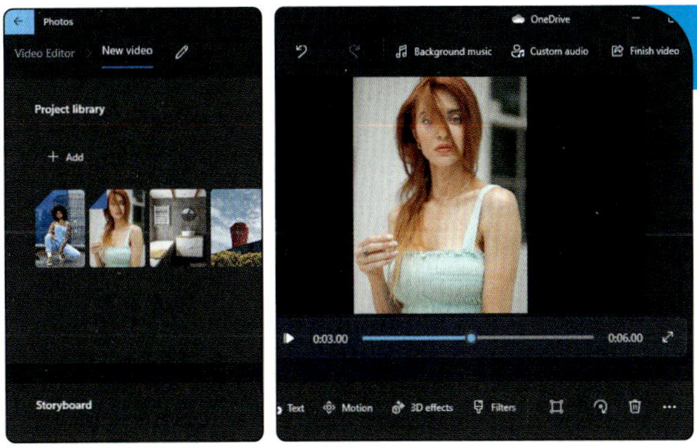


## Step 10

To begin making a video, click "New video project" and name your video. Add images or video using the "+Add" button. Then drag them down into the storyboard. You can then click on each image or video clip and make adjustments to duration, effects, etc. Click "Finish Video" to save it to your computer.

# Drawing on Images

## Step 1

Open the Photos app and select your image, or double click an image to open it in Photos if that is the default app. Along the top of the image are several buttons, click the Draw button to begin editing your image. You will see a new set of buttons and controls appear at the top.

## Step 2

These have been somewhat simplified for Windows 11. From left to right, these buttons allow you to draw/write in pen style, pencil style, calligraphy style, erase your ink and save your file. If you click on any button and see a small arrow, click again to open a contextual menu for it.

## Step 3

The contextual menus allow you to change the colour and the thickness of the pen or pencil tools. When you have picked a style, colour and size, you can begin to draw or write over the top of your image. The drawing tool in Photos works best with a touchscreen PC or stylus.

## Step 4

Once you have completed drawing or writing on your image, you can save it. Your image will automatically be saved with a slightly different file name, so you don't have to worry about overwriting the original. Your inked image will appear in your Collection.

# Editing Images in Photos

## Step 1

Open your image in Photos and click on the Edit button at the top of the screen. The image will be shrunk down slightly to fit the editing toolbar that appears down the right of the editing window. Along the top are the three main editing section tabs: Crop/rotate, Filters and Adjustments.

## Step 2

Starting with Crop and Rotate. Click this to see further options for managing the aspect of your image. You can choose a preset aspect ratio, or drag the handles at the corners to crop to a custom shape. If you need to straighten the image, you can do so using the slider in the toolbar.

## Step 3

Moving to the Filters section, at the top of the toolbar is the Enhance button. You can click this to let the software make changes and improvements to the image automatically. You will see the image change slightly, and you can then use the slider on the button to increase or decrease those changes.

## Step 4

You can, of course, apply enhancements yourself. Below the Auto-enhance button are the photo filters. Click on any of these to see the changes applied to your image. You can apply a filter and then adjust its effects by clicking on the Adjust tab at the top of the toolbar.

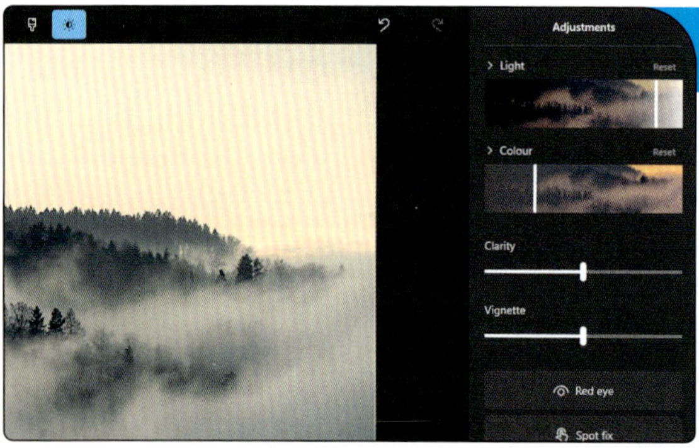


## Step 5

The tools in the Adjust tab allow you to tweak the Light, Colour, Warmth and Clarity of an image. You can also use a slider to apply a Vignette (to lighten or darken the edges of an image). Just use the sliders to adjust any of these effects until you are happy with your image.

## Step 6

At the bottom of the Adjust tab are Spot Fix and Red Eye tools. Click Spot Fix and the cursor will change to a blue circle. Place this over the part of the image you want to fix and click. The software will try to match the location of the spot to the scenery or colour around it, hopefully removing it.

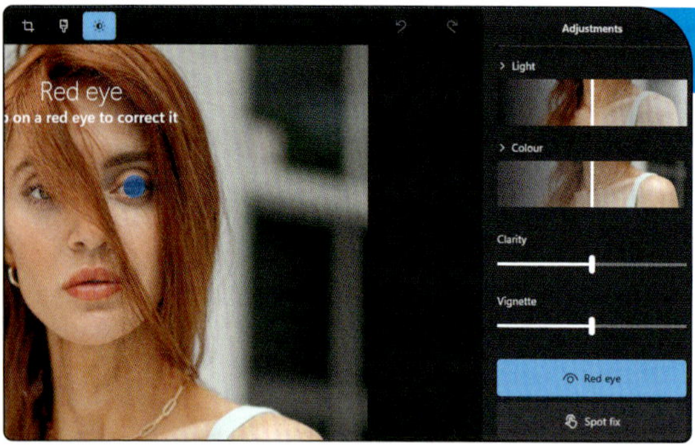


## Step 7

The Red Eye tool works in a similar way. Click the tool and move the circle cursor over the red part of your subject's eye and zoom in if you need to. The tool will try to take the red out of the image and match it to the surrounding colour. The results are usually very good.

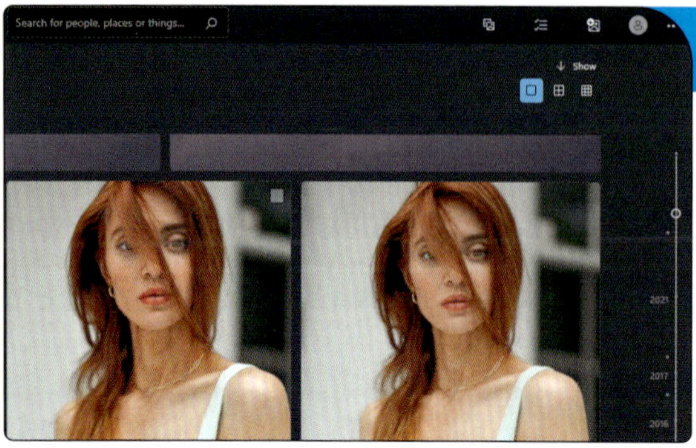


## Step 8

When you have finished editing your image, you can click the "Save a copy" button to create a new file that includes the changes, whilst retaining the original. Or you can choose "Save" from the pop-up menu, which will overwrite the original image with the version you just edited.

# Making Calls with Skype

**Skype is now a much bigger part of Windows 11 than it once was, and has its own app that comes pre-installed with the OS. Getting to grips with the different tools in Skype is fairly simple but learning how to use it more efficiently and easily takes a little more time.**

## Install and Use Skype

### Step 1

Skype has a dedicated Windows 11 app and this may be preinstalled on your Windows PC but you might need to download it from the Windows store. You can also download Skype directly from www.skype.com as well as check that you have the latest version available.

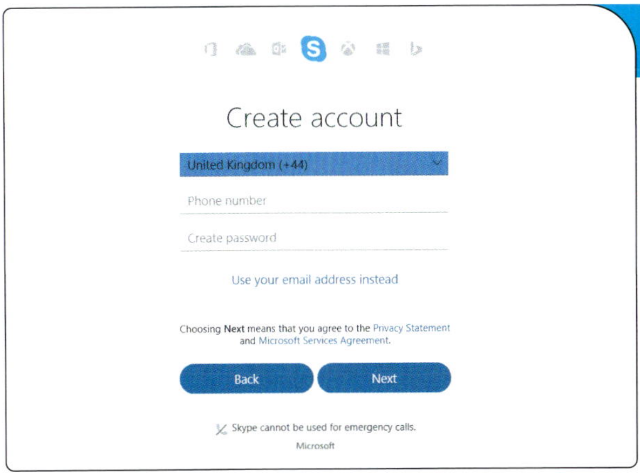


### Step 2

Once installed, you will need to sign in to the Skype app. If you already have a Skype account, which is completely free to set up, just enter your login details when prompted. If not, you can go to www.login.skype.com and simply create a new account in just a few minutes.

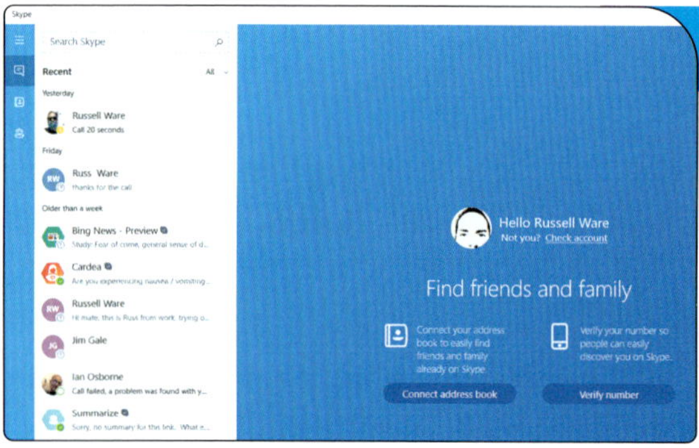


## Step 3

The Skype window should now be open on screen. The default view is the Recent conversations screen but this may be completely empty if you are new to Skype. The first thing you need to do as a fresh user, is to begin adding contacts.

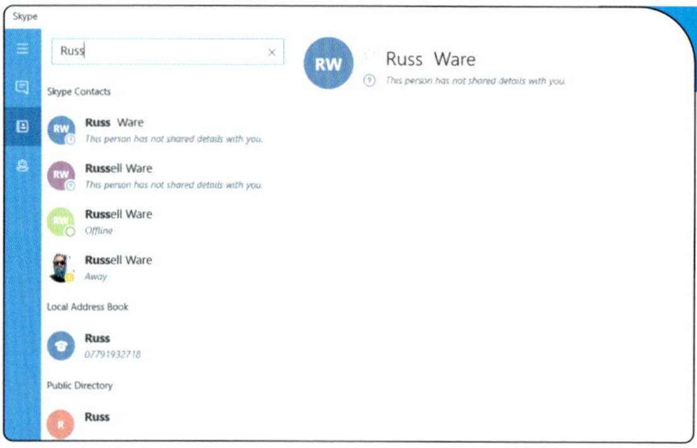


## Step 4

Click the Contacts button (2nd button down from the top) and either select the add contact icon at the bottom of the sidebar or click directly in the search text box and type the name, Skype name or email of the person you want to add. Click Search Skype.

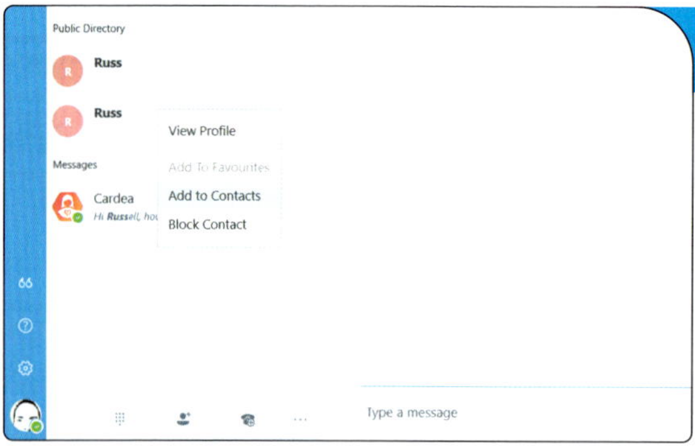


## Step 5

Select your friend from the search results, assuming you can see them in the list, and click Add to Contacts. Type a quick note to introduce yourself and then click Send. They will receive a request from you, along with the message and can choose whether to accept you or not.

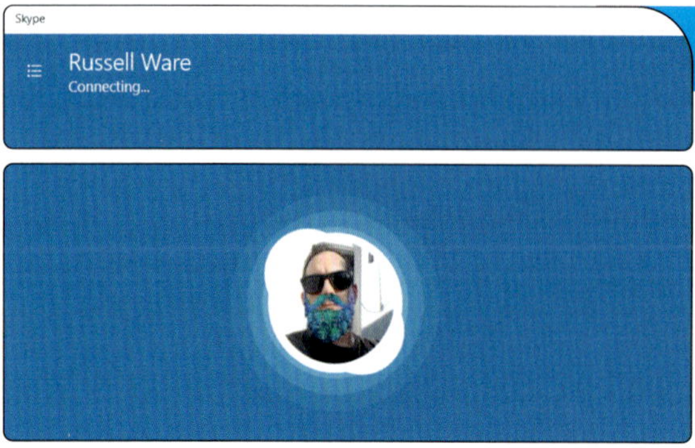


## Step 6

You can select any contact from your contacts list and then either instant message them or alternatively start a voice or video call. If the contact you click on has Skype, the call option buttons will appear in the top right corner of the window. Click the relevant button to start a call.

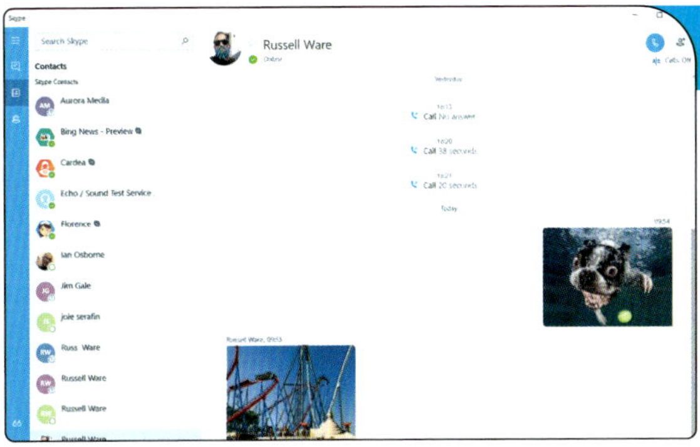


## Step 7

Skype instant messaging makes it easy to keep in touch with your contacts and groups wherever they are. You can share files, photos and also contacts. To instant message one of your contacts, select their name and start typing at the bottom of the main window.

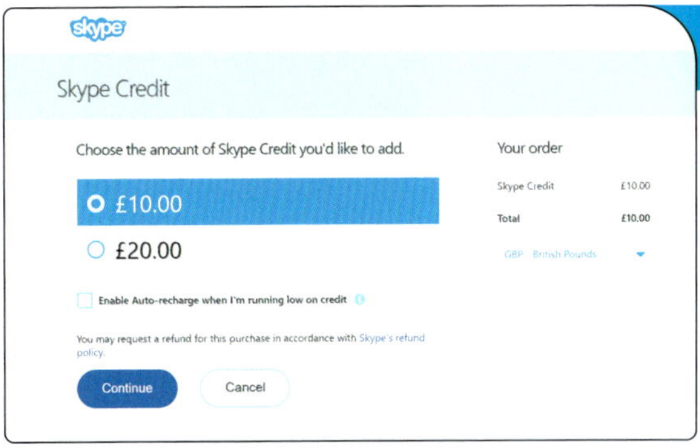


## Step 8

If you want to make calls to contacts not using Skype (you can make calls to mobiles and landlines too), you will need to add some Skype credit. To do this, click on your profile picture in the bottom left and click the 'Add Skype credit' link.

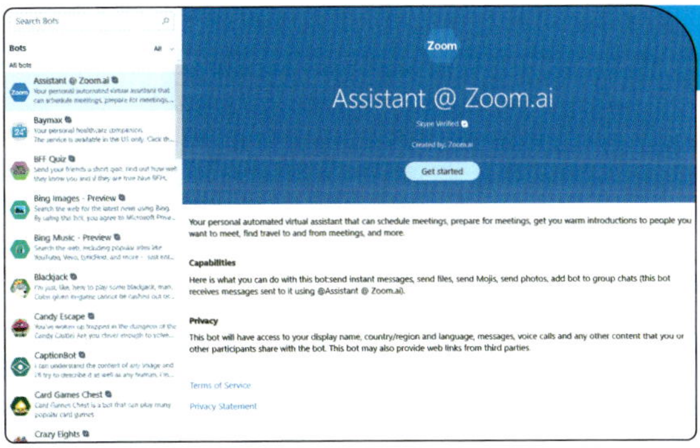


## Step 9

Skype also now includes Bots. Bots are artificially intelligent programs that can do many useful things like search for news, summarise webpages, play games and more. You can start chatting with a bot just like you chat with friends, just choose a bot and click Get started.

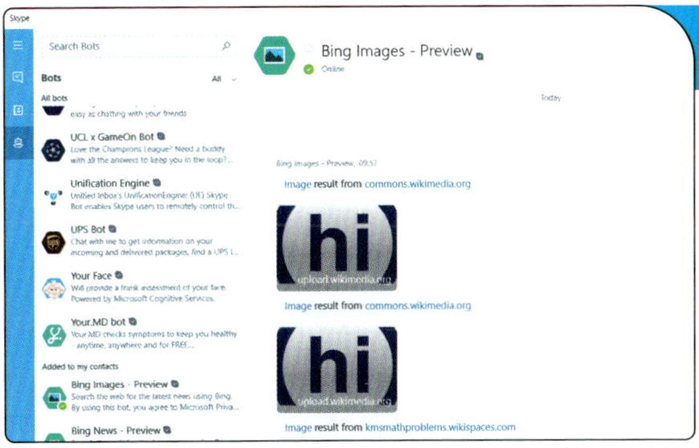


## Step 10

Bots vary in how useful they are but some are well worth taking a look at. Take the Bing News bot for example. Add this and then type a word ("Crime" for example) in the conversation window. The bot will return news stories based on that subject.

# Skype in Windows 11

## Profile

This is your Profile, click the image to open details about your Microsoft account, as well as manage your Skype profile. Further settings are available, along with Bookmarks and being able to add call credit in your local currency.

## Skype Panel

This panel details the recent chats and calls you've had with others in Skype. From here you can arrange new Skype video calls, new chats, look at your contacts and see any notifications. Click recent chats to display the contents in the main Skype window. You can also run an Echo/sound Test here, to test your microphone and camera.

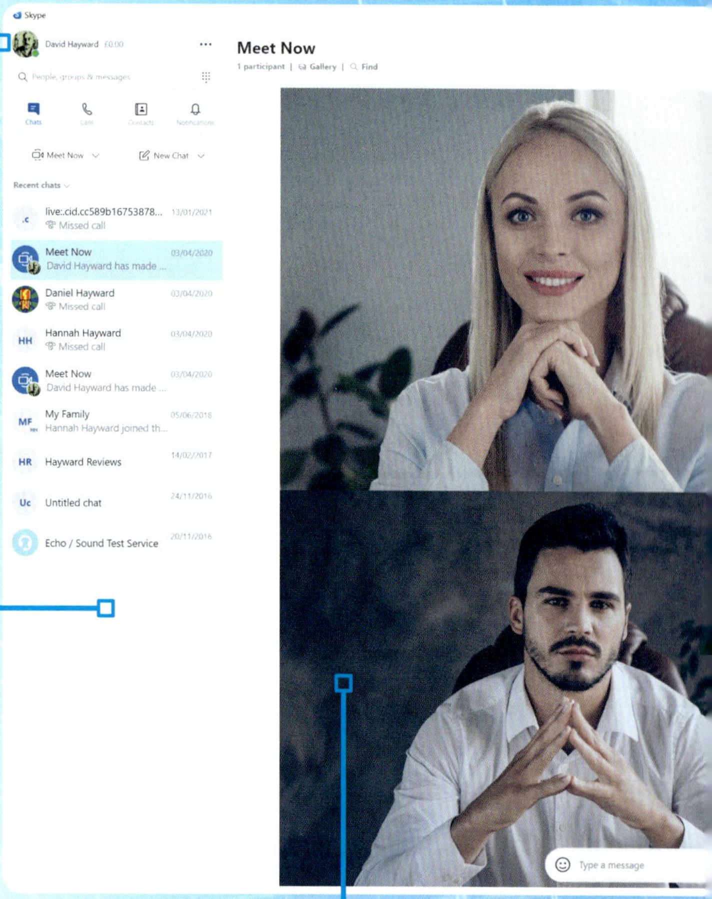


## Main Window

The main Skype window is where all your video calls and chats will take place. Grouped calls split the screen depending on how many people are in the call, and chats can have attachments added and viewed – such as images and videos.

**Although Skype took something of a backseat to Microsoft Teams during the world-wide Covid-19 lockdown, it still proved immensely useful for individuals to keep in contact with loved ones and friends all around the world.**

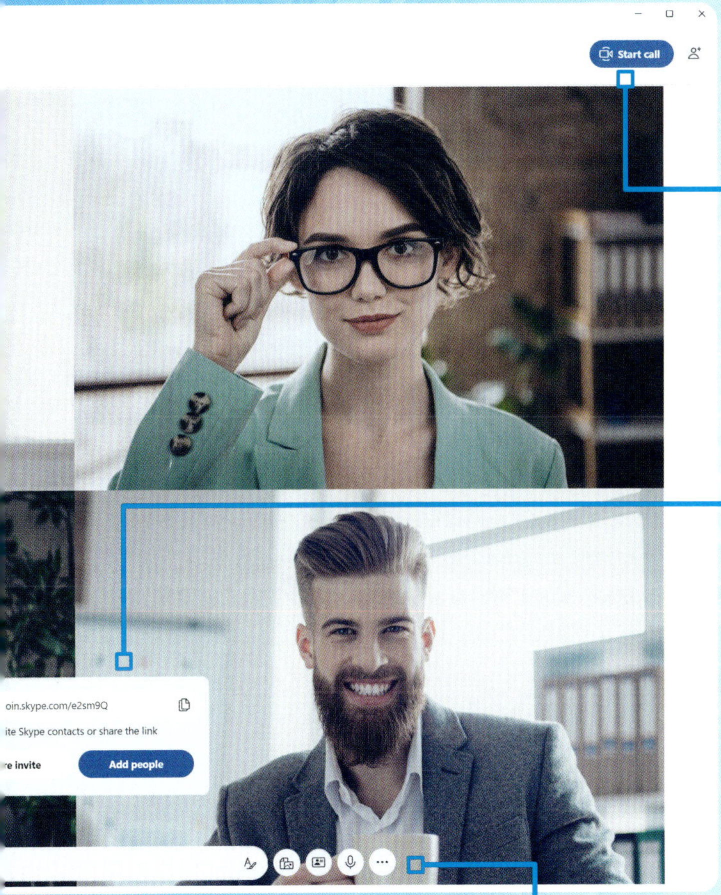


## Top Bar Options

The top bar details the number of participants, any images and videos included in the chat or call, and allows you to find any specific keyword for participants. You can also Start a Call, and add more contacts as you need from the two buttons in the top-right of the screen.

## Share Link

Use this link to send to others so they can join in the conversation. They will need access to Skype, either as their own installed app on their system, or they can use the link to access the call via the Skype webpage. You can also add more people via your contacts, or create specific shared invites.

## Chat and Messages

You'll enter your chat and video message texts in here. You can also include emoji, attach files, share contact details, create a poll, schedule a call, share your location and access your OneDrive area to collaborate with others on content.

# Explore the Facebook App

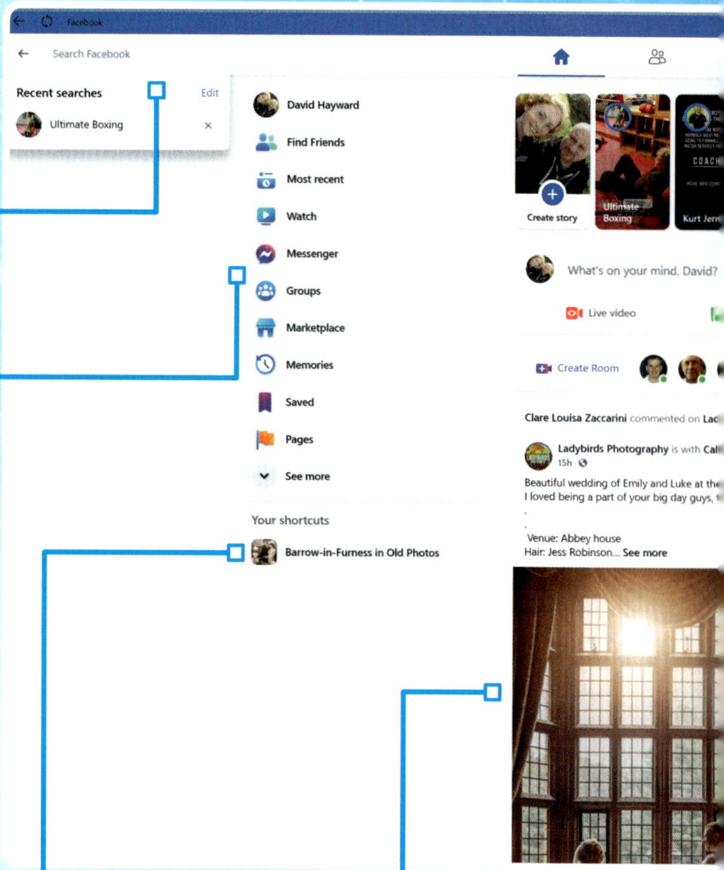


## Search

Within the app you can search for people, places, companies and Facebook pages from the Search function in the top-left of the app. A list of recent searches is displayed, which can be cleared by clicking on the 'x' next to the name, or by clicking on the Edit link.

## Options

The options to the left of the main timeline Feed allow you to switch views, browse the Marketplace for a local bargain that someone is selling, look for Facebook Groups setup by likeminded individuals, Watch Facebook Videos, Find Friends, look back at your previously posted Memories and much more.

## Facebook Shortcuts

The Your Shortcuts section is where you'll find quick launches to Groups and Pages you're a member of or have Liked on Facebook. This saves you trawling through your Facebook Feed to find any relevant new posts that may have appeared while you've been away, or have missed. You can edit your available Shortcuts by hovering over the section and clicking Edit.

## Facebook Feed

This is your main Facebook Feed, where you'll post your own comments, videos, photos and so on, and where you'll see your friends posts and any Groups or pages you've Liked and signed up with to receive notifications. You can create video chat rooms, and quickly see who's currently online via their profile image.

**Facebook's popularity peaks and falls with regularity throughout the year. However, it's still one of the most used social media platforms. Naturally, an app is available for it in the Windows Store and, once signed in, it offers the user a wealth of options.**

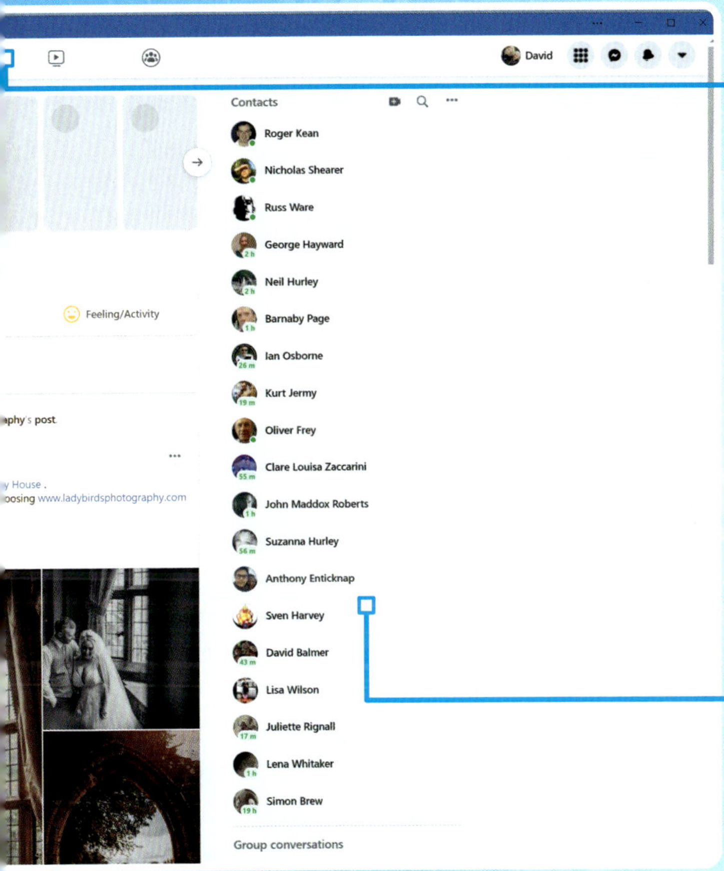


## Top Bar Options

The top bar options include: Home, your main Facebook Feed; Friends, where you can find new Friend suggestions and manage Friend Requests; Pages, which covers items like invitations and where you can create your own unique business page; Watch, which displays Facebook's video library from around the world; and finally Groups, where you can browse groups you're a part of, and find new ones. Further to the right is your Profile, followed by Menu (detailing all of Facebook's functions), Messenger for private and group chats, Notifications and finally Account settings.

## Contacts

The Contacts drop-down link will display all your friends, and whether they're online or when they were last online. You can click each contact and start a Messenger text or video chat with them, or click the Create New Group link at the bottom to group individual Contacts together for a group chat.

# Explore the Twitter App

## Twitter Menu

The menu on the left-hand side of the Twitter app will give you access to everything from your profile setup and management, through to exploring trending Tweets. Plus, any Notifications you've had from your own Tweets, DMs (direct Messages), Bookmarks and Lists you've made, and quick links to privacy settings, analytics, ads and a help centre.

## Tweet Button

The Tweet button brings up a pop-out window where you can enter a new Tweet, and post it for the world of Twitter to see, comment on and hopefully like. It does exactly the same function as the What's Happening section at the top of your Twitter Feed, so it is a little redundant these days. It would seem to be left over from older versions of the Twitter platform.

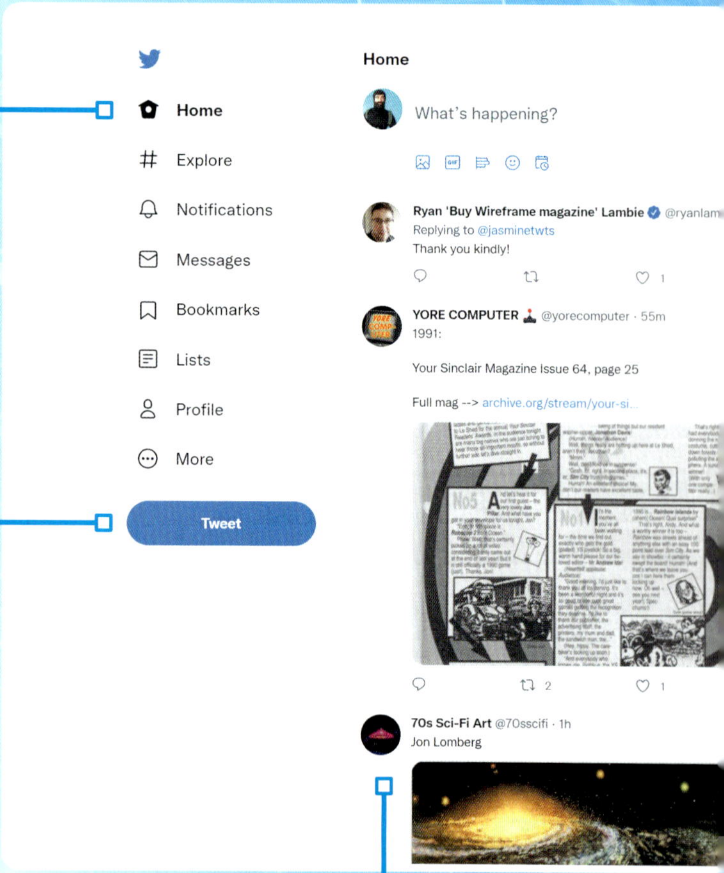


## Twitter Feed

Your Twitter Feed, where you can view your own posts, as well as those who you've liked and followed, alongside any advertising the company decides to place on your Feed. It's from here you can like, comment, share, delete, report and generally remark on how you are feeling about current issues.

**The Twittersphere is often a resting place for interesting discussions, but also a haven for news that's not published in the mainstream media. Like it or loathe it, Twitter has its uses and is freely available in the Windows Store; so you too can join the 'debates'.**

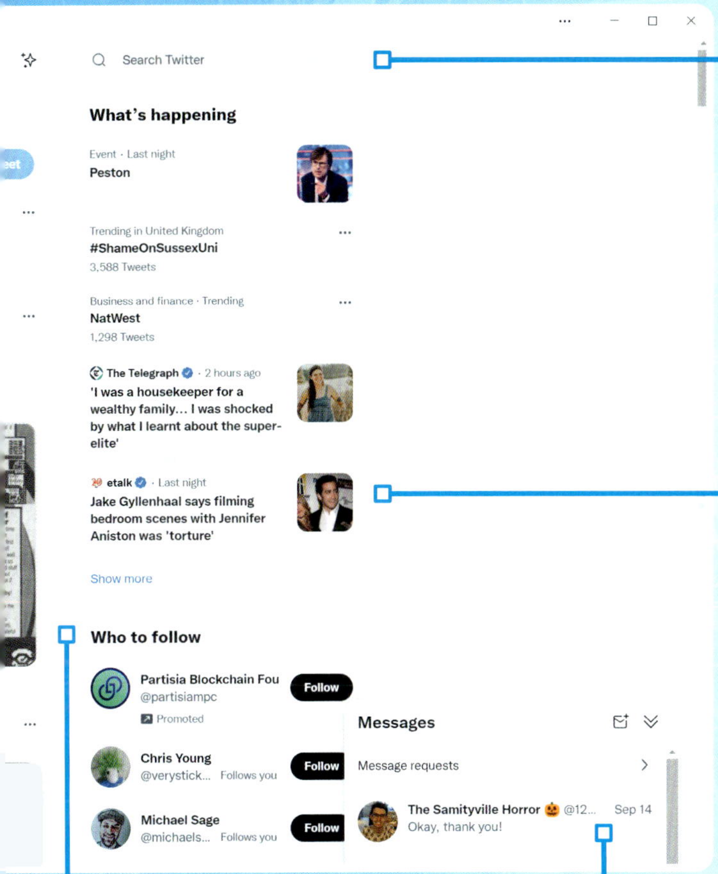


## Search

You can search for people from the Twitter Search function in the upper-right of the app. Enter a person's name, be they a celebrity, politician, or humble writer of Windows 11 books, and the results will appear here.

## What's Happening

This is the What's Happening section – which is different to the What's Happening section where you can enter your own Tweets. This section displays the current trending stories in the Twittersphere depending on your location. In the UK we'll naturally have a different set of trending feeds compared to someone in the US. Click the Show more link to display trends that have dropped off due to the limitations of your screen size.

## Who to Follow

Who to follow displays a brief list of people who Twitter thinks you'd like. Some of them may already follow you, but you don't follow them back, whereas some are promoted by Twitter to help boost their follower numbers.

## Messages

The Messages section here is collapsible, and contains all the current and previous Direct Messages you've had over your time on Twitter. Open it, click a person, and you can continue the message or start a new one.

# Exploring WhatsApp

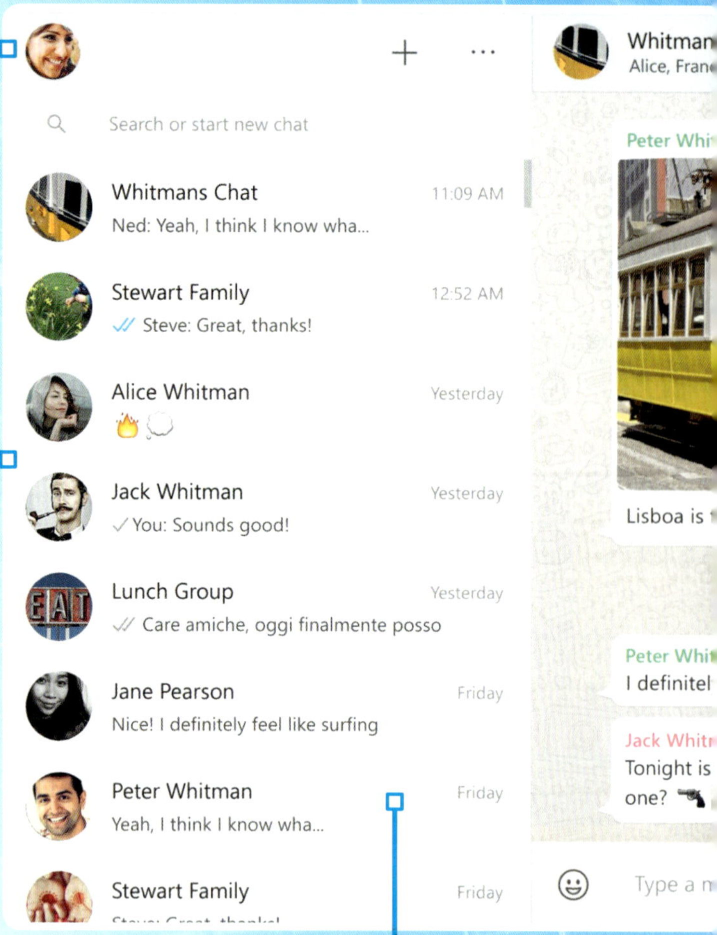


## Your Profile

This section displays your WhatsApp profile picture, as well as enabling you to start a new conversation with any of your WhatsApp contacts, or start a new Group chat. Click the Plus symbol for a new chat, or the three dots for more options and group setups.

## Contacts and Comments

These are all your contacts, along with the last comment they made on either the group chat or with you individually. You can see when they last commented, as well as be informed on any profile status updates they may post about themselves.

## Further Contact Options

Scroll down the contacts list for more, and you can also use the Search bar at the top of the contacts list to look for individuals; and even start a new chat. Click an individual to open more options, such as mute, archive, delete or pin to keep for later.

**WhatsApp has proved to be a vital addition to many of us in our daily digital lives. It's used to keep in contact with family, friends and work colleagues, and thanks to its high levels of encryption and easy to use interface, it can be used by even hardened technophobes.**

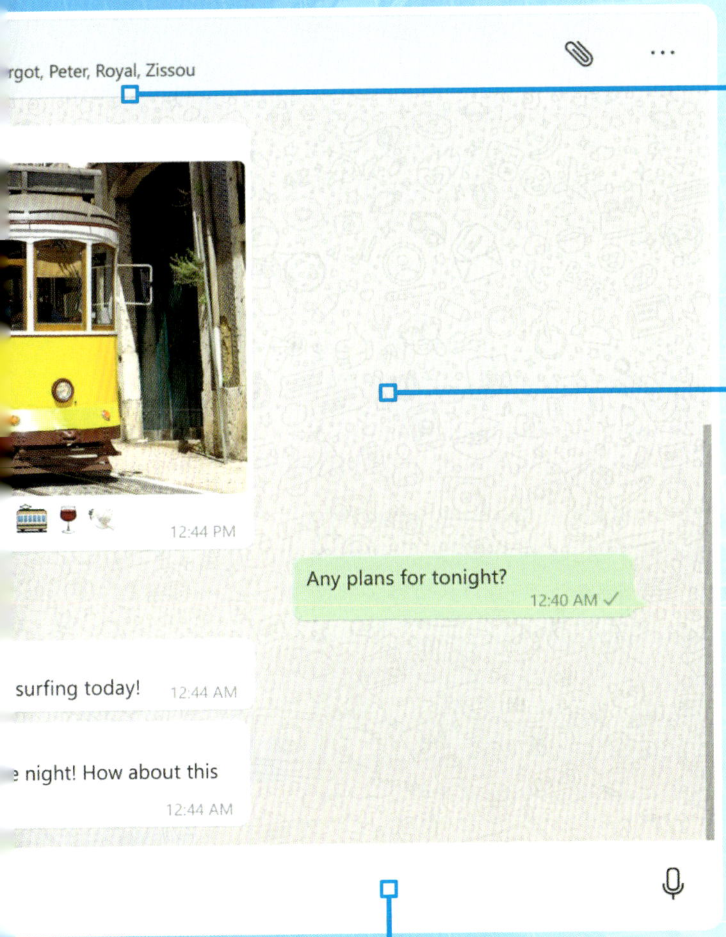


## Group Details

This section displays all the contacts currently involved in a group chat, as well as the name of the group you or someone else has created. From here, you can also attach any photos or videos, or click the three-dots more options.

## Main Chat Screen

This is the main part of WhatsApp, this is where all the chatting takes place, as well as any media you or a member of your contacts will upload. Your comments are highlighted to the right of the chat pane, whereas your contacts are put to the left of the pane. Photos and videos can be clicked to expand and then viewed.

## Chat Box

Enter your chats in this box, and then they'll appear in the main chat window. You can also click the microphone icon to begin a voice conversation. This is handy, as the voice communications are as encrypted as the text communications. Clicking the smiley face icon will open the available emoji list, where you can insert all manner of strange and useful iconography.

# Explore the Maps App

## Directions

You can use the Map app to plan routes: in a car, by public transport and even on foot. Select your chosen transportation method using the icons at the top of the Directions pane. You can either leave the A field as My Location or type a new one. In the B field, type your destination. The route will appear on the map. You can refine the route by clicking the Options button.

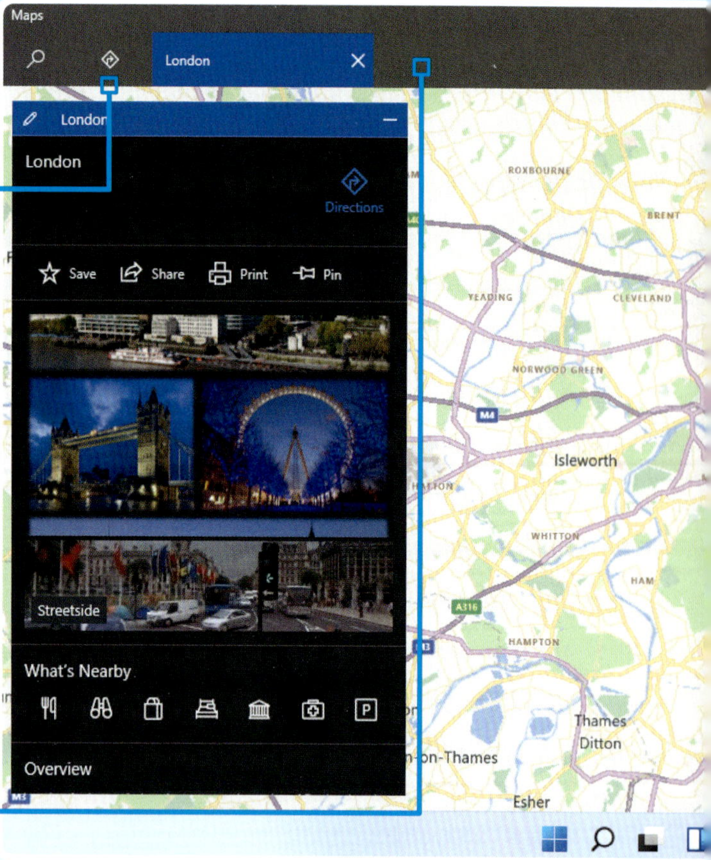


## Search

Click the Search button on the left-hand side of the map window and a new pane will open. This pane contains some search suggestions, such as hotels, restaurants and shopping, with the standard search field at the top. As you type your search, suggestions will appear in the search pane. You can click any of these to find that location.

## Maps View

The Maps view is the default one for the Maps app. This is what will greet you when you first load the app on to your PC. You can zoom in and out of the map using either the + and – buttons on the control panel on the right of the window or by scrolling back and forward with the scroll wheel on your mouse (if you use one).

## Your Location

When you open the Maps app it will try to pinpoint your approximate location. Your location will then be shown on the map as a small black and grey circle. You can click on this to see more information, if available, and then save the location as a favourite by clicking the star in the pane that opens.

**The Maps view is the default one for the Maps app. You can zoom in and out of the map, using either the + and – buttons on the control panel on the right of the window, or by scrolling back and forward with the scroll wheel on your mouse (if you use one).**

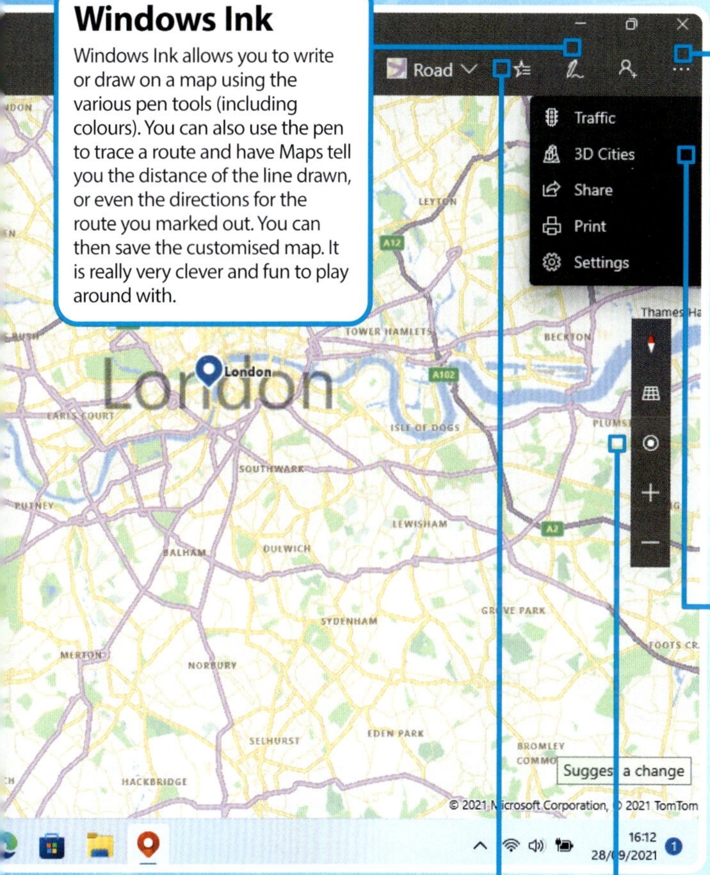


## Windows Ink

Windows Ink allows you to write or draw on a map using the various pen tools (including colours). You can also use the pen to trace a route and have Maps tell you the distance of the line drawn, or even the directions for the route you marked out. You can then save the customised map. It is really very clever and fun to play around with.

## Maps Settings

The Maps app settings let you choose the units of measurement used, depending on your preference and your preferred defaults for directions and location. This last option will be used if the app can't find you, by using location services. You can also download maps for offline use or upload maps that have been saved elsewhere.

## 3D Cities

Click the button to open the pane and you will see an alphabetical list of the cities with thumbnails that have been mapped in 3D. Click the Country/Region heading at the top to refine the list. Click on any of the thumbnails to load the 3D map; loading time will vary, depending on your Internet speed.

## Rotate & Tilt

The small floating control panel on the right of the Maps window contains useful tools for changing the current view. The top two controls are rotate and tilt, allowing you to either rotate the map around the central point or tilt the map to give you an isometric view. You can centre your location view again by clicking the third icon down.

## Saved Places

The Saved Places pane contains all of your saved locations. These can be anything from a favourite coffee shop to the street where you parked your car in a new city. To add places, search for a location and select the star underneath the correct one in the search results list. You then have the option to give the favourite a nickname or set it as Home or Work.

# Navigate with Maps

Boasting excellent mapping, great aerial photography, up-to-the-minute traffic and the ability to calculate directions by public transport, road or foot, the Maps app is one of the very best ways to navigate. New additions make the Maps app even more useful.

## Moving Around in Maps

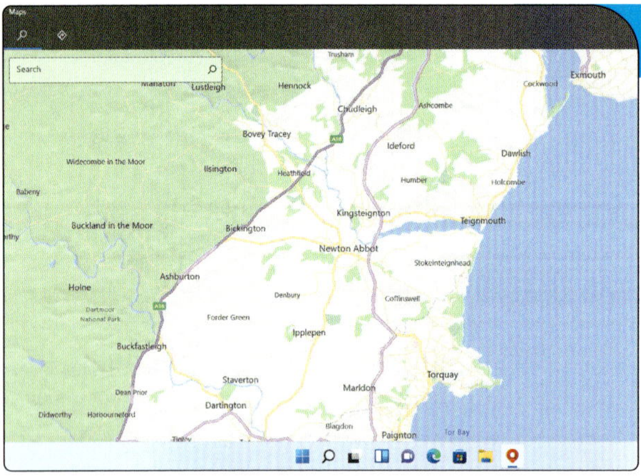


### Step 1

The easiest way to move the map around is to left-click and drag it and use the mouse wheel or trackpad slider to zoom in and out. This allows you to move the map around to focus on the area you need. If you are zoomed far out of the map, double-clicking the mouse zooms in quickly.

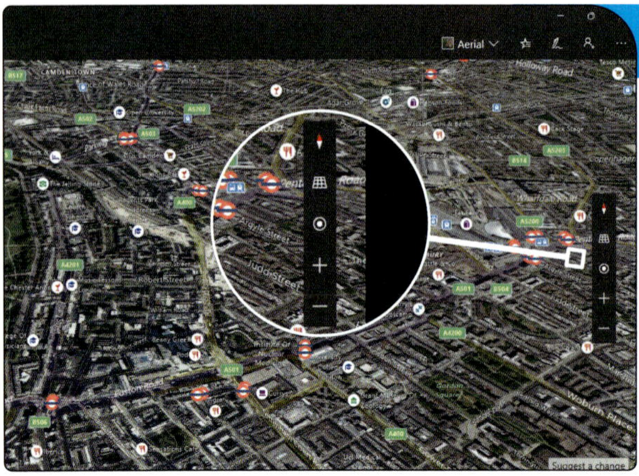


### Step 2

Maps has a dedicated control panel on the side of the window containing, from top to bottom: Rotate, hold pointer on it to see; Tilt, hold pointer over to see options; Show Location; and Zoom in and Zoom out. You can also tilt by holding the right Mouse button and moving up and down.

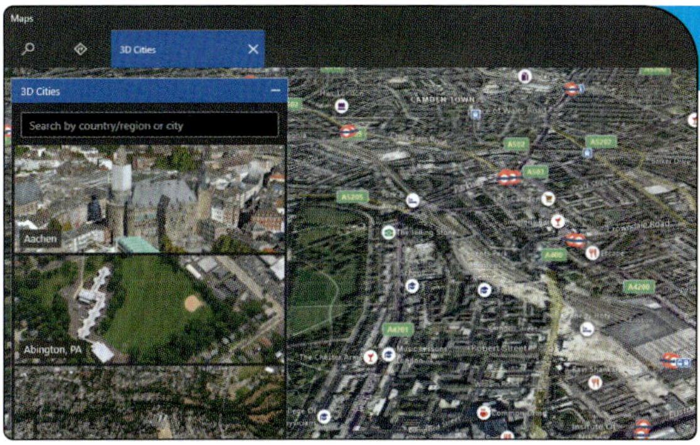


## Step 3

Clicking on things like Saved Places or 3D Cities in the top control bar, tabs will line up alongside the permanent Search and Directions buttons at the top left of the window. You can then click on them at any time to see the information contained in each pane or tab.

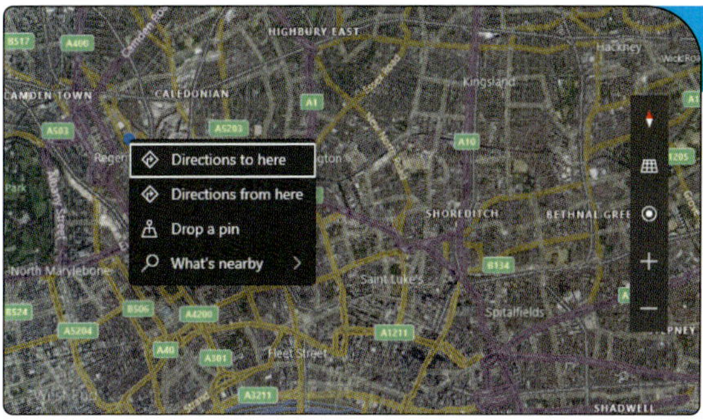


## Step 4

Right-clicking on the map brings up a small action menu. This lets you set a To location, a From location (for planning a route), add a new destination and drop a pin in a specific location. When you drop a pin, a new window opens allowing you to search for things at that location, add favourites and more.

# Planning a Route

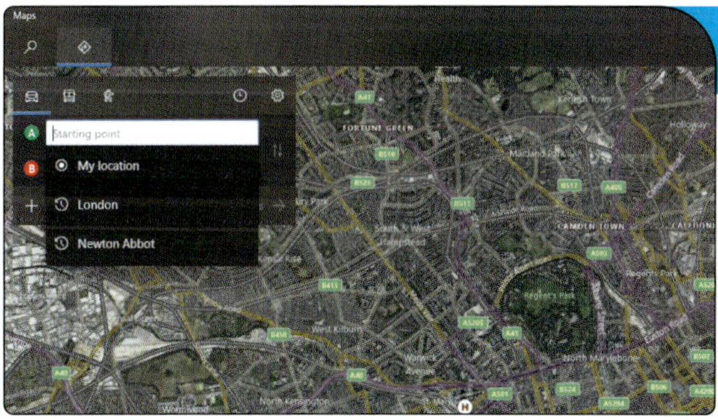


## Step 1

To start planning a route, click the Directions tab at the top left of the Maps window. A small panel opens with boxes for your starting and ending location. You can either type a destination or you can choose one from the list that appears below the box when you click on it.

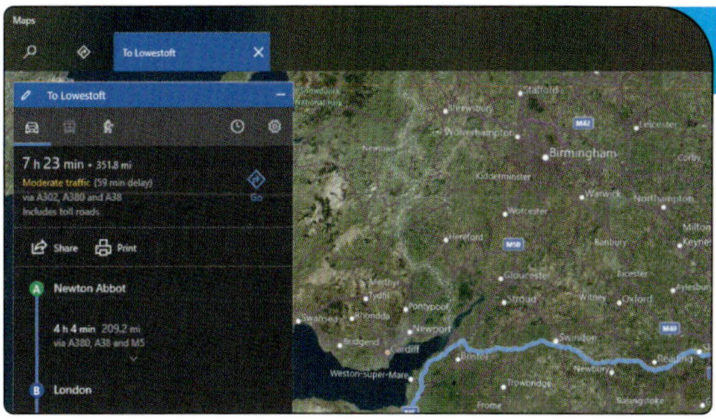


## Step 2

If you need to make detours or multiple stops along your route, you can click the + button to add more destination boxes. Each one can have a destination in it, making up your complete route. When you view directions, each of the destinations you added is marked with a relevant letter.

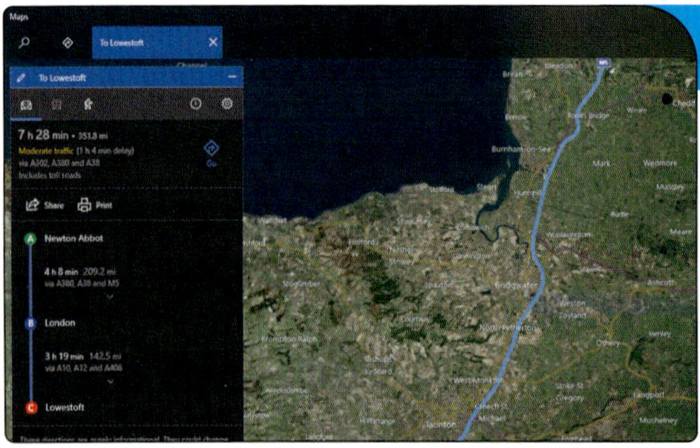


## Step 3

Routes vary depending on whether you are driving, walking or need to take public transport. You can quickly flick between these options using the buttons at the top of the directions pane. When you have your start and end points entered and travel method chosen, click Get Directions.

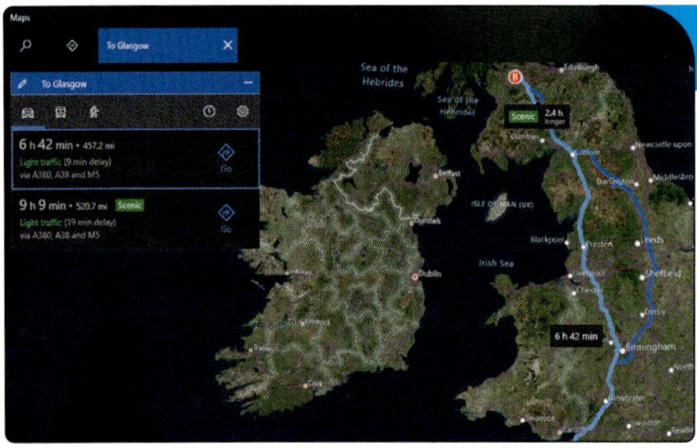


## Step 4

The route is now shown on the map, with an estimated travel time readout above the destination. If alternative routes are available, they are shown as a light blue line, with the main route shown as a dark blue line. Points along the route are marked, usually where a change of direction is needed.

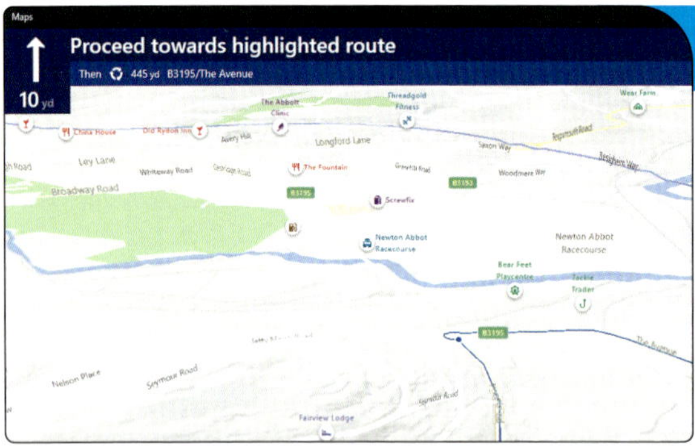


## Step 5

If you click Go in the directions pane, Maps switches to a satnav-style view and traces your route as you continue along it. This is more for portable devices such as phones and tablets that you might use for directions in a vehicle. Click the Exit button via the three dots in the bottom-right of the screen to return to the normal maps view.

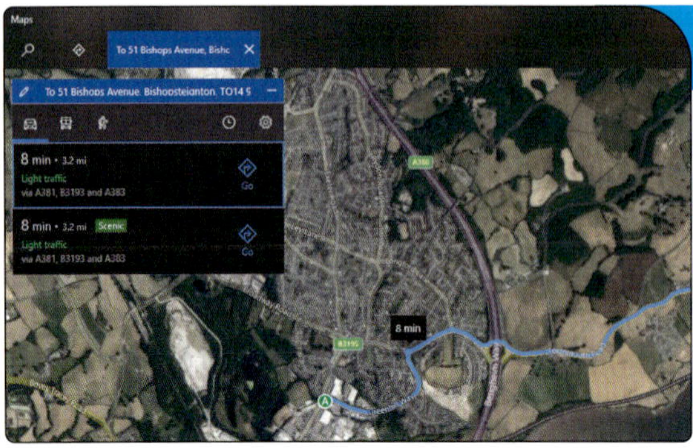


## Step 6

You can also plan a route by drawing it. Click the Ink button and then the Directions tool in the menu that opens. Draw a line along the route you wish to take and Maps refines that into a proper route along roads, missing dead-ends, etc. You can save or share the route just as with any other.

# Manage Your Contacts

The People app has been a part of Windows 10 for some time, but in the more recent update to Windows 11, it has had an overhaul. The People app is no longer a part of the traditional taskbar, but instead Microsoft has incorporated into the Mail app.

## New People, New Apps

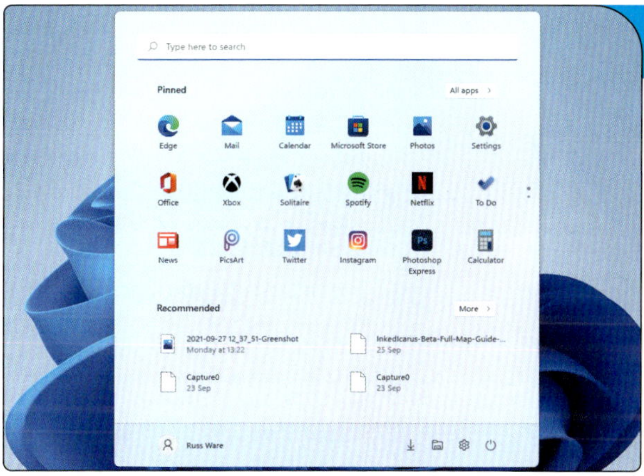


### Step 1

If you've not done so already, you will need to open the Mail app. Start the process by clicking on the Windows icon in the Windows 11 taskbar, or alternatively tapping the Windows Key on your keyboard. This will bring up the Apps menu and your last used files.

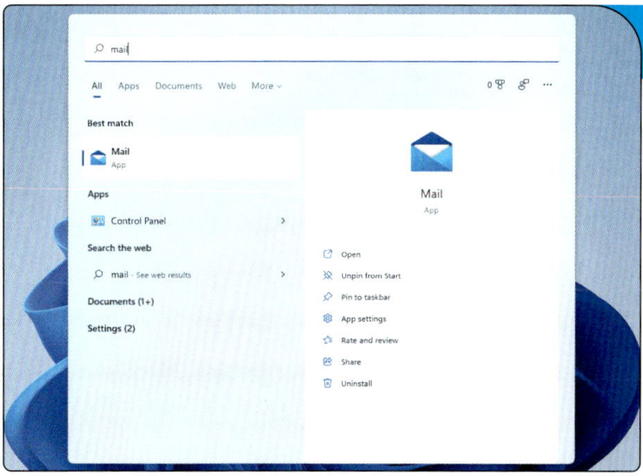


### Step 2

Then type 'mail' (without the quotes), and you'll see the Mail app icon appear on the list of available matching apps. Click on the Mail app to open, or click on the Open link from the list underneath the icon.

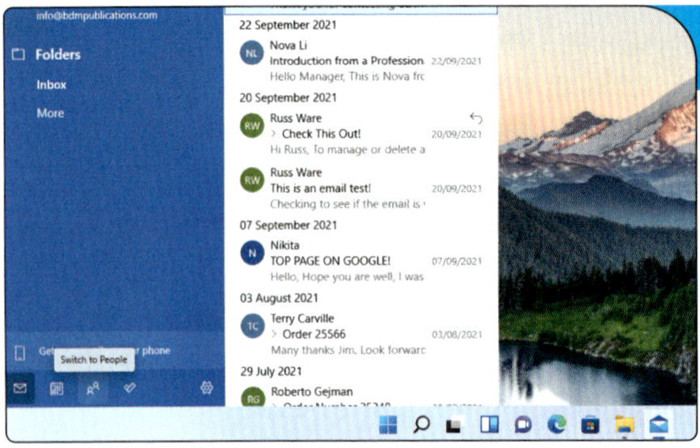


## Step 3

Within the Mail app, you'll notice a row of icons along the bottom-left of the window. The third one in, from the left, is the People button. Click on it to switch the view to the new Windows 11 People app.

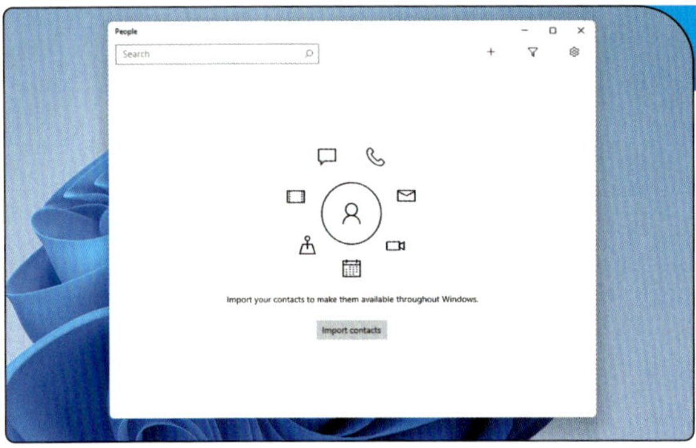


## Step 4

The new People app is significantly different from its earlier appearances in Windows 10. It still connects to the various apps within Windows that utilise contacts, such as Skype, Teams and so on, but it looks and behaves radically different.

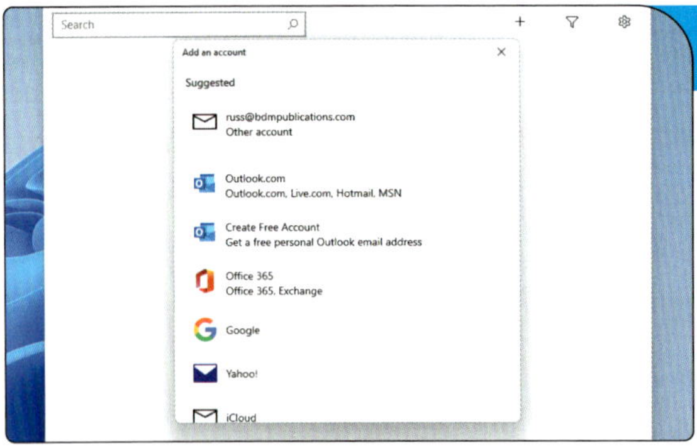


## Step 5

The first things you'll probably want to do is import your contacts from other sources. As you'll no doubt notice, there's a handy Import Contacts button on the People app window. Click it, to begin the process.

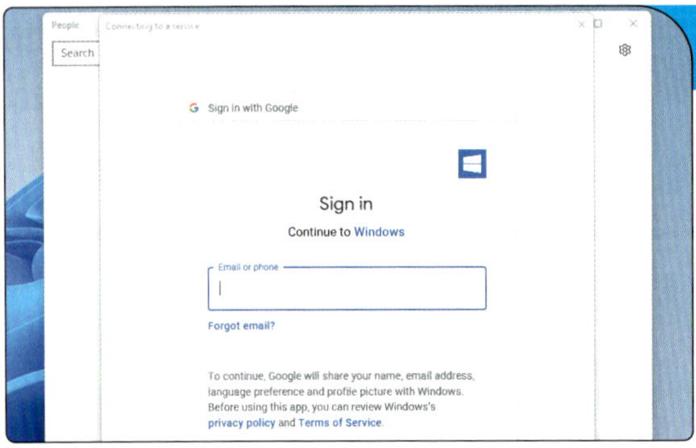


## Step 6

You've got a selection of different sources from which you can import your list of contacts. From an already created account, through to Microsoft's Outlook.com, Office 365 Exchange, Google, Yahoo!, and even from your Apple iCloud. Click the source that applies to you.

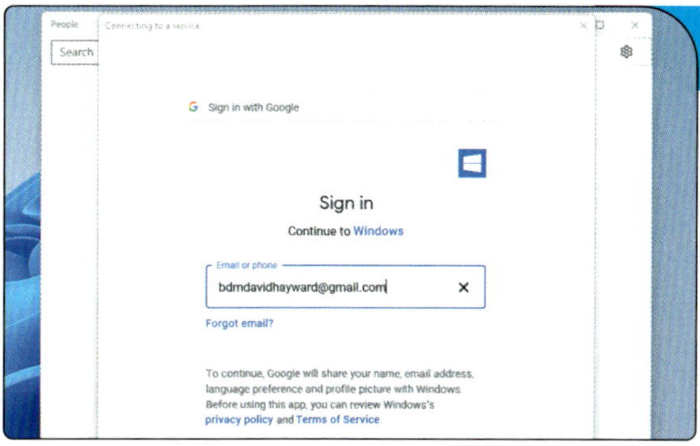


## Step 7

In this example, we're connecting to a Google Account. The People app will open the connection services needed to link your Google account with the People app, all you'll need to do is enter the correct information into the available boxes to continue.

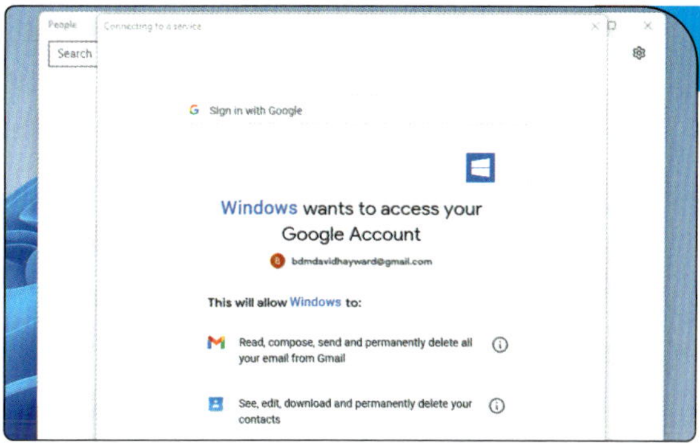


## Step 8

The People app will notify you as to what access Windows 11 will need when you've setup the account. For most of us, the legal areas involved are part of the daily routine, we need access, so we have very little choice in the matter. If you want more information, scroll down to the Privacy Policy link to read more.

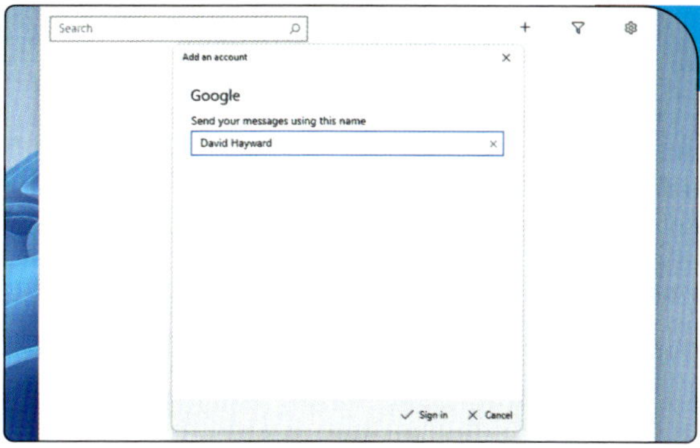


## Step 9

If you're ready to go ahead with the connection to another service, then scroll down and click on the Allow button at the bottom of the page. This will open a new window, asking for the name in which to send messages as. Enter your name, then click Sign in at the bottom of the window.

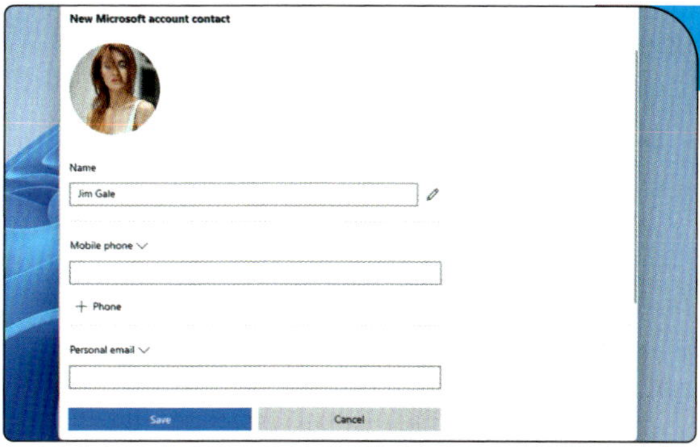


## Step 10

If you want to add individual contacts, click on the Plus sign in the upper-right of the People window. From there, you can add their name, phone, email, address, add a photo and more. Click on the Save button when you're ready to add the new contact.

# Using Sticky Notes

There are lots of Windows 11 apps for making reminder lists, but sometimes you just need a simple note to jog your memory. There is a simple, and often overlooked, piece of software in Windows that allows you to add sticky notes to your screen, quickly and easily.

## Getting Sticky

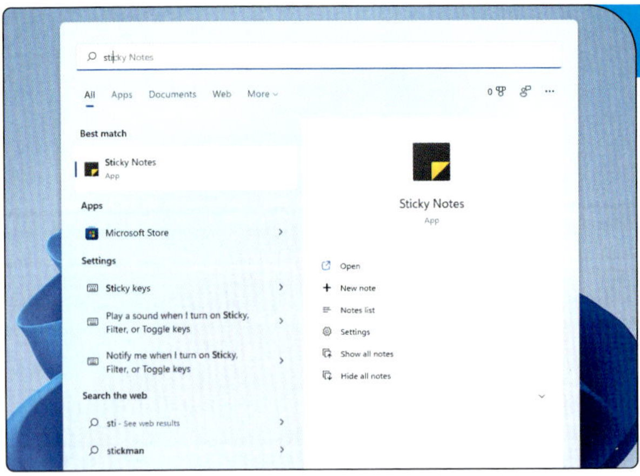


### Step 1

Sticky Notes is available via the Windows Start button, or by pressing the Windows key on your keyboard, and typing in 'sticky notes' (without the quotes). Click on the Sticky Notes app that's listed in the search results.

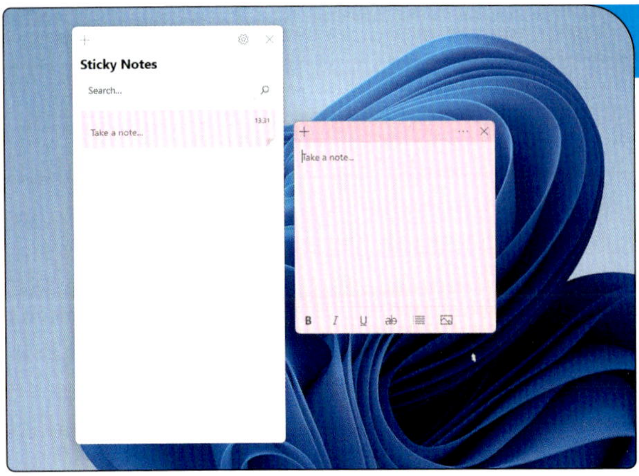


### Step 2

Sticky Notes launches with two windows: one is the main Sticky Notes control window, and the other is a blank note, ready to be filled. As you create notes, these will be displayed when you start the app.

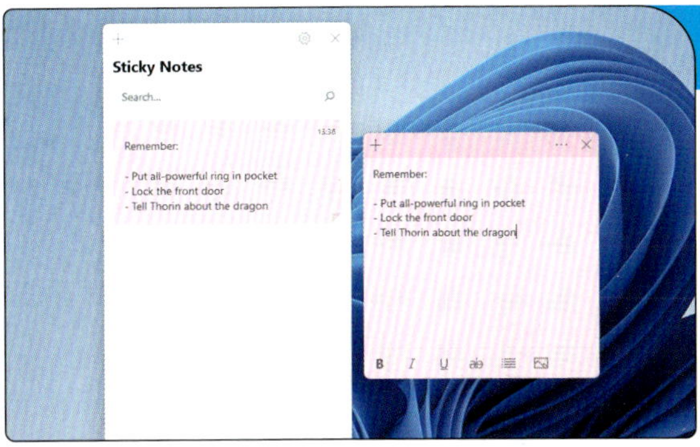


## Step 3

To quickly create a new note, click on the smaller of the two windows; the new note window. The cursor will appear where the window says, 'Take a note…', and from there you can begin typing to create your note.

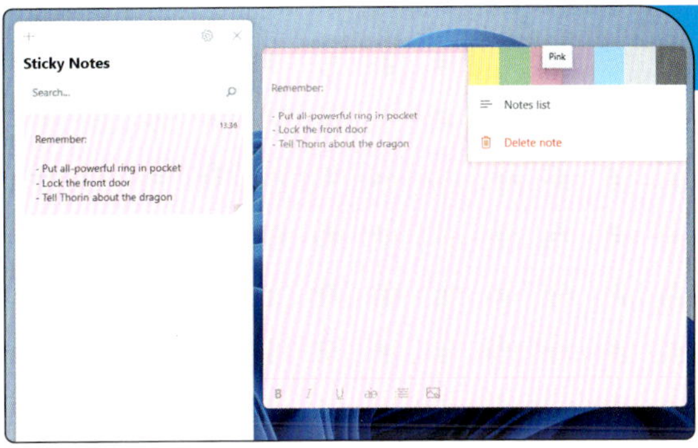


## Step 4

As you type, the note will add scroll bars down the right-hand side. You can increase the size of the note by expanding the corners of the window, and you can change the colour of the Sticky Note by clicking on the three dots in the top-right corner of the note window, and choosing one of the available colours.

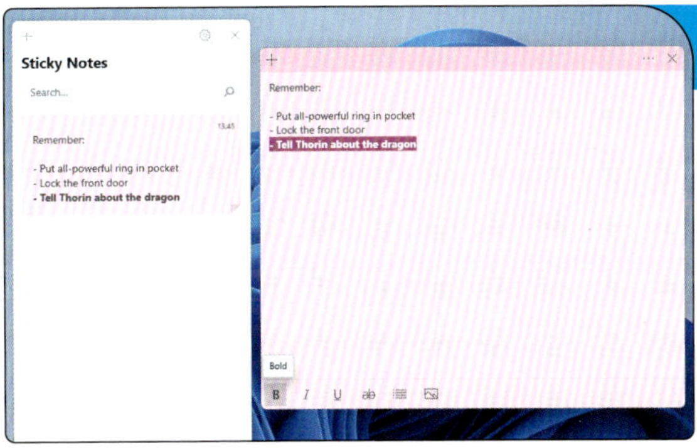


## Step 5

If you look at the bottom of the note window, you'll notice a series of options. These change the text type to Bold, Italic, Underline or Strikethrough. You can also toggle bullets or even add an image.

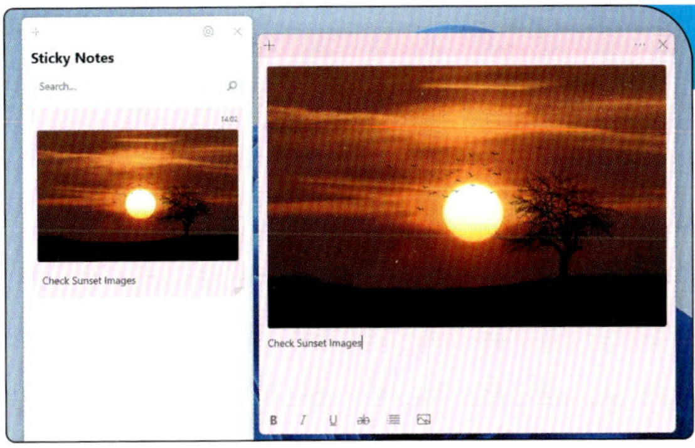


## Step 6

You'll need to highlight existing text, then click on one of the text type options to apply the result, or click the option, then start new text. To add an image, simply click the image option then use the windows File Manager to locate the image. Click on the Image file itself.

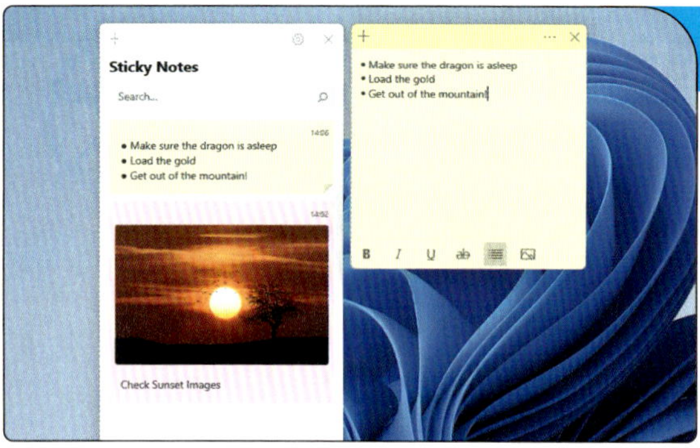


## Step 7

When you close the note, it will be automatically added to the Sticky Notes control window. If you want to create a new note, click on the Plus symbol in the Sticky Notes control window, located in the top-left.

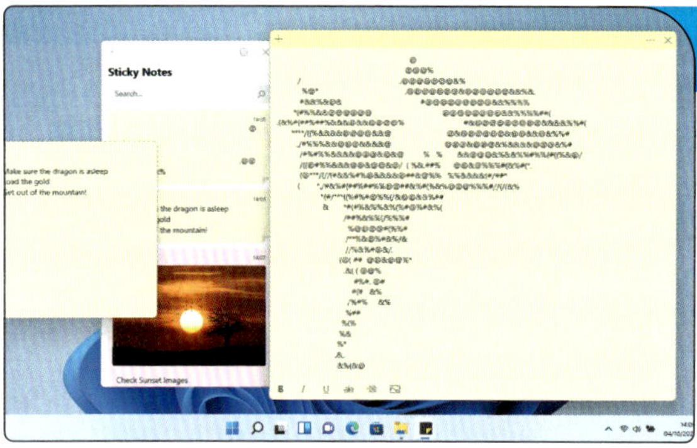


## Step 8

You will need to keep the app open for your notes to remain on the screen but as long as it is, you can shut down and reboot, and the notes will remain on the desktop. To close notes, you simply need to click on the trash icon in the top right corner. Close the last note and the software closes too.

# Troubleshooting Sticky Notes

**While Sticky Notes for Windows 11 is a marked improvement over its predecessors, it can still yield one or two problems for those who use it. One of the main issues with Sticky Notes, and this is something that has appeared in earlier versions too, is adding images. Sometimes, Sticky Notes won't add PNG images, but JPGs will be added successfully. If this is the case, you can often get around this issue by copying the image, then pasting it directly into Sticky Notes with Ctrl+V.**

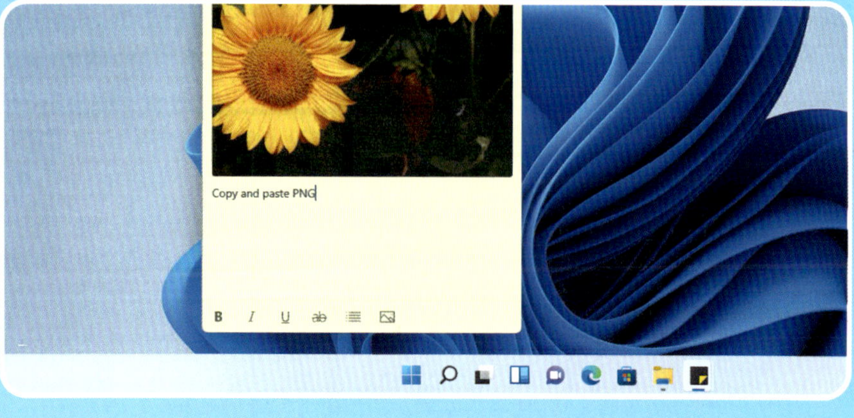

# Using the Xbox Game Bar

Windows 11 has carried on the developmental work that its predecessor put in with regards to the Microsoft Xbox Game Bar. There are a wealth of sub-apps within the Game Bar app, and it's definitely well worth looking at in more detail.

## Game On!

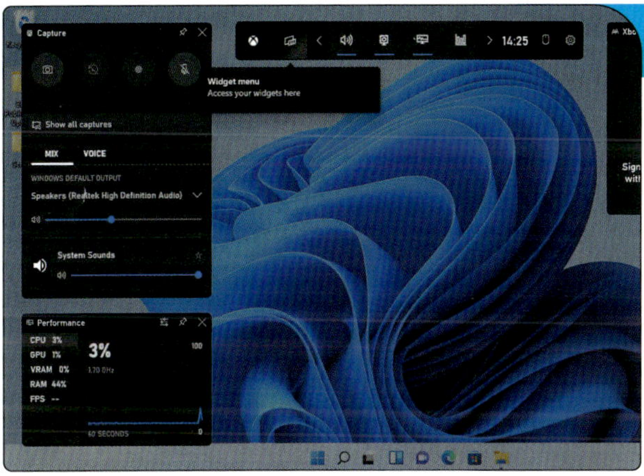


### Step 1

You can open the Xbox Game Bar simply pressing the Windows Key + G, or by searching for Xbox via the Windows button on the taskbar menu. When it loads it will dim the screen and present multiple windows.

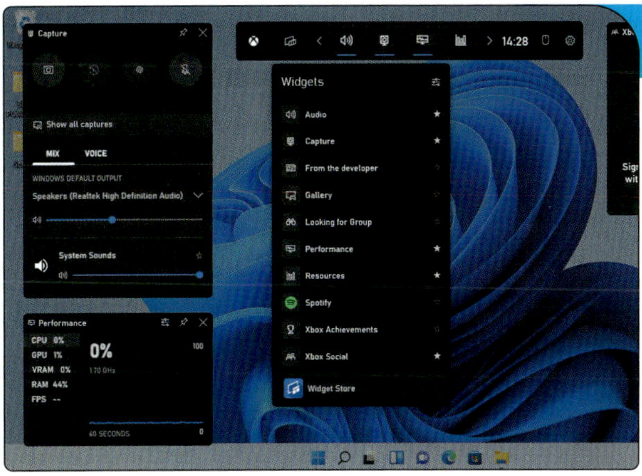


### Step 2

The multiple windows can be managed by clicking on the Widgets icon; the 3D window icon located to the right of the Xbox icon on the top, thin window in the middle of the screen. Click the star next to each item to add or remove it from the Game Bar selection.

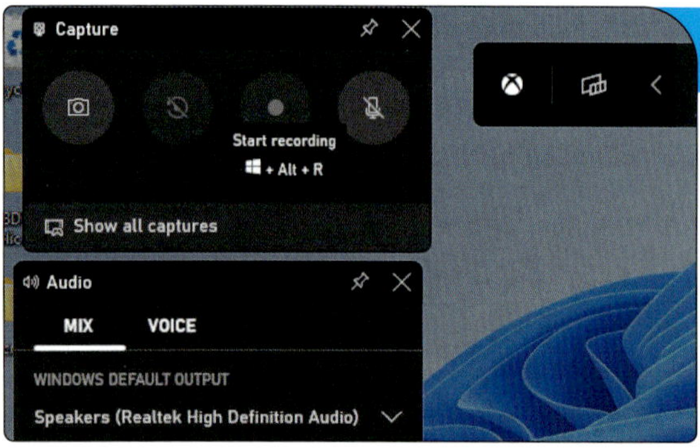


## Step 3

By default, the top-left window is the Capture section. Here you can take screenshots, start recording video, record the last thirty seconds and activate the microphone during recording. You can also view any previous screen captures. All elements are displayed together with their keyboard shortcuts.

## Step 4

Xbox Social is an element that lies in the top-right of the Game Bar windows. Here you can sign into your Microsoft Xbox account, and use voice and text chat across PC, mobile or Xbox with your friends.

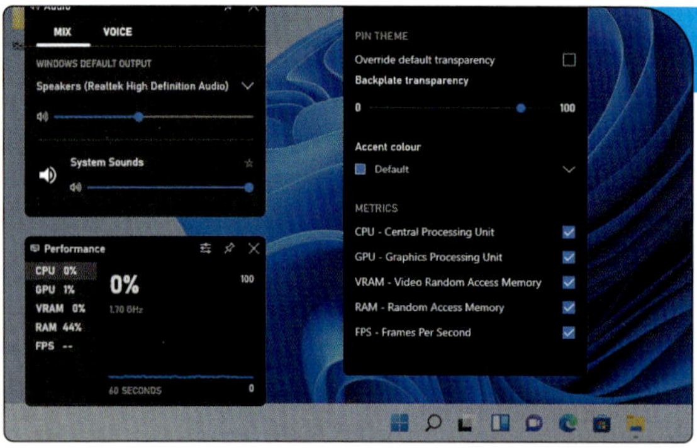


## Step 5

In the bottom-left of the Game Bar windows, there's the Performance element. It details various metrics regarding your system. CPU, GPU, available memory and more can all be viewed as a handy graph. Click the icon next to the pin, within the Performance window, and you can customise the view.

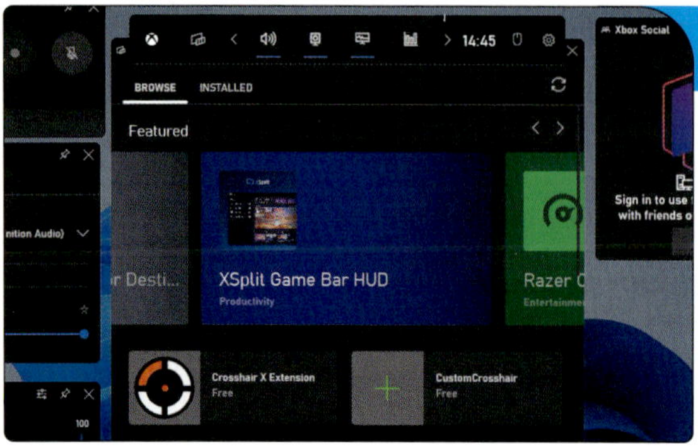


## Step 6

If you want more widgets available, click on the Widget Menu, then scroll down the menu to the Widget Store. Click this, and you can choose from a selection of available widgets to install and use whenever you open the Xbox Game Bar.

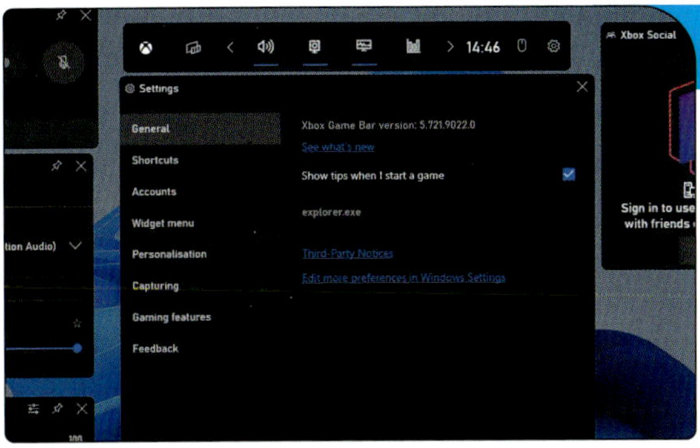


## Step 7

You can also fine-tune the Xbox Game Bar by clicking on the cog icon in the top, slim, main window section. This open the Game Bar's Settings page, where you can alter the shortcuts, create and sign in with different accounts and change other features of the app.

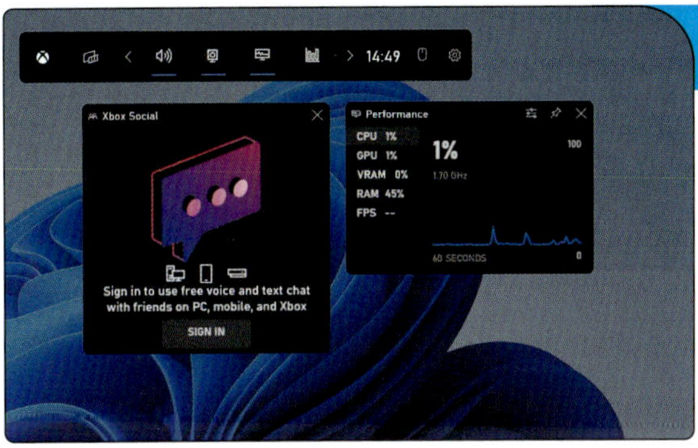


## Step 8

You can rearrange the position of all of the overlay panels by clicking on their top bars and dragging them into the desired position. Several of the panels can be pinned, meaning that they will remain visible on screen even after the Game Bar is hidden. Just click the Pin icon in the top bar.

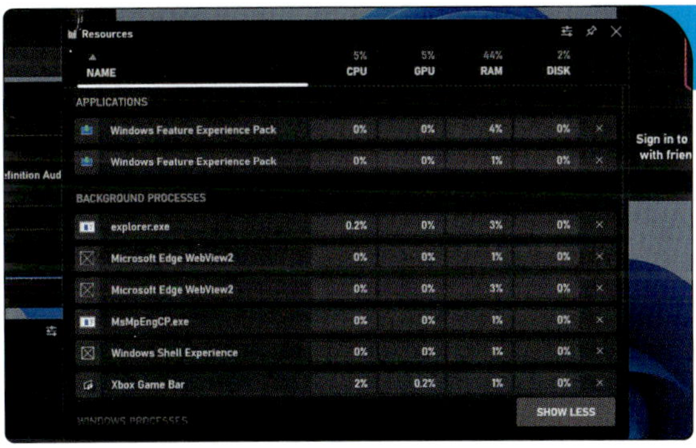


## Step 9

The Resources window, found by clicking on the bar graph icon in the top, slim, window, details the currently open tasks within Windows 11. If you find the game you're playing is slowing down, you can open this and find where the majority of your system's resources are being used.

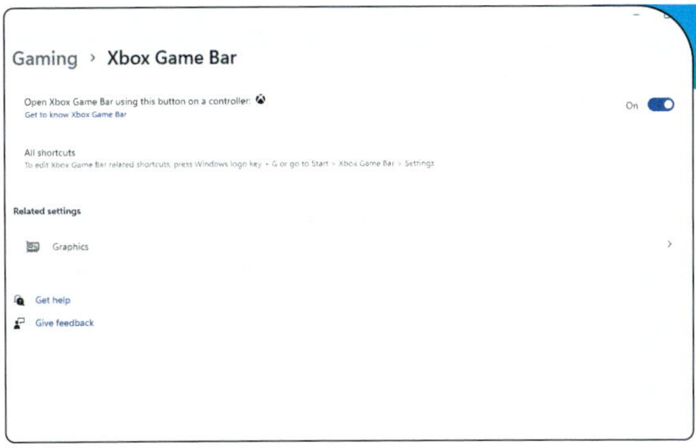


## Step 10

You can close the Game Bar overlay screen by clicking anywhere else on the screen, or by pressing Windows Key + G again. If you want to disable the Game Bar completely, open the Main settings, go to the Gaming section, and use the slider to disable the tool.

# The Cloud Clipboard

Copying and pasting is something we all do. However, what do you do if you need to copy the same few things again and again and how do you copy content across your devices? The new Cloud Clipboard solves both of those problems in a single, simple interface.

## A New Way to Copy + Paste

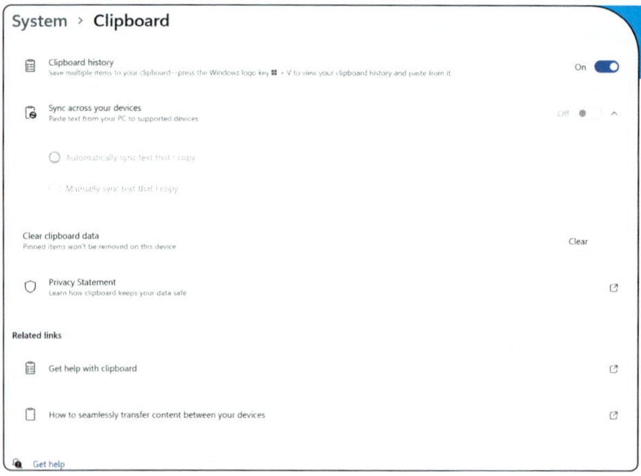


### Step 1

Before you can use all the features of the Cloud Clipboard in Windows 11, you will need to enable them in the settings. Go to Settings > System and look for the Clipboard section. You can turn on the clipboard history using the slider toggle. To sync across devices, click 'Get started'.

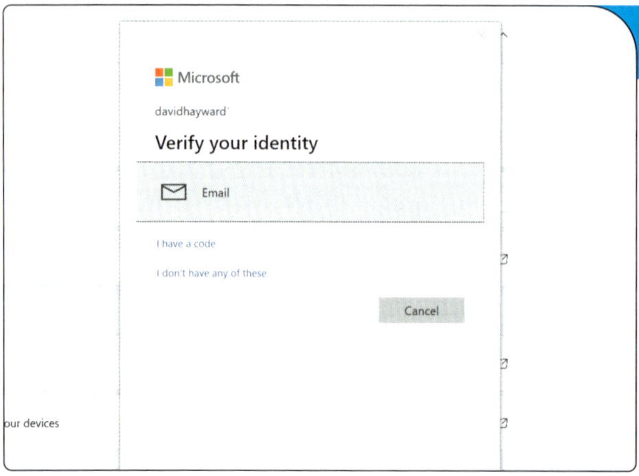


### Step 2

Follow the instructions to confirm your Microsoft account (if this is requested) and then choose whether you want to enable automatic syncing across devices or not. If you want to be able to sync the clipboard to your phone, you will also need to download and install an app on that device.

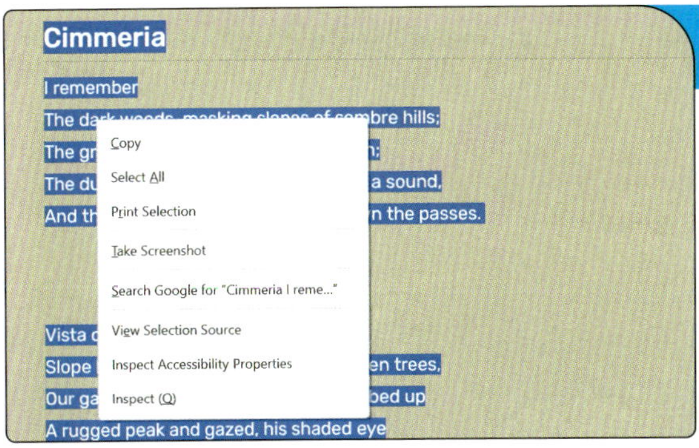


## Step 3

With the Cloud Clipboard settings configured to how you want, you can start using the feature. Just like the old clipboard, things are added to it when you copy something. This can either be by pressing Ctrl + C with some text highlighted or right-clicking on an image or file and selecting Copy.

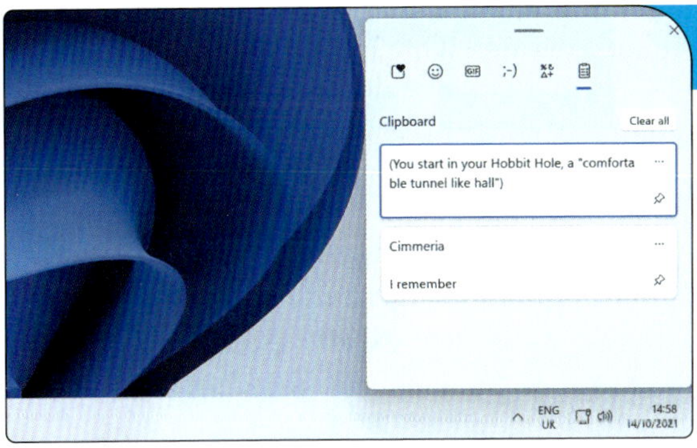


## Step 4

The difference now is each thing you copy is stored in the clipboard, rather than being overwritten by the next thing you copy. To see the things stored in the Cloud Clipboard, press Windows Key + V. In the new Cloud Clipboard window, you will see a list of the things you have copied.

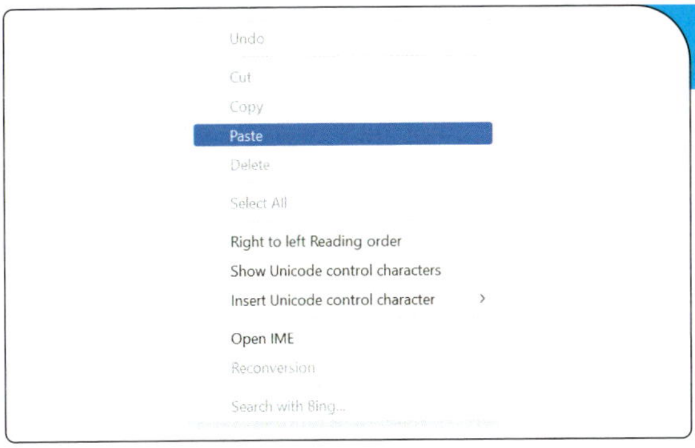


## Step 5

The things you have copied can be made ready to paste by selecting them in the Cloud Clipboard. You can then use Ctrl + V to paste or right-click and select Paste from the menu. When you select something in the Cloud Clipboard, it remains there to be pasted again.

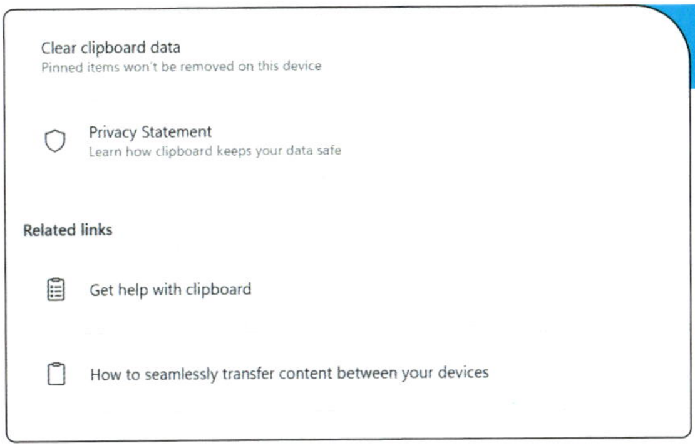


## Step 6

You can clear the items from the clipboard easily, either by opening settings > System > Clipboard and clicking on 'Clear clipboard data' or by opening the clipboard window and clicking the 'Clear all' button. Once the clipboard is cleared, you cannot recover the copied data.

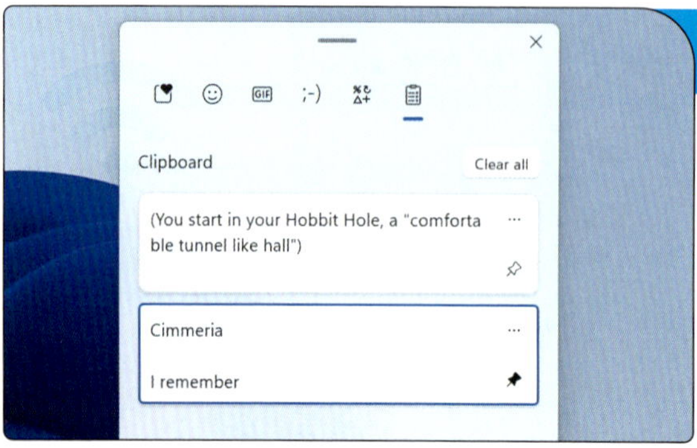


## Step 7

If there is copied data in the Cloud Clipboard that you think you will always need to keep, you can pin it. Pinned items in the clipboard do not get cleared when using the methods described in the previous step. To pin something, move your mouse over the item and then click the pin icon that appears.

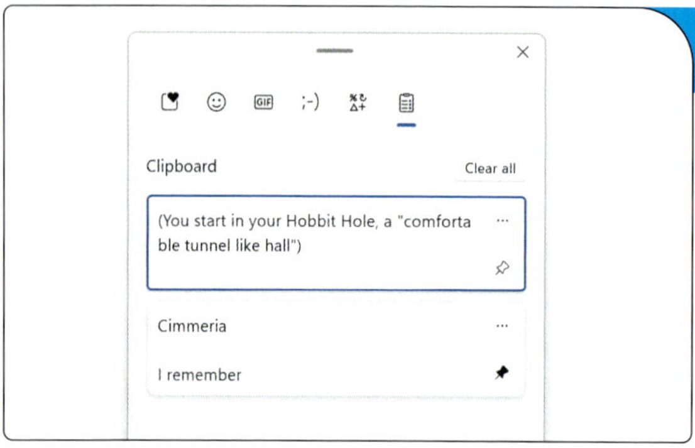


## Step 8

Pinned items even remain in the Cloud Clipboard when you restart your computer. The only way to remove them now is to unpin them from the clipboard. To do this, highlight the item again and click the pinned icon. Copying something that is already saved in the clipboard doesn't overwrite it.

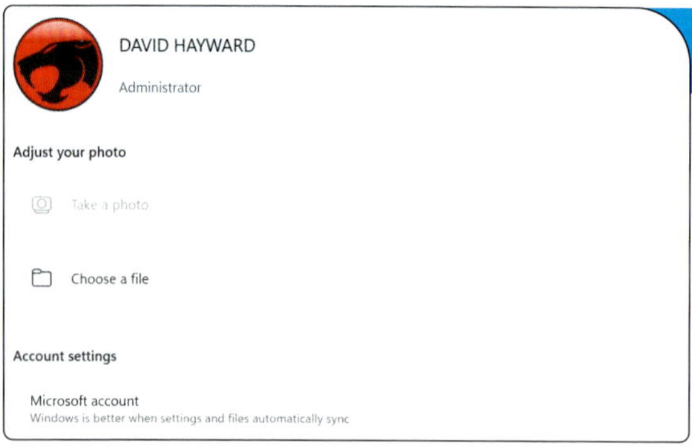


## Step 9

Syncing clipboard data between devices actually works using the same Microsoft Graph technology that powers the Timeline, introduced in Windows 10's April 2018 Update. You will need to be signed into both devices with the same Microsoft account for this feature to work.

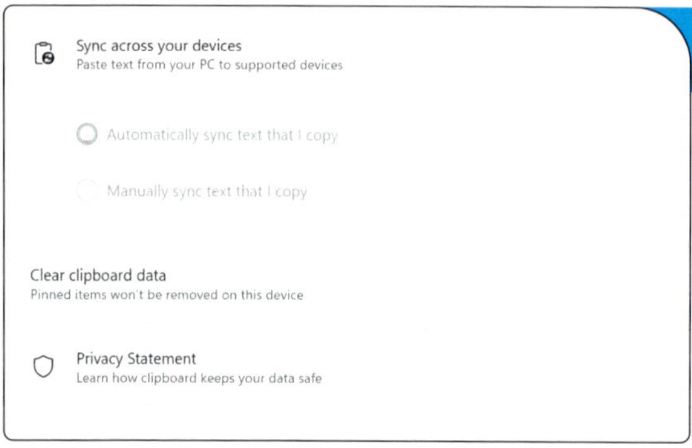


## Step 10

If you select 'Never automatically sync text that I copy', you'll have to manually choose what you want to copy. To do so, open your Clipboard history with Windows+V, hover over an item in your Clipboard history and click the cloud-shaped Sync to Other Devices icon.

# Using the Snipping Tool

In 2018 Microsoft announced that it was abandoning the much-loved Snipping Tool in favour of a new tool called Snip & Sketch. However, with Windows 11, Microsoft has reversed that decision and has merged both apps into the new Snipping Tool.

## Snip, Snip!

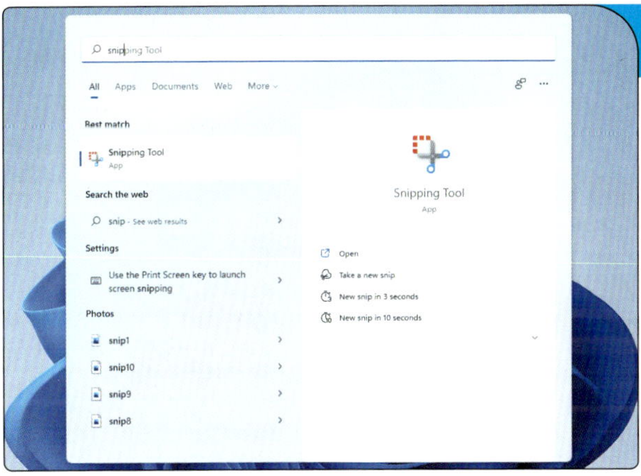


### Step 1

To open the Snipping Tool, you can click on the Windows Start button and type 'snip', then click on the Snipping Tool app as listed in the results. Or, you can press the Windows Logo Key + Shift + S to start a new Snip.

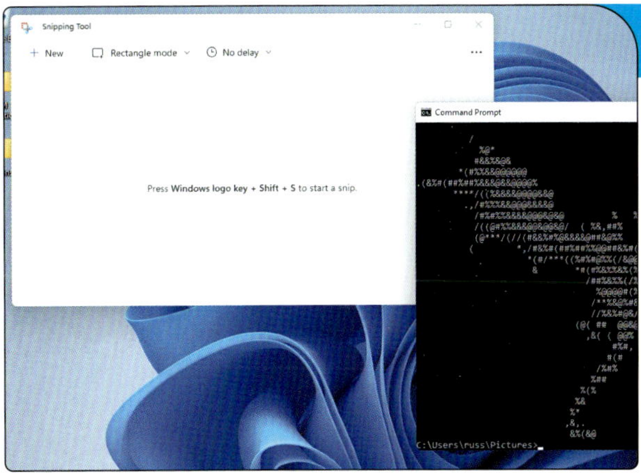


### Step 2

As you will see, the Snipping Tool is a merger of the two former screenshot apps. To begin with, let's open something so we can take a screenshot of it. Remember to keep the Snipping Tool open in the background while you do this.

## Step 3

To take a Snip screenshot, click on the +New button in the Snipping Tool window. This will darken the screen, and display an overlay reading 'Draw a shape to create a screen snip'. There are some options at the top of the screen, which represent the shape of the area you want to snip.

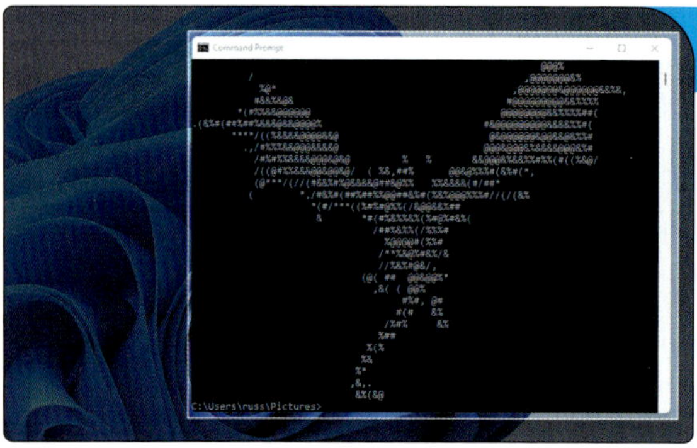

## Step 4

Now, using the mouse, and assuming we're opting for the default shape of a rectangle, draw around the area where you want the screenshot to capture. Press and hold the left mouse button while you draw, and release it when you're done.

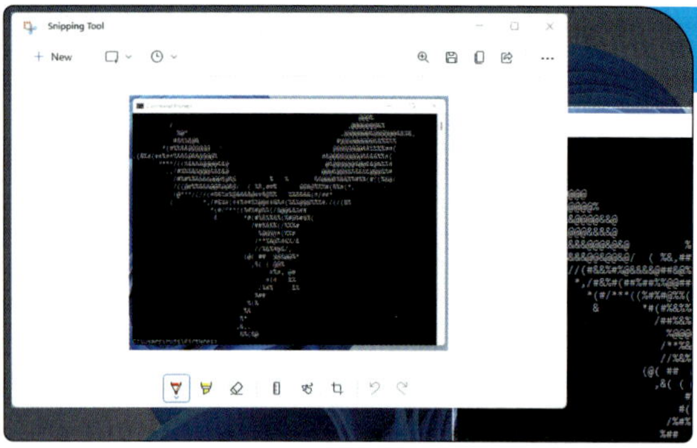


## Step 5

The screen area you are capturing will be highlighted – which means it simply returns that portion of the screen back to its normal colours. This is the area that will be made available to the Snipping Tool.

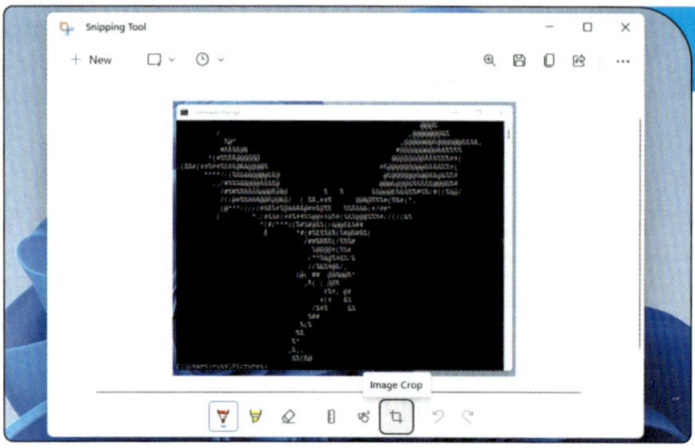


## Step 6

There are a number of options available along the bottom of the Snipping Tool window to further edit the screenshot. From left to right, you'll find: Ballpoint Pen, Highlighter, Eraser, Ruler, Touch Writing, Crop, Undo and Redo.

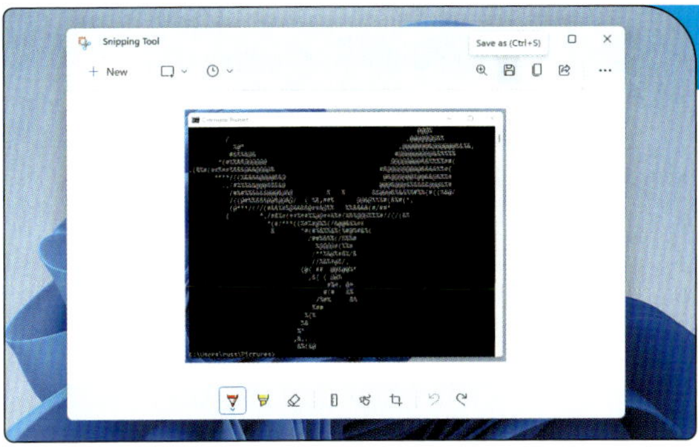


## Step 7

There are also options along the top-right of the Snipping Tool window: Zoom, Save As, Copy and Share. The top-left options will have you create a New snip, change the Shape of the snipped area and create a Time Delay for when the snip will take place.

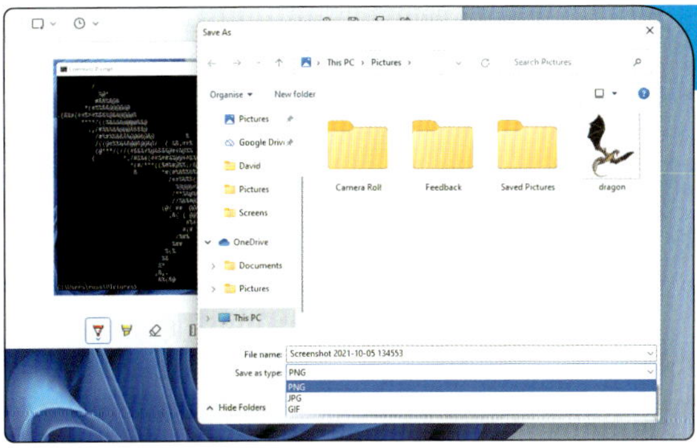


## Step 8

Save the captured screenshot by clicking on the Save As button, located in the top-right of the Snipping Tool window. This will open a familiar File Manager window, where you can locate a folder or area to save the image. You can save your images as PNG, JPG or GIF.

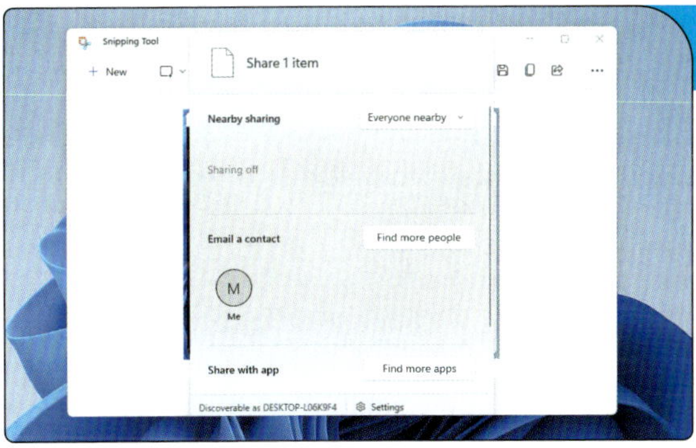


## Step 9

The Share option will enable you to send the captured image as a file to a number of different sources. You can utilise Nearby Sharing, send it as an Email or share it via an installed app – such as Mail or Teams.

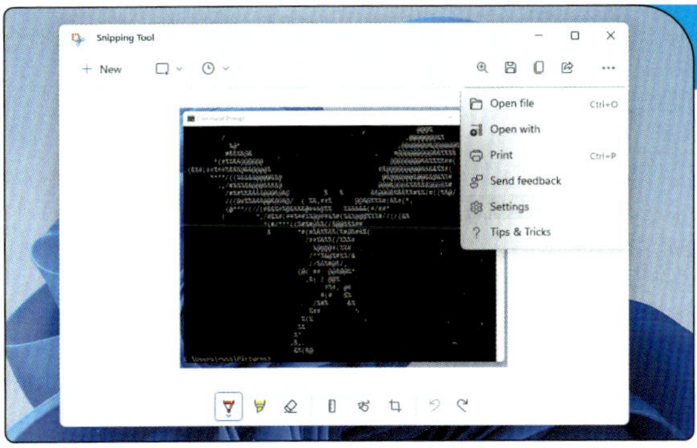


## Step 10

Clicking on the three dots in the upper-right of the Snipping Tool window will open a sub-menu where you can open files, print, send feedback and even call upon tips and tricks from the Microsoft website. There's also a Settings option, which allows to further enhance the Snipping Tool experience.

# Installing a Printer

When you connect a printer to your PC or add a new one to your home network, you can usually start printing straight away. Windows 11 supports most printers, so you probably won't have to install special software. Here's how to install printers in Windows 11.

## Install a Local Printer

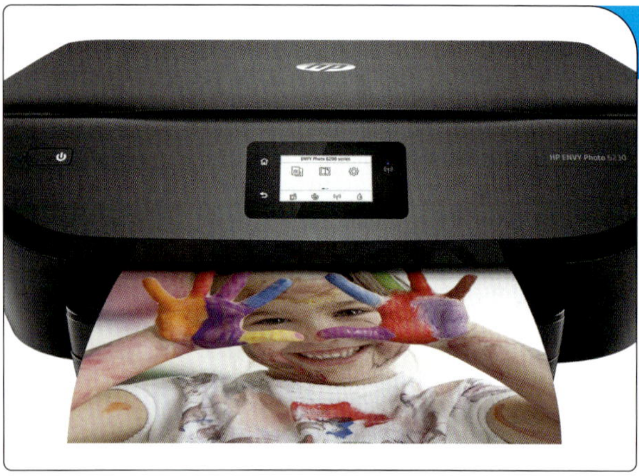

### Step 1

In most cases, all you have to do to set up a printer is to connect it to your PC and let the plug and play software do its work. Plug the USB cable from your printer into an available USB port on your PC and turn the printer on. If nothing happens, try restarting your PC with the printer connected.

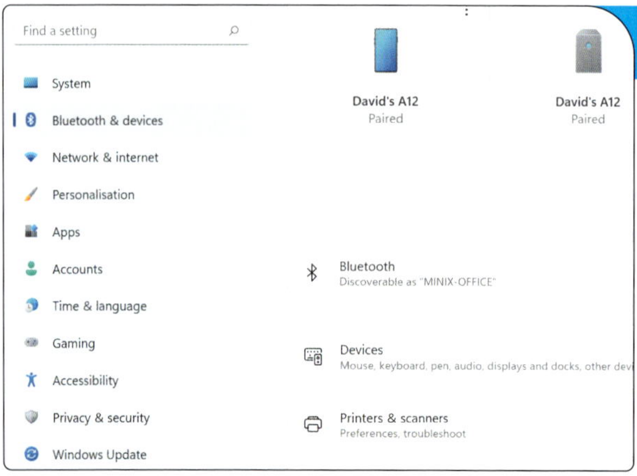


### Step 2

If the printer does not set up automatically, you will need to do it yourself. Click the Start menu button and head into Settings. Look for Bluetooth & Devices from the list on the left-hand pane, and click it. Next, expand Printers & Scanners. You should see a list of available devices, hopefully with your printer's name shown.

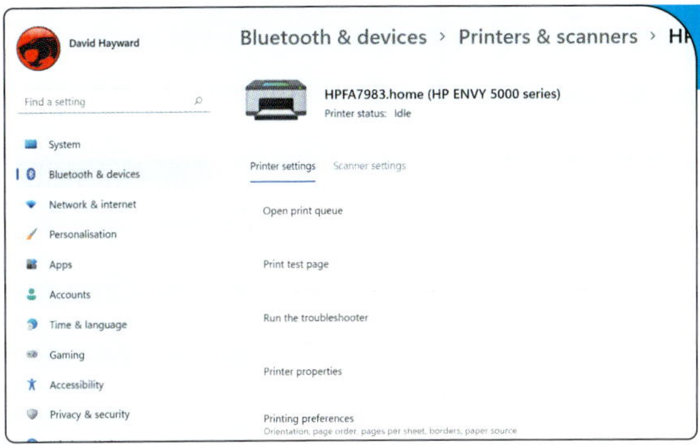


## Step 3

If so, click on it and then click Add Printer. The printer should then be installed and ready to use. If you don't see your device in the list, click 'Add Device' and see if the scan finds it. If it still does not appear, click the 'Add Manually' link that appears with, 'The printer I want isn't listed'.

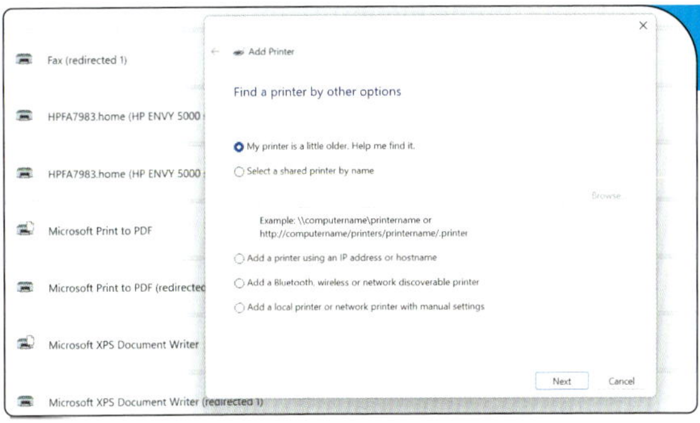


## Step 4

This opens a step-by-step tool that will show you how to find and install software for an older printer, or one which is not yet supported by drivers pre-installed with Windows 11. If that still fails, try going to the printer manufacturer's website and download an installer or drivers.

# Install a Wireless Printer

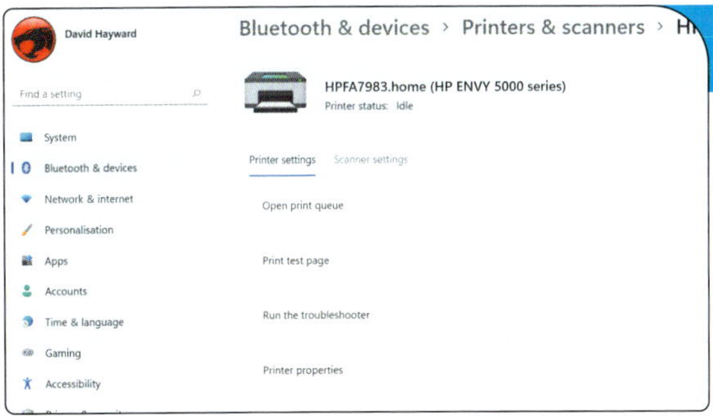


## Step 1

Open the settings, followed by Bluetooth & Devices, then Printer & Scanners. Look for your printer in the list of available devices and if it is there, click on it and then click 'Add Device'. If your printer is switched on and connected to the network, Windows 11 should find it easily.

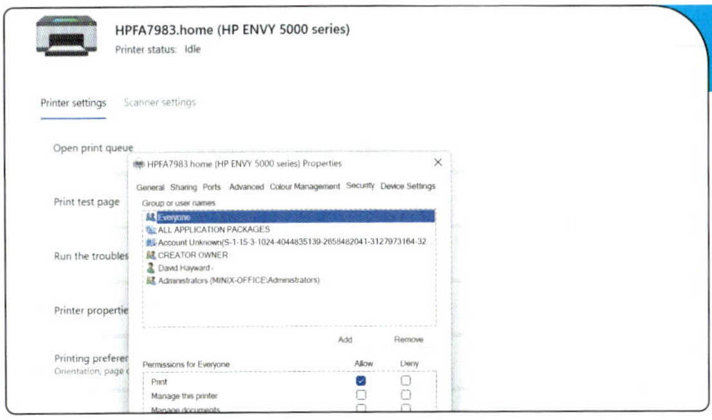


## Step 2

Available printers can include all such devices on a network, such as Bluetooth and wireless printers or those that are plugged into another computer and shared on the network. You might need permission to install some printers, depending on the type of network you are connected to.

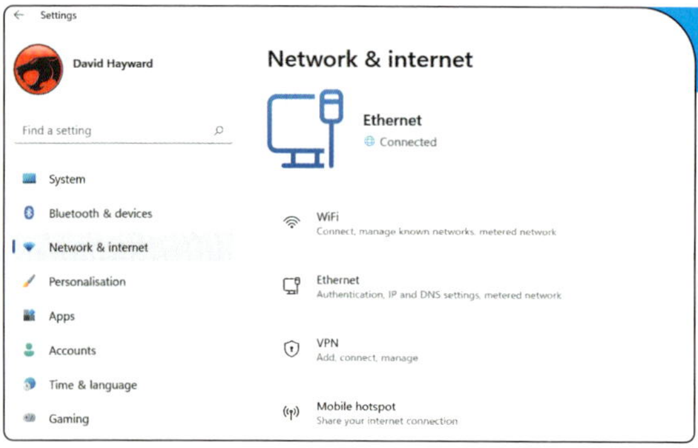


## Step 3

If you use wireless access points, extenders or multiple wireless routers with separate SSIDs, you'll need to ensure that you're connected to the same network as the printer for your PC to find and install it. If the printer does not appear in the list you may need to add it manually.

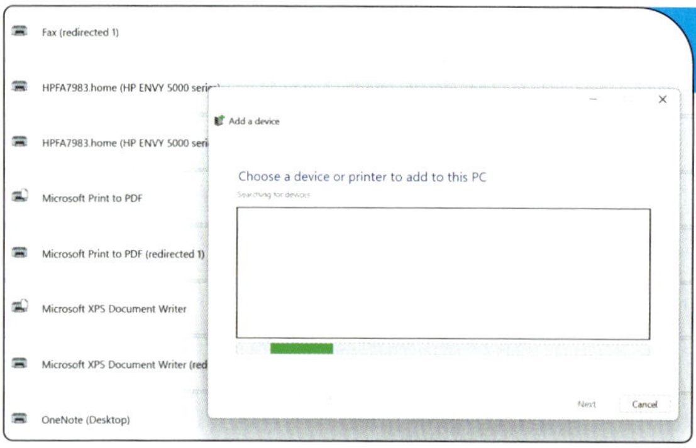


## Step 4

Click on the 'Add Manually' link when 'The printer I want isn't listed' appears. This opens a tool that will show you, step-by-step, how to find and install software for an older printer, or one which is not supported by Windows 11 drivers. If this fails, try looking for the software on the manufacturer's website.

# Common Printer Problems

**Check for Old Drivers**
**Most printers require driver software to work properly. If you recently upgraded from one version of Windows to another, it's possible that the current printer driver is for the previous version of Windows and may not work (or work well) with Windows 11. Check Windows Update for new drivers.**

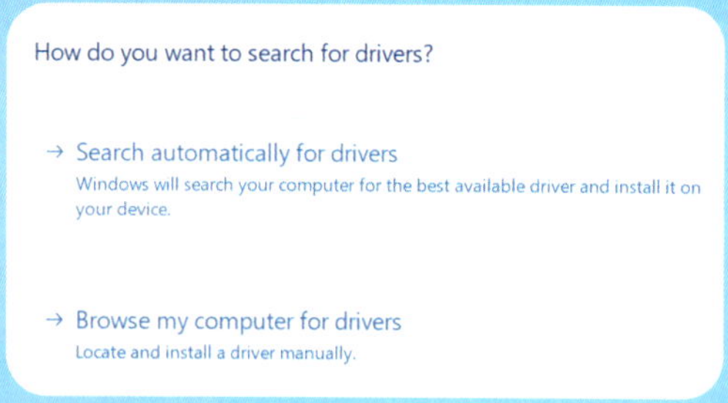


**Run the Troubleshooter**
**Head in to settings > Update & Security > Troubleshoot and run the Printer Troubleshooter. You can also type 'Printing problem' into the search box, select the search result labelled 'Help from Microsoft' and then select the troubleshooter to download it.**

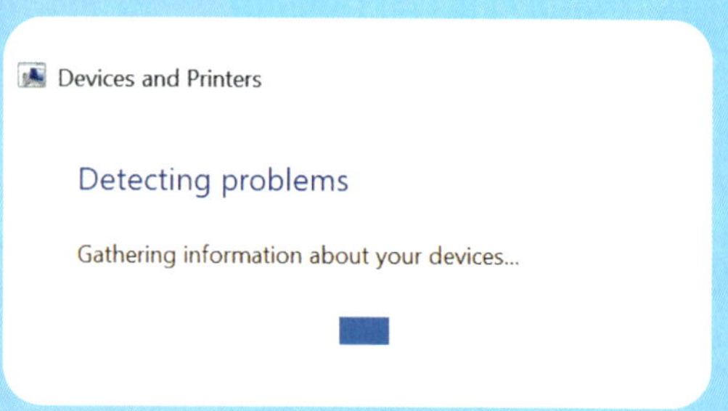

# Setting Up Dual Monitors

With a second monitor and the required connectors on your PC, setting up Windows 11 to display over two screens is easy. Having a second monitor can really help to increase productivity, and allow you to stay more organised when you're at your computer.

## Setting Up a Dual Display

### Step 1

You will obviously need to ensure that your PC has the requisite connections for two monitors (two HDMI, VGA or DVI ports, or a combination of these). Check the back of your PC tower or the side of your laptop to find out. With your PC turned off, connect both monitors to the available ports.

### Step 2

Boot up the computer and log in. Windows should automatically detect that two displays are connected and you should see both of them displaying a desktop. Your main display will have all of your icons on it, whilst the new second display will be blank apart from the taskbar along the bottom.

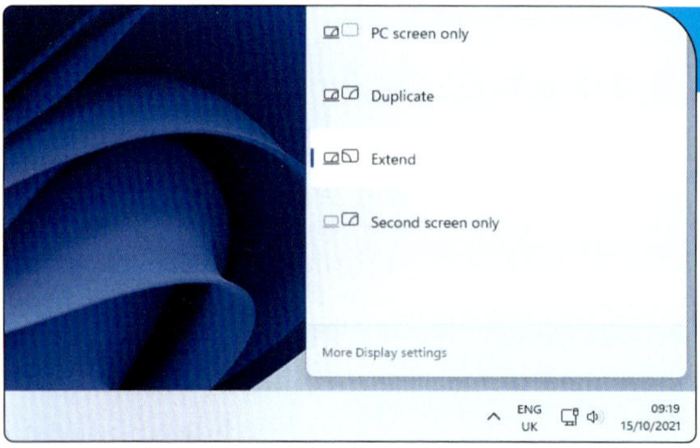


## Step 3

You will now need to configure the dual monitor setup to your liking. Windows 11 allows you to easily choose how the dual monitors display. Press Windows Key + P to see the Project side panel. Here you can choose from PC Screen Only, Duplicate, Extend or Second screen Only options.

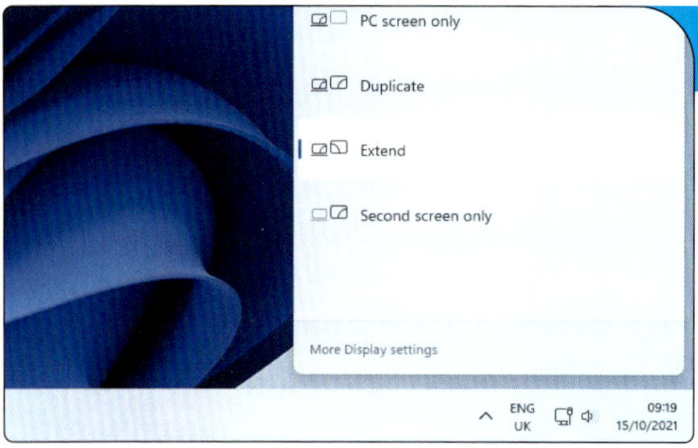


## Step 4

PC screen Only and Second Screen only are fairly self-explanatory, displaying an image on one or the other screens. Duplicate is also fairly easy to understand, showing exactly the same display on both screens. Extend turns the two monitors to one long screen that you can spread out across.

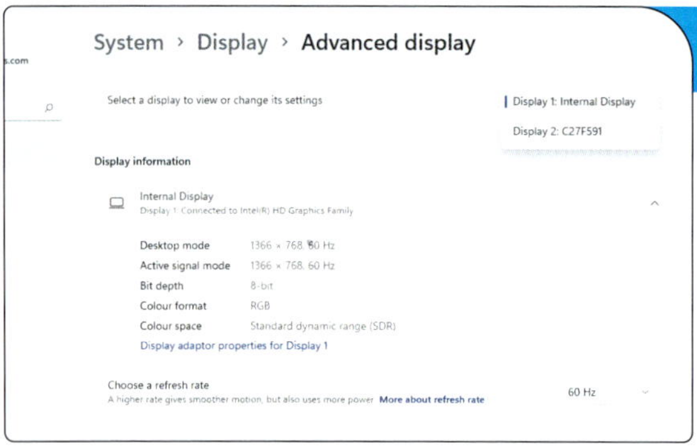


## Step 5

The Extend option is the one which needs the most setting up. On the main display, right-click anywhere on the desktop and choose Display settings from the Action menu. Scrolling to the bottom of the display settings gives you another way to choose the display mode.

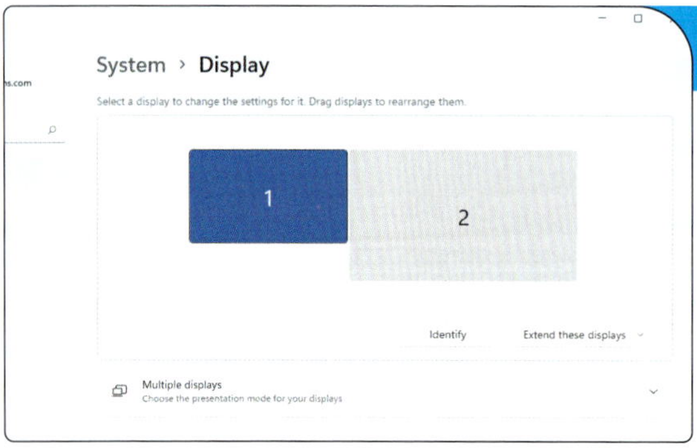


## Step 6

At the top of the display settings are the two displays side-by-side. 1 is your main display and 2 is the secondary display. Which side of the screen the two monitors "join" at (which side allows you to move on to the second monitor) is controlled by dragging the display boxes here to the left or right.

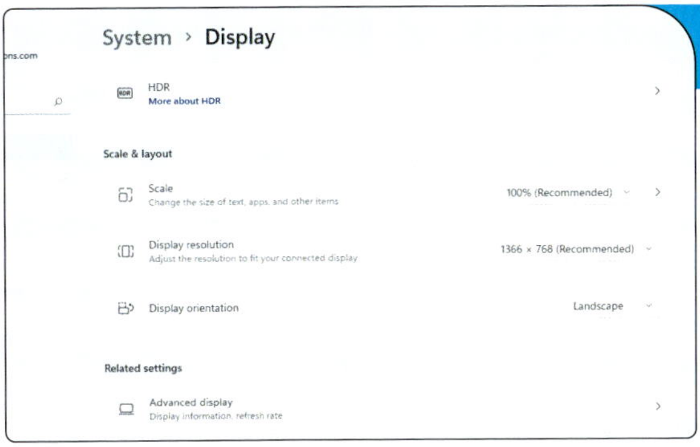


## Step 7

You can view settings for each display independently, by clicking on one you want to see, and then scrolling down. You can change the scaling, orientation and resolution of each display to best suit the specification of the monitor, if it is the case that the two monitors have different maximum resolutions.

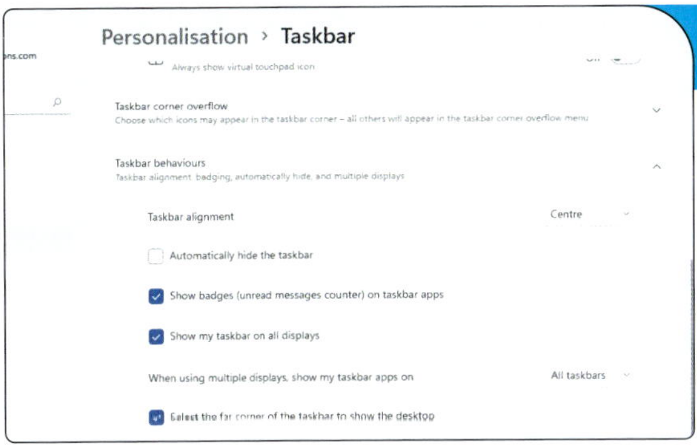


## Step 8

If you don't want to see the taskbar on both displays, go to Settings > Personalisation > Taskbar, and scroll down to Multiple displays. You can then choose to turn off the taskbar on the second display. You can also spread a single wallpaper across both screens by selecting Span in Background settings.

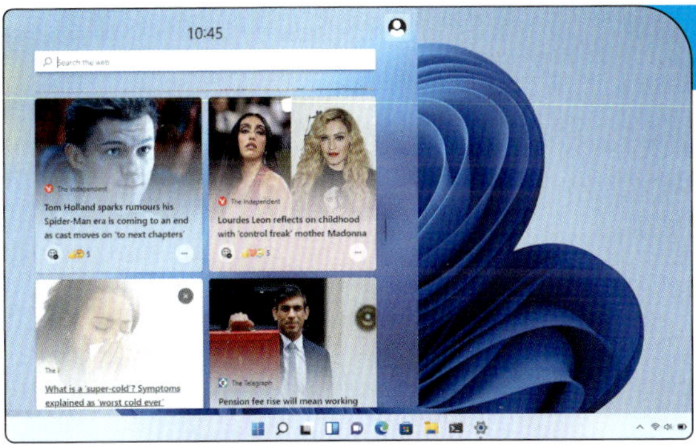


## Step 9

Spreading out across the two monitors in Extend mode is as easy as clicking and dragging a window, be that a browser window, app or anything else, to the "joined" side of the main screen. Just keep the mouse pointer moving and it will continue on to the second screen seamlessly.

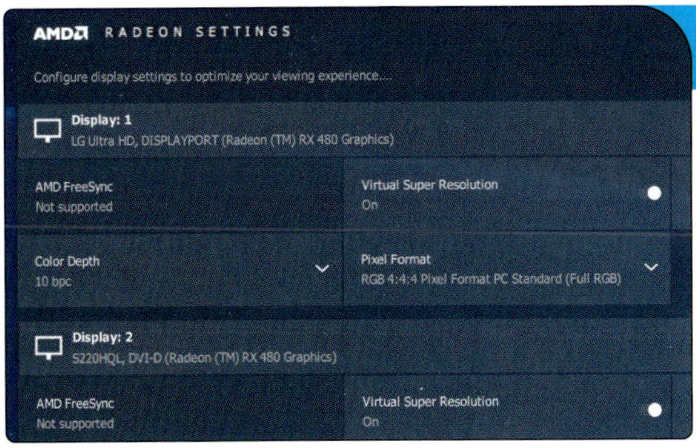


## Step 10

Depending on the graphics card software you have installed (Radeon for example), you will usually have further display options for the second monitor in the graphics adapter settings. This might include Virtual Super Resolution and GPU scaling, helping you match up resolution settings.

# Find My Device & Remote Lock

Remotely tracking, locking, or disabling mobile devices has been the norm for several years now, helping to increase security when a device is lost or stolen. Microsoft has decided to make these features available to Windows 11 users with its own "Find my device" option.

## Enable Find My Device

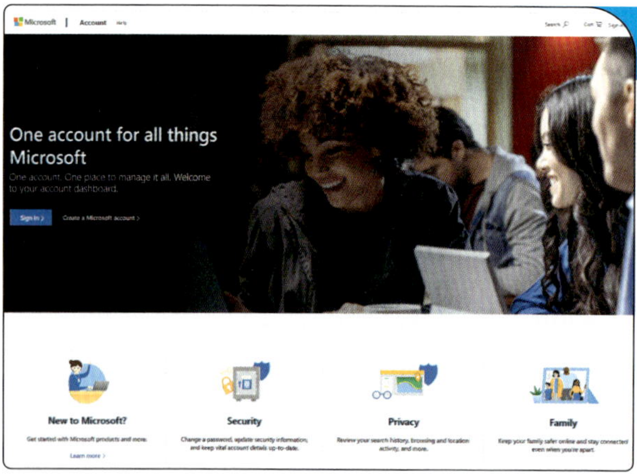


### Step 1

Go to the Microsoft account login page (account.microsoft.com) in the browser on your computer. Sign in using your Microsoft account details (if trying to enable Find my device for a different device, make sure you sign in with the correct details) and then click the Devices tab at the top.

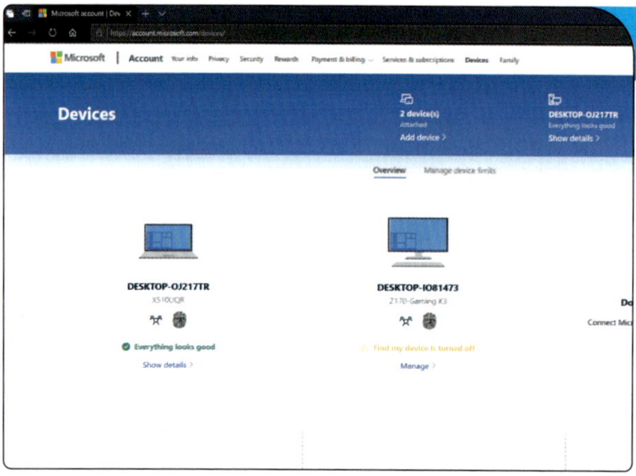


### Step 2

You should see your device listed on the Devices screen. On the panel, click "Manage" for the device you want to locate and then click "Enable location". This is found above the map image, below the battery power indicator. You need to wait for the setting to be enabled.

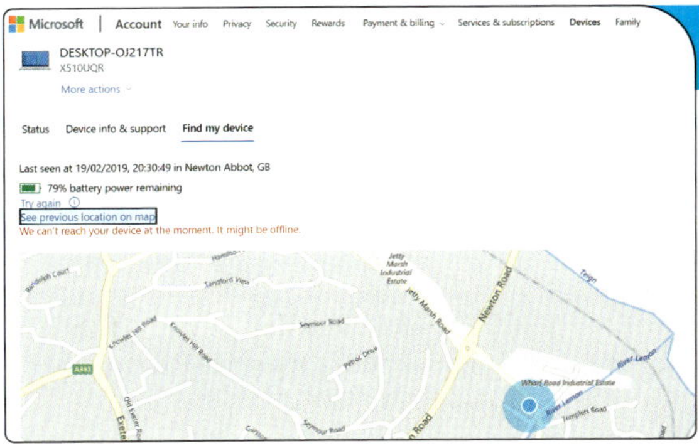


## Step 3

If able to, your device turns on Location access, and after a few seconds, the map image updates to display the last registered location of the device. You can scroll and zoom the map using the controls, or your mouse/ trackpad. You can also change the view style.

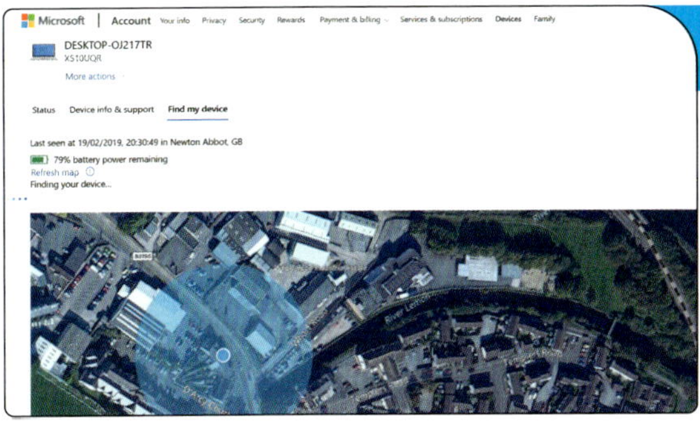


## Step 4

If the device is offline, you won't be able to activate Find my device, and you will see a warning telling you so. You should still be able to see the previous last known location by clicking the link that appears above the warning message. This will be updated when the device is next online.

# Using Remote Lock

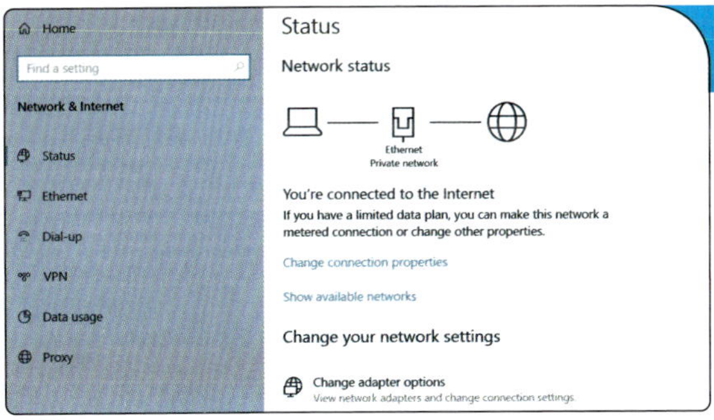


## Step 1

For the Remote Lock feature of Find my device to work, your laptop needs to be connected to the Internet, the feature must already have been enabled and set up, and you must be using a Microsoft account (not a local account) with administrator privileges enabled.

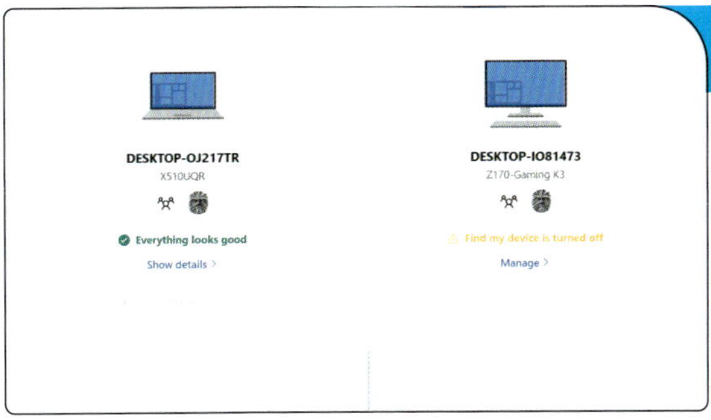


## Step 2

Sign in to your Microsoft account (account.microsoft.com) in the web browser on your computer. Click on the Devices tab at the top, or select All Devices from the panel on the account homepage. Any devices that use this Microsoft account are displayed on the screen.

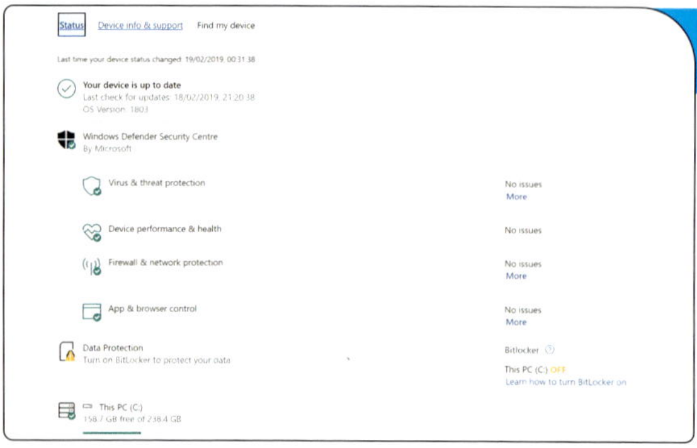


## Step 3

You see a warning on each device panel, telling you that "Find my device is turned off". Click the Manage button for the device on which you want to set up the feature. The next screen should show a large map, along with options to enable location, and a large blue "Lock" button.

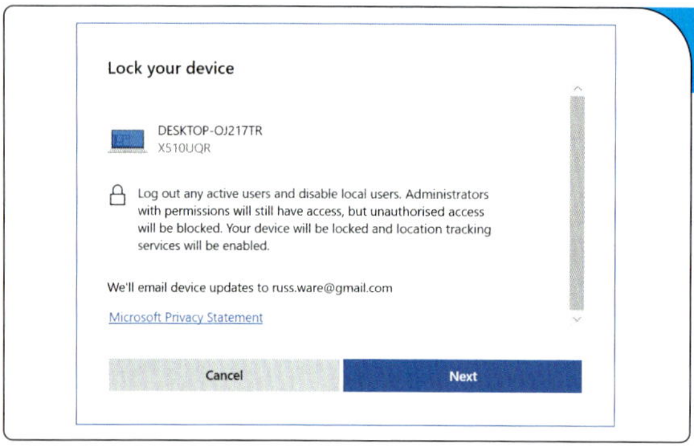


## Step 4

Click on the Lock button and a new window opens explaining what will happen to the device once it is locked. This includes logging out active users and disabling local users, enabling location tracking and locking the device. An email is sent to the account address once the lock is complete.

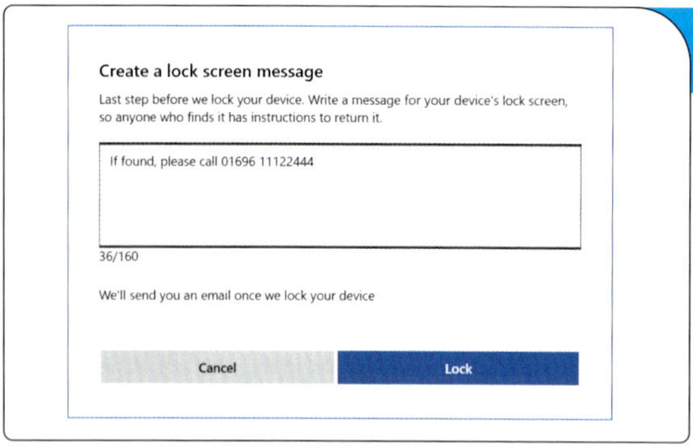


## Step 5

Click Next, and you have the option to create a custom message to appear on the lock screen of the device. This could be a message asking anyone who finds the locked device to contact you (with contact details included, obviously), or anything else you can fit into 160 characters.

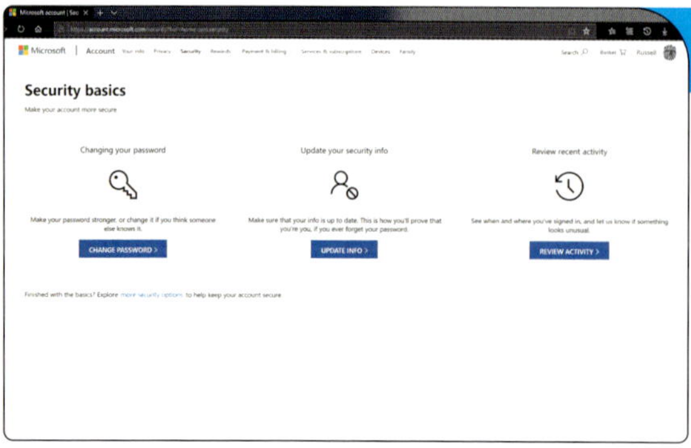


## Step 6

Finally, click the Lock button to complete the process. Remember, if you manage to retrieve the device, you will need to have administrator privileges to get back into it. If you think the device is lost forever, or even if you get it back, it is a good idea to change your Microsoft account password.

# Essential Apps for Windows

The new Windows Store is crammed full of useful apps for your computer. You'll find everything you'll ever need in here; from music to movies and performance to productivity. Here are some of the top apps we think are worth taking a closer look at.

## A World of Apps

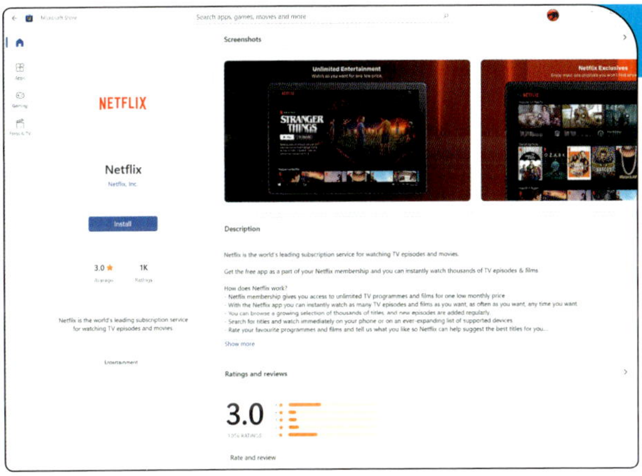


### Netflix

The king of the streaming services, Netflix has become one of the most installed apps across any platform. Watch your favourite films, and binge on top series until the wee hours of the morning; there's something for everyone within the ever-growing genres on Netflix. Don't forget though, after the first month, Netflix is a paid subscription service.

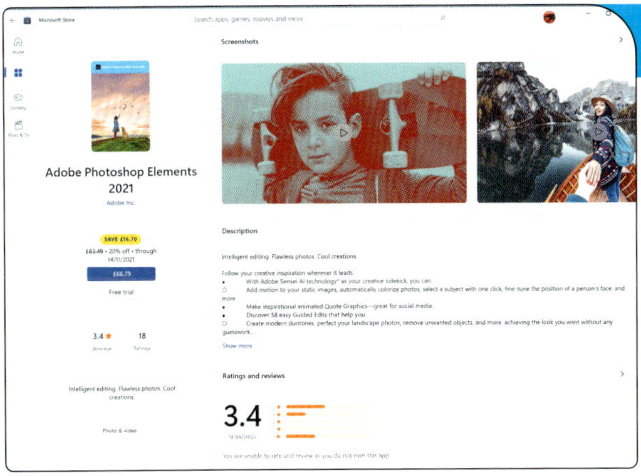


### Photoshop

Unleash your inner digital photographer and artist with Adobe's Photoshop Elements. If you don't want to go down the Adobe Photoshop Professional route, then this is the app for you. There's tons of features available that will greatly enhance your photos and unlock your hidden potential.

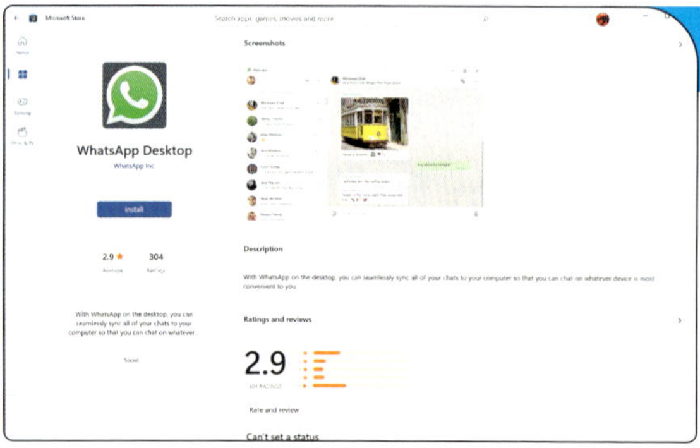


## WhatsApp

WhatsApp has increasingly become an essential part of communications between colleagues, friends and family. Thanks to encrypted chats, group communications, and voice and video calling over Wi-Fi, it's easy to see how important the app is in today's modern, digital world.

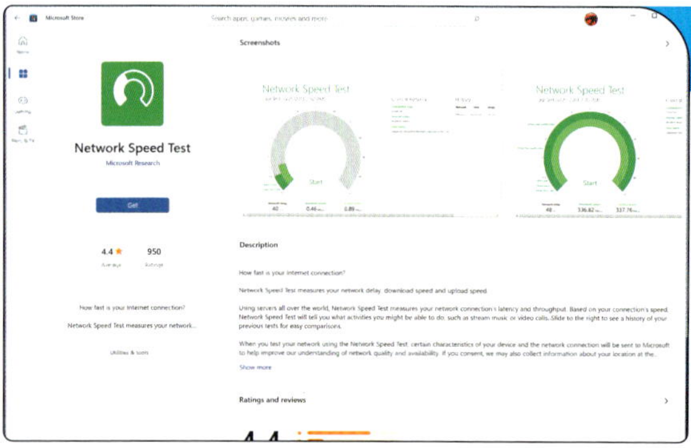


## Network Testing

Working from home over the last year has proved just how vital our Internet connections really are. A drop in connectivity can cause havoc, especially when you have deadlines to meet. With Network Speed Test you can closely monitor your bandwidth, and ensure you're getting the maximum from your ISP.

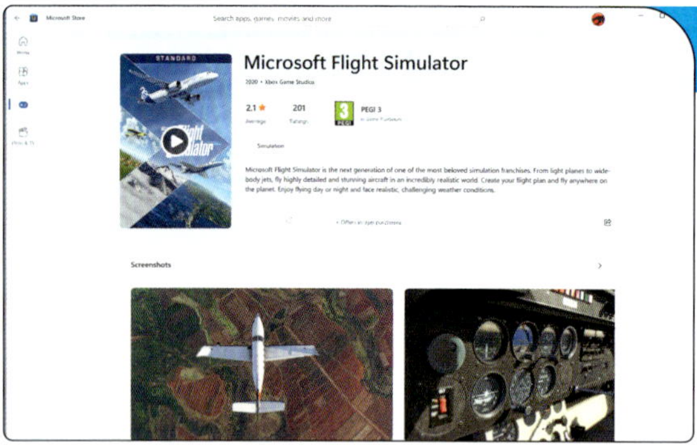


## Flight Simulator

If you like a different kind of gaming on your PC, then why not give Microsoft's latest Flight Simulator a try? This is the next generation of the famous, and long-running sim, and features incredible realism and graphics that will blow your mind. According to Microsoft, the sim uses actual satellite terrain footage, so you could fly over your own house!

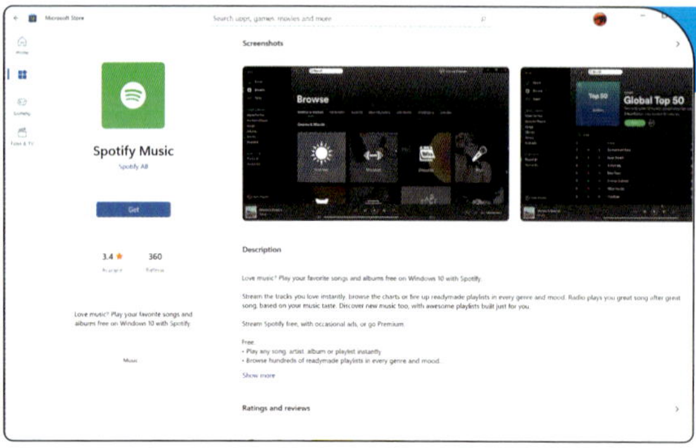


## Spotify

With a catalogue of music numbering the tens of thousands, Spotify enables you to browse everything from Abba to ZZ Top. You can go free and tolerate the occasional ad break, or pay for a Premium subscription and play across multiple devices without any adverts.

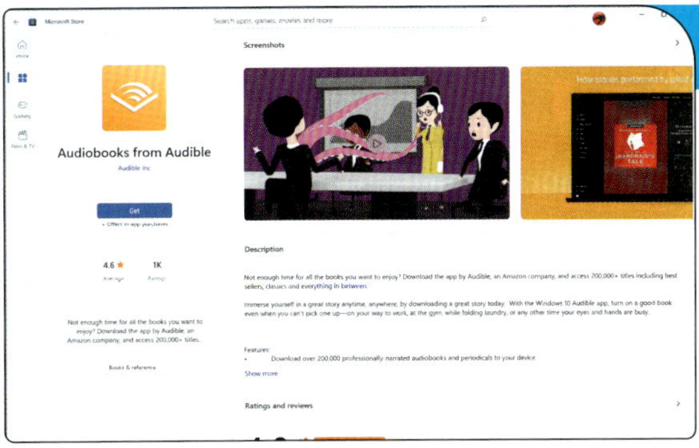


## Audible

Audio books are a great way to get into the classics, as well as new titles without having to read the book. For many, that's an ideal setup, as work and life can get in the way of a good book. Listen to the Adventures of Sherlock Holmes while doing your work, or The Handmaid's Tale during your break. Audible will open even greater worlds for you to explore.

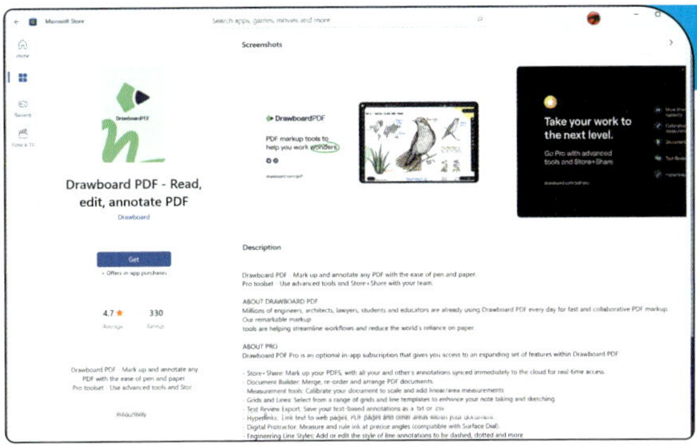


## Drawboard

Drawboard PDF allows you to mark-up, read, edit and annotate any PDF. You can create hyperlinks, linking text to web pages, or other PDF pages within the document; add grids and lines to enhance note taking; choose colours for annotations, and more. It's free, but there's an Advanced Toolset you can buy to further the experience.

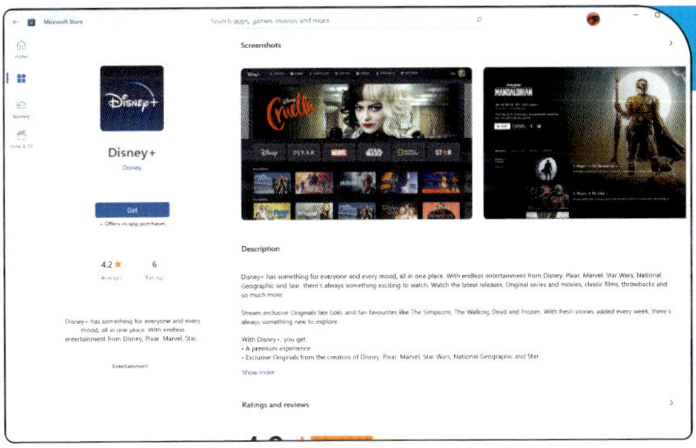


## Disney+

Despite being the newcomer to the streaming video service model, Disney+ has quickly become one of the most downloaded apps in the Windows Store. With shows such as The Mandolorian, What If..?, and WandaVision, you can catch up on everything that's Marvel, Star Wars, and Pixar. Remember, though, it's a subscription service.

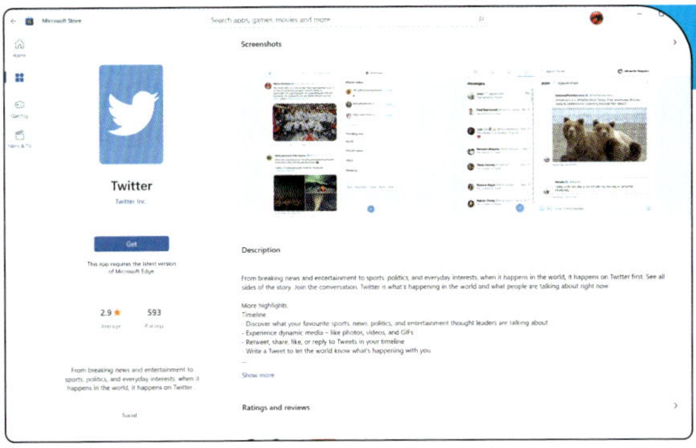


## Twitter

Say what you like about Twitter, you can't ignore the fact that it's often better informed than the news presented on the TV or in the paper. Instead of going to the website, install the app, and you too can join the many millions who enjoy the platform for its varied discussions.

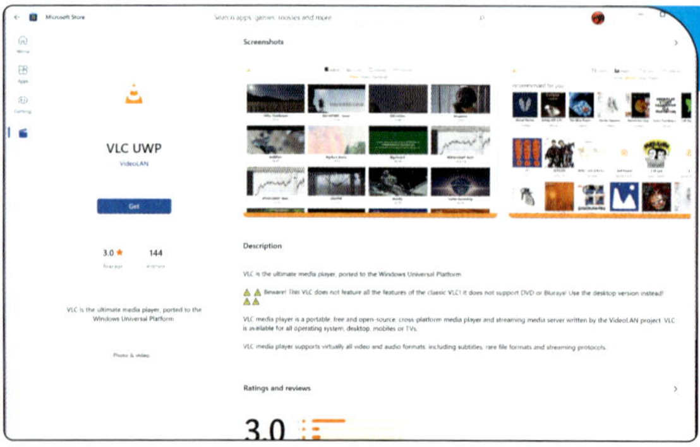


## VLC

Known as the Ultimate Video Player, VLC can play pretty much anything you throw at it without the need to install extra codecs. This particular version is cut-down slightly, so you won't be able to play DVD or Blu-Ray discs, but any digital media file can be played without a problem – and it's free!

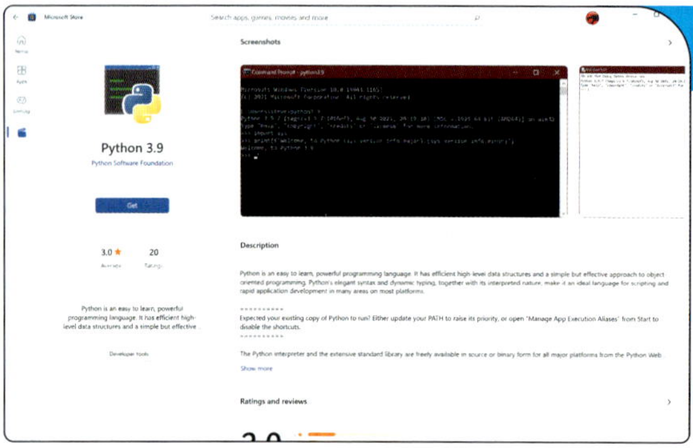


## Python 3.9

Python is a powerful programming language that's easy to learn and use, and can be found throughout the Internet, as well as onboard the ISS. This is the latest version of the free-to-use language, and can help open many doors for you in terms of career opportunities; as well as just enjoying learning how coding works.

## Minecraft

Cited as one of the greatest video games of all time, Minecraft is now considered an essential app for a huge number of Windows users. You don't have to be an avid gamer, nor do you need to be of a certain age. Minecraft allows you to freely explore a world that's estimated to be bigger than the surface area of Neptune.

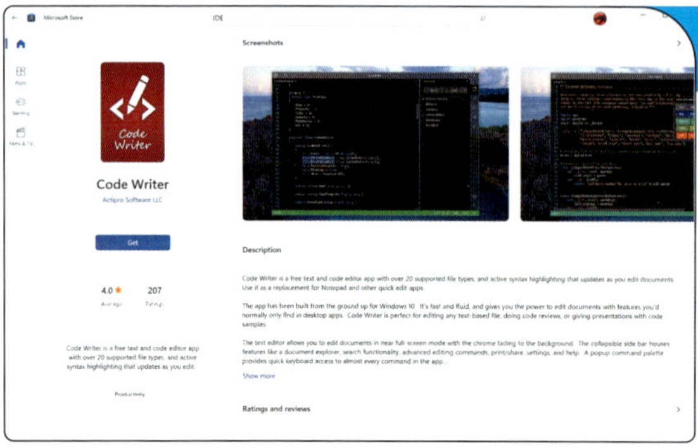


## Code Writer

If you're interested in learning how to code on Windows 11, then you'll need a comprehensive IDE (Integrated Development Environment). Code Writer is one of the best freely available IDEs, with over twenty syntax-highlighted file types that support HTML, CSS, Python, C++, Ruby, SQL, C#, VB, Perl and many more.

Chapter 3

# Windows 11 Advanced

**What do you do if you are hacked? How do you protect your devices on a public Wi-Fi? What exactly is encryption?**

**These and many more questions are answered throughout this chapter, as you begin to move into the more advanced user techniques and skills needed to make Windows 11 secure; while keeping it in tip-top shape.**

# Windows 11 Security Tools

## Virus & Threat Protection

This is where to check and scan for viruses and other threats to your Windows 11 security. Here you will find tools for preventing viruses and other malware from ever taking hold of your computer, as well as the tools needed to check for anything which already got through your defences.

## Account Protection

This is where you manage account and sign-in security for Windows 11. This includes the Microsoft account you are signed in to (or the option to sign in to one), Windows Hello and Dynamic lock. Clicking on any of the options here will simply take you to the relevant area of the main settings.

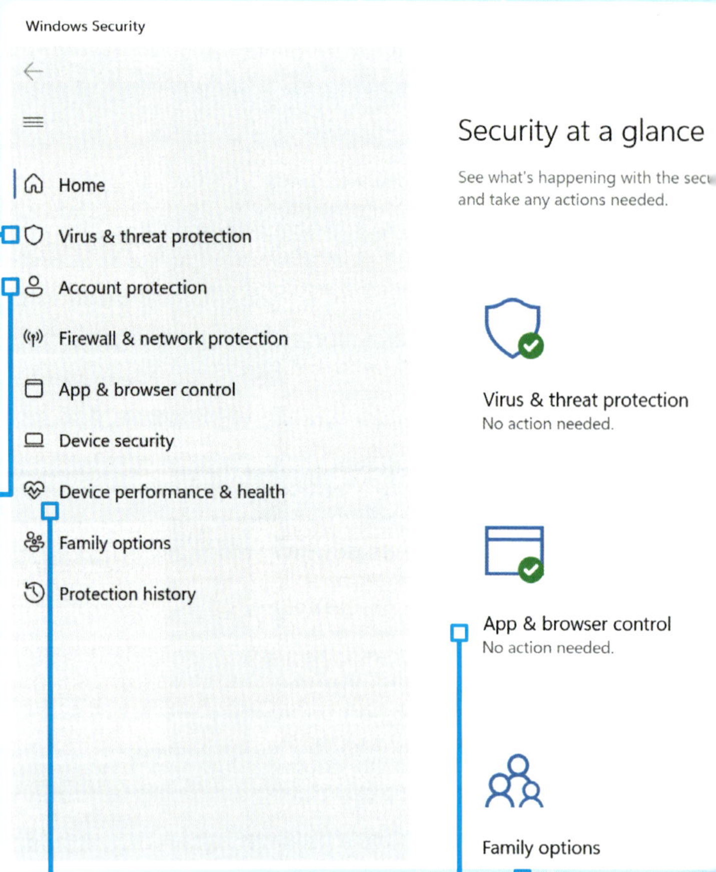


## Device Performance & Health

Displays issues with the health and performance of your computer, including the status of the Storage capacity, Apps and software and the Windows Time service. This is also where you come if you want to begin the process of performing a Fresh Start on your computer.

## Apps & Browser Control

This section contains the settings for Windows Security SmartScreen. This helps to protect your Windows 11 device from potentially dangerous apps, files, websites and downloads. It also includes a link to download Application Guard and lets you control Exploit protection.

**The Windows Security set of tools may not be quite as comprehensive as one of the bigger Anti-Malware suites, such as BitDefender, but it does a good job of protecting the average user from the wealth of nasties out in the Internet.**

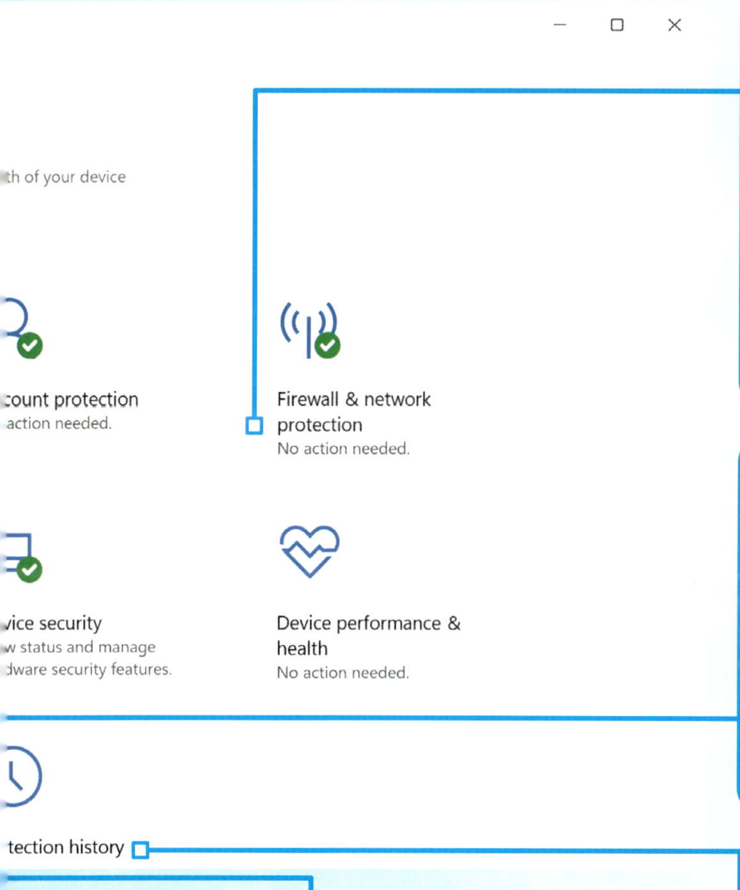


## Firewall & Network Protection

Windows Security includes three firewalls, for: Domain network, Private network and Public network. You can turn each of these firewalls on or off at will, although you will normally only be connected to one type of network at a time (if you are at home, usually a Private network).

## Device Security

Despite the title, this isn't really a hub for device security. You can learn more about Core isolation (virtualisation- based security) and enable the memory-integrity feature, helping to prevent malicious attacks to core, high-security processes. Note: The exact options here can vary depending on device.

## Family Options

The Family options feature in Windows Security provides you with easy access to tools for managing your children's digital life. Use Family options to help keep your children's devices clean and up to date with the latest version of Windows 11 as well as protecting your kids when they're online.

## Protection History

The Protection History option really speaks for itself. In here you will find a history of all the actions and recommendations that the Windows Security system has discovered. You can look through the history and see if any trends form, so you'll know what to avoid in the future.

# Manage Disk Partitions

Disk partitioning is the creation of one or more separate regions on a PC hard disk (hard drive) and all modern drives need at least one partition to begin storing files. A partition could be the size of the whole drive or just a tiny part of it.

## System Imaging

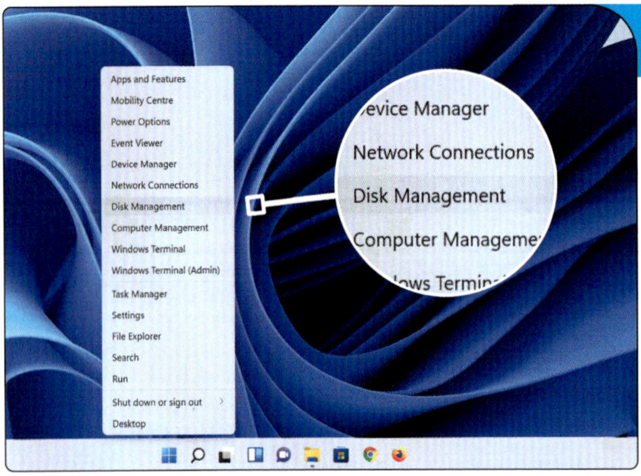


### Step 1

The first thing you need to do is find the Disk Management tool. The easiest way to open the tool is to use the hidden Start button menu. Right-click on the Start menu button and select Disk Management from the menu that appears. There are several system tools here, so it is a useful trick to know.

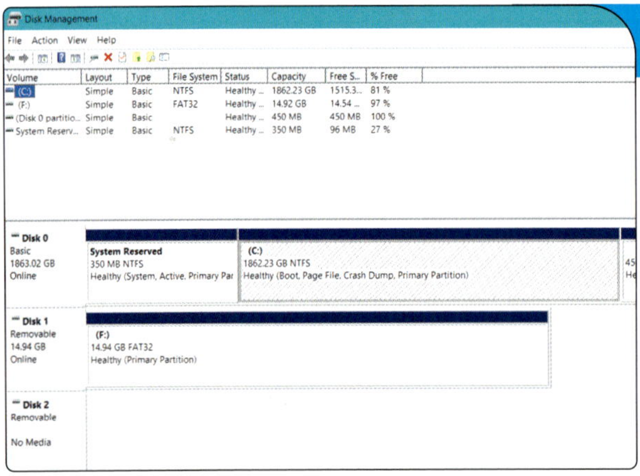


### Step 2

The Disk Management tool shows all of your internal and removable drives (even USB flash drives, etc.) along with details of the capacity and current amount of space being used. Depending how your hard drive was initially configured, you will see one or more partitions in place.

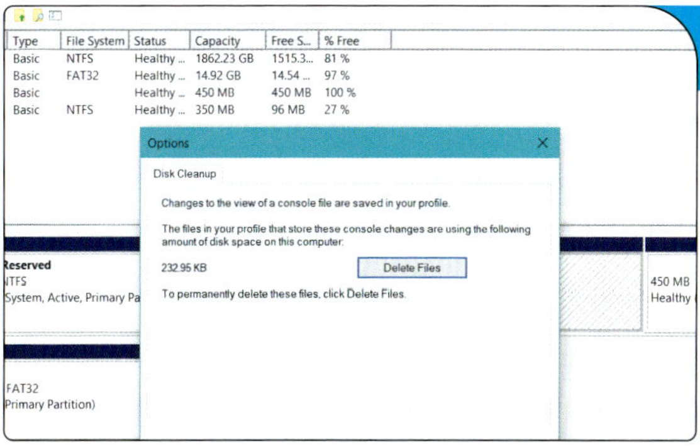


## Step 3

You can use the seemingly simple Disk Management tool to resize, create, delete and format partitions and volumes, as well as change their drive letters and all without downloading or paying for any other software. You can also simply use it to check the health of your disks.

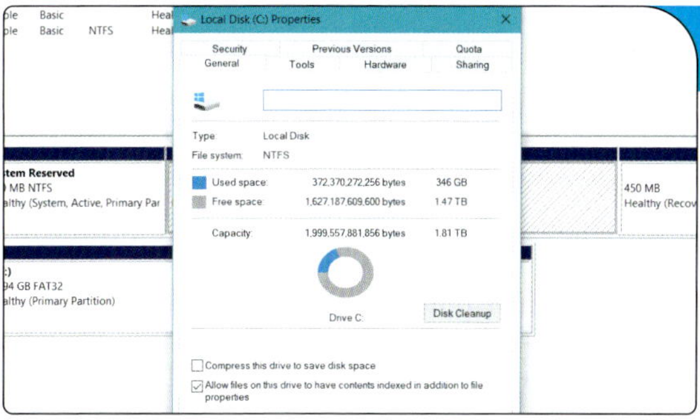


## Step 4

The tool shows partitions and volumes, which are similar but different. A partition is space that's set aside on a disk separate from the other space on that disk. A volume is a partition that's been formatted with a file system. We will mainly be talking about volumes in this guide.

# Resizing a Volume

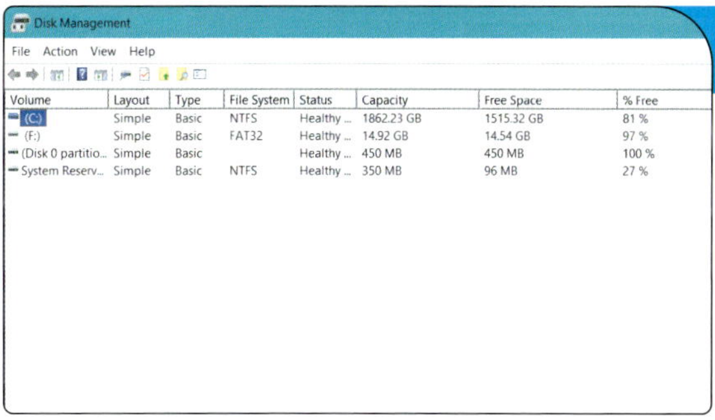


## Step 1

You will need to make sure that there is enough free space on the drive before you can shrink a volume. For example, if you have a 500GB volume which has 200GB of data already stored on it, you will only be able to shrink it by a maximum of 300GB, the amount of remaining space.

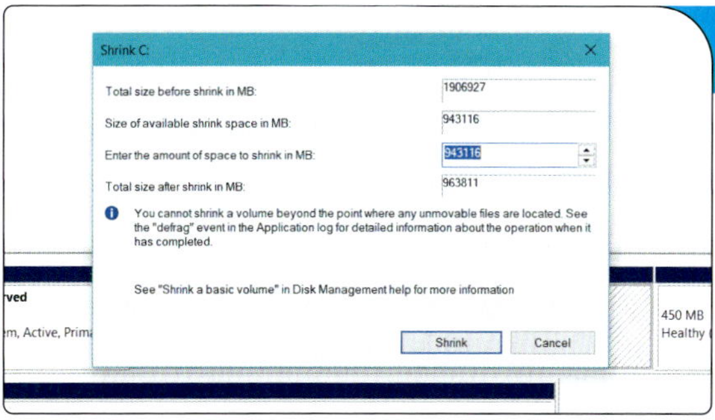


## Step 2

Right click on the volume you want to shrink in either the top panel or the bottom one and click 'Shrink volume' from the Action menu. You will then need to enter the amount you want to shrink the volume by in MB. So if you wanted to shrink it by approximately 500GB, you enter '500000MB'.

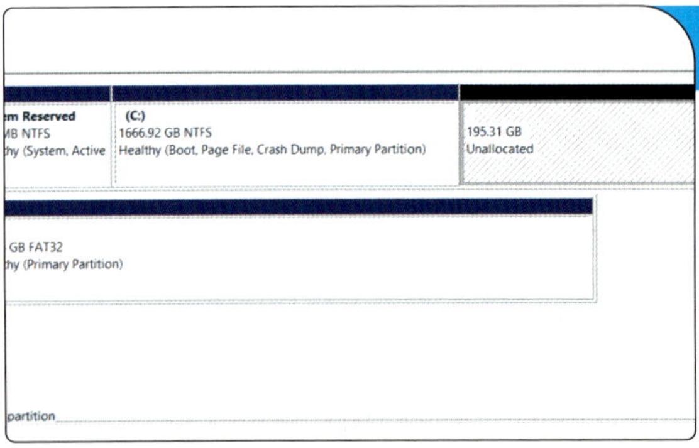


## Step 3

When you have clicked the Shrink button, you should see that the disk now contains the shrunken volume and some new, unallocated space. If desired, you could now extend the volume back into that space, by right-clicking and selecting 'Extend volume' from the Action menu.

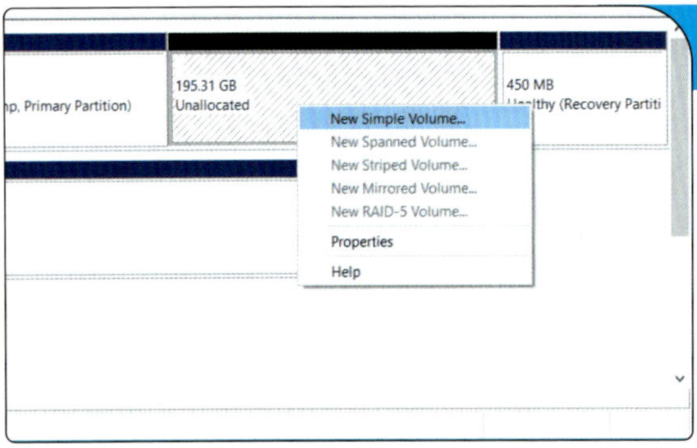


## Step 4

To create a new volume in that unallocated space, right-click on it and select New Simple Volume from the Action menu. In the New Simple Volume Wizard window, click Next to get started. Specify the volume size you want to create and then assign it a drive letter on the next screen.

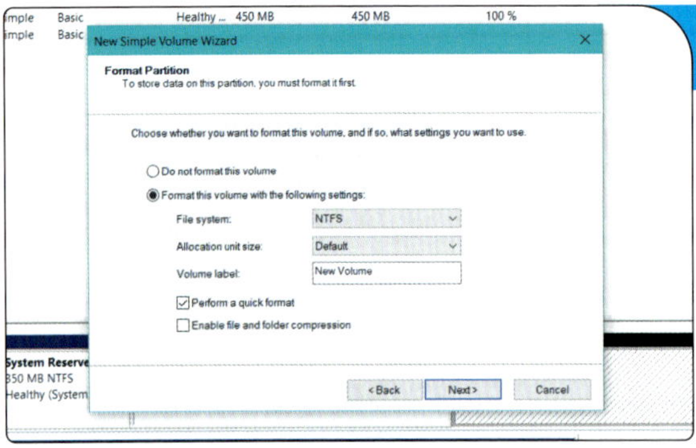


## Step 5

You will then need to decide whether to format the partition. You will need to format it before you can begin using it but if you are planning on installing a second operating system, in order to dual-boot, you will need to let the new OS format the partition during its installation.

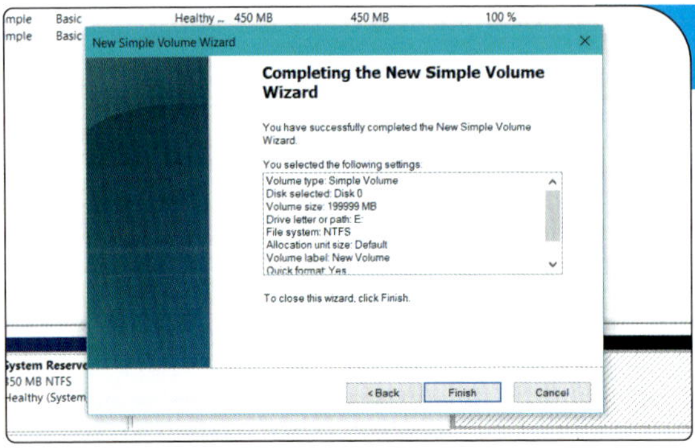


## Step 6

Otherwise, go ahead and format the disk; pick a file system to use and assign a volume label. Click Next when you're ready and then click the Finish button; Windows will now start to create the volume and, if you chose to, format it. When finished, you will see your new volume listed.

# Optimise RAM Usage

**Adding RAM, or Random Access Memory, is a good way to give your PC an instant boost but before you go to the expense and trouble of installing new RAM modules, it is worth checking what is using your existing RAM and whether it can be optimised.**

## Checking Memory and RAM Usage

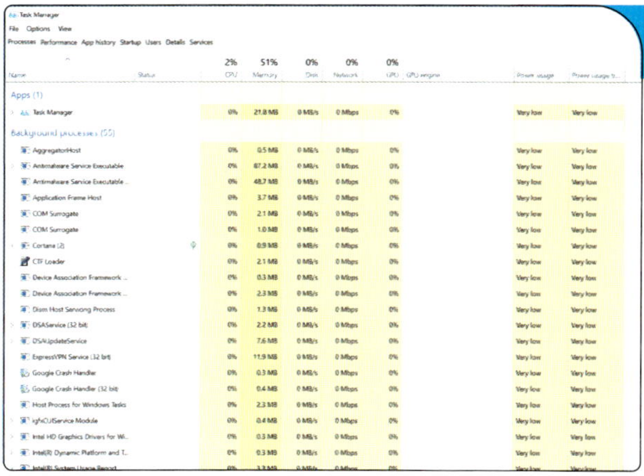

### Step 1

To check up on your RAM, you need to open the Task Manager. Press Ctrl + Alt + Delete on the keyboard and then select Task Manager from the list that appears. If Task Manager opens showing just a simple list of tasks, click the More details button to see a more advanced view.

### Step 2

Click the Performance tab at the top and then the Memory tab on the left side. You can now see how much you have in total and then check the graph to see how much RAM is being used. Try opening a few different apps while Task Manager is open, to see RAM usage increase or change.

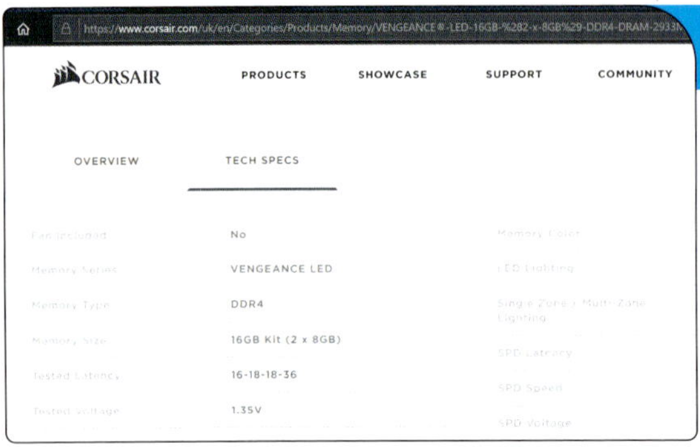


## Step 3

If it seems like most of your available RAM is regularly being used, and if less than 8GB is installed, consider adding more RAM. You can find out what kind of RAM your PC model uses by looking at the memory info in Task Manager. Then visit the PC manufacturer's website for more specific info.

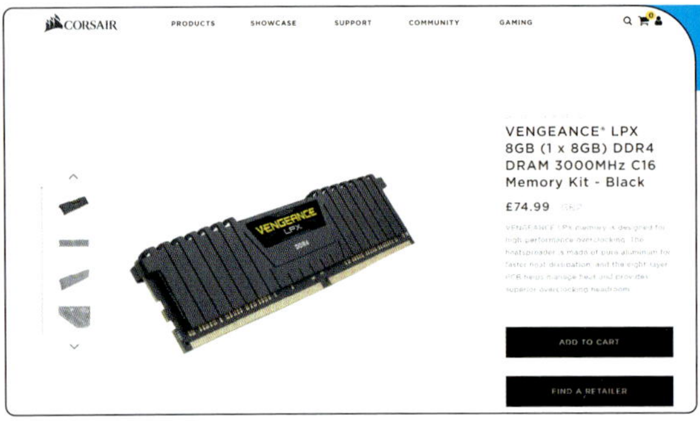


## Step 4

Windows 11 can run on a PC with 4 GB of RAM, as per the specifications from Microsoft, but in reality you will want at least 8GB for regular use. If you can afford to double this to 16GB, you will improve performance and also add more time to the long-term lifespan of your computer.

# Using Windows ReadyBoost

## Step 1

ReadyBoost is a way to boost memory performance by creating an extra memory cache on an external USB-connected drive, such as a flash drive. You will need a USB drive with at least 500MB of free space and a high data transfer rate. A USB 3.0 drive can peak at a data rate of 600MB/s.

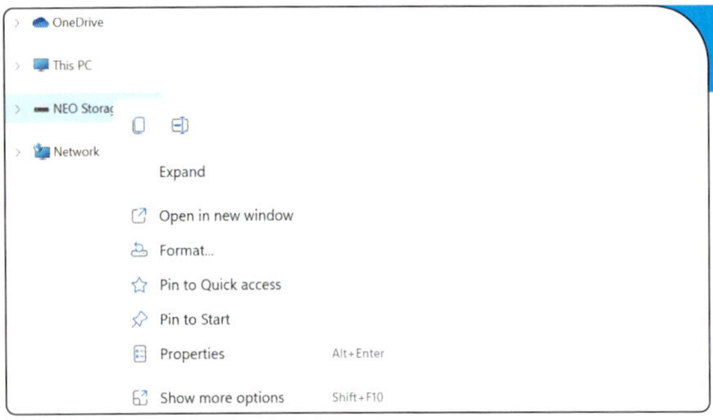


## Step 2

Insert the drive into a free USB port on your PC and then open the File Explorer. Right-click on the name of the drive in the left-hand sidebar and select Properties from the action menu. Be aware that computers with a solid-state drive (SSD) installed, will not be able to take advantage of ReadyBoost.

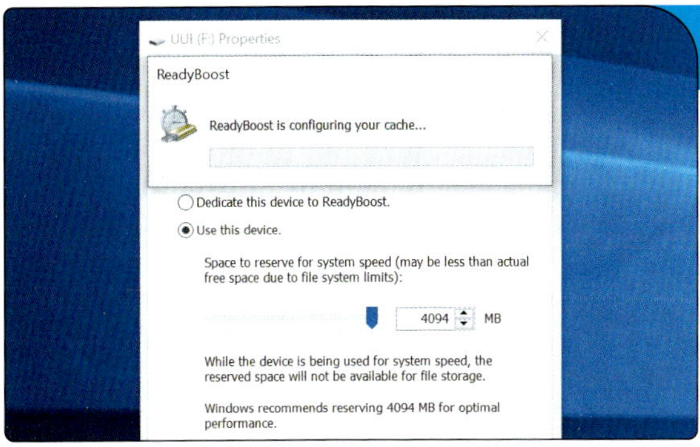


## Step 3

Select the ReadyBoost tab, then select 'Use this device'. Windows 11 determines if the device can use ReadyBoost. If it is not able to use the feature, it will let you know. Windows will then determine how much free space to assign to memory. Click Ok to reserve this space on the connected drive.

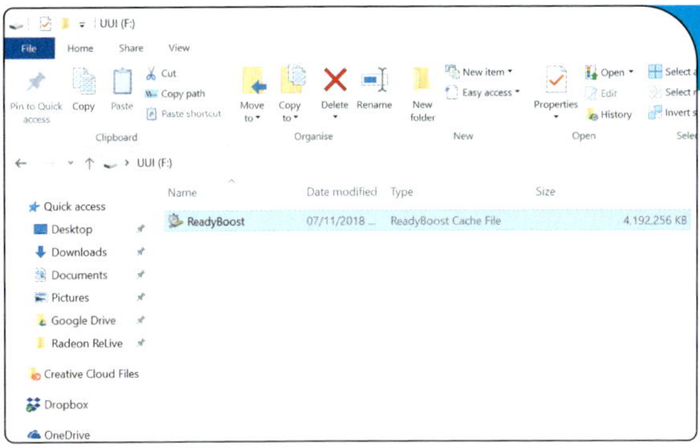


## Step 4

If you look at the contents of the drive in File Explorer, you will see a file called ReadyBoost.sfcache. This file shows how much space is reserved for ReadyBoost. If you don't have a USB flash drive handy, you can sometimes use a smartphone, connected via USB, as a temporary ReadyBoost drive.

# Change Paging File Size

**In the search box on the taskbar, type 'advanced system' and then select 'View advanced system settings'. In System Properties, on the Advanced tab, select Settings in the Performance area, and then select the Advanced tab > Change in the Virtual memory area.**

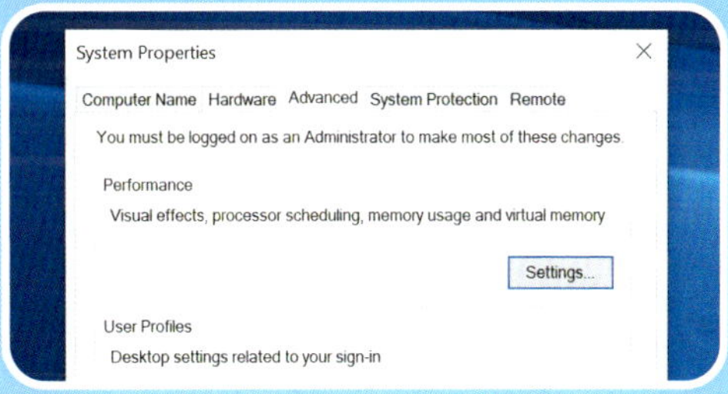


**In Performance Options, Clear the 'Automatically manage paging file size for all drives' check box. Select Custom size, then enter an initial size (in MB) and maximum size in the corresponding boxes. Select Set > OK and then restart your PC by selecting the Start button > Power > Restart.**

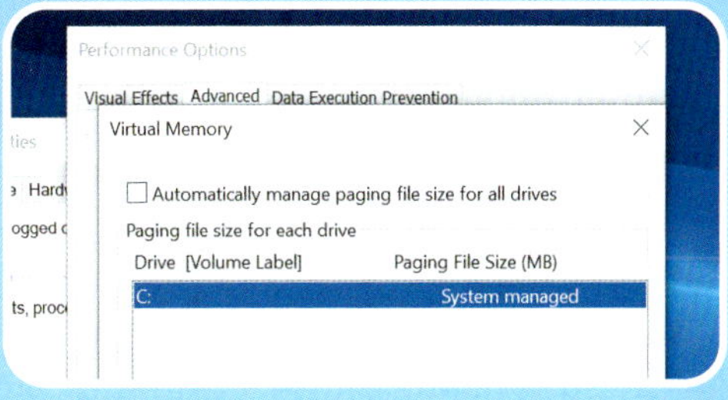

# Create a System Image

Backing up your files is perfectly fine, but in the event of having to wipe your hard drive and start again, getting everything back in order can be time-consuming. However, creating a system image means you can almost instantly restore the entire system.

## System Imaging

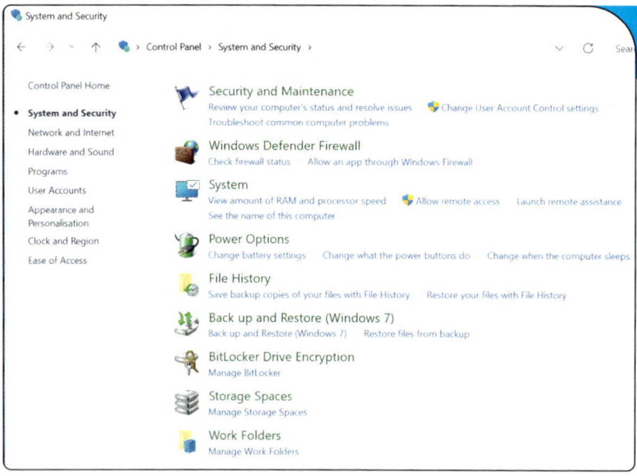


### Step 1

To begin, click on the Windows Start button and start typing 'control panel', then click on the Control Panel app. From there, go to System and Security > Backup and Restore (Windows 7). Odd as it sounds, it still uses the old Windows 7 backup technology here.

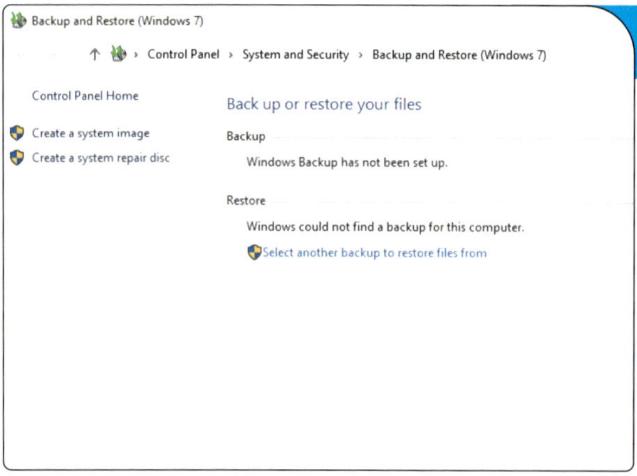


### Step 2

This launches a new window, the Backup and Restore (Windows 7) console. Microsoft has kept this feature intact through Windows 8.1, 10 and 11, purely due to compatibility support for backups created under older versions of the OS. To the left, there are two links, click on the Create a system image link.

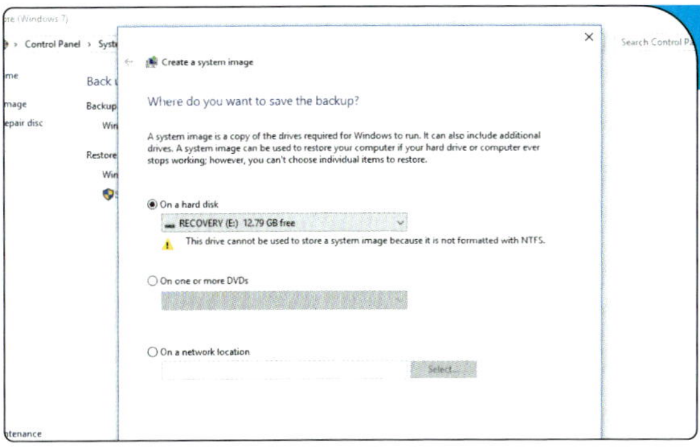


## Step 3

Windows now scans your system for a drive capable of housing the system image files. You may need to make some changes to any drives according to what messages you get back from the scan. In this example, the drive we're using needs to be formatted as NTFS before Windows 11 can use it.

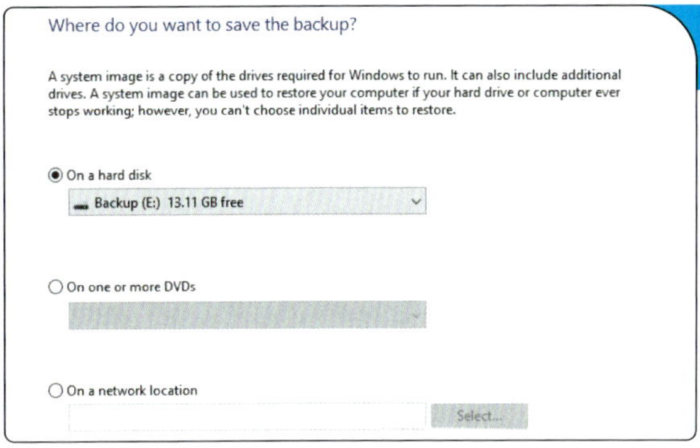


## Step 4

Providing you've met the requirements, you're offered a choice of to where the system image can be written. A drive is the quickest solution when it comes to restoring the image, but you can opt for DVDs; it depends on the size of the image as to how many DVDs you need. You can even select a network location.

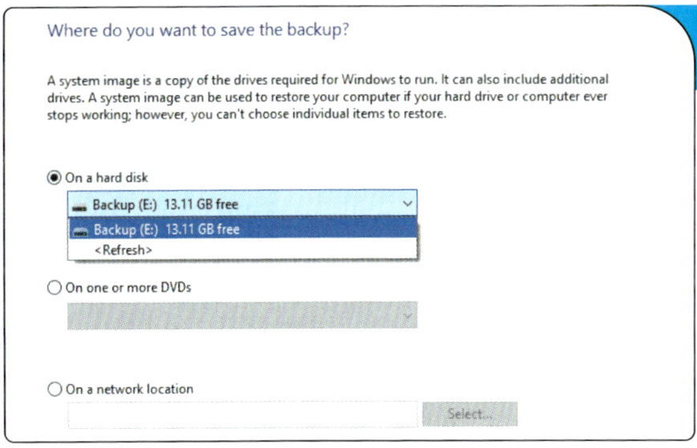


## Step 5

For this example, let's use an internal second hard drive. Make sure that the correct drive (it could be a high capacity USB stick or even a portable USB hard drive) is selected, and then click the Next button to continue the process.

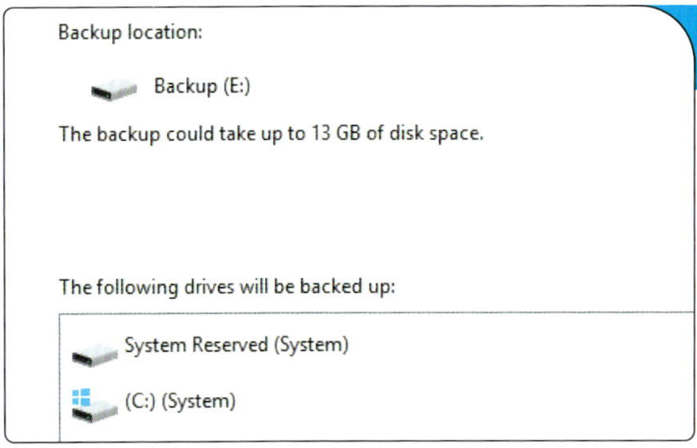


## Step 6

The next window displays the drives included in the system imaging process. In this example, the C:\ drive, the System drive and the System Reserved partition are all to be backed up. When it comes to restoring the system, you'll need both partitions for Windows 11 to be able to boot up correctly.

## Step 7

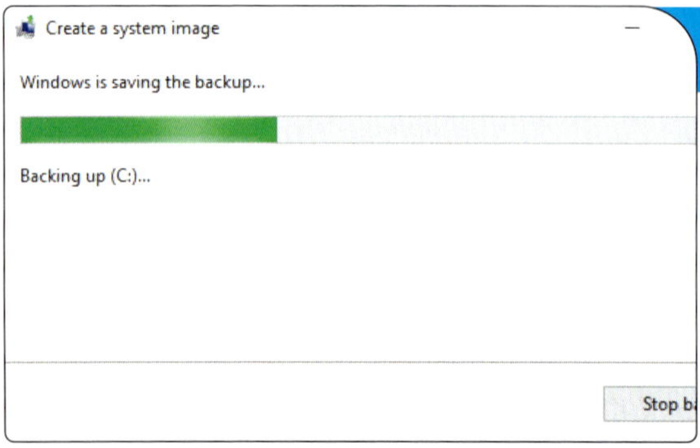


When you're ready to continue, click the Start Backup button. This begins the imaging process, which can take some time depending on the amount of space used on the C:\ drive and the speed of the drive to which you're writing. Allocate ample time if you're writing to DVDs.

## Step 8

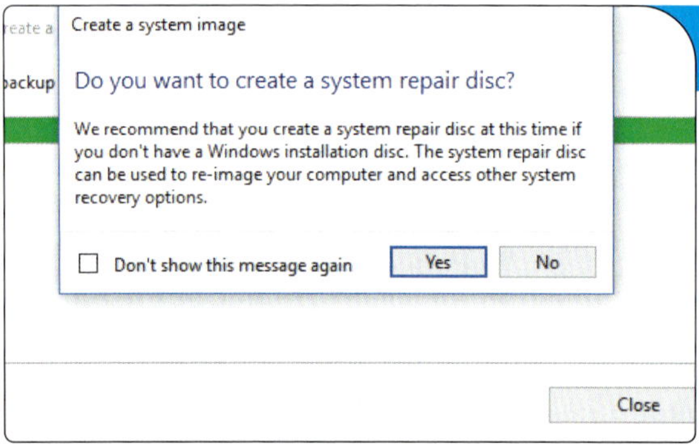


Once the process is complete, Windows will then ask you to create a System Repair Disc. This disc will allow you to boot into the environment, where you are then able to launch the system image restore.

## Step 9

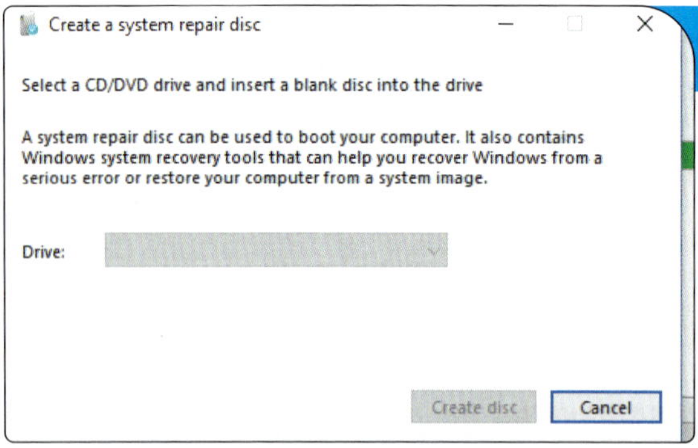


If you click Yes to creating the System Repair Disc, you need to make sure you have a blank DVD to hand. Follow the on-screen instructions and click on the Create Disc button to burn the repair files to the disc.

## Step 10

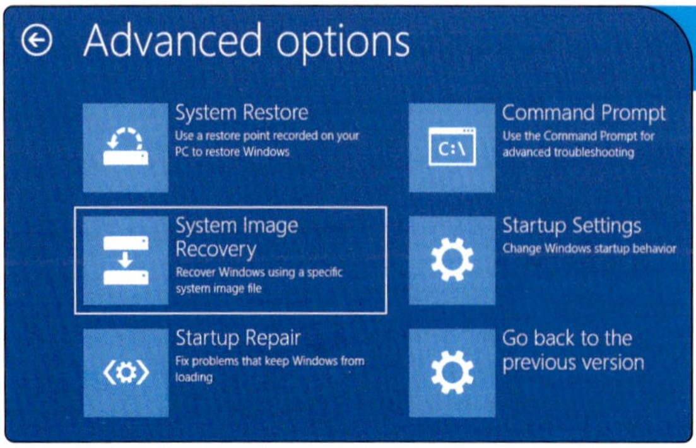


Should you need to restore Windows 11 from the system image, you can boot into the System Repair Disc and select the System Image Recovery option from within the Advanced Options of the Trouble Shoot menu. Follow the instructions, and within minutes, Windows 11 is back as it was when the system image was taken.

# Creating a Recovery Drive

A recovery drive is a useful way to ensure that you don't lose everything on your PC in the event of a critical malfunction. It can help you troubleshoot and fix problems, even if the PC won't start as it normally would. All you need is a blank, formatted USB flash drive.

## Protecting Your PC and Files

### Step 1

The first thing you need to do is find a USB drive that is large enough and then make sure it is ready to be used. The USB drive you decide to use won't be able to be used for anything else like storing other files, etc. so make sure it is a spare, or bought specifically for the task.

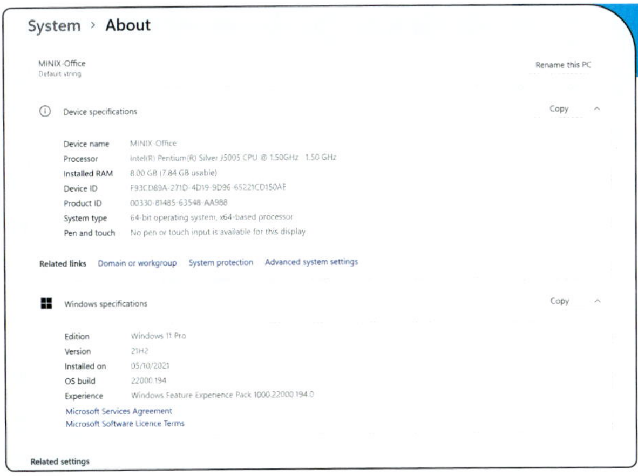


### Step 2

A basic Windows 11 recovery file will be less than 500MB but if you choose to include system files in the backup (recommended), so you can use it to reinstall Windows, you will need much more space. A basic recovery drive can be as small as 1GB but a full recovery drive needs to be at least 8GB.

## Step 3

Your USB drive needs to be wiped of everything currently on it before the recovery drive is created. You can do this during the set up process later or you can format it yourself right now: a useful thing to know how to do. Insert your USB drive into a free USB slot on your computer.

## Step 4

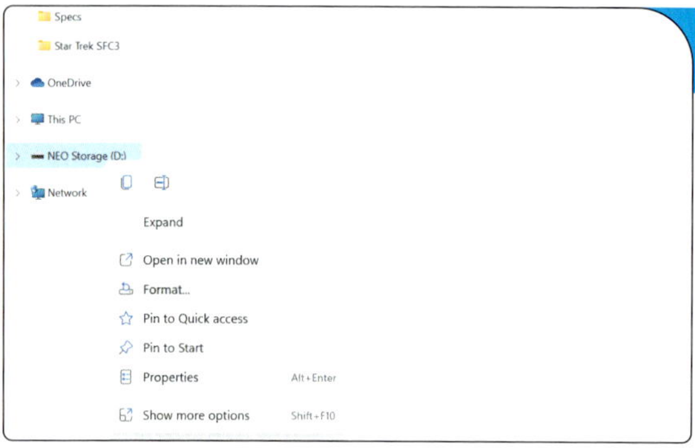


Open the File Explorer on your computer and you should see the USB flash drive listed in the sidebar. It will probably be labelled as the (E:) or (F:) drive. Right-click on the drive label and select Format from the action menu. Leave the settings as default (should be FAT32) and then click Start.

## Step 5

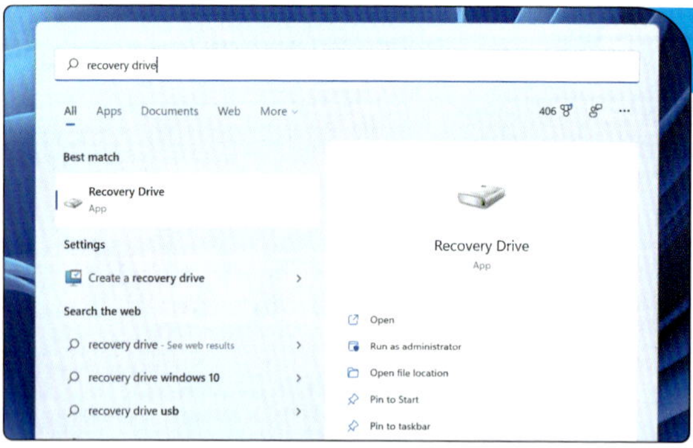


You should now be ready to create your recovery drive. In the search field, type "Recovery Drive" and select the Recovery Drive app result. In newer versions of Windows 11, you might also be able to find the Recovery Drive in the main apps list, opened by clicking the Start menu button.

## Step 6

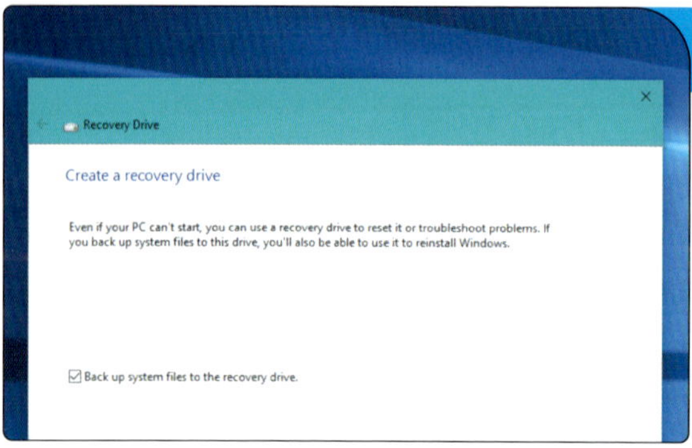


Allow the software to "make changes to this PC" and the setup wizard will open. This first screen is where you choose whether you want to back up system files with the recovery drive, so you can use it to reinstall Windows 11. If you do, tick the checkbox and then click Next.

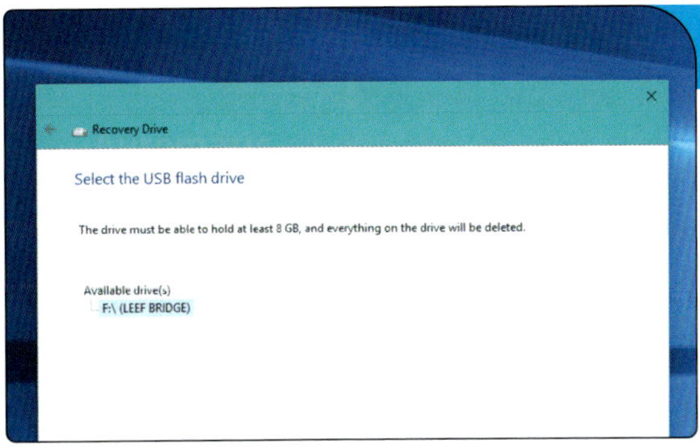


## Step 7

After a few moments, you will be asked to select the USB flash drive you wish to use. If you only have one USB drive inserted, it will be the only one shown and will be automatically selected. You are reminded again how much storage space the drive needs, and that all existing data will be wiped.

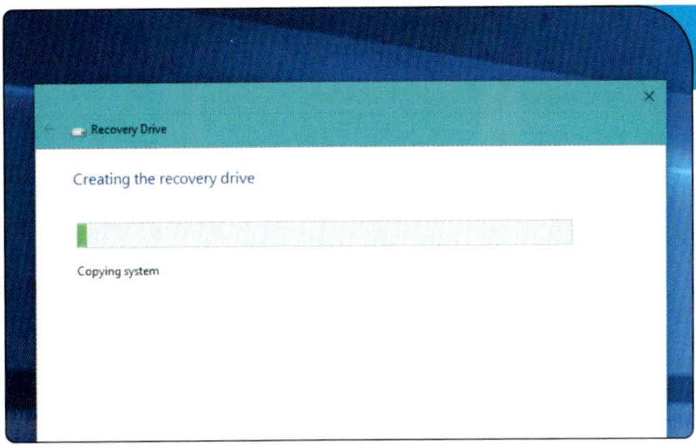


## Step 8

Click Create on the next screen and the process will begin. This may take a while to complete, so go make a coffee and leave it to run. A progress bar shows how far along it is, should you need to check. Do not remove the USB drive, or turn off your computer, before the process finishes.

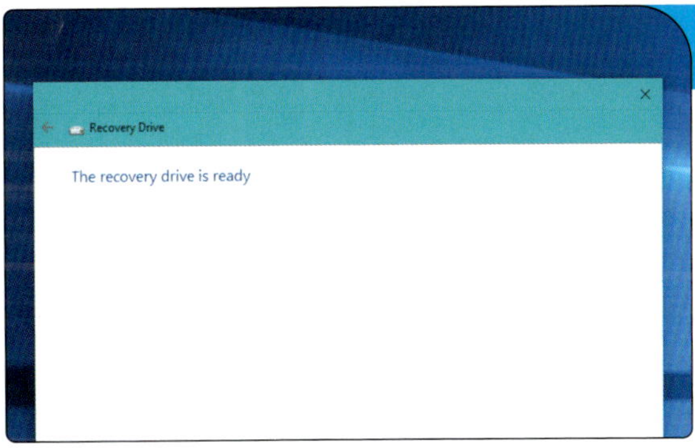


## Step 9

When the process is complete, you should be prompted to delete the recovery partition on your PC, to save some space; as long as you plan to keep your recovery drive, this is safe to do. If you are not sure, you can leave the recovery partition in place; it can be deleted at a later date if you wish.

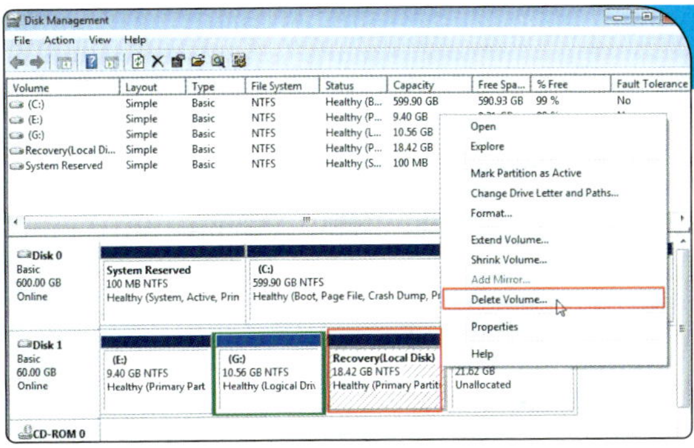


## Step 10

If you did not already have a recovery partition on your computer, you won't see this step. You will simply be informed that the recovery drive is ready, and to click Finish. Remove the USB drive from your computer and put it somewhere safe. It is a good idea to label the drive so it is not reused.

# Fix Wireless Networks

**It's frustrating when you're browsing YouTube videos or playing online games, only to find that you have no Internet connection. If the same problem occurs when least needed, it can cause you to panic. Try these solutions to try and fix the issue.**

## Make Sure Wi-Fi is On

If you are trying to connect wirelessly, check that Wi-Fi hasn't somehow been switched off: click the Start button, select Settings > Network & Internet > Wi-Fi. Next, select "Show available networks" and if your network appears in the list, select it, then select Connect. If using a laptop, make sure the physical Wi-Fi switch (if there is one), is turned on. An indicator light usually shows when it's on or off. Again, if using a laptop (or Windows 11 tablet), check to see that Flight mode is turned off: select the Start button, then select Settings > Network & Internet > Flight mode and if it's on, turn it off.

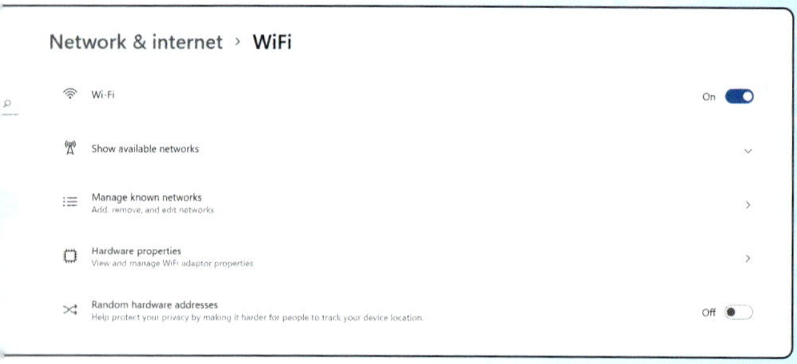


## Restart Your Modem or Router

If you've never experienced network problems before, you may never have touched your modem or wireless router, however, occasionally problems arise with its configuration and it needs to be reset to establish a new connection to your Internet service provider (ISP). When you do this, take into consideration that everyone connected to your Wi-Fi network will be temporarily disconnected.

**Step 1:** Unplug the power cable for the router and/or wireless modem from the power source.

**Step 2:** Some modems have a backup battery, if so, remove this and wait around 30 seconds.

**Step 3:** Replace the battery and plug the modem/router back into the power socket. The lights on the modem will blink for a few minutes as it reconnects.

**Step 4:** Wait until the status lights on the box stop blinking (if any fail to come on or light up red, there is another problem) and then try again to connect your PC to the network.

# Create a Wireless Network Report

With the simplest attempts at a fix out of the way, it is time to dig a little deeper by generating a Wireless Network Report. This takes a bit of work with the Command Prompt, but is actually nothing to be scared of and quite simple if you follow these steps. Generating the report creates a HTML file that you can open in your web browser (even with no Internet connection). The report will contain a lot of information that will most likely be hard to decipher, but the main thing you need to look out for are the Connection Successes/Failures, where information about network connection attempts will be shown.

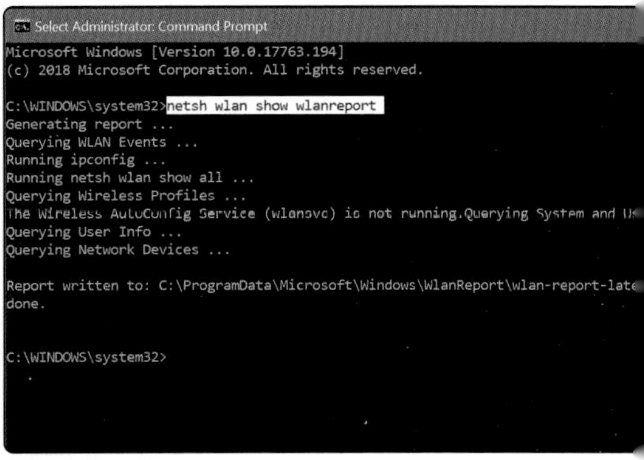


**Step 1:** Click in the Search box on the taskbar and type "Command Prompt", right-click on the Command Prompt listing in the search results and then select "Run as administrator" from the action menu.

**Step 2:** In the Command Prompt window, type netsh wlan show wlanreport.

**Step 3:** "At the bottom of the Command Prompt it shows where you can find the generated report on your PC (e.g. C:\programdata\Microsoft\Windows\WlanReport.html).

# Perform a Ping Trace

To check if the problem is with your ISP or router, rather than your PC or software, you can perform a ping test. This tests to see if data can be sent and received over the network. If the ping test is successful, but you cannot connect to the Internet on your PC, it means there is more likely a problem at the ISP end and you will need to contact them for help.

**Step 1:** In the Search box on the taskbar, type "Command Prompt", select it in the results and then select "Run as administrator".

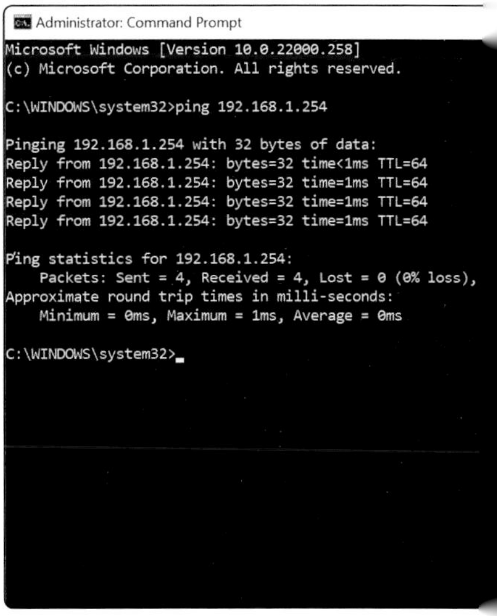


**Step 2:** At the Command Prompt, type ipconfig and look for the IP address listed next to Default Gateway (something like 192.168.1.254).

**Step 3:** Now type: "ping <Default Gateway IP>" and press Enter. It should look something like "ping 192.168.1.254".

A successful result should be something like this:
Reply from 192.168.1.254: bytes=32 time=5ms TTL=64
Reply from 192.168.1.254: bytes=32 time=5ms TTL=64
Reply from 192.168.1.254: bytes=32 time=5ms TTL=64
Reply from 192.168.1.254: bytes=32 time=5ms TTL=64

Ping statistics for 192.168.1.254: Packets: Sent = 4, Received = 4, Lost = 0 (0% loss), Approximate round trip times in milli-seconds: Minimum = 4ms, Maximum = 5ms, Average = 4ms

# What is Encryption?

**To better understand what encryption is, it's worth taking a moment to learn about its origins, how it has developed over the years and how it now applies to every aspect of our modern-day communications.**

The word encryption comes from the ancient Greek word Kryptos, which means hidden or secret. Interestingly, the practise of hiding messages from others can be traced back to early Egyptian scribes who inserted non-standard hieroglyphs within other communications in order to hide the message from casual viewers. According to historians, the Spartans used strips of leather engraved with messages. When the strips were read, they were meaningless, but when wrapped around a staff of a certain diameter, the characters would be decipherable.

Of course, the modern forms of encryption are far more advanced, but the overall core concept has remained the same: to be able to send a message to others without anyone else being able to decipher it. However, modern encryption now requires more than merely sending coded messages. Not only is confidentiality required, encryption must perform a level of authentication, so the origin of the communication can be verified; integrity of the communications, where both the sender and those who receive the communication can be sure that the message hasn't been altered in between; and some form of nonrepudiation, where the sender cannot deny having sent the communication in the first place. During the early digital age, the only users of encryption were the government and military. As such, between them they created a set of algorithms and standards to protect the communication on the battlefield and from one government agency to the next. These algorithms grew in complexity as technology advanced and it wasn't long before the military-based forms of encryption were being used in commercial modes of communications. Within a few short years, bank transfers, cash withdrawals and data sent to and from modems began utilising these new protocols to protect sensitive information. Today we're regularly seeing and using devices that boast 'military-grade 256-bit AES' forms of encryption, a standard that is regarded as nearly impossible to break without spending billions on specialist hardware and software. In plain English, the modern form of encryption takes data and passes it through an algorithm together with a key. This creates a garbled file of characters that can only be read if the correct key is applied to decrypt the data. Algorithms today are divided into two categories: symmetric and asymmetric. Symmetric key cyphers use the same key to both encrypt and decrypt data. The most popular symmetric cypher is AES (Advanced Encryption Standard), developed by the military and government to protect communications and data. This is a quick form of decryption that requires the sender to exchange the key used to encrypt the data with the recipient before they're able to read it. Asymmetric key cyphers are also known as public-key cryptography and utilise two mathematically linked keys, public and private. The public key can be shared with everyone and is usually generated by software or provided by a designated authority. The private key is something that's usually only known by the individual user. Interestingly both types of keys can be applied, where one user has a public key and another a private key, which can be combined to form a shared encryption level. These keys are many characters in length, making it nigh impossible for someone to Brute Force hack them. The Brute

**Forms of encryption can be traced as far back as ancient Egypt, using non-standard hieroglyphs.**

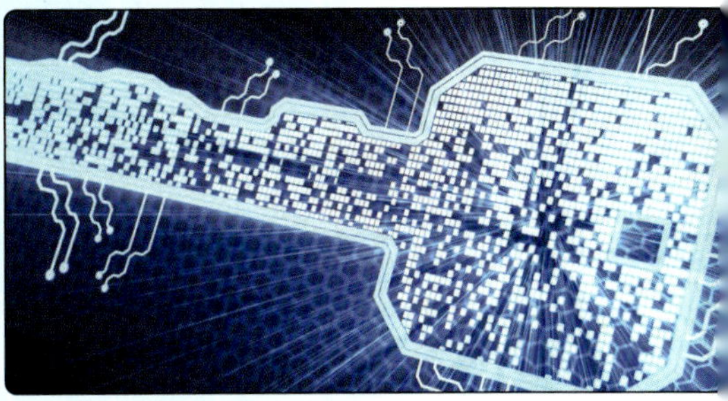

**Making data impossible to read is just one step; you also need the key to decrypt that data**

Force method involves using a program on a computer to try every possible combination of a key until the correct one is found. In the case of the 256-bit encryption, it would take $2^{256}$ different combinations to break the key. If you were able to force one trillion keys per second, it would still take you somewhere in the region of $10^{57}$ years in order to crack 256-bit encryption. However, a powerful computer can probably manage around two billion calculations per second, so in theory, it would take $9.2^{50}$ years for your standard desktop to crack it. Keep in mind that the universe has theoretically only been in existence for $1.4^{10}$ years. Numbers this big are generally far too mind-boggling to comprehend. Suffice to say that if you're able to use 256-bit encryption for your communications or to protect your data, then you're going to be protected for at least seven times the current age of the universe.

**The universe is 14 billion years old, but it would take seven times that amount to crack 256-bit encryption.**

# Encrypting Your Laptop

Windows 11 Pro comes with Microsoft's BitLocker program to encrypt the file system; however, Windows 11 Home versions do not have this feature. Thankfully, there are many encryption programs available for download; we're using DiskCryptor in this tutorial.

## Windows 11, Under Lock and Key

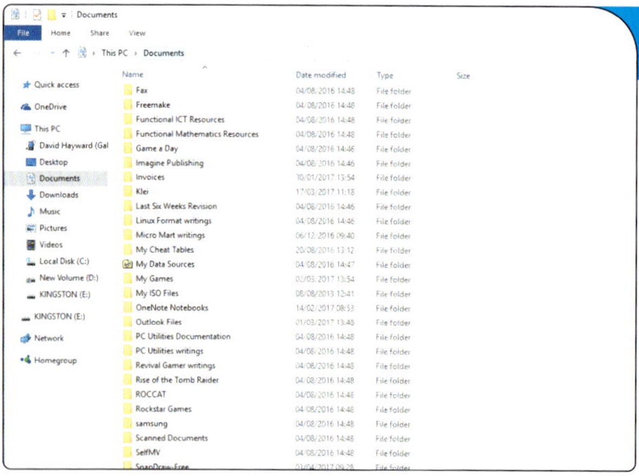


### Step 1

Encryption doesn't affect the core data, other than making it impossible to read without the decryption key. Still, it's always worth making sure you have a backup of all your data prior to any system related changes. If you normally store your work or data in the Documents folder, then start by opening it in Windows Explorer.

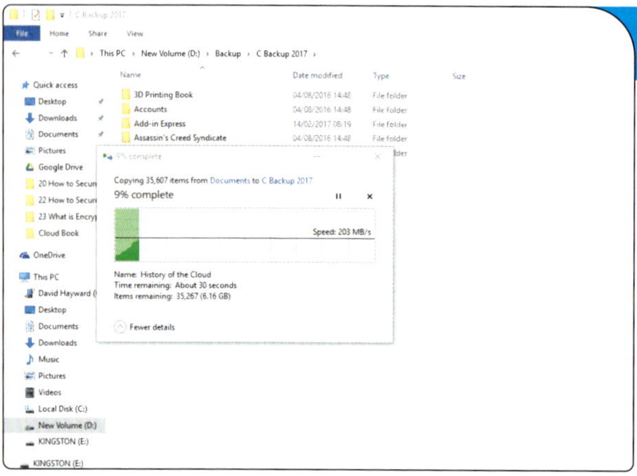


### Step 2

Press Ctrl+A to highlight all the files, then press Ctrl+C to copy them to the clipboard. Next, choose a suitable backup location – such as an external or network drive – and when ready, press Ctrl+V to paste the copied data into the new location. Then, should something go wrong, you have a recent backup of your most used data.

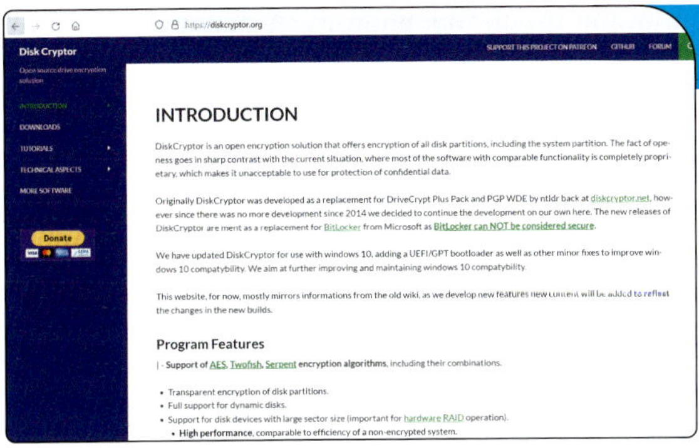


## Step 3

It's always best to save data before commencing with anything like this. It's also always worth doing (as we are), a test of the software first; on a disk that you don't mind messing up, should you get the process wrong. Let's start by navigating to the DiskCryptor homepage, at: https://diskcryptor.org/.

## Step 4

From the top-left menu, click on the Downloads link. This will tell you to get the latest version from the official GitHub page. On the GitHub page, scroll down to the Last Version Officially Released section, and expand the details to view the installation instructions and get the file. Click the Assets header to locate the file and download it.

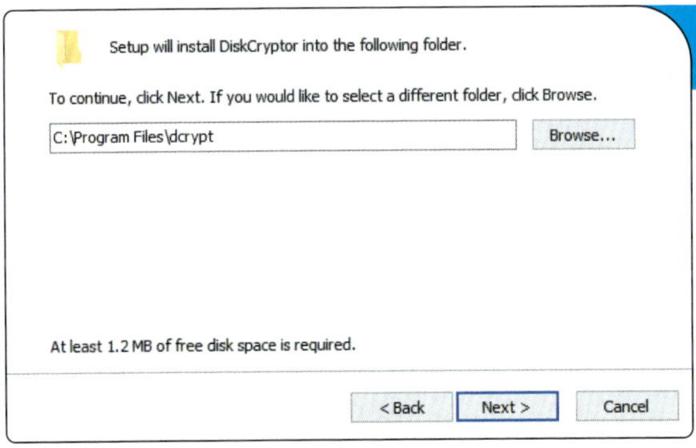


## Step 5

The dcrypt_setup.exe file should be in your Downloads folder. Double click it and select Yes to accept the Windows confirmation. With the DiskCryptor setup window open, click the Next button and accept the license agreement. Choose the default options by clicking Next. When done, click the Install button and reboot the computer.

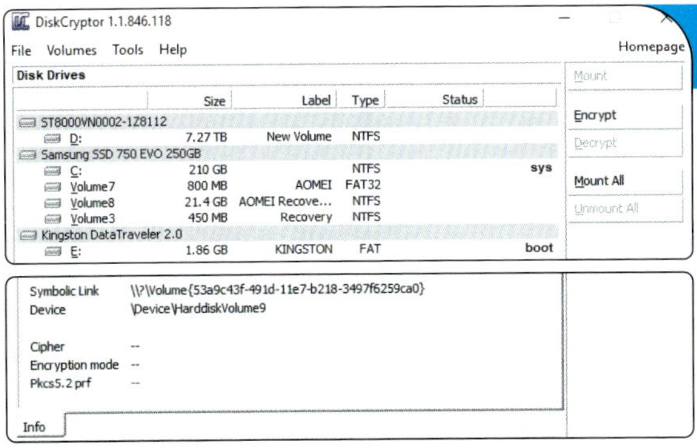


## Step 6

After a reboot, click the Windows Start button and locate the newly installed DiskCryptor program. You need to click Yes to authorise its administrative access. With DiskCryptor open you can see the list of currently installed hard drives in your system. You can click each in turn and view its information at the bottom of the DiskCryptor window.

## Step 7

Start by selecting the disk you want to encrypt. As mentioned before, in our example we're going to test this out on a USB stick. We recommend you also do this until you're comfortable with the process. With the correct drive selected, either click the Encrypt button to the right or right-click and choose Encrypt from the menu.

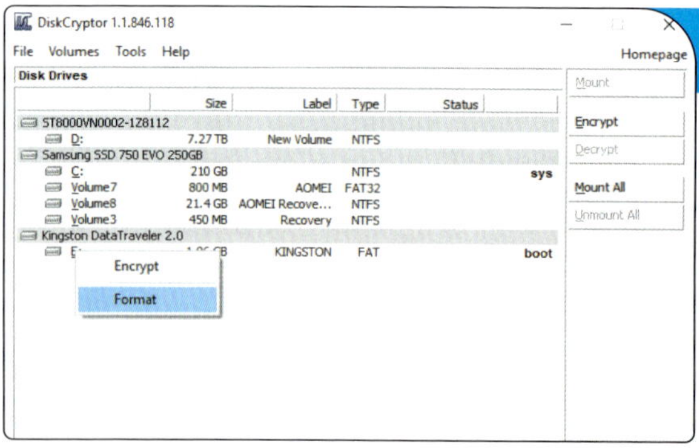


## Step 8

You're now offered a selection of available algorithms from which to choose. Click the drop-down box to view them all, however, we recommend staying with the default AES algorithm for the time being. Leave the Wipe Mode box as None and when you're ready, click the Next button.

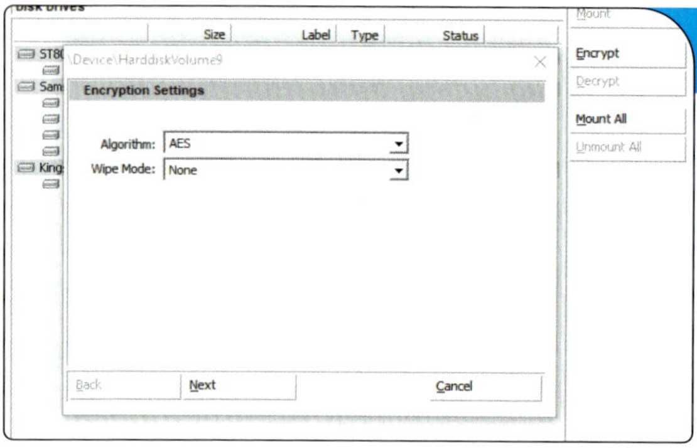


## Step 9

In the next section, choose a unique password for accessing the encrypted disk; you're notified how strong the password is. When you're ready, enter it again in the Confirm box. Click the OK box to start the encryption process.

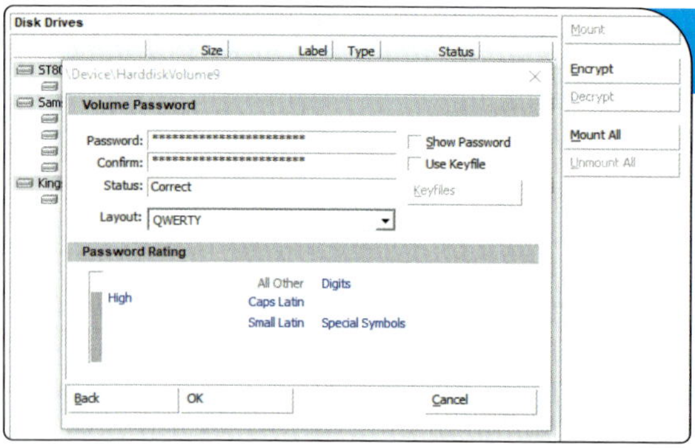


## Step 10

Depending on the size of the drive, and how much data is on it, the encryption process could take some time. When it's complete, you're notified and the selected drive will be fully encrypted, with you able to access and decrypt it using the password you set up in the previous step.

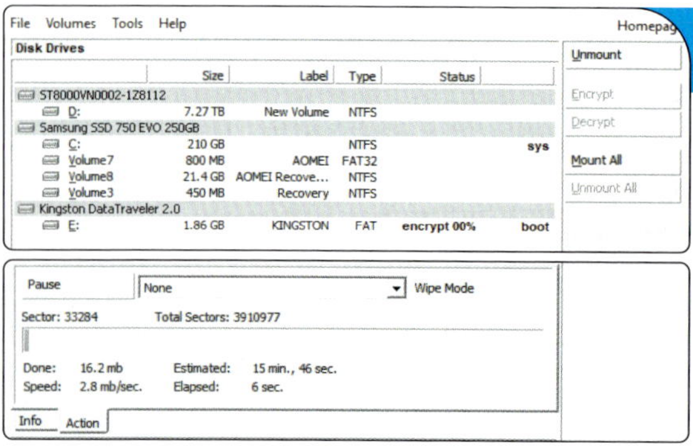

# Windows 11 Power Options

**If you use Windows 11 on a desktop PC, you might adjust the power options for how long the PC sleeps or when the display turns off when inactive. With a laptop, the Windows 11 power options should definitely be something with which you are more familiar with.**

## View, Switch, and Create Power Plans

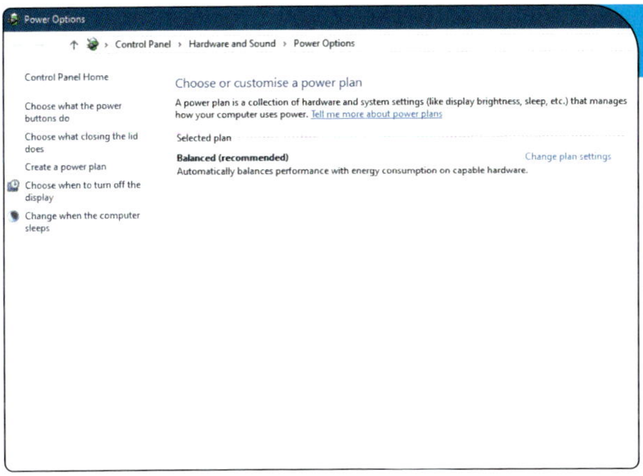


### Step 1

Click on the Windows 11 Start button and enter: Control, then click the first result, Control Panel App. From there, select System and Security > Power Options. Windows 11 will, by default, have selected the Balanced power plan. This is designed to balance performance and energy consumption, and is best for PC's that are connected to the mains.

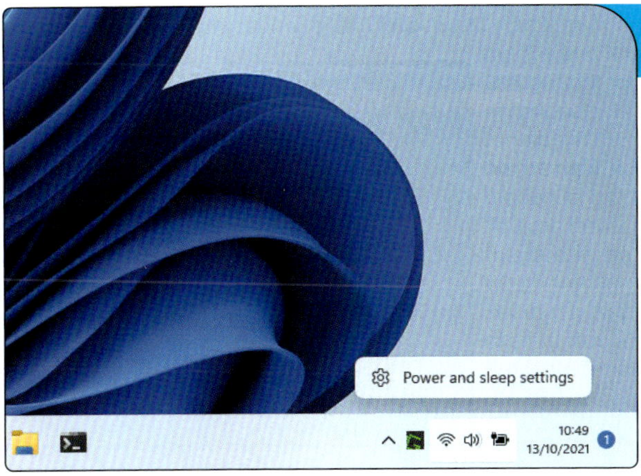


### Step 2

On a laptop, you can access the power options by right-clicking on battery indicator in the taskbar tools. There are two other, default power plans alongside Balanced; Power Saver is designed to reduce energy use by scaling back performance when possible. Good for laptops using battery power.

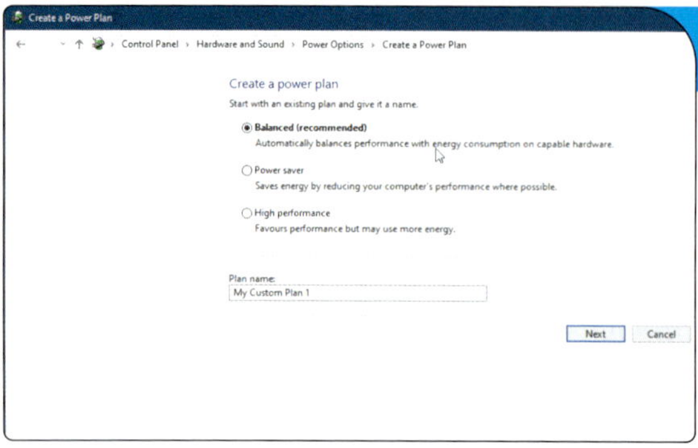


## Step 3

The High Performance power plan is, as the name suggests, best for overall performance, but will use more power and is unsuitable for use on a laptop using battery power. To switch between power plans, simply select the one you want to use. For many users, this is all you will need to do.

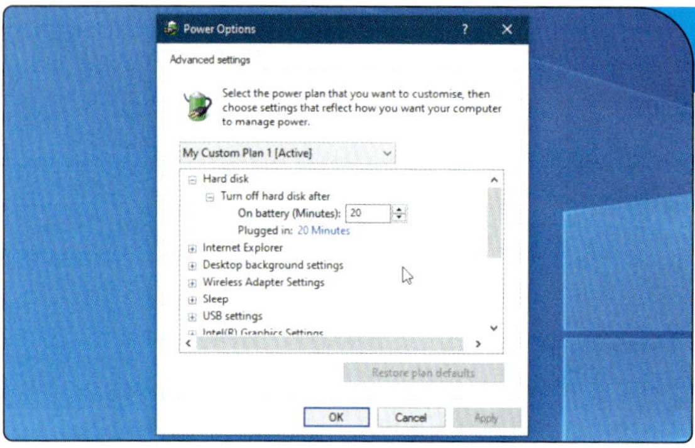


## Step 4

To customise any of the power plans, click the link next to the relevant one. The next screen will let you set when the display turns off and when the computer sleeps after inactivity. You can also click "Change Advanced Power Settings" to see settings for the hard disk, desktop, USB and processor and more.

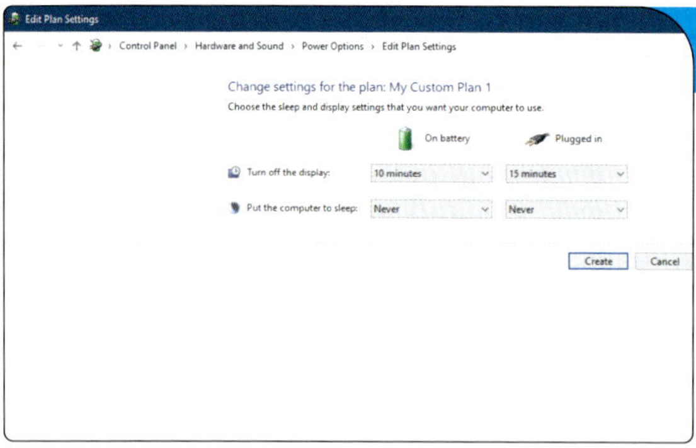


## Step 5

You should be fairly careful when changing these advanced settings, especially for things like the processor (although Windows should prevent you from making a damaging change). It is best to make small changes, and then test to see if the change has had the desired effect, before making more.

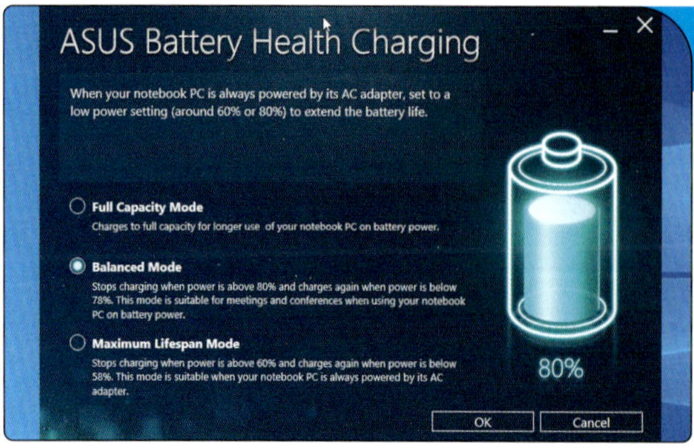


## Step 6

Your laptop might have software installed that automatically switches power plans, depending on whether it is working on battery power or plugged into the mains. The settings for this can usually be found in the taskbar tools panel at the bottom right of the screen.

# Use Your Laptop with the Lid Closed

## Step 1

When you close your laptop lid, the default setting will be for Windows 11 to go into low power sleep mode. This is obviously no good if you are using your laptop with an external monitor, as it will make the laptop unusable. To solve this problem, click on the Battery icon > power and sleep settings in the taskbar.

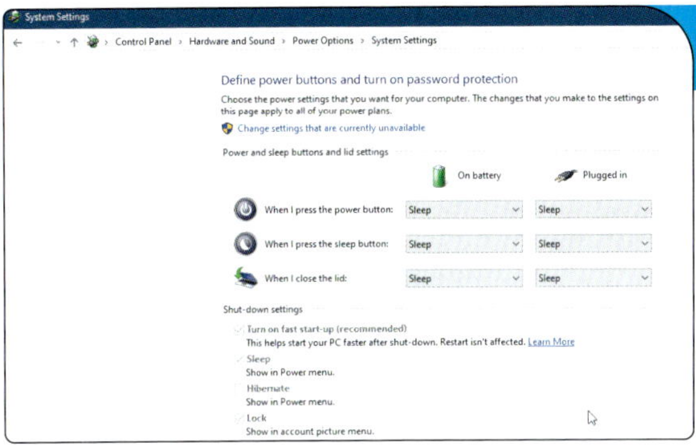


## Step 2

In the Power Options panel, look in the left sidebar for the option to "Choose what closing the lid does". Click this and you will see the Power button, Sleep button, and lid closing settings. You can change the settings for each individually. Settings include: Do Nothing, Sleep, Hibernate and Shut Down.

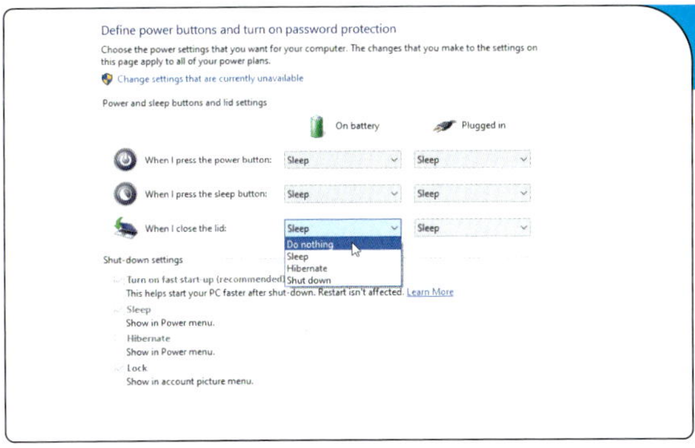


## Step 3

Use the drop-down menus to select what happens when you close the lid, both when on battery and when the laptop is plugged into the mains. When you are happy with your settings, click the Save the changes button and you will be able to use the laptop as a desktop replacement with the lid closed.

## Step 4

If you also take your laptop to different locations out of the house, it is a good idea to revert these changes. If you don't, you run the risk of having the laptop continue to run while in a bag, etc., which, if the cooling vents are covered, can be damaging to the hardware.

# Managing Your Privacy

Being in control of security on your computer is important but almost as important is being able to control your privacy settings. Microsoft launched a web-based privacy dashboard tool and this has since become available to everyone.

## The Privacy Dashboard

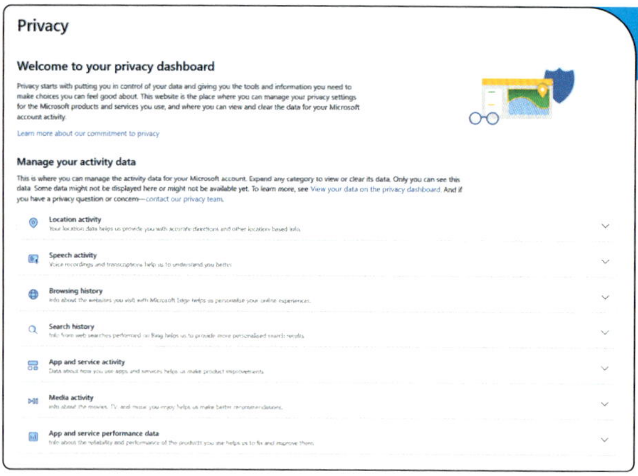


### Step 1

Open your browser and navigate to www.account.microsoft.com/privacy. If prompted, use your Microsoft account details to log in. You will be logged in to the privacy overview page that lets you quickly see what privacy settings the dashboard contains and controls.

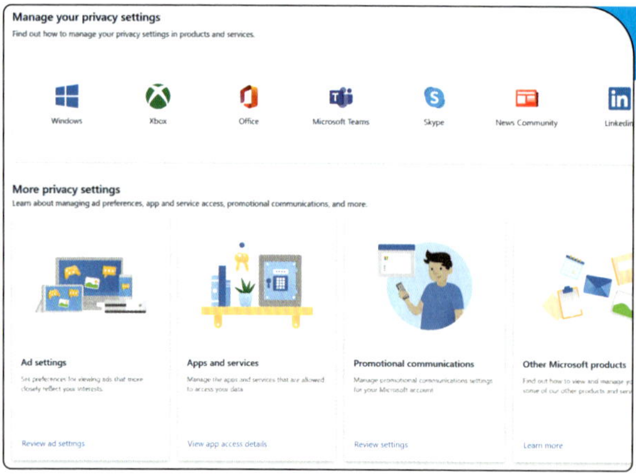


### Step 2

Along with the main Search, Browsing and Location privacy categories, if you scroll down to the bottom of the page you will see entries for everything from Apps to Xbox, with simple links to take you to the settings and options for those privacy areas.

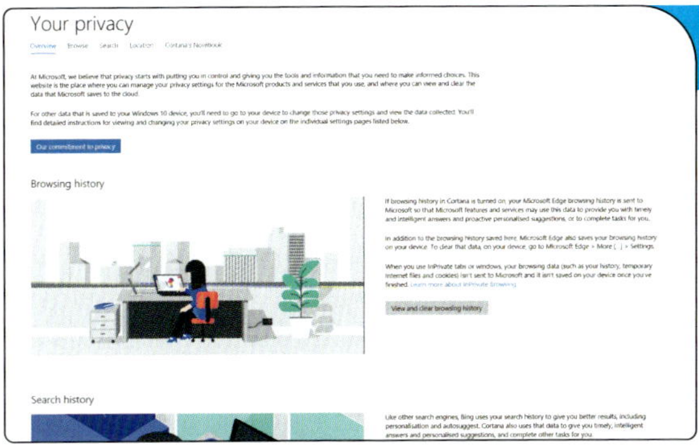


## Step 3

Click on one of the main categories, Search, Browsing, Location or Cortana, and you will see more information. This could include a list of searches you have made or websites visited (in Edge only, not other browsers), interests Cortana has saved for you or locations you have been.

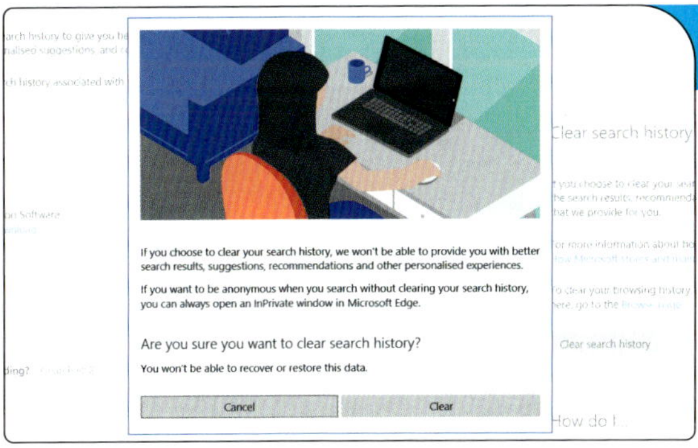


## Step 4

Each section has a Clear button, to clear browsing history, search history and so on. It is next to a warning that states clearing data will stop Windows being able to provide you with accurate and relevant information. You need to decide what is more important, privacy or recommendations.

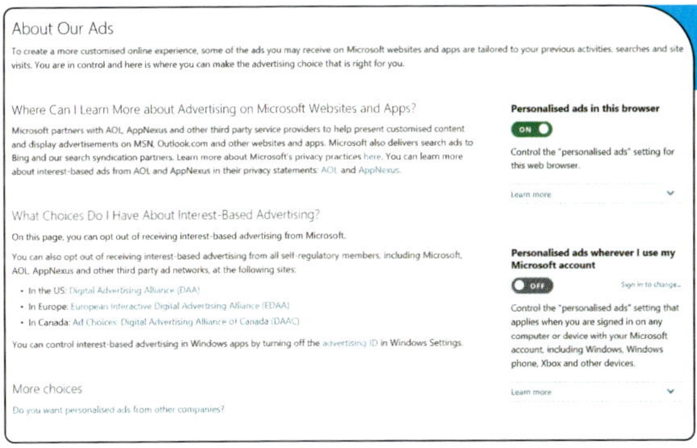


## Step 5

Another useful privacy section in the dashboard is the Advertising Preferences. This lets you control whether personalised adverts are shown to you in the Edge browser. Some of the ads you may receive on Microsoft websites and apps are tailored to your previous activities and searches.

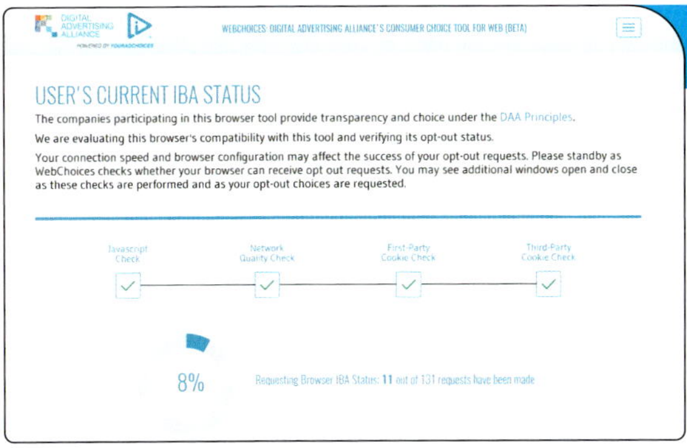


## Step 6

There is also a browser tool that lets you choose if the adverts you see come from companies other than Microsoft. Click the option under More Choices and wait for the Digital Advertising Alliance scan to finish. You can then choose from the list to see adverts from different advert providers.

# Privacy Settings

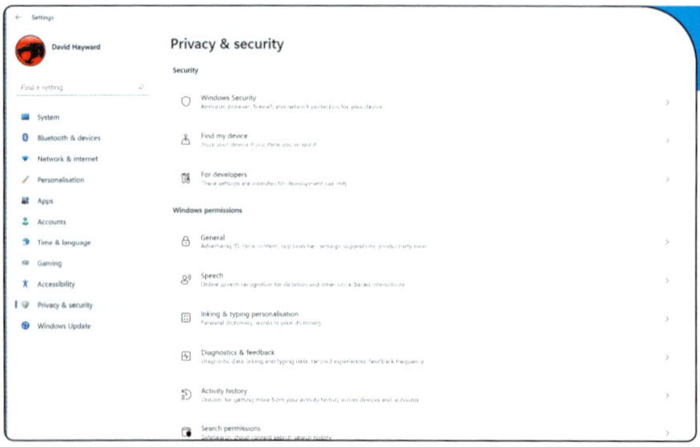


## General Privacy

Privacy has its own section within the settings; here there are many different categories covering everything from Location to Background Apps. Click on each of the privacy categories to see the options within that category. Use the slider switches to allow or block privacy actions.

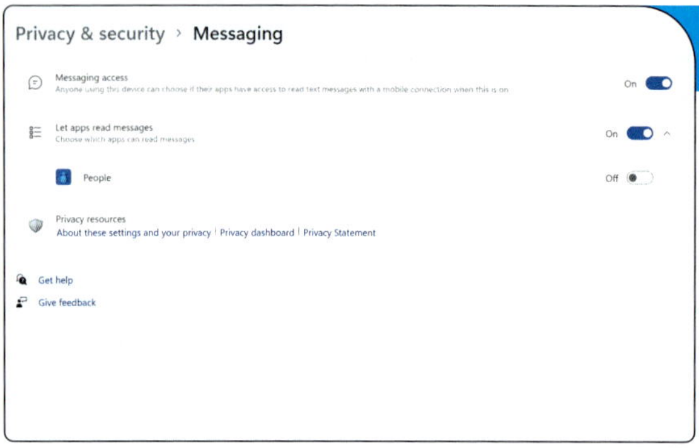


## Messaging Apps

We're using Windows 11 on a laptop here but if we had a tablet with a SIM card we would be able to get control over which apps were able to send messages over SMS and MMS. You probably want this to be restricted to just your Messaging app; most apps really shouldn't have access to your texts.

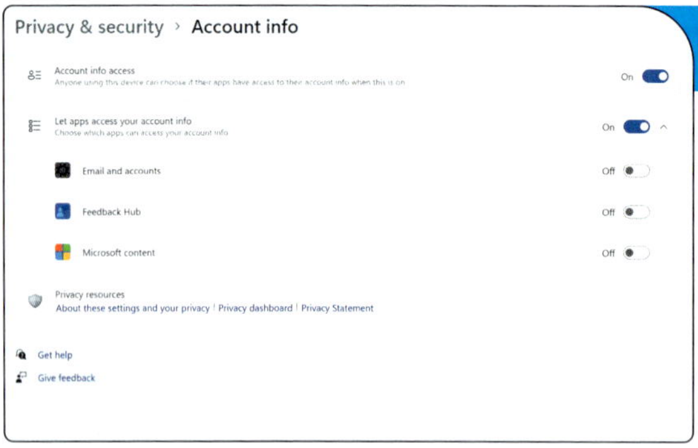


## Account Info

Apps are able to access very basic personal settings such as your name and account information. This is so they can sign you in automatically to your Windows account for things like Xbox Live or the Windows Store. You can turn this off wholesale or on an app by app basis.

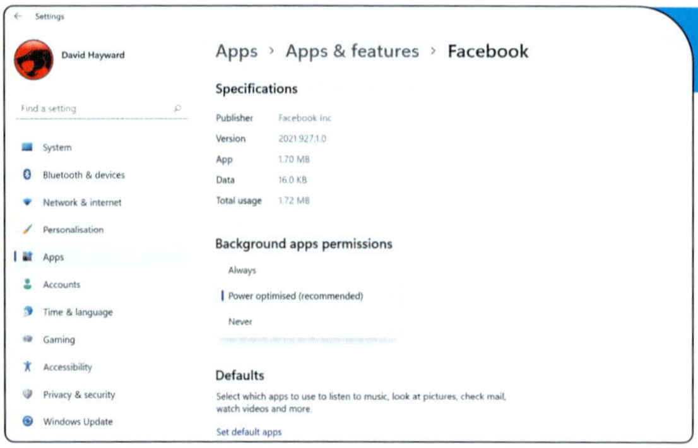


## Background Apps

You can control which apps you allow to run in the background. Go to the Apps section, then Apps & Features, and locate an app you don't want running in the background. Click the three dots to the right of the app, select Advanced Options and change the Background Apps Permissions via the drop-down box.

# Maintaining Windows 11

Before you start to add software to help with maintenance, it is worth checking out the numerous tools included with the OS. These are spread out over several menus but once you find them you will see that they can really help with security and performance.

## Storage Sense

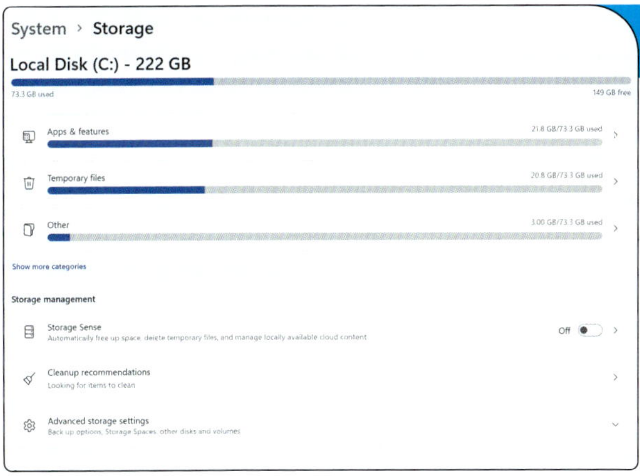


### Step 1

Activating Storage Sense lets the system software automatically free up storage space by getting rid of files you no longer need. These can include temporary files such as cookies and the contents of your Recycle Bin.

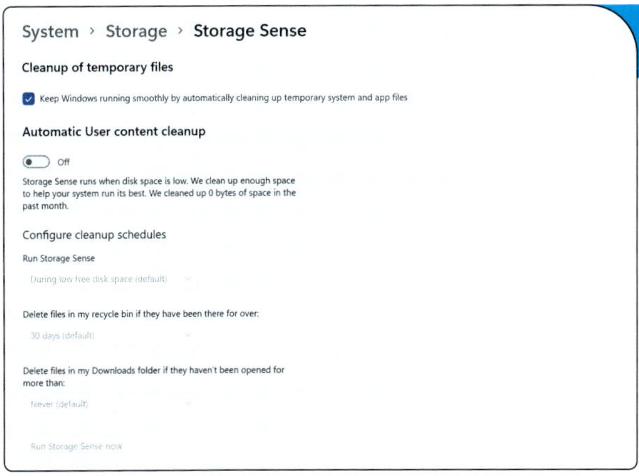


### Step 2

You can choose when files are deleted, e.g. after 30 days in the Recycle Bin or if apps don't use them for a certain amount of time. Alternatively you can simply click a button to Clean Now rather than setting automatic cleaning. You can find the Storage Sense option in Settings > System > Storage.

# Background Apps

## Step 1

One of the easiest ways to conserve power (for laptop users) and reduce processor strain, is to take control of Background Apps. These are apps that are, by default, allowed to receive info, send notifications and update in the background.

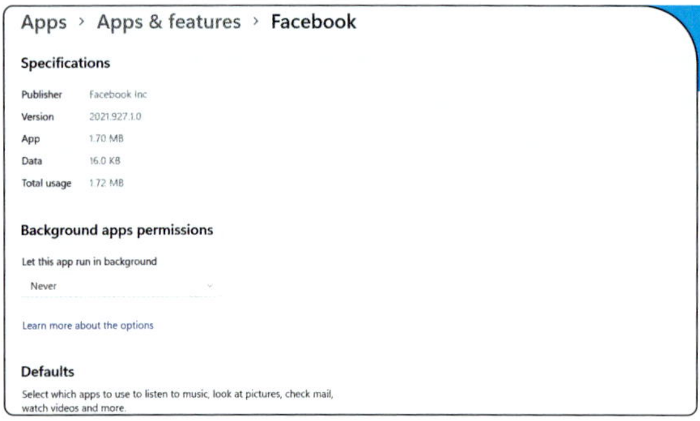


## Step 2

You can either stop all background apps with a single slider click, or prevent individual apps from running in the background. Go to Settings > Privacy > Background Apps. If you see apps in the list that you don't need notifications or updates from, click the slider to disable its background activity.

# Troubleshooters

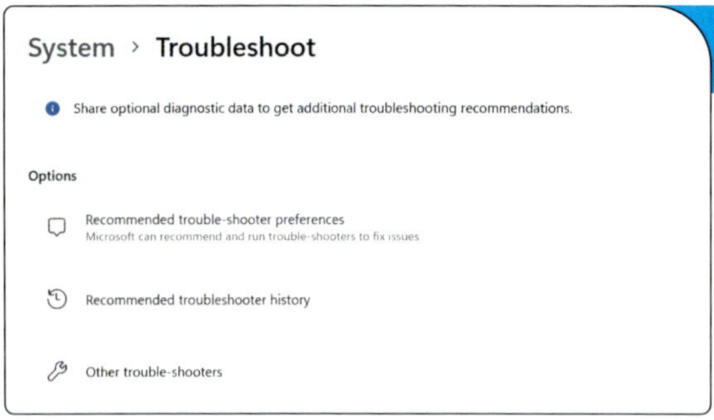


## Step 1

Windows 11 includes a number of troubleshooting tools, aimed at problems such as audio loss or patchy Internet connection. This is often the best place to start when trying to solve issues, as the OS contains many drivers for common devices and may just need a small software update.

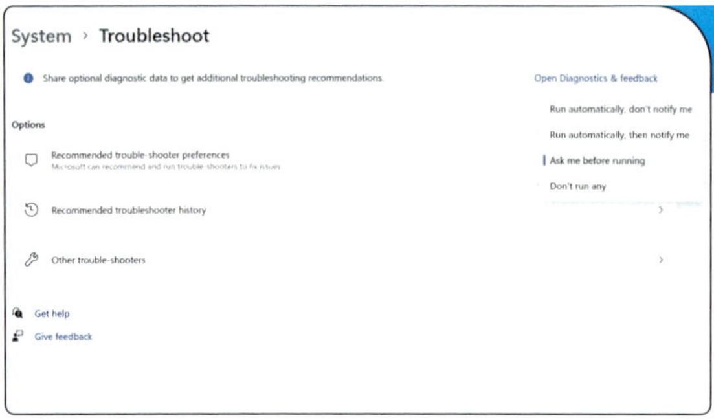


## Step 2

You simply look through the list of troubleshooters and click on the one which applies. Choose Run the Troubleshooter and then follow the instructions to try and solve the problem. You can find the troubleshooters in Settings > System > Troubleshoot.

# Disk Tools

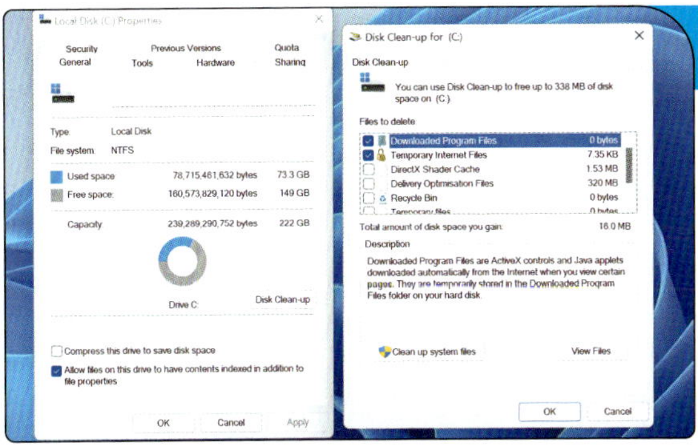


## Step 1

There are several tools built in to Windows that allow you to clean, fix and manage your hard disk. Open the File Explorer and look in the left-hand column for 'This PC'. Select it and then right click on Local Disk (C:). In the General tab, you will see a button for Disk Clean-up that lets you get rid of temporary Internet files, old program files and so on.

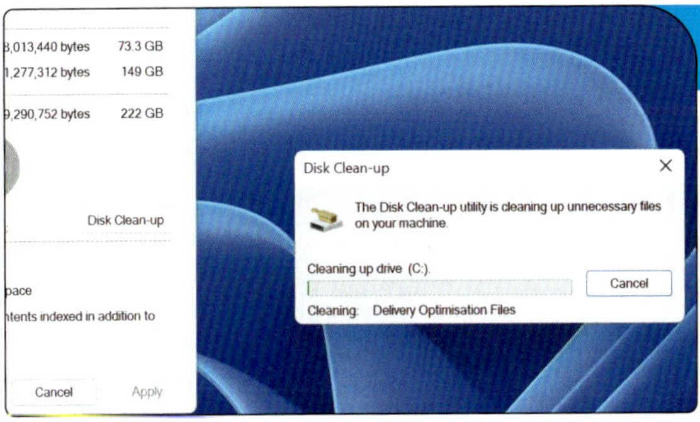


## Step 2

If you click the Tools tab, you can use the Error Checking tool and the Disk Defragment tool. Both of these tools can help your hard disk run more efficiently. Click on either button and follow the instructions for each.

# Disk Management

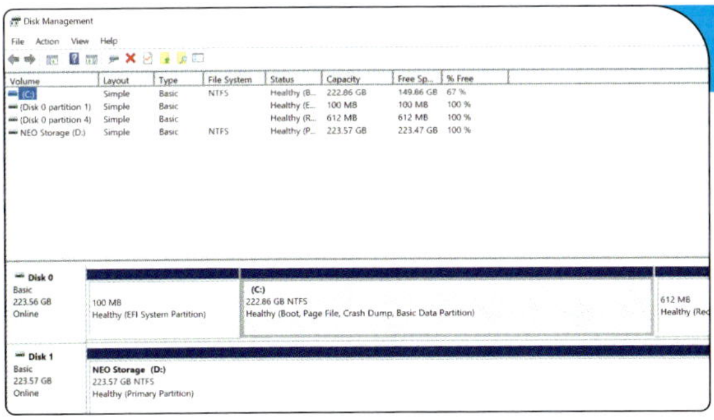


## Step 1

The Disk Management tool is more about diagnostics than actual maintenance but it is a useful way of checking whether your hard disk has space available and is healthy. The panel will show all of your disks, as well as all of the partitions.

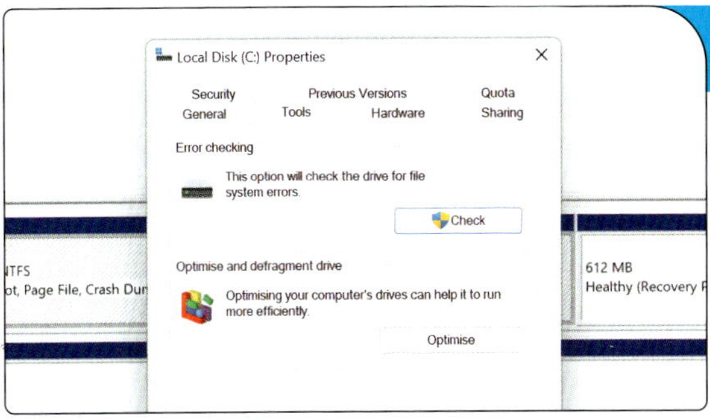


## Step 2

Each column contains information about capacity, free space in MB, percentage of free space and health status. There are further options, such as the ability to change drive letters and mark partitions as active but they are probably not worth playing around with unless you know what you are doing.

# Removing Malware

The Windows 11 Defender and Security suite is actually very good, but what if you're unlucky enough to already have some form of digital infection? Thankfully, there's a way to remove malware and viruses from your Windows computer.

## Malware Busters

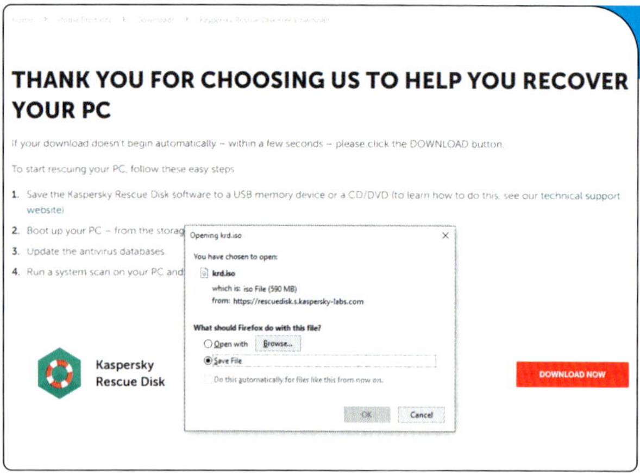


### Step 1

Make sure you have a blank CD or a USB stick that's at least 1GB in size. The Kaspersky Rescue Disk is downloaded as an ISO (which is an image file containing all the disk information), and can be downloaded from https://www.kaspersky.com.au/downloads/thank-you/free-rescue-disk.

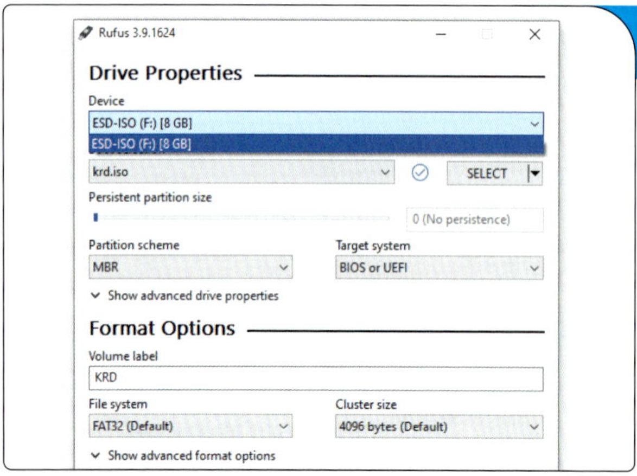


### Step 2

To transfer the ISO to a USB, download Rufus; which is an executable that doesn't require any installation, from: https://rufus.ie/. Insert your USB stick and double-click Rufus. Check that the Device label is pointing to your inserted USB stick, if not then you may need to close Rufus, remove the USB, then re-insert the USB and re-start Rufus. The remaining options can be left as their defaults.

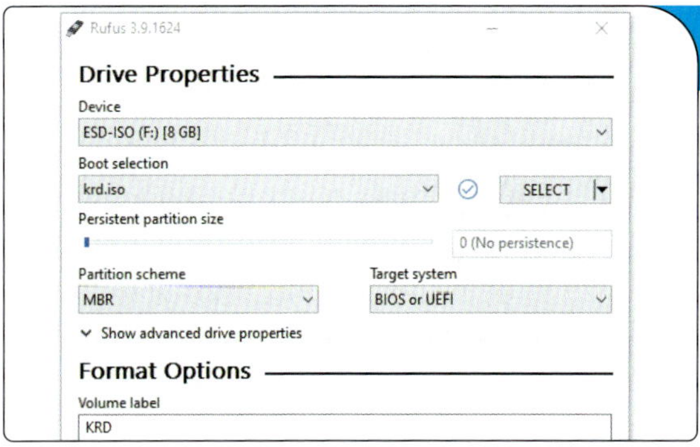


## Step 3

Click the Select option, and using Windows Explorer, locate the downloaded Kaspersky Rescue ISO – it'll be called krd.iso. Click the Start button to select the image and continue with the process. This will copy the contents of the ISO to the USB while also making the USB a bootable device.

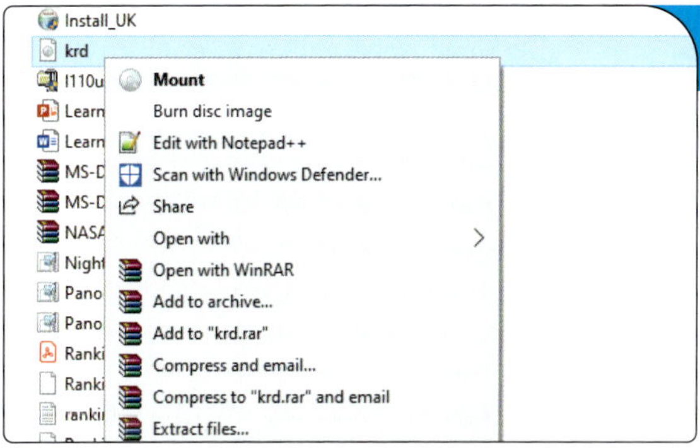


## Step 4

If you're using a CD, start by inserting the CD into the drive. Locate the downloaded Kaspersky Rescue ISO, right-click it and choose Burn Disc Image from the context menu. Tick the 'Verify disc after burning' option, and click the Burn button to start the process. Once the ISO is burnt to the disc, you can power off your computer.

## Step 5

You'll now need to allow your PC to boot up into the Kaspersky Rescue CD environment. Power up your PC and open the Boot Option Menu. This could be accessed by pressing F12 (depending on the make and manufacturer of your PC motherboard). With the boot options available, select either the CD or USB stick and press Enter.

## Step 6

The PC will now boot into the Kaspersky Rescue Disc environment. This is a custom Linux operating system with all the necessary security tools pre-installed. First, you'll need to choose which language to load the environment. Use the arrow keys, and press Enter for your language choice. After that, choose the Graphic Mode.

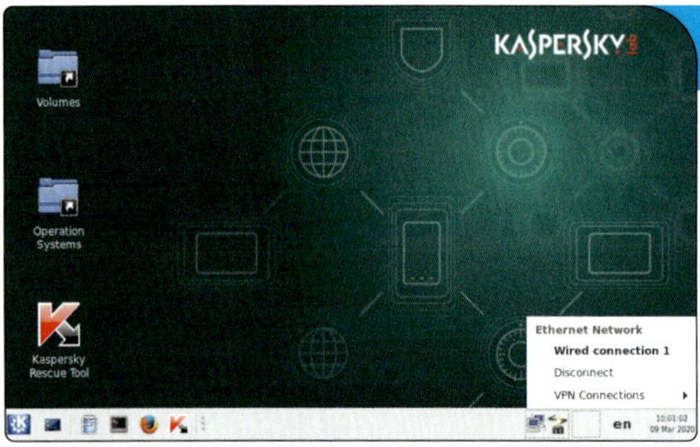


## Step 7

First accept the license agreement. Then, the rescue disc will check its status and open a window asking for you to start scanning the system. It's best to check you've got access to the Internet in order for it to update first. Close down the Rescue Tool window, and click on the Network box in the bottom right. Connect to Wi-Fi, or Wired as required.

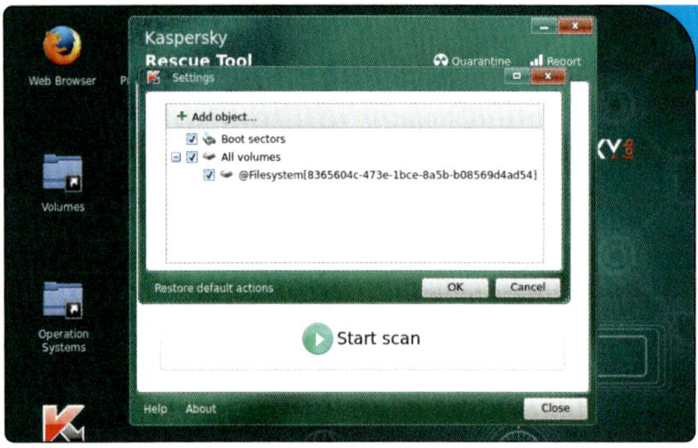


## Step 8

Once connected, relaunch the Kaspersky Rescue Tool from the desktop icon, agree to the license once more. Before you begin, click on the Change Parameters link in the Kaspersky Rescue Tool window. This will enable you to choose which drives the tool can scan for infections and malware. Tick all the drives in your system.

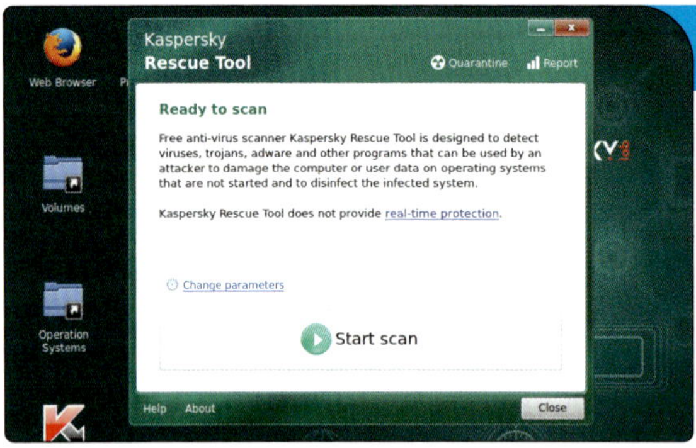


## Step 9

When you're ready to continue, click on the Start Scan button in the Kaspersky Rescue Tool window. This will begin the process of scanning all the drives selected in the previous step. Be aware, that, depending on the size of your drives and the amount of data on them, this could take quite some time.

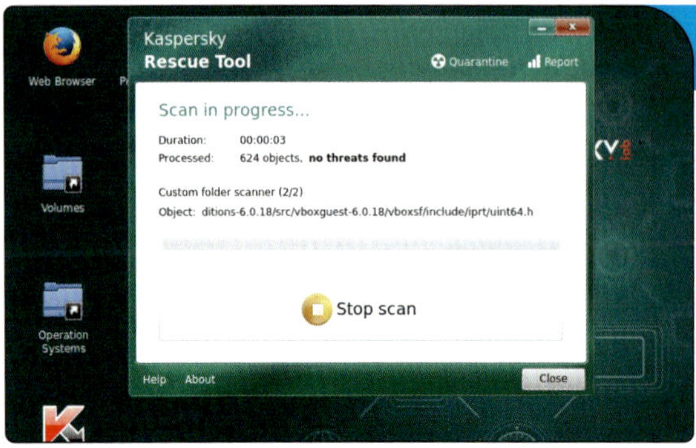


## Step 10

While the scan is working, you'll see the area that the tool is currently processing. You'll also get a brief run-down of any threats currently found, time taken, and number of files scanned. Once complete, you can view a report by clicking on Details. Hopefully, you're malware free, and you can remove the USB/ disc and reboot the system.

# Securing Home Networks

We've mentioned previously that an attack doesn't always come from the other side of the globe but can indeed be a little too close to home at times. Home network hacking is possible with the simplest of tools; easily found on the Internet.

## Network Protection

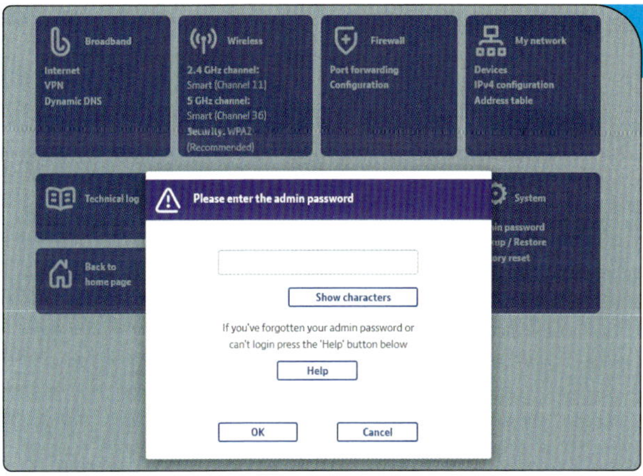


### Step 1

The most common entry point to gain access to your network is via the router. The router from your ISP may well be offering the latest forms of encryption but it doesn't take a genius to trawl the less reputable sections of the Internet to obtain a list of passwords. Therefore, change the default username and password needed to access it.

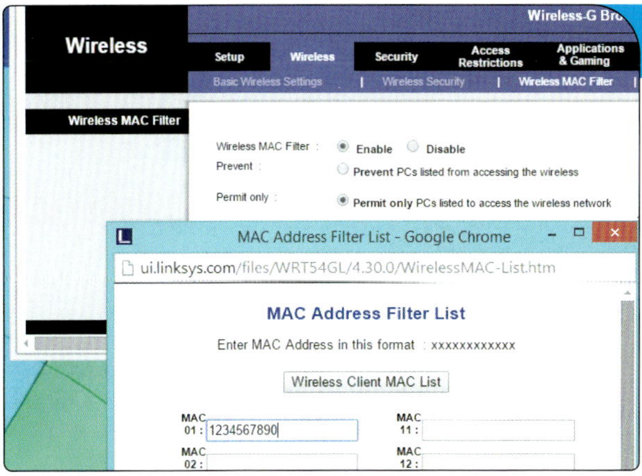


### Step 2

Most routers these days come with a form of authentication called MAC (Media Access Code) address filtering. Every networkable device, computers, tablets, games consoles, come with a unique MAC address. The filtering allows you to enter the MAC addresses of your devices, so only they can be used on your router. Consult your router documentation for more details.

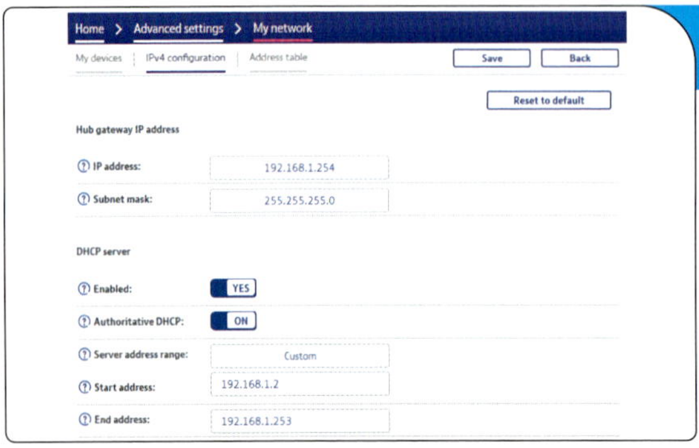


## Step 3

It can be a pain but try disabling DHCP on your router and opting for static IP addresses. Every device that connects to a DHCP router will receive an IP address. By eliminating that you get to specify the address range available. It's not fool proof but it's worth considering.

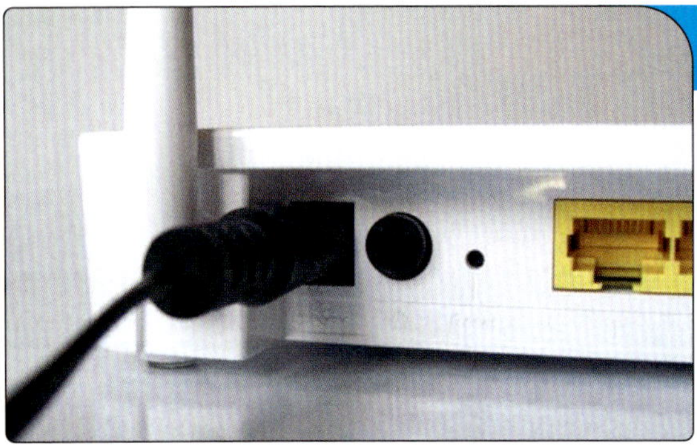

## Step 4

According to Trustwave's 2013 Global Security Report, many home network hacks are conducted when the household is away or asleep. This leaves the hacker with ample opportunity to steal bandwidth and view files you may have on a NAS drive. The short, simple solution is to power off the router at night or if you go out for the day.

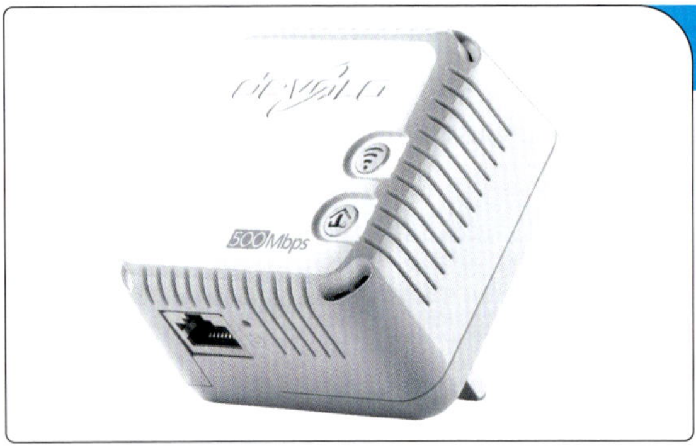


## Step 5

Powerline adapters are an excellent resource for connecting wired network devices. However, depending on the adapter, it is possible to use another adapter to gain access to yours. In newer homes it's an easy enough task to pick up another user's network, so use the Encryption button if the adapter has one.

## Step 6

Networking a home with Ethernet cables isn't a difficult project and it offers faster connection speeds than that of wireless. However, if you're living in shared accommodation or a block of flats, make sure that any unseen cable lengths can't be accessed by a neighbour. It's easy enough to splice into an Ethernet cable and steal bandwidth.

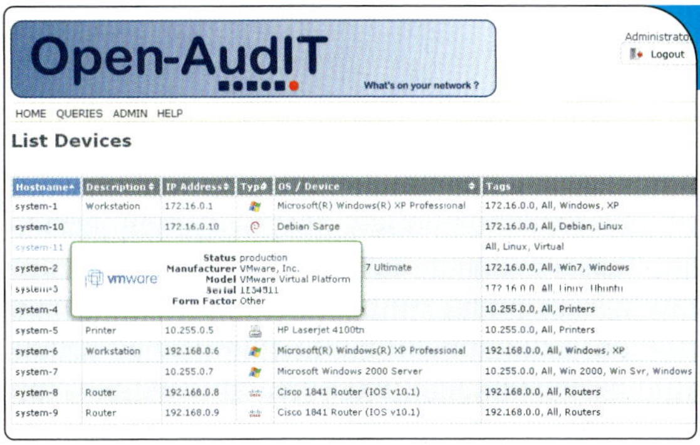


## Step 7

Consider using a network mapping program, such as Open-AudIT, to gain a better understanding of what devices are attached to your network. Become familiar with the addresses, manufacturer, model IDs and so on of every connected object. That way, should anything new appear, you'll know it's not something you allowed.

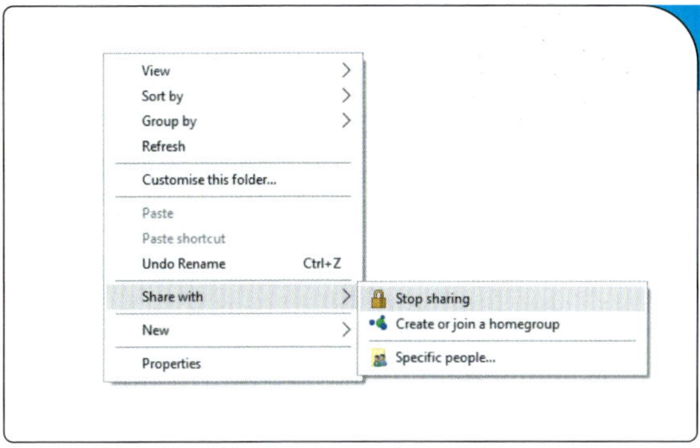


## Step 8

Sharing resources and files from one computer to another is perfectly fine but consider sharing less if you live in close proximity to others. Once a hacker has gained access to your network, getting to any shared folders you have will be a doddle. In extreme cases don't share anything, but generally tighten password control.

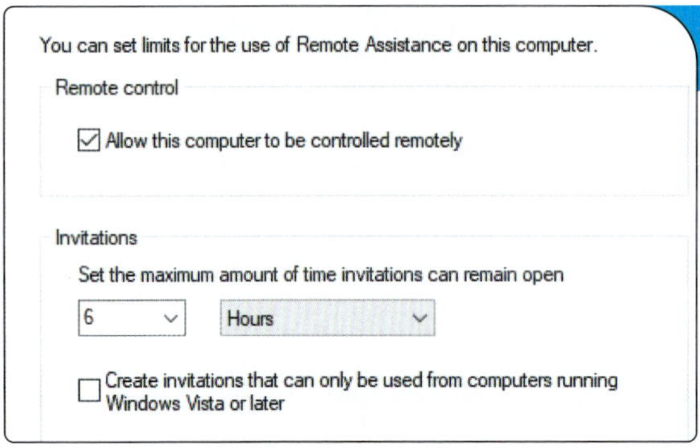


## Step 9

Remote administration on both the router and computer certainly can help you out when you're not at the keyboard. Perhaps you connect to your home network from work? Whatever the reasons, it does leave a potential gap in your home network security. Consider closing it completely or double-checking the authentication is top notch.

## Step 10

If you run a small office make sure that all your wall ports are located in areas where they are secure. Behind desks and generally away from where the public or any visitors may be able sneakily plug a laptop in.

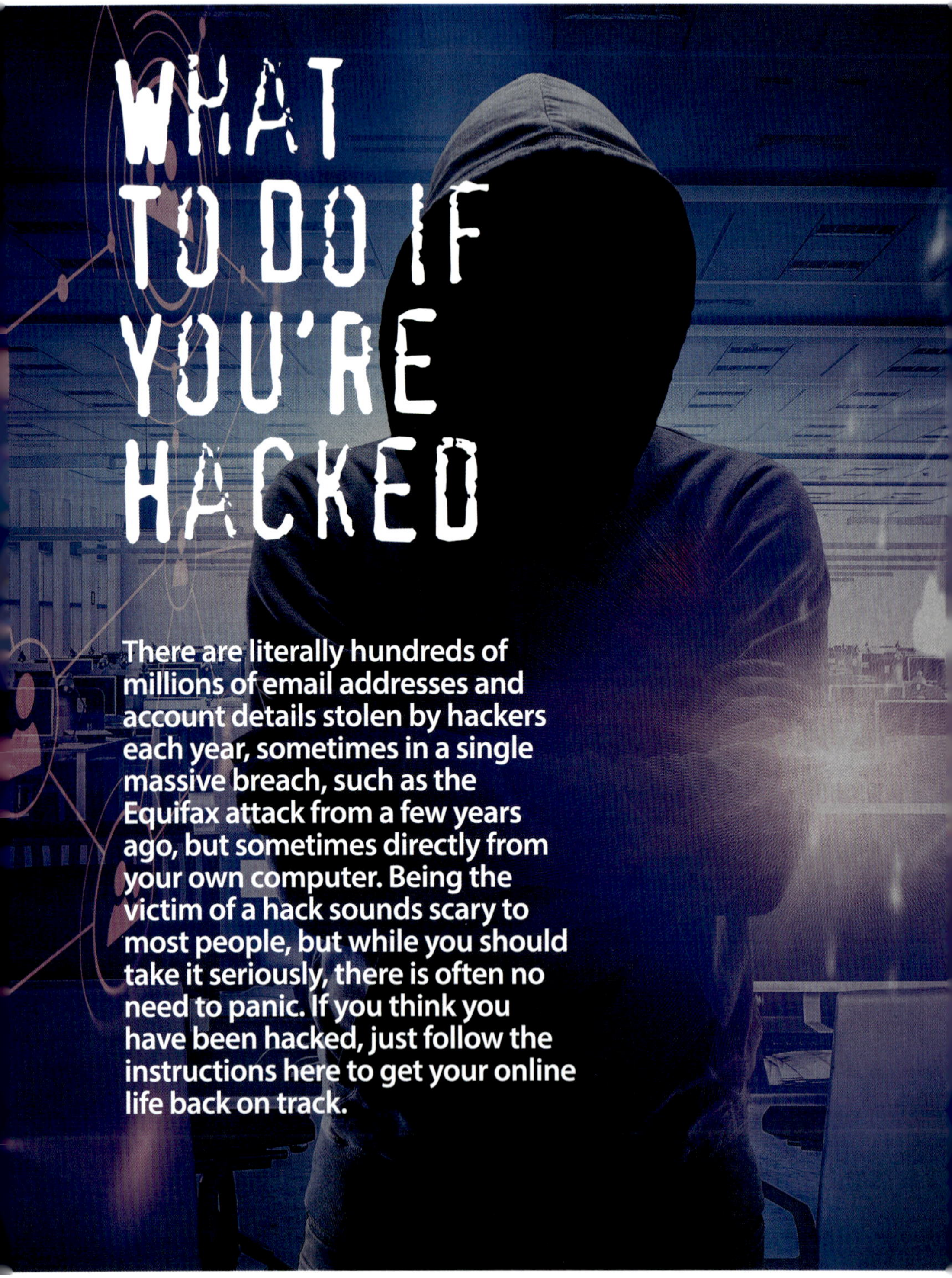

# What to do if you're hacked

There are literally hundreds of millions of email addresses and account details stolen by hackers each year, sometimes in a single massive breach, such as the Equifax attack from a few years ago, but sometimes directly from your own computer. Being the victim of a hack sounds scary to most people, but while you should take it seriously, there is often no need to panic. If you think you have been hacked, just follow the instructions here to get your online life back on track.

## HOW WILL YOU KNOW?

You may hear about a big data breach in the news, or from friends and colleagues, and if the company hacked is one you have accounts with, it is worth following all of the steps below just in case. Often, the first you will know about being hacked is a call from your credit card company or bank about unusual activity, or from friends/relatives suddenly receiving strange requests for money from you.

Many of the large email providers, such as Gmail, will alert you if there is a new login to your account from an unrecognised location or device. Or you may simply find that you have been logged out of an account and your password is no longer working. The most important thing is not how you discover how you have been hacked, although we urge you to keep a close eye on all your online activity, but how you act immediately after you find out.

You can check if your email address has potentially been involved in a data breach by entering it in to the Have I Been Pwned website.

https://haveibeenpwned.com/

## WHAT TO DO NEXT

Even if you think only one account has been targeted, you should still move to protect ALL of your important accounts. This is especially true if your main email account has been breached, or if you use the same  email and password for all of your online accounts.

## CHANGE YOUR PASSWORDS

The very first thing you need to do is change all of your passwords, especially for your email account, banking accounts, credit card accounts, PayPal, etc. Many online accounts now offer 2-step verification, which adds an extra layer of security by sending you a passcode each time you try to log in. If this is available, set it up as soon as possible.

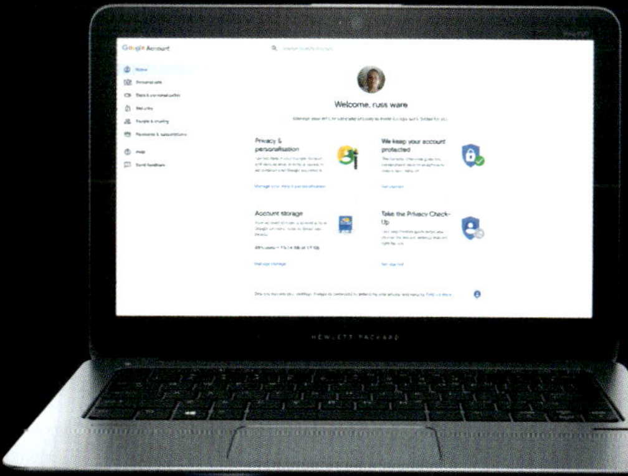

If your email account password has been changed by the hacker, you will need to contact the provider and prove you are the rightful owner of that account. For Gmail, there are instructions for recovering a hacked account on the Google support pages (https://support.google.com). The other main email providers should offer similar advice.

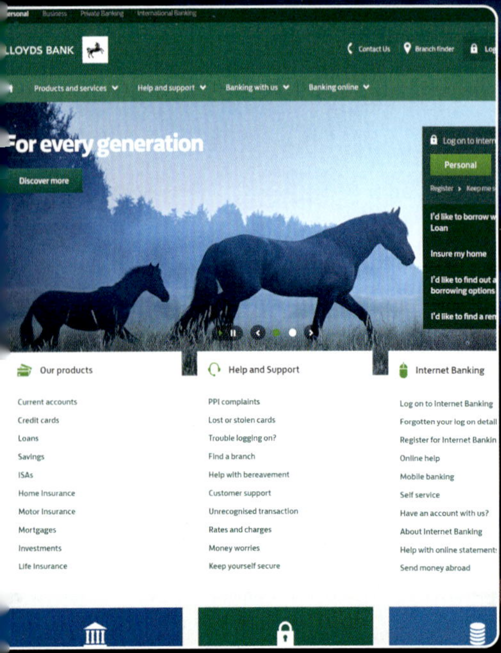


# EXAMINE ALL YOUR ACCOUNTS CAREFULLY

This includes banking, email, online shopping accounts, especially if you use the same password for multiple logins. Check your email inbox and sent mail box for things you haven't signed up to or sent. Think about how you recover a forgotten password on almost any website: You request a password reset to your email address. If someone has got hold of access to your emails, they could do the same.

Look for any unusual activity at all, and if you spot some, contact the website or company to let them know your account may have been breached. Often, they can help you sort it out the fastest way.

If your email account has been taken over, and the password changed, you will need a way to prove that you are the rightful owner. This is why it is important to have two separate email addresses, as you can usually use a second email address as the alternate contact for the main address.

# CHECK YOUR BANK AND CREDIT CARD STATEMENTS

Check both your bank account and credit card statement for any unusual activity (online and immediately if possible, but if not contact your bank/credit card company and ask for a statement). It is also worth informing both your bank and credit card company what has happened, so that they can be aware and alert for any unusual activity in the near future.

Having to get new cards issued may be a hassle, but it is less hassle than trying to sort out the mess left when a hacker starts buying things using your card details.

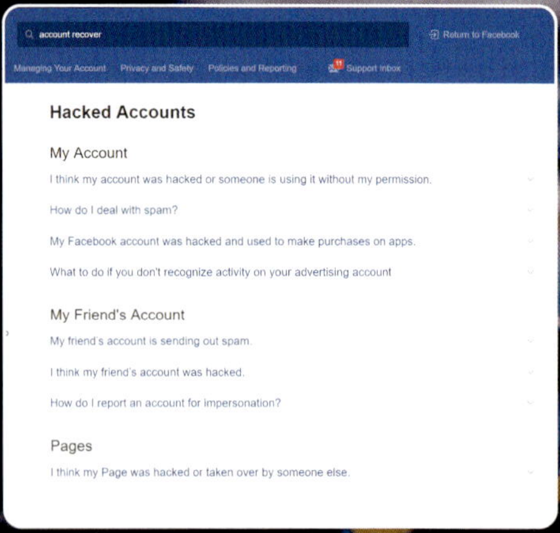

## SCAN FOR VIRUSES/MALWARE

If your computer has been infected with a virus or malware, this could be where the hacker got your details, so none of the steps above are any use if the underlying source of the breach is still sitting on your device waiting to send all of your updated information to the hacker. Run a complete virus scan, using reputable scanning software from the likes of Norton, Kaspersky, Panda or McAfee.

If using Windows 11, then the Windows Defender tool offers an Offline Scan, which can find even particularly well-hidden malware on your computer. This scan will take at least 15 minutes to complete, but is the most in-depth scan offered by the free anti-virus software.

## CONTACT FRIENDS, FAMILY AND COLLEAGUES

If you think that your email or social media account has been hacked, contact friends, family and colleagues to let them know. There have been many cases where a family member or friend has received an email supposedly from a stranded person, asking for help (in the form of money) so that they can get home. Making people aware, means they will be less likely to fall for this sort of scam.

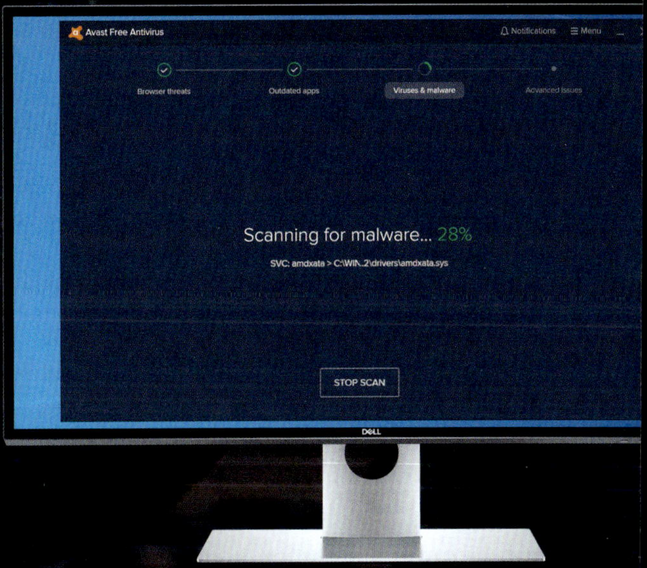


## RECOVER YOUR ACCOUNTS

Major companies such as Google, Facebook, Twitter and Microsoft are well aware of the possibility of accounts being hacked, and most offer processes to get the account back to normal. Indeed, the company may well be the first to realise an account has been hijacked and shut it down for you. Head over to the homepage of the website in question and check the knowledge base/help desk for advice on what to do next.

Just remember that if you get an email from Facebook, Twitter, etc., telling you that your account has been breached, make sure that it is legitimate and not someone phishing for your login information. You can read more about spotting scam emails at https://bdmpublications.com.

# Limit Data Tethering

Tethering means connecting your phone to the mobile data network and then connecting a second device via Wi-Fi to the phone to make use of that connection. Windows 11 can be data-heavy; a problem if your phone has limited mobile data allowance.

## Set Tethered Connections to Metered

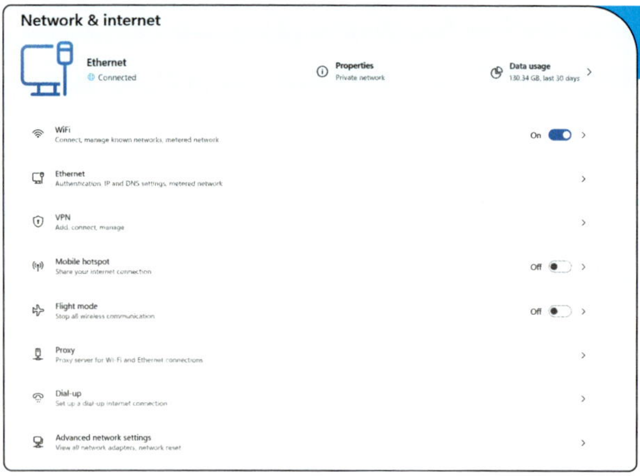


### Step 1

Cellular data connections are set as metered by default. Wi-Fi and Ethernet network connections can be set to metered but aren't by default. Some apps might work differently on a metered connection to help reduce your data usage. Some updates for Windows won't be installed automatically either.

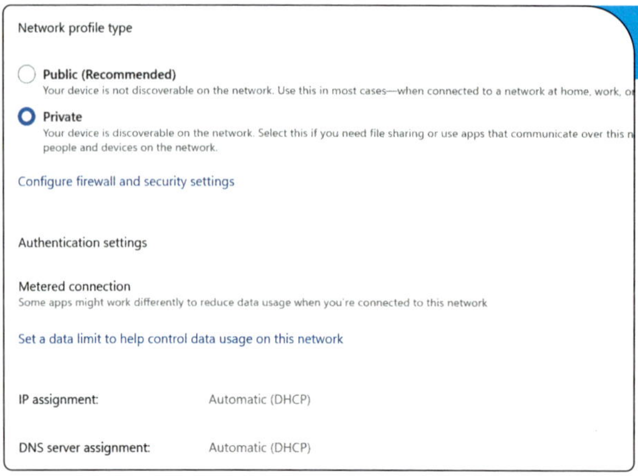


### Step 2

To set a Wi-Fi network connection as metered, click Start > Settings > Network & Internet > Wi-Fi > Manage known networks. Select the Wi-Fi network > Properties > turn on Set as metered connection. Unfortunately, many Windows apps completely ignore the metered connection setting.

# Check Network Usage Details

You can also view a log of how much data applications on your PC have used in the last 30 days. This can help you identify applications that might be using data in the background. To check this, head to Settings > Network & Internet > Data usage and click the graph to see more details.

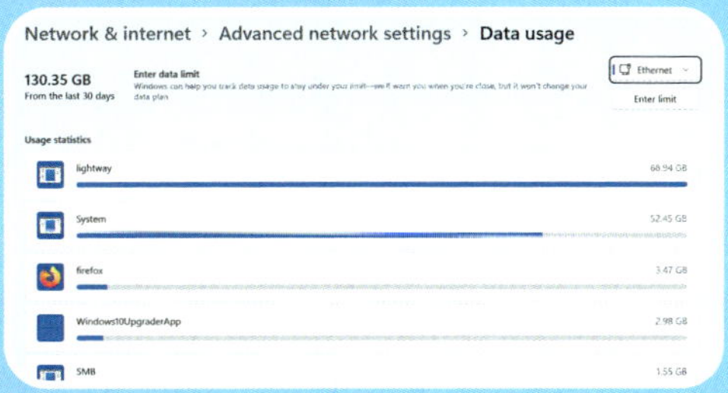


# Manage Browsing Data

You should now have reduced background data use, including updates and cloud syncing, so data use will be in the apps you use; for example, Google Chrome. You can install a handy extension for Chrome which limits data. Go to www.chrome.google.com/webstore/ and search for Data Saver.

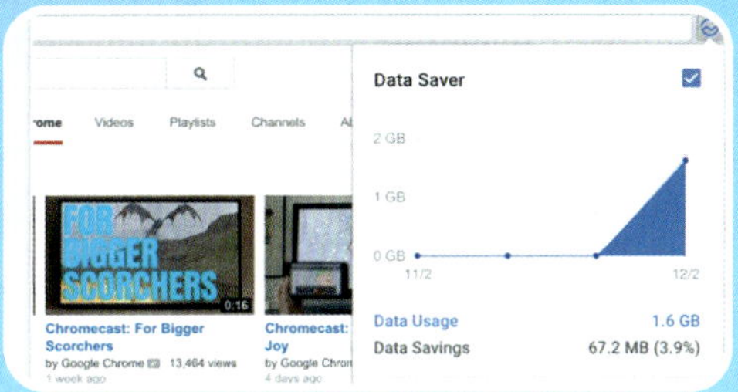


# Pause or Disable OneDrive

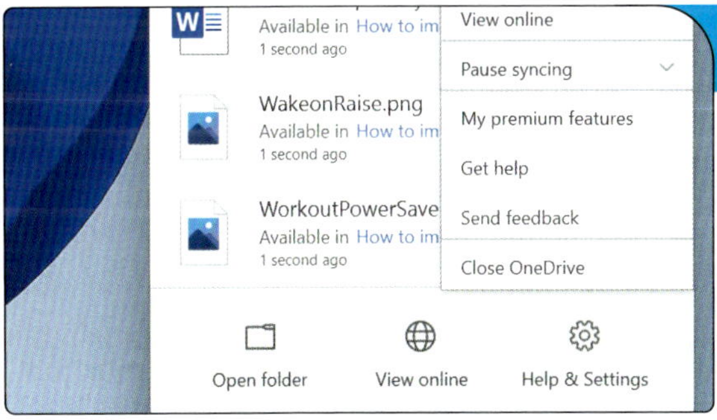


## Step 1

When you close your laptop lid, the default setting will be for Windows 11 to go into low power sleep mode. This is obviously no good if you are using your laptop with an external monitor, as it will make the laptop unusable. To solve this problem, click on the Battery icon > power and sleep settings in the taskbar.

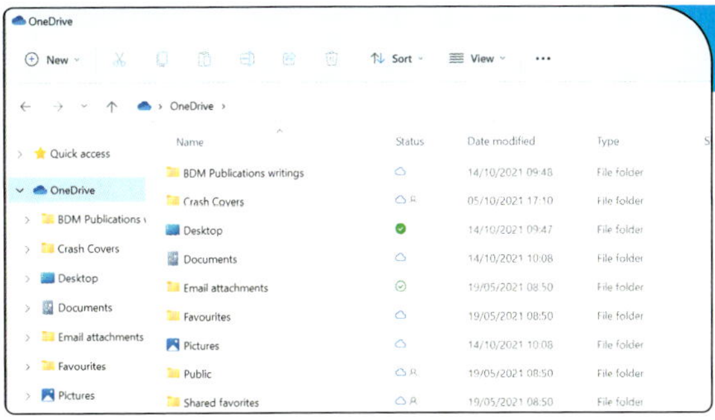


## Step 2

OneDrive in Windows 11 can be disabled through your computer's Local Group Policy Editor. This doesn't remove OneDrive from your PC but it stops it from syncing with the cloud or connecting with other apps, and removes it from the navigation pane in File Explorer.

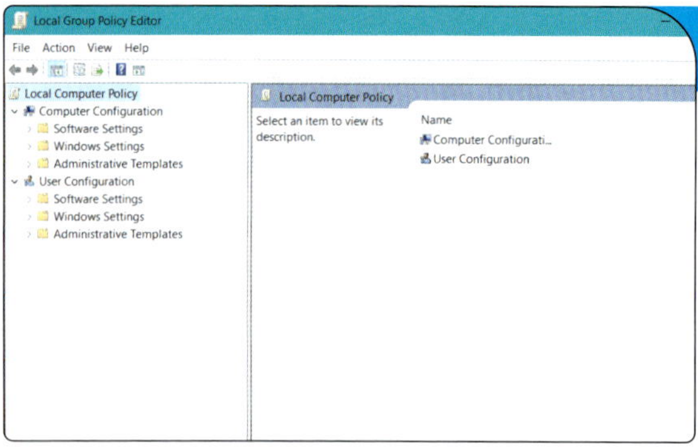


## Step 3

Press the Windows key + R to open the Run box. Type gpedit.msc and click OK. In the Local Group Policy Editor, in the folder list under Local Computer Policy, navigate the folders to Local Computer Policy > Computer Configuration > Administrative Templates > Windows Components > OneDrive.

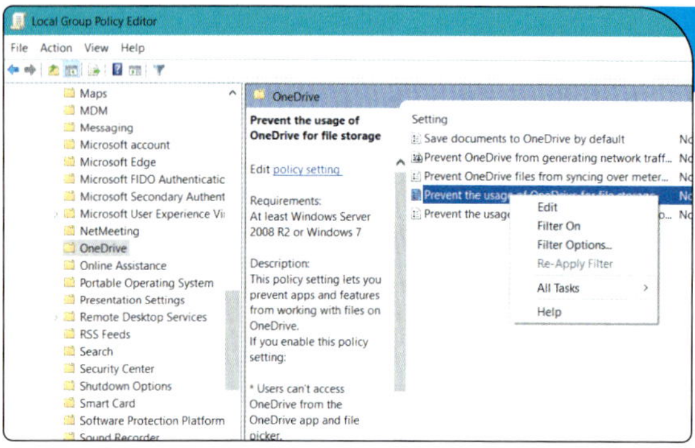


## Step 4

On the OneDrive screen, under Settings, click Prevent the usage of OneDrive for file storage. In the Prevent the usage of OneDrive for file storage box, select Enabled, then click OK. Be aware that disabling OneDrive like this will disable it for all users of the PC, not just you.

# Check Task Manager

**The Task Manager is a great tool for checking to see which apps or services are using a lot of data at any time. To open the Task Manager, press Ctrl+Shift+Esc or search for it in the Start menu search field. Click at the top of the Network tab to display high usage services at the top.**

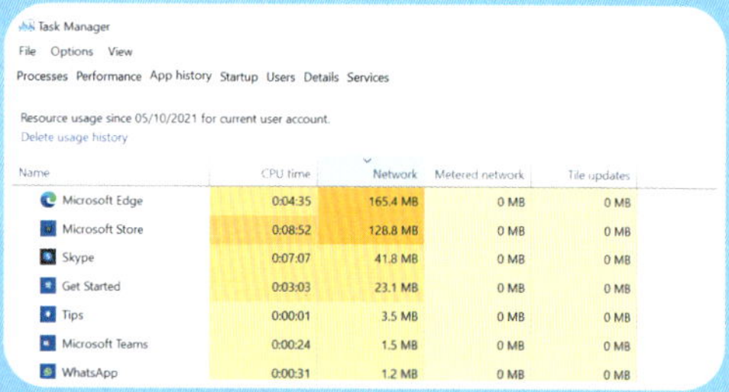


# Reduce Video Streaming Quality

**Streaming or downloading videos is a surefire way to burn through your data quickly and is best avoided when tethering. However, if you need to view video over a tethered connection, you can tell Windows to reduce quality in Settings > Apps > Video Playback. Click 'Allow video to play at low res'.**

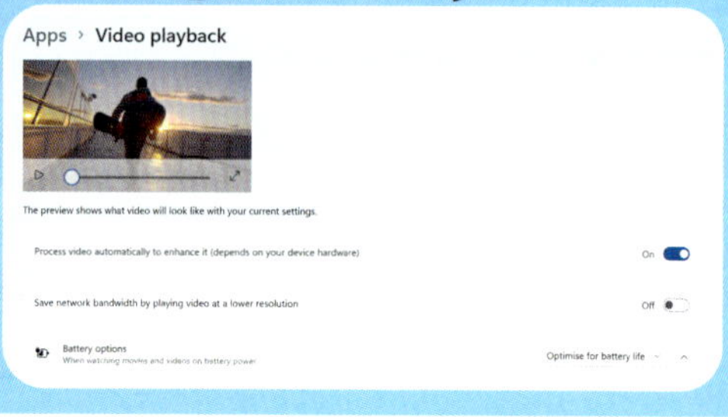

# Windows 11 VPN Security

A VPN offers incredible levels of encryption and heightened anonymity when you're connected to one of the many supporting services; but what security benefits does a VPN bring to a Windows 11 computer with an antivirus program already installed?

## Network Protection

### ISP Leaks

This doesn't happen often, but an ISP can become compromised and details of user activities leaked or stolen. Using a VPN can hide your browsing activity from trackers and even your ISP, enabling you to browse without the fear of having your details leaked or accessed by others.

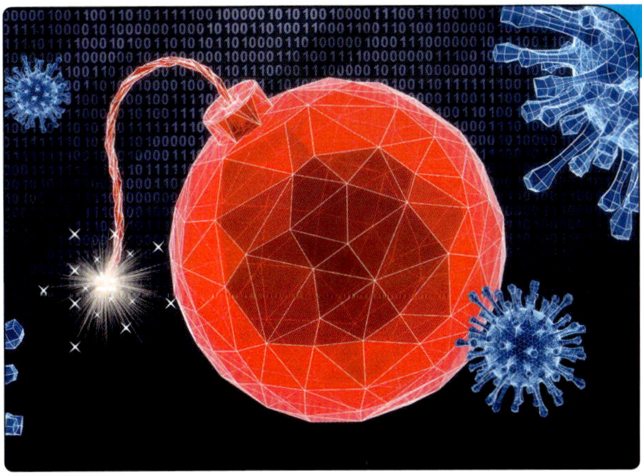

### Anti-malware

Many VPN providers utilise a level of anti-malware into their security layers. This enhances your security by filtering any downloads through the VPN first. Should there be a virus present, then it can be removed or stopped at the VPN before it even reaches you.

## Filter Web Pages

To expand the previous feature, VPNs filter web pages that are dangerous or contain threats. Even with a good antivirus client installed, you can still access a dangerous site. Using a VPN actually prevents the site from even being loaded.

## Encrypted Data

The connection between you and the VPN server is encrypted to the highest possible standards. This makes it near impossible for some external element to gain access to the data you're transmitting. Online banking and shopping are extremely secure with a VPN.

## Public Wi-Fi

Public and free Wi-Fi hotspots are notorious when it comes to mobile security. Anyone with a little knowledge and some free tools via the Internet can intercept public Wi-Fi networks and hijack your connection, revealing all your data. A VPN encrypts the data and protects you.

## Remote Working

If you're working abroad, or you're a remote worker, a VPN connection to the company's servers ensures that all the sensitive business data remains secure. It's difficult for a company to ensure 100 per cent security with mobile and off-site workers, but a VPN provides a secure tunnel straight to the company itself.

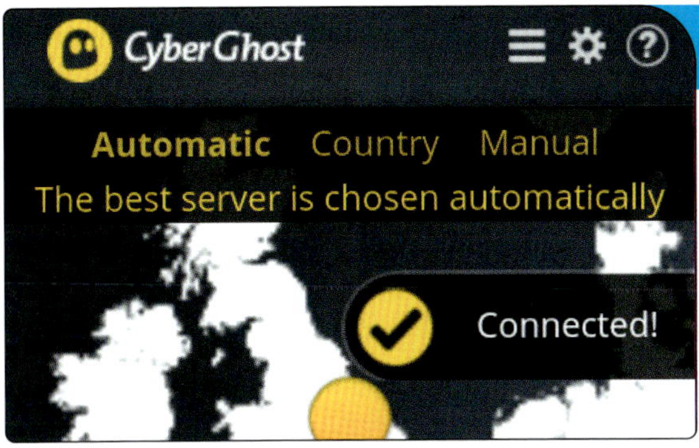


## Mobile VPNs

The availability of iOS and Android VPN clients means that your call data and data stored on your device is also secure. Mobile VPN apps use the same levels of protection and security, so your data can't be stolen when you're not even aware of it.

## Block Ads

Most VPNs also add an extra layer of security, whereby they actively block any advertising from websites. Internet ads are a necessary evil in some ways, as they provide much-needed funds for your favourite, freely available websites. However, some contain malicious content and do need to be blocked.

## HTTPS

Using HTTPS instead of HTTP utilises the secure side of the Internet protocol. Sadly, it's not always implemented either in browsers or by users. Many VPNs force all websites to use the secure connection that a HTTPS site offers, thereby enhancing your browsing security.

## Browsing History

In some countries, data retention laws are quite archaic, meaning governments and other bodies are able to access your data log for as long as you've been able to access the Internet. A good VPN won't detail any logs of your browsing and in most cases won't even hand over any personal information relating to you to other agencies.

# Protect on Public Wi-Fi

**There are few places where you can't now find a wireless connection for your laptop. And while this is great for those of us that want to stay connected day and night, accessing Wi-Fi in a public place does bring with it some dangers not found on your home network.**

## What Makes Public Wi-Fi Unsafe?

The very same features that make publicly accessible Wi-Fi hotspots desirable for all of us, such as the lack of authentication needed to connect, also makes them very desirable for hackers to exploit.

Let us start by saying that not all public Wi-Fi is equally unsafe. A coffee shop that has a new Wi-Fi password chalked up on the board every day is probably safer to use than one where the password has been the same for five years, but not by much. As a rule of thumb, you should assume that any network

connection you do not control will have fewer defences against interception and should be treated as unsafe.

Hackers are able to insert themselves (virtually) between your device and the network connection point, so all of the information sent to and from the network passes through the hacker, who then passes it on. As this information passes, it can be collected without you even knowing it has passed through a third party device.

Even if a hacker doesn't want to farm your data directly, if you allow file-sharing across a network then public Wi-Fi connections can be used to distribute malware. This malware could hide itself on your device and cause all sorts of problems, from logging keystrokes to sending spam emails to contacts as if they are from you.

As the use of public Wi-Fi increases, you can expect the number of different ways hackers can find to attack those using it to increase, as well. That doesn't mean you need to stop using Wi-Fi Hotspots, you just need to ensure that you are not the easy target most hackers are looking for.

If you want to stay connected, but also want to keep yourself and your device safe, there are a few simple things you can do to tighten up security without compromising your Internet access.

# Ways to Make Public Wi-Fi Safer to Use

## Keep Your Device Updated

Software updates, as well as providing new features, will often include security updates, so it is important to make sure all of your device software is the most recent version. This includes apps and programs, as well as OS updates. Almost all modern devices, from your laptop to the smartphones and tablets you use, make it very easy to keep things updated, often alerting you to the availability of an update or processing updates automatically.

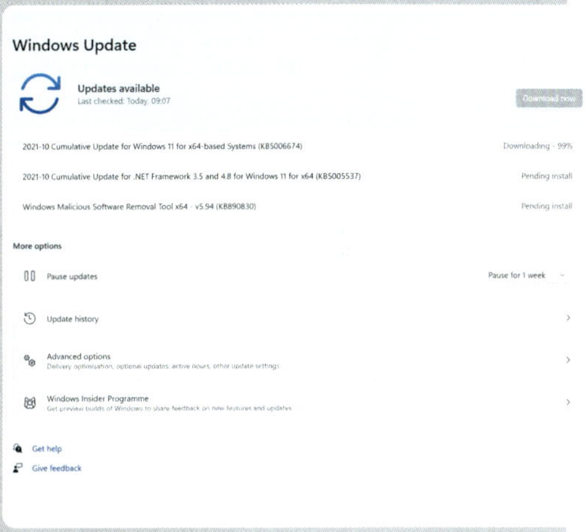


If you have turned off automatic updating on your device (and don't want to turn it back on in the settings), make a point to regularly check for them yourself and of course apply them, as soon as possible, especially on devices that may be used to connect to public Wi-Fi.

In Windows 11, you can find update information in Settings > Windows Update. If updates are available to download, they will be displayed here (along with any previous failed updates, etc.).

## Turn Off Sharing

Your PCs, phones and tablets are designed to interact easily with other devices you own, using a system known as Sharing. Sharing, as the name suggests, allows data or files to be shared or accessed from devices on the same network. This is normally perfectly fine when all of your devices are connected to your home network, but not so fine when you are connected to a public Wi-Fi hotspot.

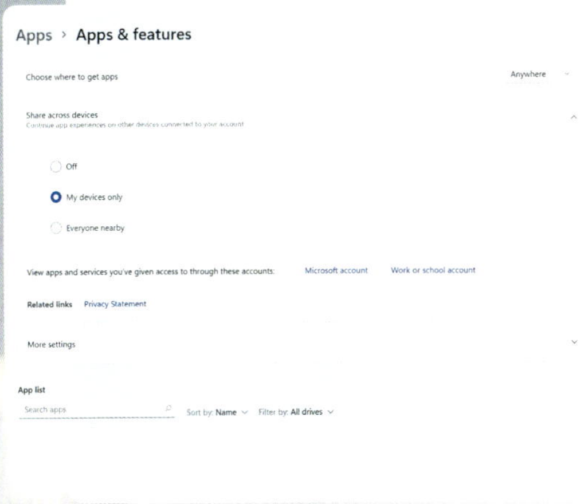


When using your devices online in public, you should always turn Sharing off. This can be done in Network and Sharing (on a Windows PC). In Windows, you can also just select "Public" when asked about a new network connection.

Many mobile devices also allow you to turn off Network Discovery or Device Visibility, meaning it is hidden from other devices connected to the same network. You can normally find this option in the Connections or Wi-Fi settings. In Windows 11, you can find further sharing options in Settings > Apps > Apps & Features > Share Across Devices.

## Use a VPN

A VPN, or Virtual Private Network, is a great way of protecting yourself and your device from hackers. They are becoming increasingly popular and therefore increasingly cheap and easy to use. A VPN provides you with a secure, private and encrypted network to log in to, from your device. Any data sent to and from your device is then encrypted by the VPN at both ends (known as end-to-end encryption). Anyone trying to access your data would need the encryption key to decode it. There are hundreds, if not thousands, of VPN services available, for computers, smartphones and tablets. Some of these are free and others charge a small monthly fee, depending on the level of security offered. Even a basic, free VPN is better to have than no VPN at all! Once the VPN is set up, all you need to do is log in to it from the device you want to protect before using the public Wi-Fi connection as you normally would to browse the Internet, send emails, etc.

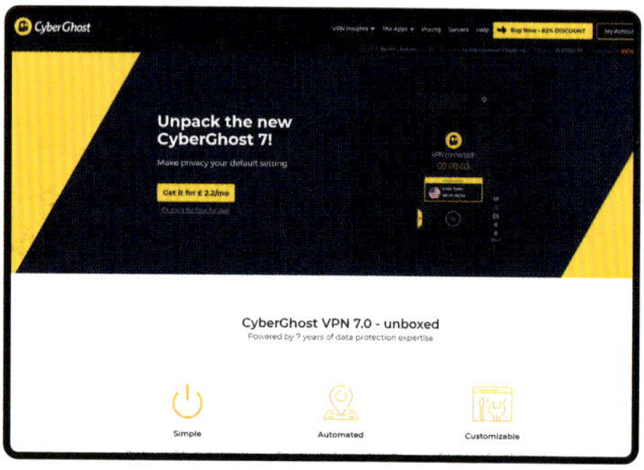


## Use Only SSL Connections

Many of the biggest, frequently used websites, now use SSL connections (particularly since Google suggested that websites not using the HTTPS protocol would be flagged as unsafe and potentially appear lower in the search results). As a general rule, even when not browsing through public Wi-Fi, any websites you use regularly and that require you to log in or enter your credentials, should be set to "Always use HTTPS". Most websites that ask for details about you have an HTTPS option somewhere in their account settings (if they don't already force HTTPS across the site). This might not seem as important on a videogame forum as it does on a banking website, but hackers are aware that people use the same passwords over and over again, so seemingly "safe" websites can be a goldmine of information about you for those clever enough to realise it.

## Install and Maintain Antivirus Software

Having a good antivirus package installed is important at home, and even more important if you use public Wi-Fi hotspots. Many modern antivirus packages offer browser protection, helping you to identify malicious websites before you click a single link on them. They also make it very hard for hackers to install malicious software on your device remotely, by offering improved firewalls and malware scanning. It is not enough simply to have antivirus software installed. You also need to make sure that it is regularly updated with the latest malware definitions, so that it knows about the latest threats and is able to counter them effectively. Some of the biggest names in Antivirus software include: Norton, McAfee, Bitdefender and Kaspersky. You can also find very good, free software from the likes of AVG, Panda Security and Avast.

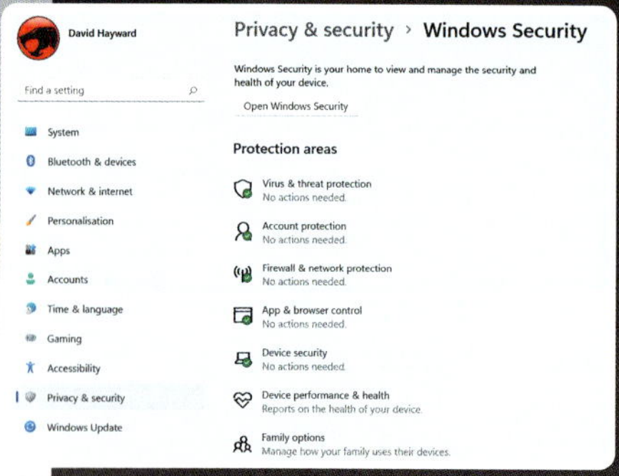

# How to Reset or Fresh Start

Resetting a PC reinstalls Windows, with a choice to delete your files, settings and apps, and main system files. Restoring will undo recent system changes, without deleting files. A Fresh Start completely removes all apps and reinstalls Windows.

## Fresh or Reset?

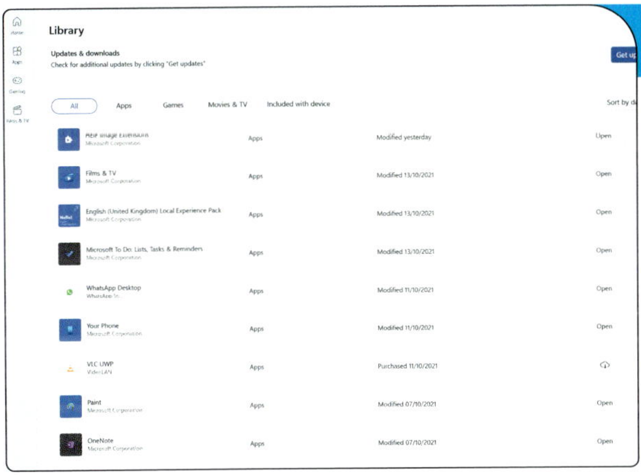


### Step 1

If your PC isn't performing as well as it once did, and you don't know why, you can reset your PC without deleting any of your personal files or changing your settings. Apps or software not installed through the Store will be removed but Windows store apps will be reinstalled.

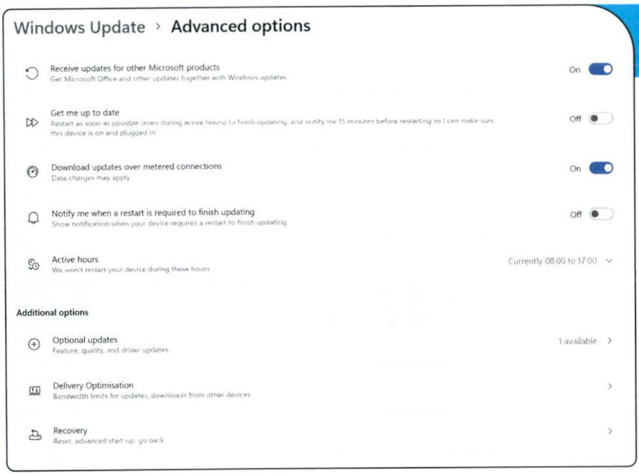


### Step 2

Open the main Settings app and head into the Windows Update > Advanced Options section. Click on Recovery and you will see several options, including Reset this PC. If you can't get into Settings, you can access reset by restarting your computer while holding the Shift key; then select Troubleshoot > Reset.

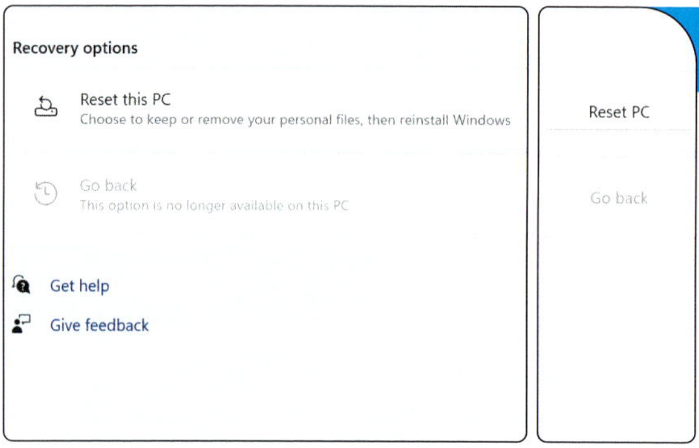


## Step 3

In System > Recovery, click on 'Reset PC' button to begin the process. You will now need to choose whether to keep your files (just remove apps and settings), or remove everything. If you choose Remove everything, you will then need to choose whether to 'Remove and clean the drive'.

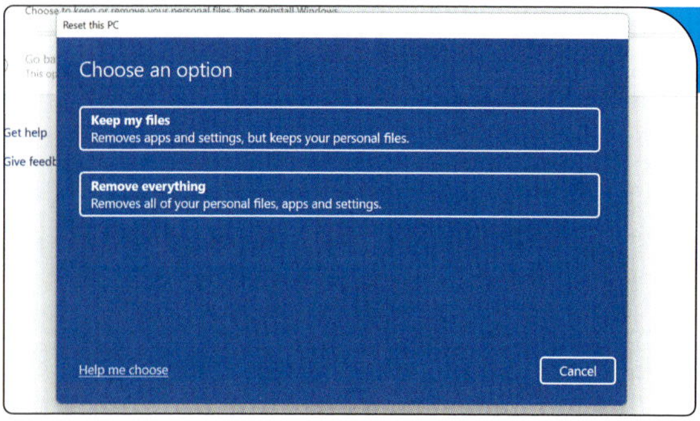


## Step 4

You will be warned that you won't be able to roll back to a previous version of Windows after the reset (old Windows files will be deleted). Click Next and then Reset when prompted. Windows will restart and take several minutes to reset itself. Click Continue when prompted.

# Perform a Fresh Start

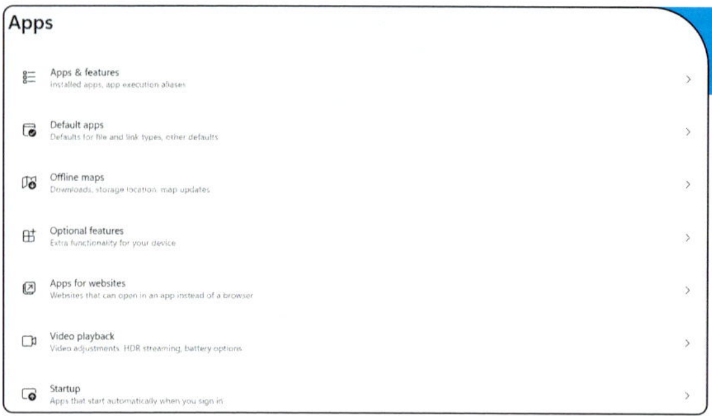


## Step 1

Fresh Start will remove most of your apps from your device, so you will have some reinstalling to do. In some cases, a clean installation may improve your device's start-up and shutdown experience, memory usage, Microsoft Store apps performance, browsing experience and battery life.

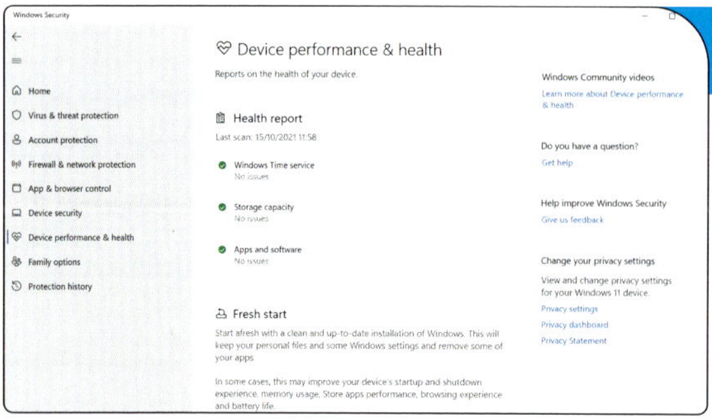


## Step 2

To find the Fresh Start tool, open the Windows Defender tool, and then click on the Device Performance & Health section. You will need to click on Additional Info and then click Give your PC a Fresh Start. If Fresh Start has previously been performed, the date will be displayed here.

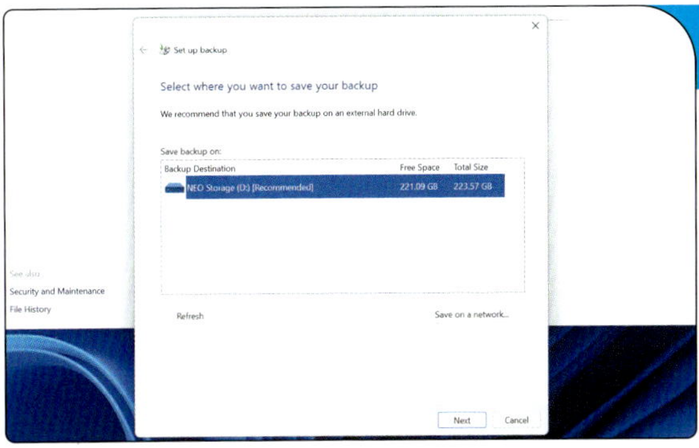


## Step 3

Microsoft recommends that you back up your files before making changes like a clean installation of Windows to your device. Make sure that you have access to all reinstallation media (such as CDs), product keys, license or login information and other materials needed to manually reinstall apps.

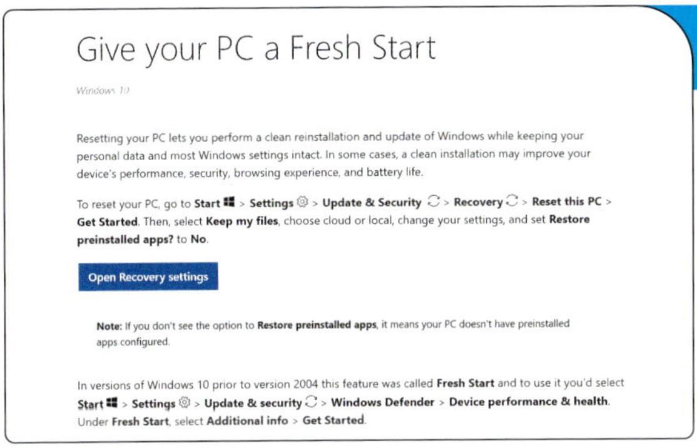


## Step 4

Looking at the website that Windows 11 sends you to when you click on the Give your PC a Fresh Start link, there will be a blue Open Recovery Settings box. Click this, and you will automatically open the Recovery Settings section, or you can access it via System > Recovery.

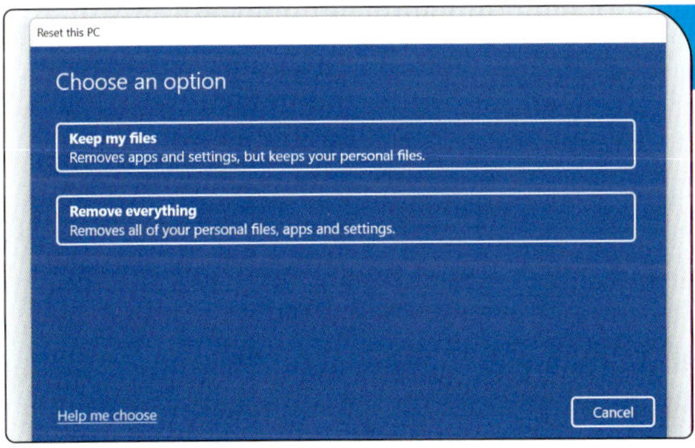


## Step 5

As you can see, all roads lead back to the Recovery section in Windows 11. To perform a Fresh Start, you'll need to click the Reset PC button. This again brings up the option pop-up window. For a Fresh Start, you'll need to click the Remove Everything button. It's worth saying again: Ensure your data is backed up before doing this.

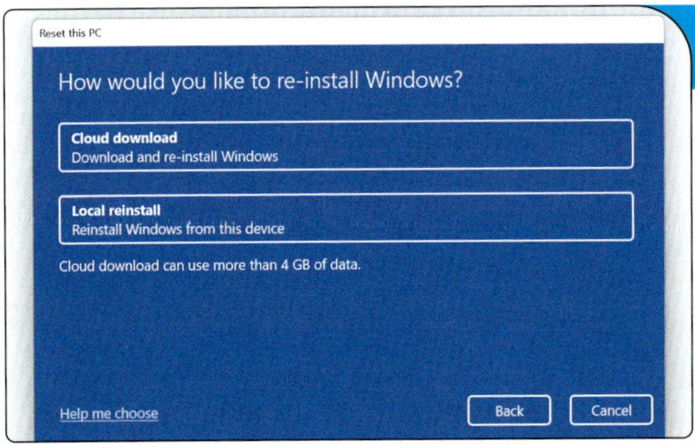


## Step 6

You'll now have the option to download Windows 11 and re-install it using the Cloud (meaning you'll download it from the Microsoft servers), or as a local reinstallation (which means you'll have a physical copy of Windows 11 either on disk or as a USB). Whichever method you prefer, click the box and the process will begin.

# Six Steps to a Faster PC

## Update Windows 11 and Drivers

The first step along your path to a faster computer is making sure that the Windows OS and all of the various drivers installed are up to date. Simply updating drivers to the latest versions can have a noticeable effect on the overall loading speed of any PC and fortunately, this is very easy to do.

Open Settings > Update & Security > Windows Update and click "Check for updates". Windows 11 will scan for available updates (to both the OS and drivers), before displaying all those available as a list.

If no updates are available, it will say "Your device is up to date" and you can move on to the next tip.

If updates are available, select those you want to download and install, then click "Install". When installation is complete, restart your PC.

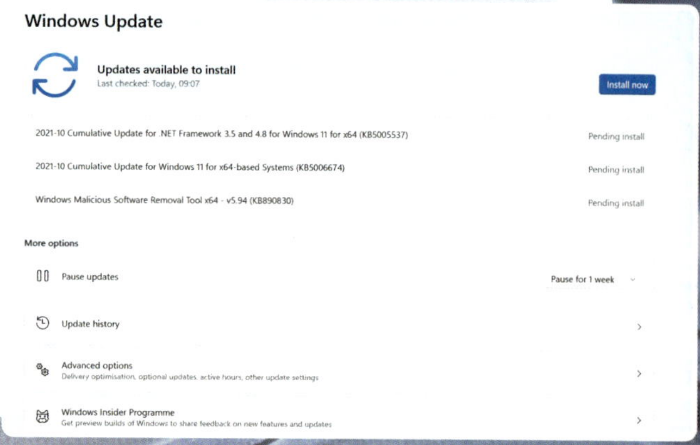


## Check Program Compatibility

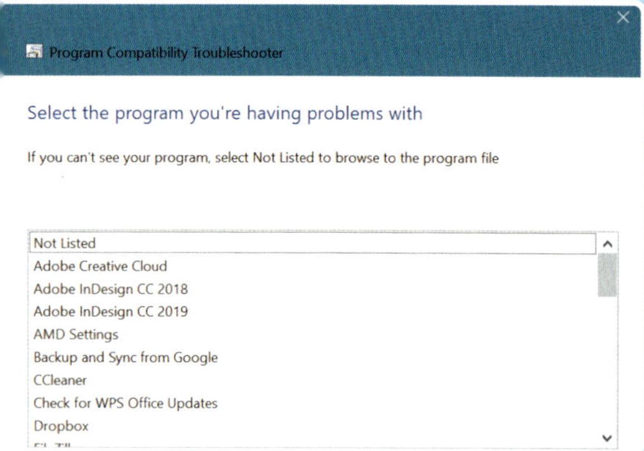


Software that is designed to run on older versions of Windows can sometimes cause Windows 11 to slow down as it struggles to manage this incompatibility issue. To find out if this is a potential problem, run the Program Compatibility Troubleshooter. In the taskbar search field, type "program compatibility troubleshooter" and click the first result in the search panel. Run the troubleshooter; testing any software you think is causing problems. The troubleshooter will offer you various ways to test and fix software compatibility issues.

**A slow computer is frustrating. When everything you try to do takes twice as long as it should, you might be tempted to think about buying a new PC; before you do, there are several things you can try to make your Windows 11 PC run faster and smoother.**

## Check and Clear Disk Space

If your hard drive is very full, it can affect performance. To check: open Settings > System > Storage and see how much space you have left. If your storage is looking full, try the following options to make some space:

**Delete Temporary Files** – Click the "This PC" bar and then click the "Temporary files" bar. Select everything you want to delete, click the "Remove Files" button and then restart your PC.

**Remove Unwanted Apps** – Open Settings > Apps > Apps & Features, click on any app you want to remove and then click "uninstall". Repeat this for all unwanted or unused apps before restarting.

**Move Files to an External Drive** – Connect a removable hard drive to your PC (a small USB flash drive for example) and open the File Explorer. Select the files you want to move, click "Move to" in the Home tab at the top and select the external drive. Files will still be instantly accessible as long as the drive is still connected.

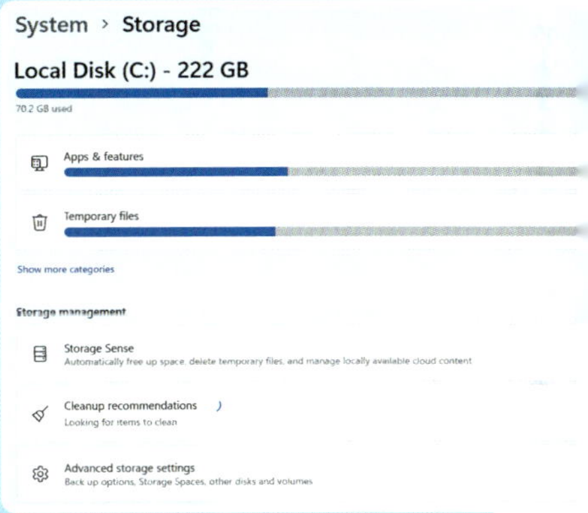


## Disable Unneeded Startup Programs

Now that you have removed any unwanted apps and software, it's time to check if any remaining apps are running unnecessarily at startup. Many software manufacturers will set their programs to start-up in the background when Windows 11 starts up. This helps the programs to open more quickly and is useful for software you frequently use, but not for software you only use occasionally. A quick way to see what software is running in the background is to look at the icons on the right side of the taskbar and open the hidden icons panel by clicking the small arrow. You can hover the mouse over icons to see what they are. If you want to have a deeper look at which software initiates during startup, open Settings > Apps > Start-up. Here you will see a list of all startup apps, along with an estimation of their performance/speed impact and a slider to prevent each one from starting automatically.

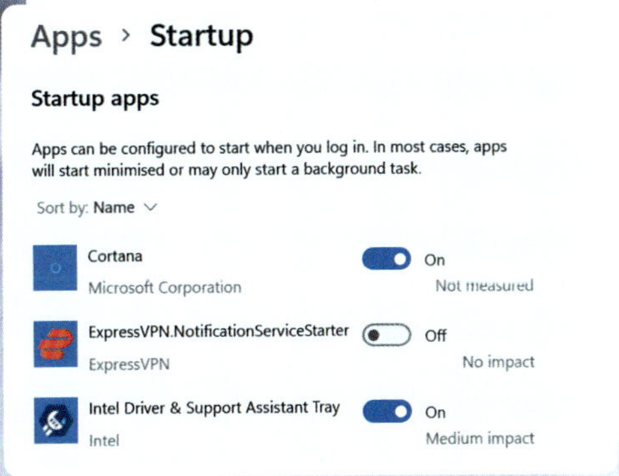

# Scan For Viruses and Malware

Viruses, malware and other malicious software could cause your computer to run slowly or behave strangely. Things to look out for include: unexpected pop-up messages, programs that suddenly start or stop, or the sound of your hard disk constantly working.

To scan for and remove viruses, open Settings > Update & Security > Windows Security (previously Windows Defender) > Open Windows Security, click on "Virus Threats & Protection" and then click the "Quick Scan" button. You can do a more advanced scan by clicking "Scan options" and choosing which you want to perform. If viruses or malware are found, you will be given options to quarantine and remove them.

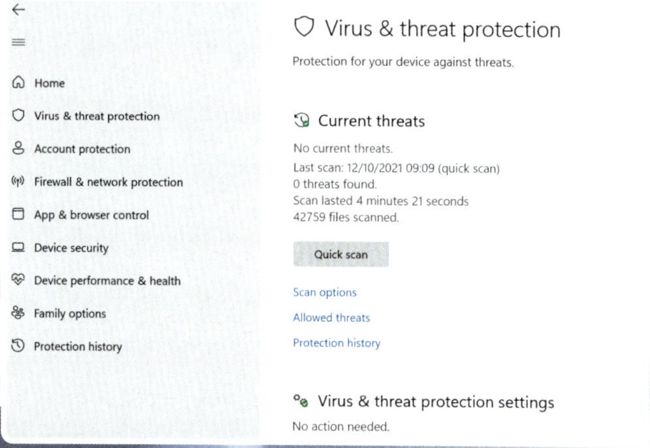


# Check for Corrupted System Files

Occasionally, the core system files in Windows can become corrupted (for a variety of reasons) and cause performance problems. Windows 11 includes a tool: the Deployment Image Service and Management Tool, that will check for such files and automatically replace them, either with a cached version or by downloading a new version.

Use the DISM Tool – In the Search box in the taskbar, type "powershell". Right-click on "Windows Powershell" in the results and choose "Run as Administrator" from the menu. At the Command prompt, that opens in the blue Powershell window, type "dism.exe /Online /Cleanup-image / Restorehealth" without the quotation marks (note the space between "dism.exe" and "/" and each switch (/)). If the tool finds and replaces any corrupted files, restart your computer and see if it has helped with your performance issues.

# Improving the Firewall

The built-in Windows 11 firewall is a surprisingly good security application. While it may not be as efficient as something offered by one of the third-party security suites, it's certainly more than adequate for the average Windows user.

## Getting to Know Your Firewall

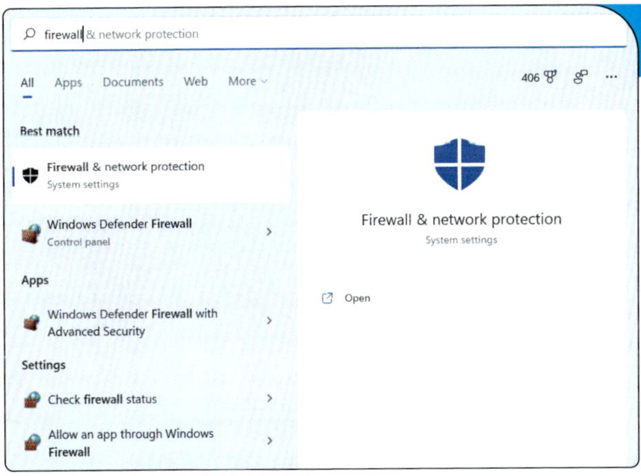


### Step 1

You can open the main Windows 11 firewall console window by clicking on the Windows Start button and entering 'firewall' into the search box. Click the returned link, Firewall & Network Protection, to launch it.

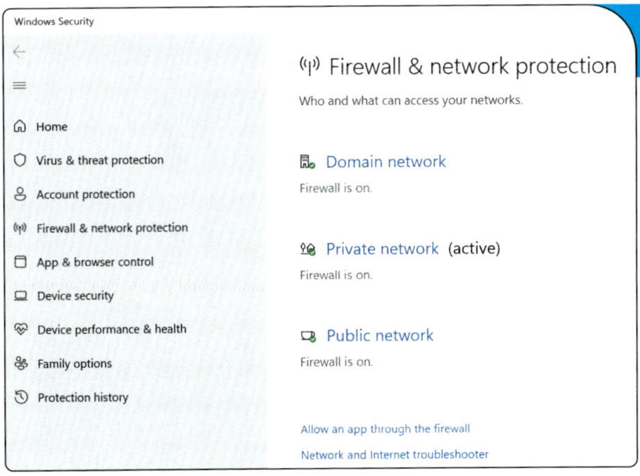


### Step 2

The Windows 11 firewall console window should be On by default, unless you've installed a third-party security suite which contains its own firewall. There are two kinds of network listed: Private and Public (and Domain if you have Windows 11 Pro version). Private is for home or work, whereas Public is for cafés and the like.

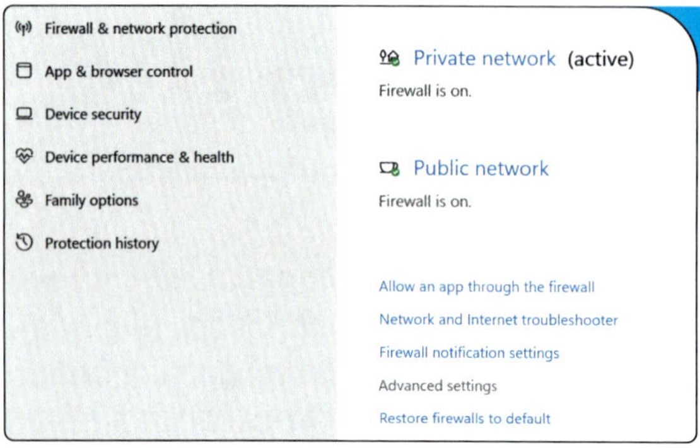


## Step 3

Under the status of the networks are some links that will help you configure and improve the firewall, as well as turning it on or off (which isn't recommended under any circumstance other than the installation of an improved third-party firewall). To begin with, start by clicking on the Advanced Settings link.

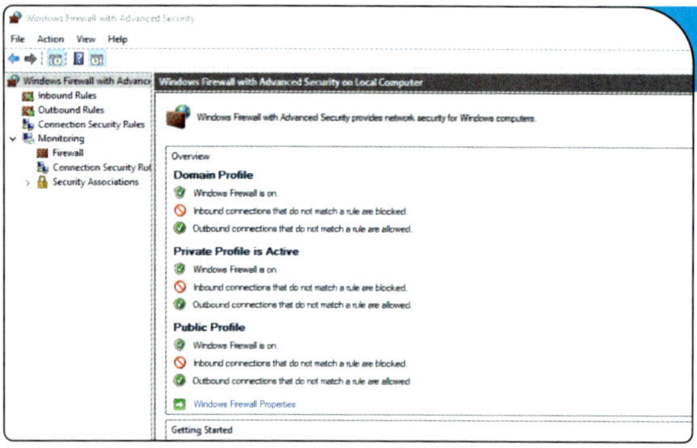


## Step 4

The Advanced Settings link launches a new console window. This defines the inbound and outbound rules for the entire system and its installed programs and applications. You can set authentication rules between computers, view and create new firewall rules, view the current firewall policies, and even monitor what's being blocked in real-time.

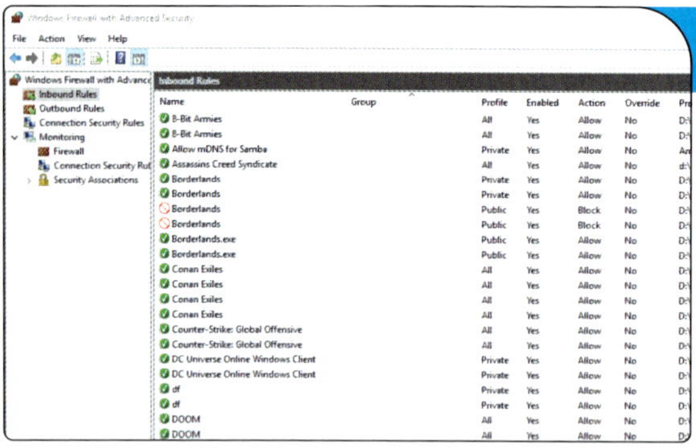


## Step 5

Click on Inbound Rules to the right-hand side of the main console window. This will list the current rules that allow traffic onto your computer and to the applications that require it. In this screenshot there's rules for various games that allow multiplayer interaction and the ability to 'talk' to the game server, as well as install updates.

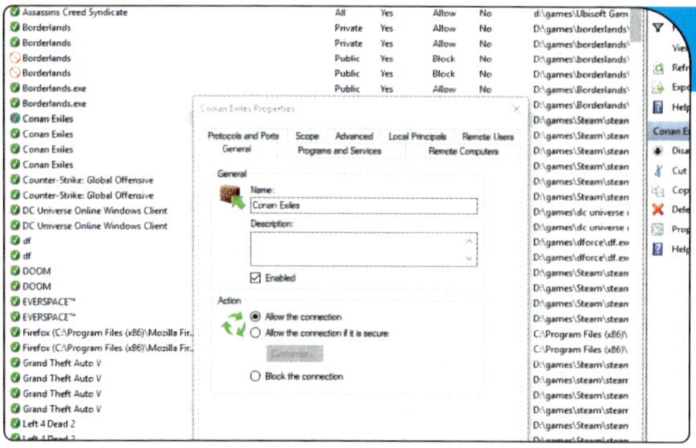


## Step 6

These rules are automatically entered into the firewall when you install the program, game or app. When you install a program you're required to accept and authenticate the process, clicking on Yes to start the installation. This level of administrative access also allows entry of the program into the firewall. Pick one of the entries and double-click it.

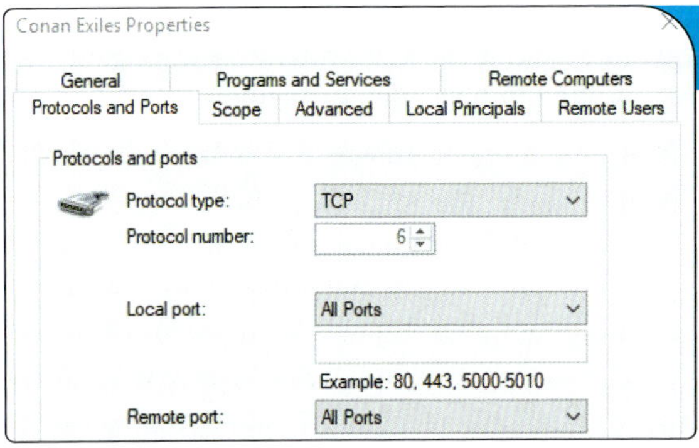


## Step 7

The properties of each firewall entry allow greater control over each program. You can change the name, allow or block the connection, define the physical location of the program on your computer, allow access to the program from remote computers, set the protocol and port number it'll use, and even which network controller to use.

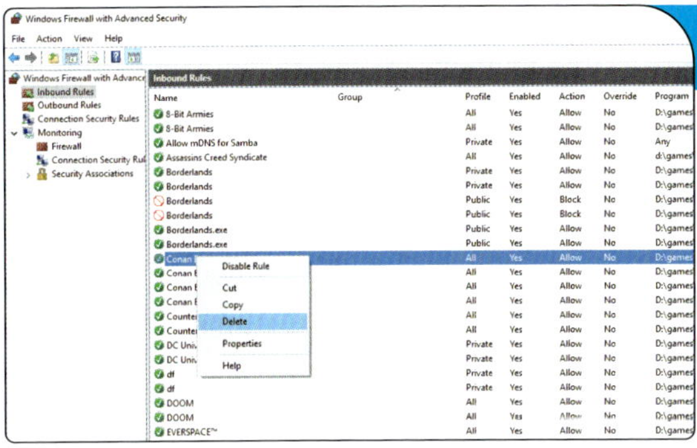


## Step 8

Sometimes, uninstalling a program doesn't automatically remove it from the firewall. The reasons why vary, but to help improve the efficiency of the Windows firewall, whenever you remove a program from your system, it's worth checking the firewall to see if its entry has been deleted. To delete it, right-click then select Delete from the menu.

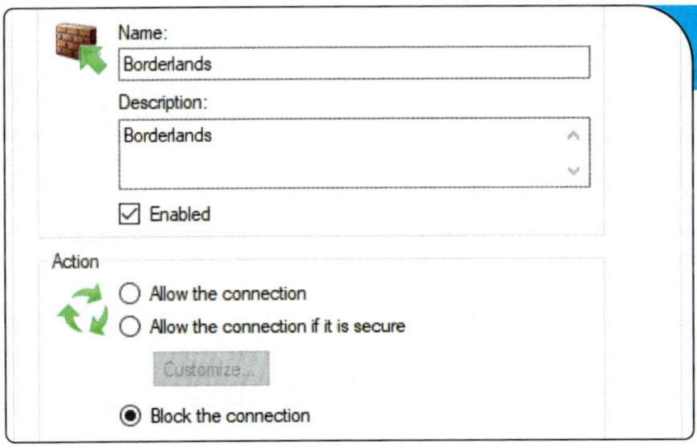


## Step 9

You may not want to delete a rule as it could be used later, or if you re-install the program and it fails to re-create the firewall entry. The recommended process then is to block the rule from communicating with the outside world. To do this, double-click the rule, and from the General tab click the Block the connection button.

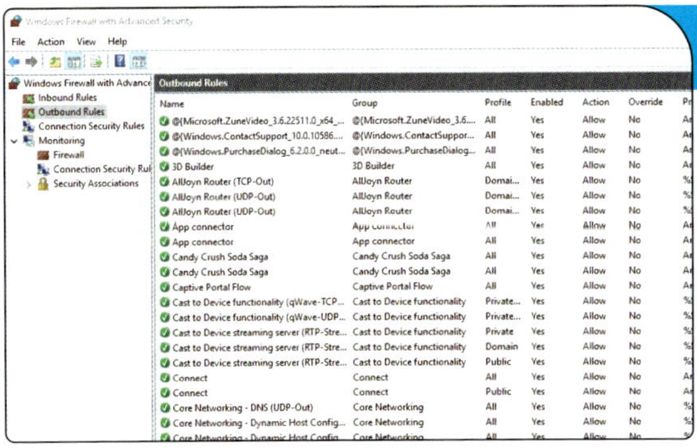


## Step 10

Similarly, the Outbound Rules link will detail the various programs that are allowed to communicate from your computer to an external destination. It's good practise to familiarise yourself with the rules of the firewall, as a rogue program will need to set a rule to communicate. You can then block that rule and stop the threat from reporting out.

# Use Defender to Stop PUPs

PUPs, Potentially Unwanted Programs, are sneaky bits of software that can sometimes be stealthily installed when you are installing other free software; usually achieved by making it a default installation option with the choice to opt out.

## Enable PUP Blocking

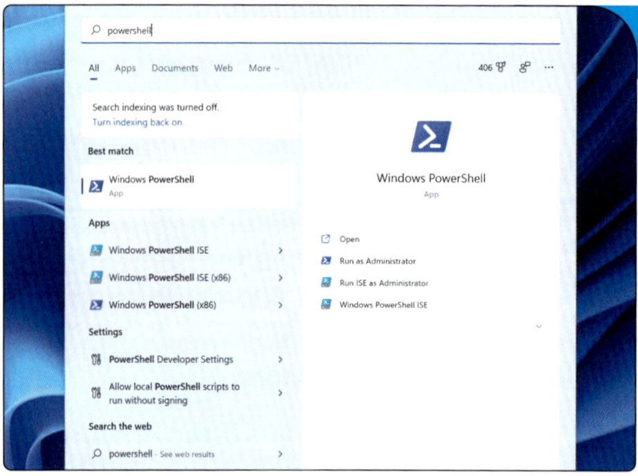


### Step 1

You can enable PUP protection with System Centre Config Manager, PowerShell or Microsoft Intune. For this guide, we'll be using the PowerShell, as this is available within Windows 11 without installing any additional software; as long as you follow the instructions carefully, it isn't as scary as it sounds.

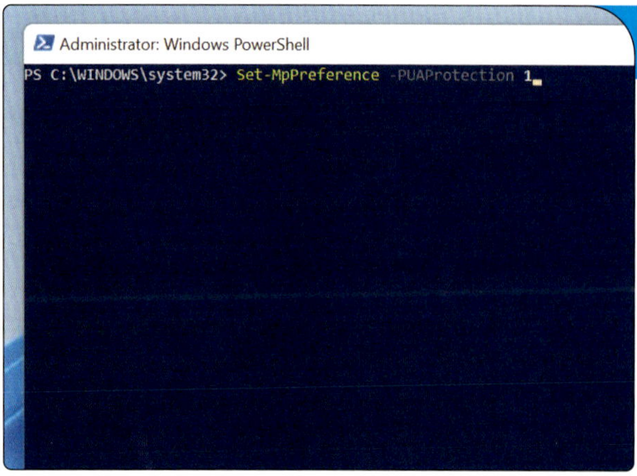


### Step 2

To access the PowerShell interface, first click the Windows Start button and type 'powershell'. Within the returned result, for Windows PowerShell, click on the Run as Administrator. Then type the following command at the prompt: Set-MpPreference -PUAProtection 1, and finally press Enter.

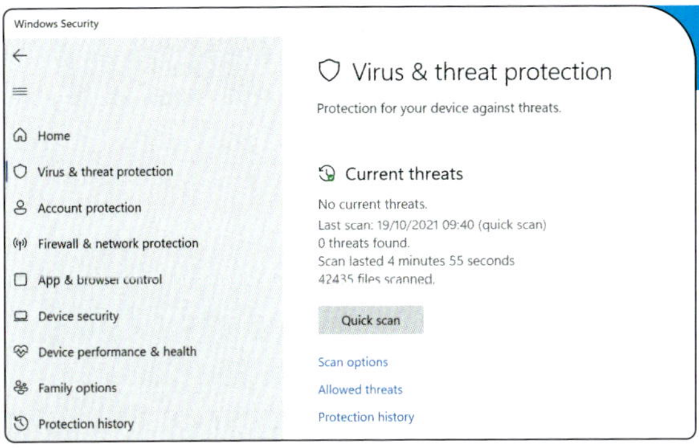


## Step 3

The PUP blocker is now enabled on your PC. You will not see any new options displayed in Windows Defender but you will see "Potentially unwanted software" listed once something is blocked. If you want to disable it in the future, just run the above command again, replacing the 1 with a 0.

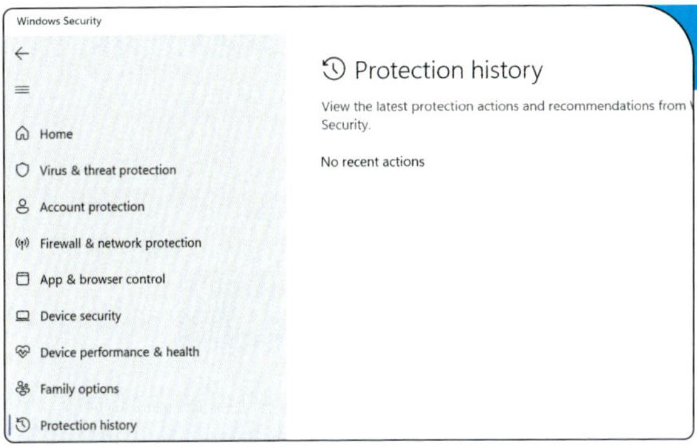


## Step 4

PUPs are blocked when a user attempts to download or install a suspicious file or if the file meets one of these conditions: the file is being scanned from the browser, it is in a folder with "downloads" in the path; or it is in a folder with "temp" in the path. The file is placed in the quarantine section.

# PUPs and Foistware

**As mentioned, a PUP is a program that's commonly installed on your system without you knowing. Most of the time, they come as part of a bundle of software or part of the installation of a piece of software. For example, if you install an app and it asks you in the installation routine if you want to also install a new add-on for your browser, then this is a PUP – or more correctly, foistware.**

**One of the first examples of a PUP (or foistware), was a toolbar that installed itself into a browser and claimed to pay the user for surfing the, then infant, Internet - via banner advertising. These days, the model hasn't changed a great deal. PUPs are mostly used to push advertising, usually through browser extensions, which also falls under the Adware category.**

**In short, always double-check everything you install on your Windows 11 computer.**

# Installing New Fonts

Windows 11 now includes a new, easier way to install and manage system fonts. This is part of Microsoft's ongoing process of moving all the system options and features to the main Settings interface. It even allows you to download from the Store.

## Install and Manage Fonts

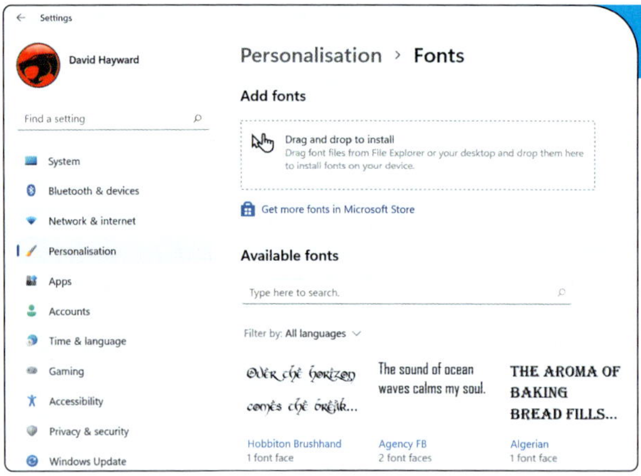


### Step 1

You can now find the fonts controls in Settings > Personalisation > Fonts. Here you will see a scrollable list of your current fonts, each with a visual example of how they look. This is a much more user-friendly way of viewing your fonts, letting you see exactly what each will look like when used.

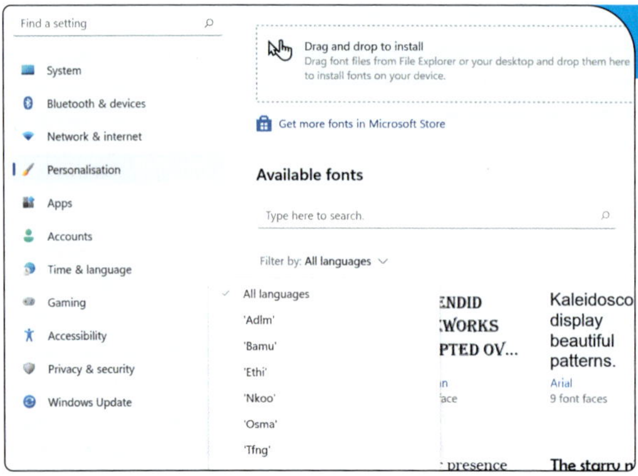


### Step 2

You can search for fonts using the search field at the top or just look through the alphabetical list. You can also filter the list by language. Each font is shown with the number of font faces it includes. A font face is a different version of the same font, i.e. regular, bold, italic, italic bold, etc.

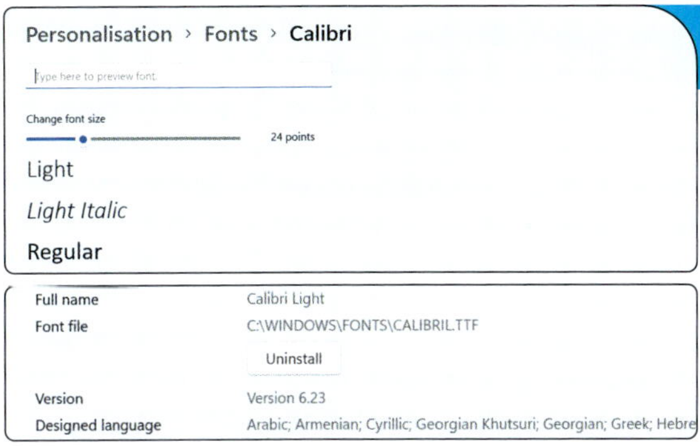


## Step 3

Click on any font in the list to view the available font faces and to see the font as it will display at different sizes, using the slider. You can type a word or sentence into the box at the top to see how it will look in that font. To uninstall a font, simply click the Uninstall button on the font preview screen.

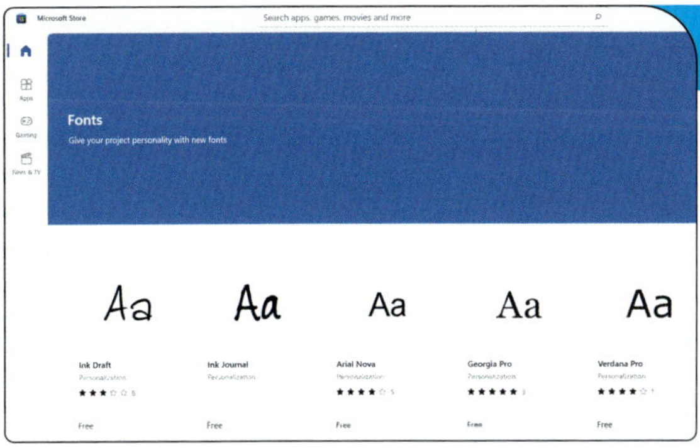


## Step 4

To find new fonts, click the Store link at the top of the main fonts page in the settings. The Store will open with all available fonts displayed. To install one, click on it in the Store and then click the Get button, or the Buy button if the font is not a free one. Installation is automatic, and now complete.

# Free Fonts

**The Internet is strewn with countless sites offering fonts. With everything from classic, typewriter and newsprint fonts, through to Lord of the Rings Elven runes, Star Trek and other fantasy and sci-fi favourites; you're spoiled for choice.**

**However, as we've mentioned throughout this book, you need to be cautious of what you download from the Internet. Most of the time, a free font is exactly that, you'll just get a compressed file which, when opened, will contain the font; but there are some examples out there that will intentionally package a virus or some other form of malware.**

**We recommend you check the site out before you download anything from it, and if you do, then every download should be scanned with Windows Security before you open it. Doing so will take longer, but will save you a lot of bother should you end up getting a virus.**

# Using the Power Menu

Windows 11 has a secret power menu that gives you access to several useful system and maintenance tools and features. We'll show you how you can use it to your advantage, to quickly access networking settings and extra features that power users need.

## Power Up

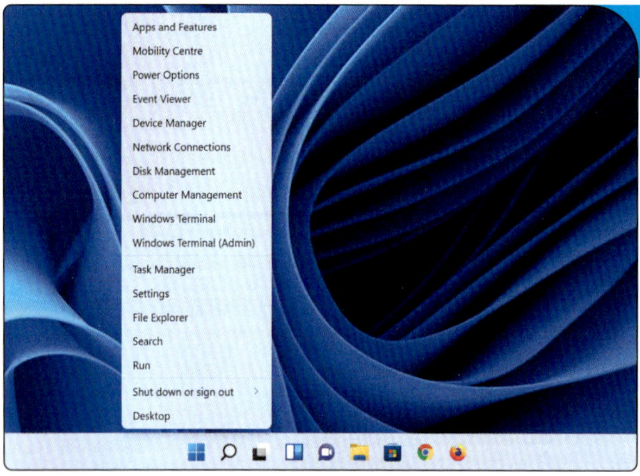


### Start it Up

Open the Power Menu using the Start button, but instead of just left-clicking it to open the Start menu, right-click the button. Note that you can also shut down or sign out here, too. This menu was originally created for users who felt the old Windows 8 Start screen didn't give them access to what they needed.

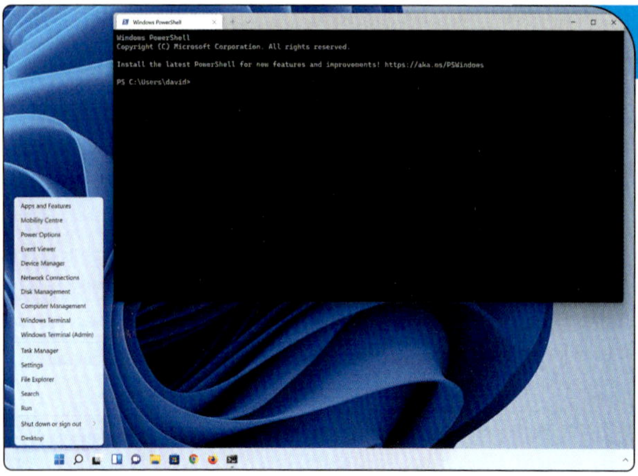


### Command

There are numerous shortcut access options available in the Power Menu. For example, you can access the new Windows 11 Terminal, both as standard access or as an elevated, Administrator access. You can also Run commands directly from the Power Menu, Search for files or folders, and more; plus view your Windows 11 Events and logs.

## Uninstall Apps

The topmost available option within the Power Menu, Apps & Features, takes you directly to the Apps section within Settings. From here, you can modify, uninstall and get to advanced options for all the apps you currently have installed on your system. It may only save a couple of clicks, but every shortcut saves time.

| Option | HotKeys | Description |
|---|---|---|
| Programs (Apps) & Features | F | Opens Windows Programs & Features |
| Mobility Center | B | Launch Windows Mobility Center |
| Power Option | O | Opens Windows Power Options |
| Event Viewer | V | Opens Windows Events viewer |
| System | Y | Opens Windows Systems Properties |
| Network Connections | W | Opens Network Connection pane |
| Disk Management | K | Opens Disk Management on Windows |
| Computer Management | G | Opens Computer Management settings |

## Hot Keys

You can access the Power Menu by pressing the Windows key + X on your keyboard. As well as opening the Power Menu, it enables you to use hot keys to quickly launch any of the options within the menu. At this point in time, you can only use the hot keys if you use the Windows shortcut key to open the Power Menu.

# God Mode

**Did you know that there is another set of menus and items that isn't so well-known by the average user: Windows God Mode!**

**Well, to be fair, it's not strictly God Mode. You can't re-write the kernel or anything, but it does offer a lot of access to background elements you won't normally come across. It's affectionately called God Mode by some, so the popular media use it every time a new version of Windows comes out. Anyway, here's how it works:**

**Right-click the desktop, and select New > Folder. Name the folder: GodMode.{ED7BA470-8E54-465E-825C-99712043E01C}, and press Enter.**

**The name of the folder will vanish, and when you double-click to enter it, there are over 200 items to manage and view. Quick warning though, as some settings can make Windows 11 unusable if you're not careful.**

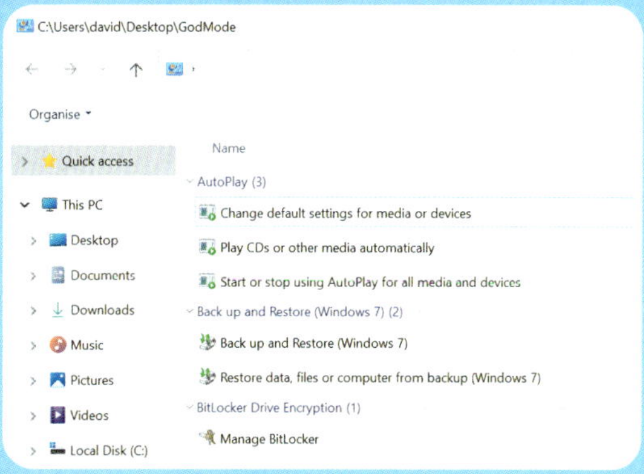

# Using Storage Sense

A feature carried over from Windows 10 is Windows 11's Storage Sense. It helps keep your computer in tip-top shape by deleting unwanted content as your hard drive begins to run out of space – something which it inevitably will do.

## Sense and Sensibility

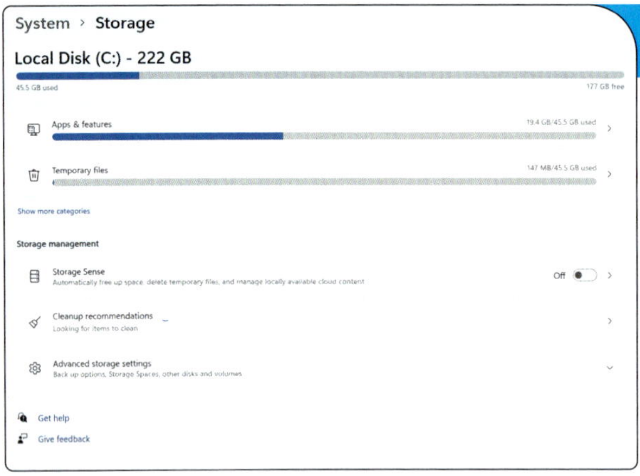


### Step 1

To get to the Storage Sense options, click on the Windows Start button, and go to Settings > Storage > Storage Sense. Alternatively, you can get there via the Power Menu (right-click the Windows button, or press the Windows key + X) and choose Settings, then Storage.

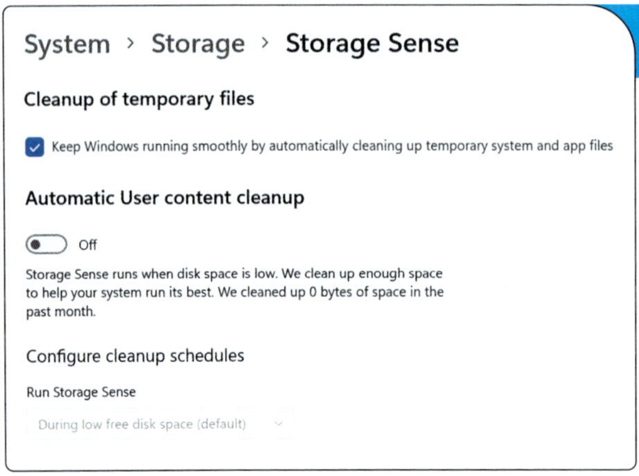


### Step 2

Click the Storage Sense option within the Storage section, if you haven't already done so. Don't worry about turning on just yet, though. In Storage Sense you have a number of options available. The first is enabled by default: 'Cleanup of temporary files', which will remove unnecessary temp files from your system as you update Windows 11.

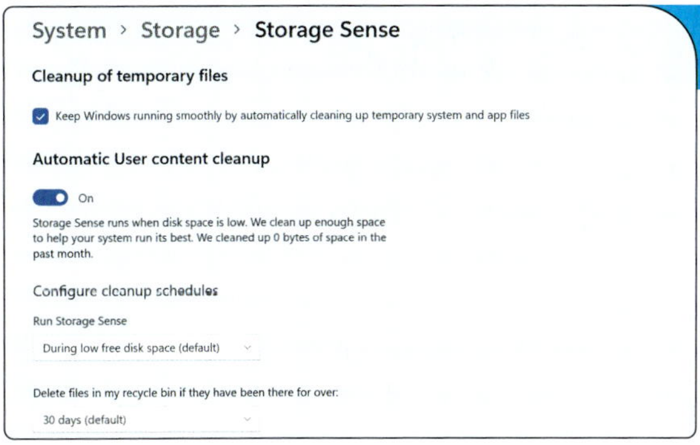


## Step 3

Click the sliding button to enable Automatic User Content Cleanup. Here you can opt to configure cleanup schedules, such as removing files every day, week or month; or just when Windows 11 reports that your hard drive is running low on space.

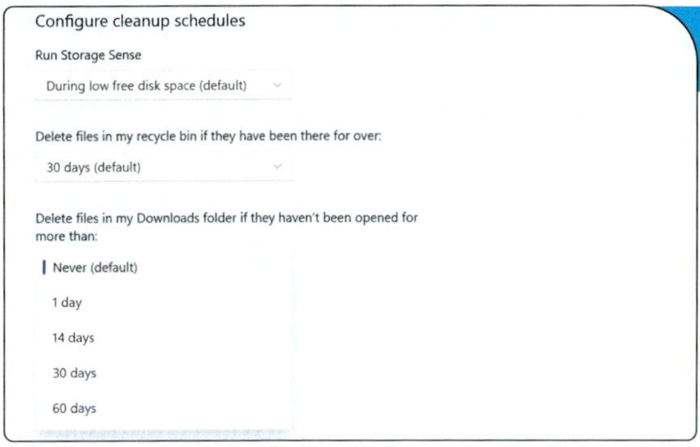


## Step 4

You can choose when to delete files in your Recycle bin. The default is 30 days, but you can opt for 1, 14 or 60 days. Files in your Downloads folder can be auto-deleted if they haven't been opened for more than 1 day, through to 60 days. However, if Storage Sense deletes them from the Downloads folder, ensure you backup your files.

# Housekeeping Your System

**Storage Sense is a great fire-and-forget element to help your Windows 11 system keep in shape; however, it's not perfect.**

**Eventually, even with Storage Sense running in the background, you'll run out of space. This is only because of the number of apps, updates and everything else that will be installed on the computer; even those with hundreds of gigabytes of free space will run out in time.**

**To best combat this, you'll need to create a housekeeping routine into your digital life. Every month, for example, take the time to clean your system out and remove anything that you don't need. You don't have to delete it, just move it to another hard drive, or cloud storage if you want. Right-click your hard drive in File Explorer, select Properties and in the General tab click Disk Clean-up, to remove stray temporary files.**

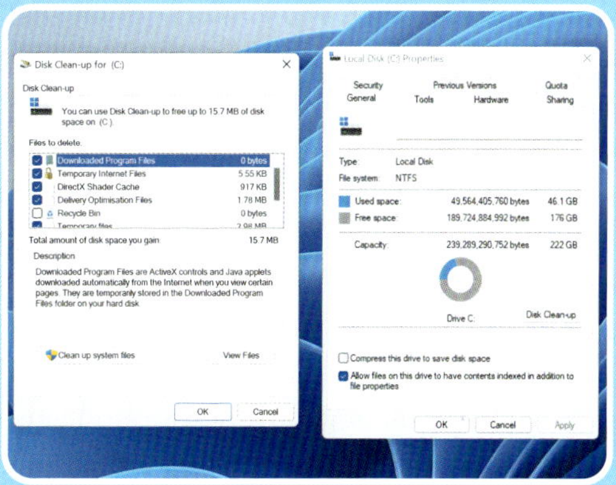

# Using the Task Manager

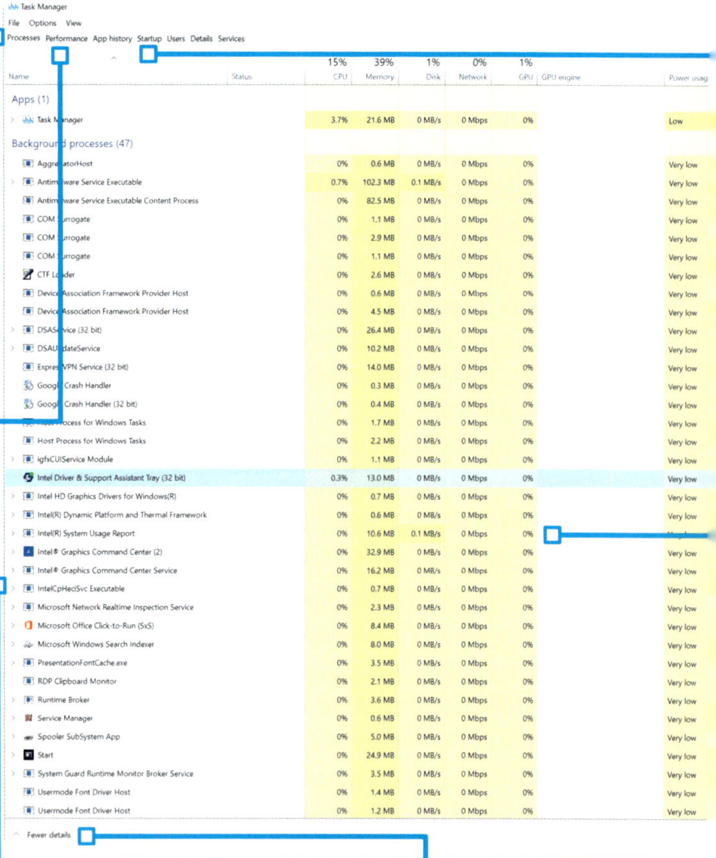


## Processes Tab

The Processes tab is the default tab when the Task Manager is opened. You can open the task manager by simply searching for it in the main search panel. Just as with any other app or piece of software in Windows 11, you can pin a shortcut to the Task Manager, to the taskbar or as a desktop icon.

## Performance Tab

Another useful tab in the Task Manager is Performance. This gives you a real-time performance overview, allowing you to pinpoint exactly how well your hardware is coping with whatever you are doing at the time. If Task Manager is the only app open, the performance chart should be very stable but if you are running several apps, it will show any power spikes.

## Process List

With the Processes tab selected, a list of all processes is shown. Processes are bits of software that run in the background, either running or waiting to run when a corresponding action is taken. As you can see from the list here, things like Microsoft Office are shown; you would most likely want to leave this alone.

## Fewer Details

You can view a limited version of the Task Manager by clicking on the "Fewer Details" button at the bottom of the window. This makes the window small enough that it can be left open, in the corner of your desktop for example, but still show relevant information. You can get more information at any time by clicking "More Details".

**The Task Manager is a useful tool, but you might never have looked at it. The Task Manager contains information on PC performance, the number of running apps, how many processes are pulling power from the processor and much more.**

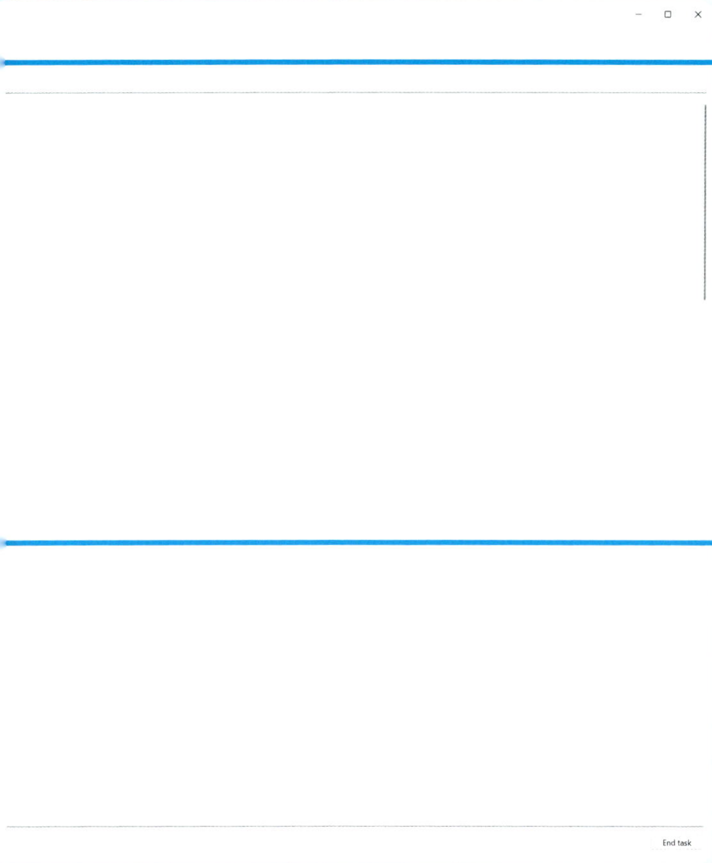


## Start-up Tab

The Start-up tab contains a list of all the apps, programs and processes that are enabled every time you start your computer. If your computer is brand new, this list should be fairly small and filled with essential items. But as you install new apps and software, this start-up list can become bloated and slow down boot up. You can disable auto start-up here.

## Resource Usage

If you find your PC becoming slow and sluggish during normal use, you may have too many processes running. By looking at the resource usage chart, you can see exactly which apps are taking up the most processing power, physical memory, disk space and even network bandwidth. If something is particularly resource hungry, you can right-click and stop it.

## View Options

The View options at the top of the Task Manager window allows you to do several things. You can manually refresh the current tab and also change the automatic update speed. For example you can change how the processes are displayed. Either by grouping them by type, expanding or collapsing the list, or showing status values.

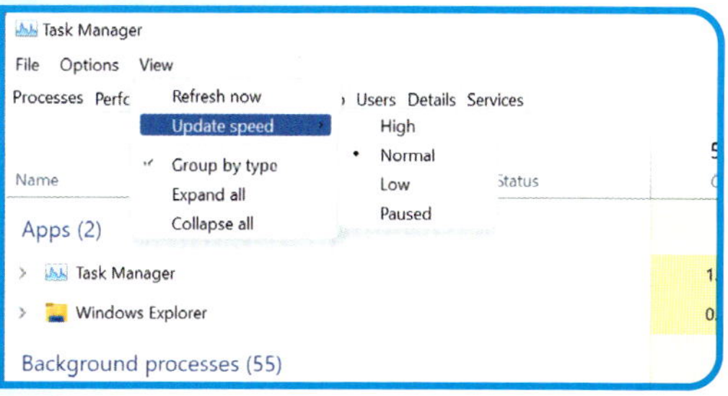

# Defragment Hard Drives

**The act of Defragging your drive goes back to the early days of computing, where data was written to the drive in various sectors across the disk platters. This data could be spread all over, taking time to read, so a Defrag packs it all neatly into readable areas.**

## Defrag

**Most of us have a modern PC with a relatively modern operating system installed on it, regardless of whether that's Windows 11, macOS or the latest distribution of Linux. These systems have been updated and tweaked in accordance with the advanced hardware technology that's now available, and will more than likely see you through a good year or so without you ever having to even look at a defrag tool.**

Defragging is one of those utilities that exist to cause arguments. The for camp declare it the best thing you can do with a PC, and therefore it must be done every week. The against camp laugh heartily at the amount of time wasted, watching little blocks being moved around the screen while your hard drive has the computing equivalent of an extreme workout.

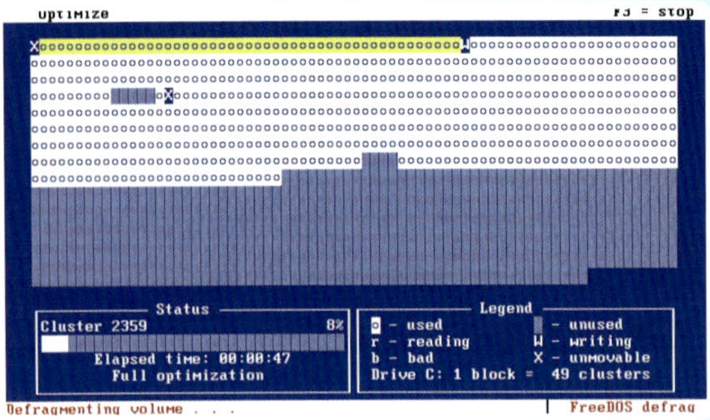


Although there are studies that show defragging every so often can help older operating systems and hardware, there's nothing concrete that suggests a weekly defrag will help out a modern operating system and hardware. In fact, if you've got a solid-state drive (SSD) installed you shouldn't be defragging at all, especially if the SSD is one of the first or second generation models. But, and here's where things get a little grey, there are also many experts who think that defragging a modern SSD won't do too much harm, and won't necessarily impede the overall lifetime of the device – since SSDs have a significantly lower read/write lifespan compared to a more traditional, mechanical hard drive.

In truth, a monthly check of the state of fragmentation of your drives is considered a good idea. If Windows 11 recommends that you perform a defrag, then go ahead and do one. Otherwise, stick to the old adage: if it ain't broke…

## So, What is Defragging?

As explained in the main intro of this page, over time the operating system will write numerous files to your hard drive. Those files can be the data you're working with, your personal data, work and such, and it can be temporary files that the OS works on in the background. For example, when you browse the Internet, temporary files are created for every page you visit, sometimes many per page depending on what's going on with the page in question. Most of these files are deleted once the browser has been closed down, some aren't. This creates areas of a drive that files now exist on, and areas where files did exist, which causes fragmentation.

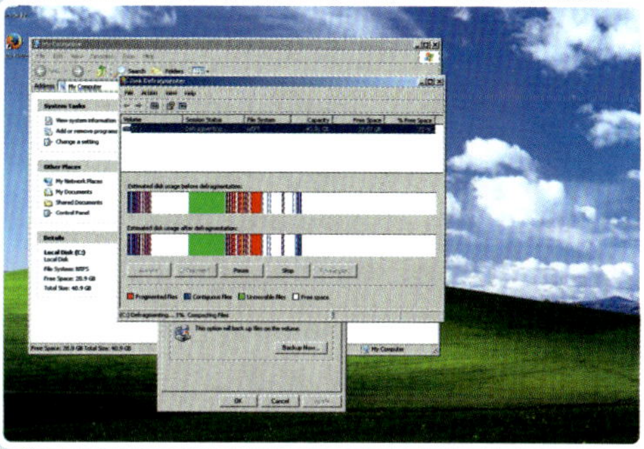

Each of these blocks of saved, deleted and moved data soon create fragmented sectors across the physical disk platter (we're talking about hard drives here, not SSDs). As the drive heads move along the platters to retrieve and write data – much like the needle on a vinyl record player – it has to travel more and from one end to the other to fetch the data, due to the inconsistencies created by the frequent writes and deletes.

Defragging will move all that readable data to areas at the front of the drive platter, so the drive heads don't have as far to travel to read the data. This speeds up the reading of data, and helps get rid of any unwanted leftovers from the number of times a disk is accessed.

Granted it does go into further depth, but we're not going to delve too deep here. If you want to understand more, then we'd recommend you look up defragmentation online.

## Do SSDs need Defragging?

Ask most folks in the know, and they'd say no, an SSD does not need to be defragged. This is understandable, as there are no physical platters or drive heads. The data written to an SSD via a modern operating system is often put into a temporary position first, then committed to an area of the drive. If you defrag an SSD, then you're moving temporary files around before they're committed, then moving them once they are, so you're doubling the workload of the SSD. And, as we've already mentioned, an SSD has a much lower read/write lifetime than a mechanical drive.

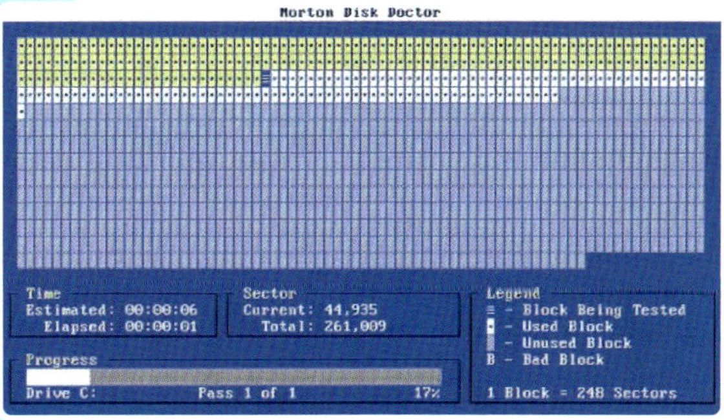


Plus, mechanical drives have average read/access times of around 15ms, whereas an SSD has access times measuring in the 0.1ms mark. So a defrag won't make any difference in access times.

However, even ones and zeros written to solid state memory can get slightly fragmented over time. In which case, it's often best to check the state of the drive.

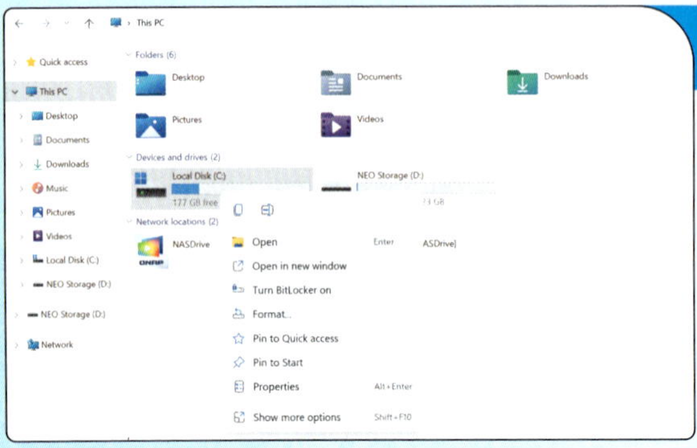


## Step 1

To do this, right-click the drive you want to check and Defrag in Windows 11 File Manager, and select Properties from the menu. Now click the tools tab, then locate and click the Optimise button in the Optimise and Defragment Drive section – it's the bottom section of the Tools tab window.

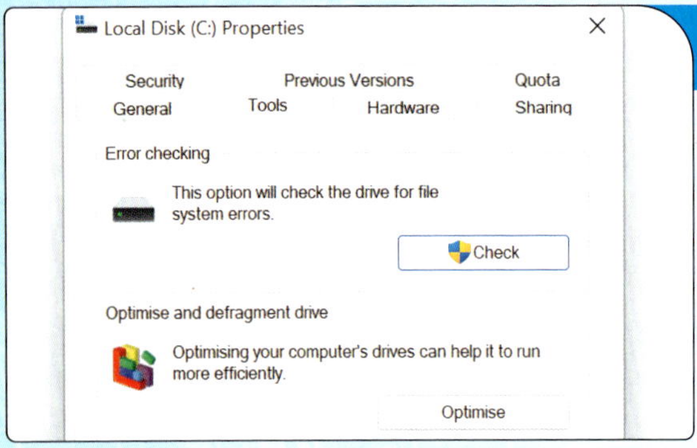


## Step 2

The new window will display the physical hard drives installed in your system. In the Optimise Drives window click the Analyse button to check the current state of the drive in question. If Windows 11 recommends a defrag, which is displayed in the Current Status of the drives section, click the Optimise button.

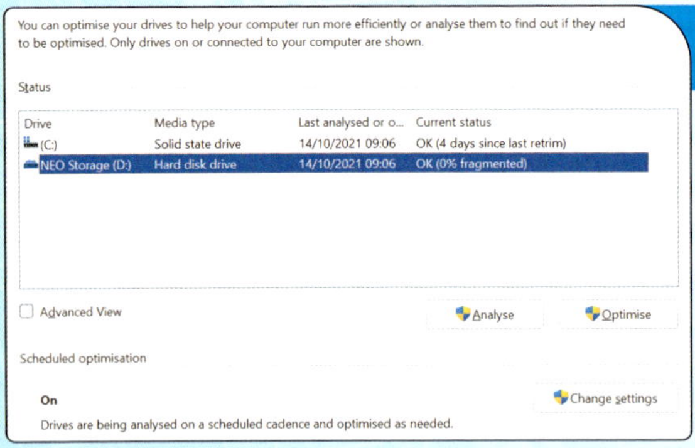


## Step 3

In short, checking on the health of your drive(s) is something you should factor into your monthly computer checks – updates, AV updates, drivers etc. However, you may never need to use a defrag during the lifespan of your Windows 11 PC.

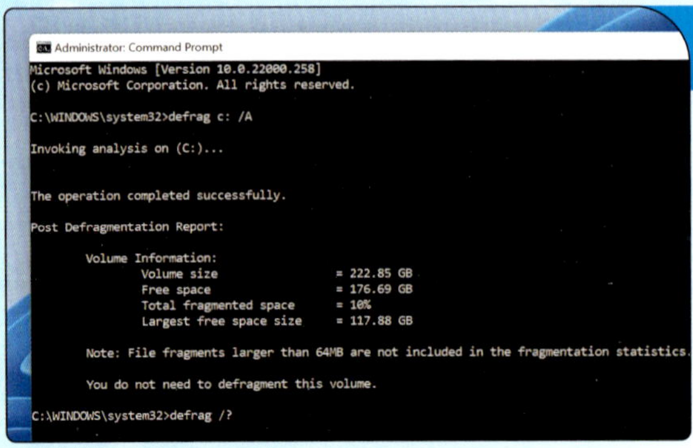


## Step 4

You can Defrag from the command line. Open a command prompt with Administrator access, then enter: **defrag c: /A**. This will run a quick report on the state of the drive, if it needs to be defragged or not. For more information on the command line Defrag tool, enter: **defrag /?** This displays all the available switches and uses of the command.

# Using Office Online

If you're out of the office or away from home, and you need to edit an existing Office document or create a new one, then try Office Online. These versions of Word, Excel, PowerPoint and more are extremely handy, and all you need is a Microsoft account.

## Office for Everyone

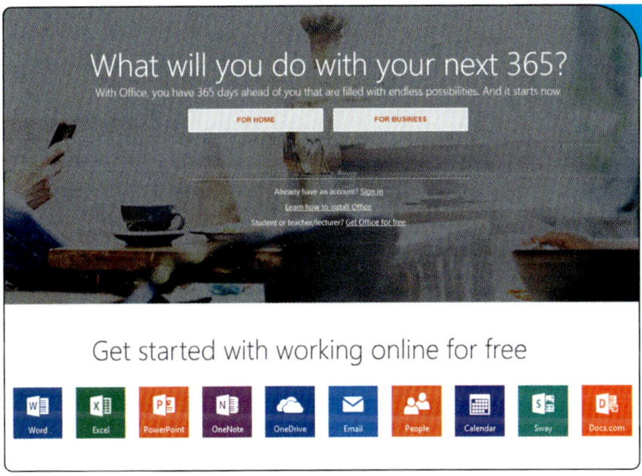


### Step 1

There are ten Office cloud options available from the office.live.com site. The more familiar and well-used Word, Excel and PowerPoint take the first three places, with OneNote, access to your OneDrive account, Mail, and so on after. The last option is Docs.com, the Microsoft collaborative portal; similar to that of Google Docs.

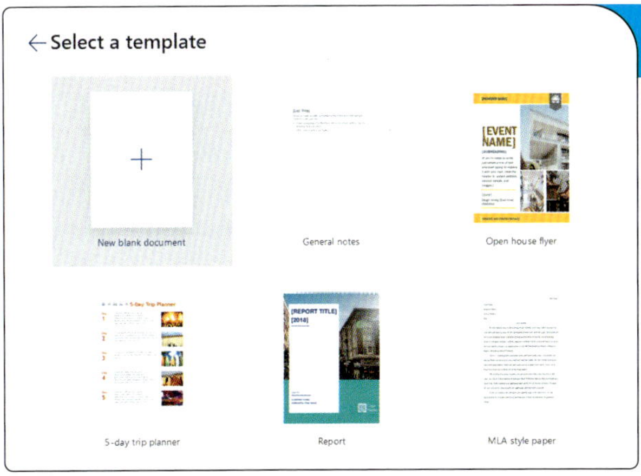


### Step 2

Clicking on each of the Office cloud icons will launch the product, asking you to sign into your Microsoft account and linking the cloud app with your OneDrive account. There are numerous templates to choose from within each of the main Office apps; or you can load up one already in your OneDrive account, or upload from a local source.

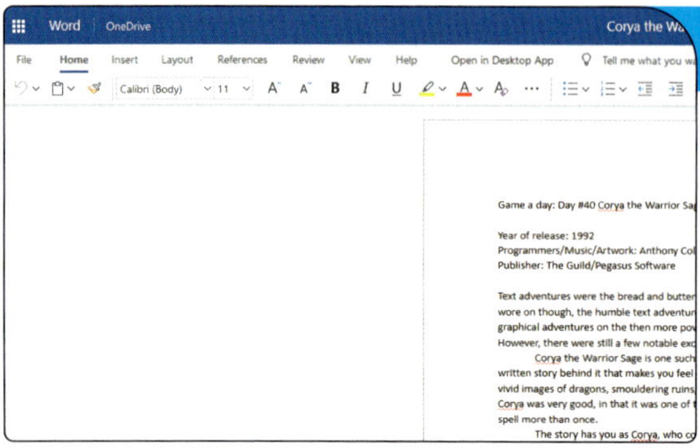


## Step 3

The layout of the individual Office cloud apps is similar to that of the latest version of Office, so you'll not need to re-learn how to use a particular app. Compatibility is taken care of across older versions of Office too, allowing you to load up content from Word 2003 and work within a Docx format.

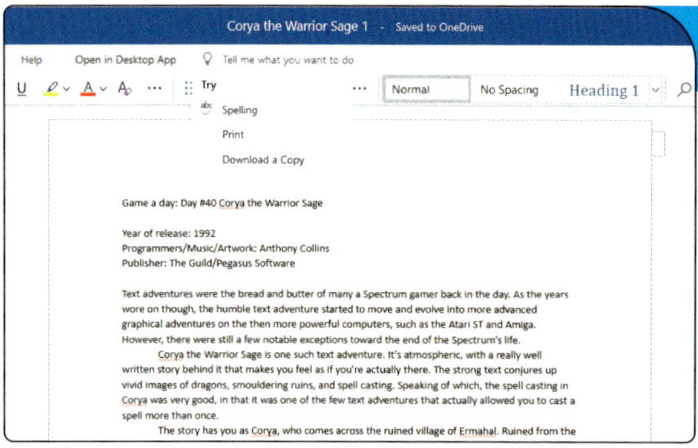


## Step 4

In addition to the usual Ribbon menus, Office Online also incorporates the latest help features from Office 2016 and 365. There's a 'Tell me what you want to do' section in the top menu, which, when clicked will reveal several suggestions to start you off.

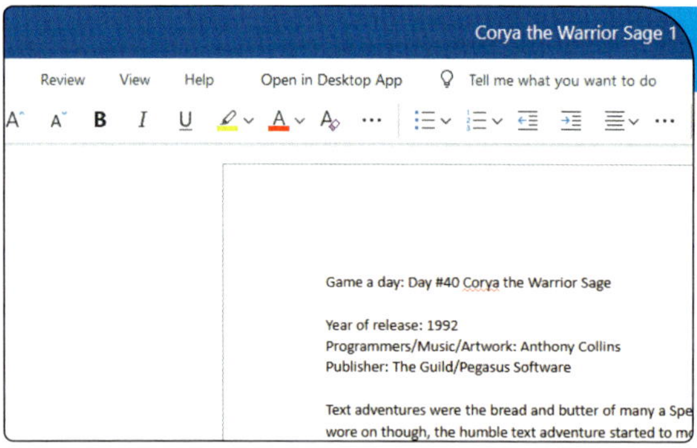


## Step 5

Clicking the 'Open in Desktop App' link will launch the locally installed version of 365, so you'll be able to continue working on the file from the desktop installed app; as opposed to the online version of the app. This is handy if the file requires the use of a feature that isn't available in the online version.

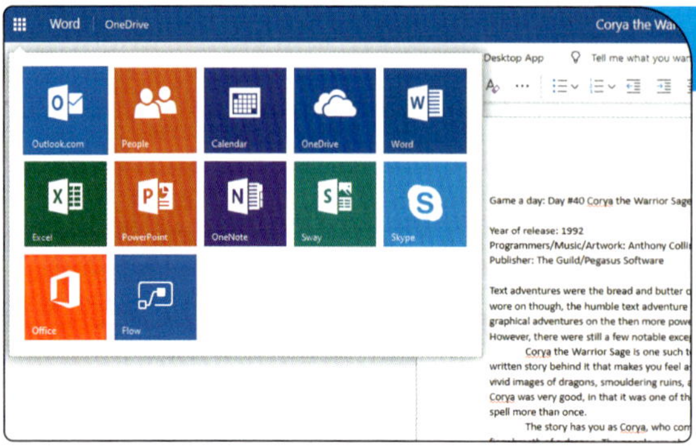


## Step 6

In all the Office Online apps, clicking the box of nine squares in the upper left of the app screen will open a quick-launch area where you can access the other cloud apps; known as the App Launcher. This way you don't need to keep returning to the main office.live.com page to launch each individual app.

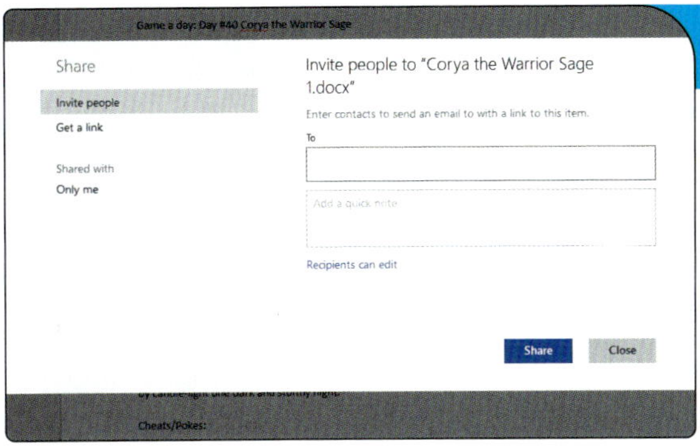


## Step 7

Sharing a file from within the Office Online apps is particularly easy. Just click on the Share button in the upper-right of the app's interface, and you'll be asked to enter the contacts who will be granted access. You can also generate a link for the file, and alter the permissions of each collaborator.

## Step 8

Any of the files you create within the Office Online cloud apps can be saved to the local system, or a USB stick if you're working off a public computer. You can download and save them as the Office format document they're created in, or you can opt to save them as a PDF or an Open Document file, ODT.

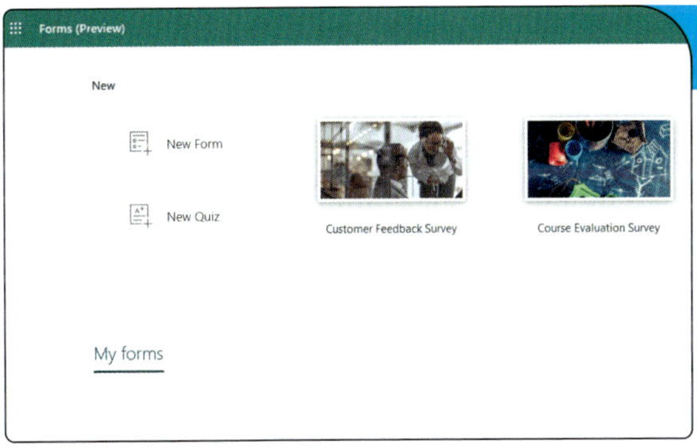


## Step 9

Forms is an interesting cloud app from the Office Online suite. Once signed in, you can create customer feedback forms, course evaluations, event registration and much more. There are loads of templates available, and you're able to create your own unique forms and even quizzes.

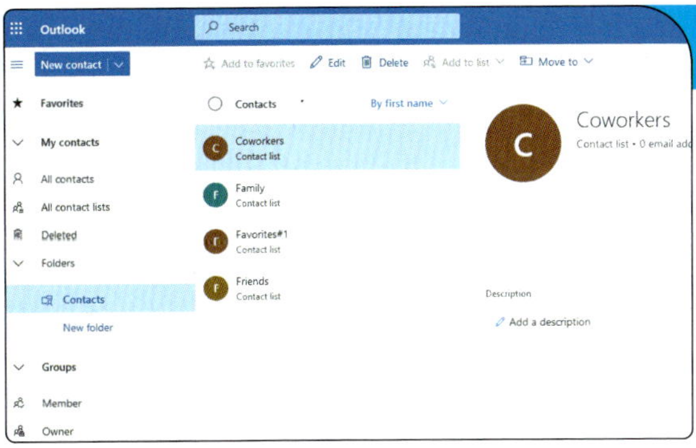


## Step 10

The People app links to your Microsoft Outlook account, and will then display any contacts you have created. With it you can create new contacts and connect to social networks such as Twitter, Google, LinkedIn and so on.

# How to Use Autoplay

Windows AutoPlay is a feature that was first introduced all the way back in Windows 98. It helpfully allows newly discovered media, based on content such as images, video or music, to begin playing via the appropriate Windows application.

## Rediscovering AutoPlay

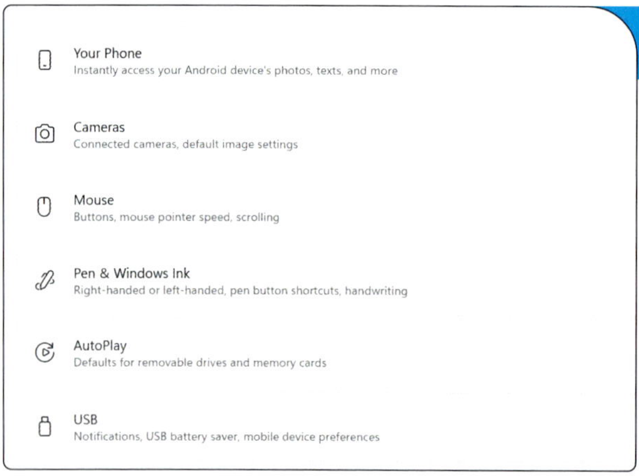


### Step 1

AutoPlay is one of those features that can be both a blessing and a curse. It's great when you want to simply insert some media, sit back and start to watch, or use it. Other times, you might just want to browse the contents of the media, instead of it auto-playing. Either way, here's how to enable or disable it.

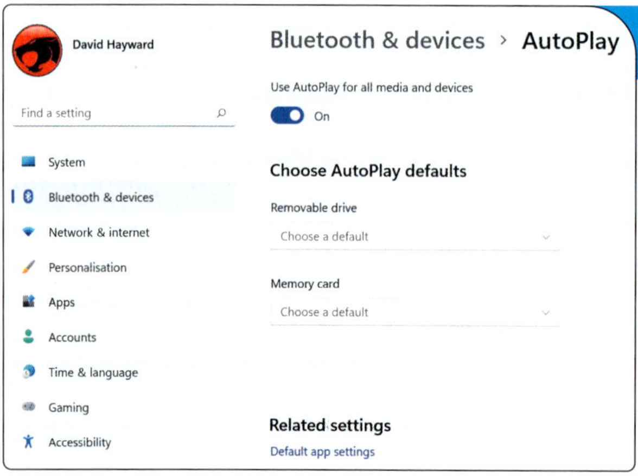


### Step 2

In our example, the AutoPlay feature was enabled. This means that whenever we insert some media, be it a disc of some description or memory card, Windows 11 will auto launch the appropriate app. However, if your AutoPlay isn't working, start by clicking on the On button at the top of the screen.

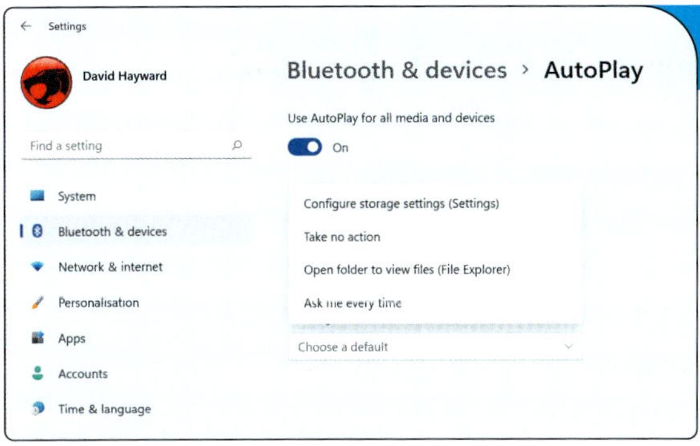


## Step 3

If nothing happens when you insert any media, despite the AutoPlay feature being turned on, you may need to specify an AutoPlay default. Under the On button are two options for AutoPlay defaults: Removable Drive and Memory Card – you may have more options available. Click the Removable Drive drop-down box - Choose a default.

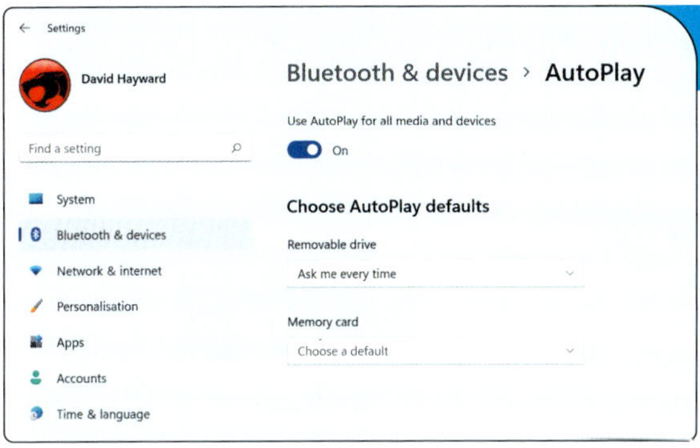


## Step 4

Here you'll have multiple options available, depending on the apps you have installed, but by default they allow you to access the Storage Settings in Windows 11 for removable drives and are: Take no action, when a removable drive is inserted; Open File Explorer or Ask me every time, what you want to do with the type of media inserted.

# AutoPlay Group Policy

**For most people, using the steps mentioned to turn on, or off, AutoPlay works perfectly well, and they'll not need to do anything else. However, if you have Windows 11 Pro installed and you want to disable/enable AutoPlay for multiple users on the same Windows 11 Pro computer, then you can use the Group Policy Editor to do the job.**

**Press the Windows Key + R, to open the Run dialogue box. Enter: gpedit.msc, and click the OK button or press Enter. Go to: Computer Configuration > Administrative Templates > Windows Components, and double-click AutoPlay Policies. From here, double-click the Turn off AutoPlay item (or other items in the window), and select Enable or Disable.**

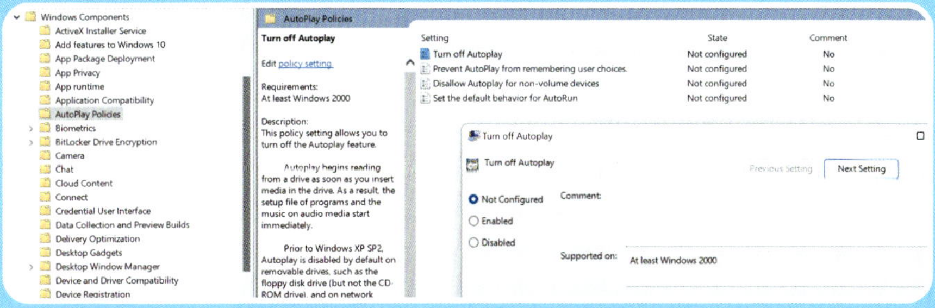

# Managing Libraries

Libraries are virtual containers for users' content. A library can contain files and folders stored on the local computer or in a remote storage location. In Windows Explorer, users interact with libraries in ways similar to how they would interact with other folders.

## Quiet in the Library

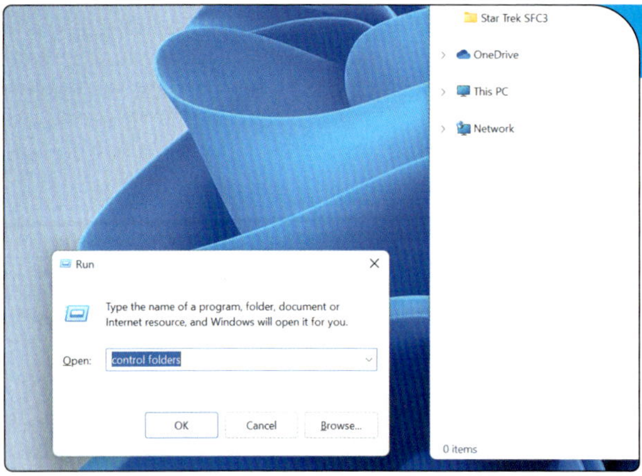


### Step 1

If you open Windows 11 File Explorer, you'll notice that Libraries are no longer visible by default, which is a shame as many users rely on them. However, they can be returned, and the process is remarkably simple. Start by pressing the Windows Key and R, then enter: control folders.

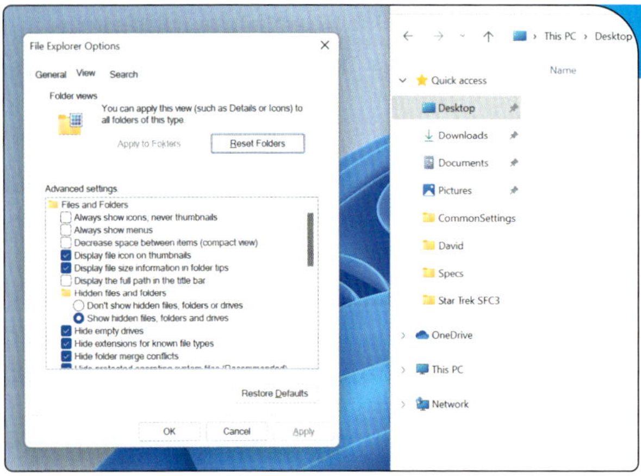


### Step 2

Hit enter, or click the OK button and the File Explorer Options window will pop up. The options available in here can drastically alter the way Windows Explorer works, so be careful what you enable or disable. Head to the View tab, and scroll down to the bottom of the Advanced Settings section.

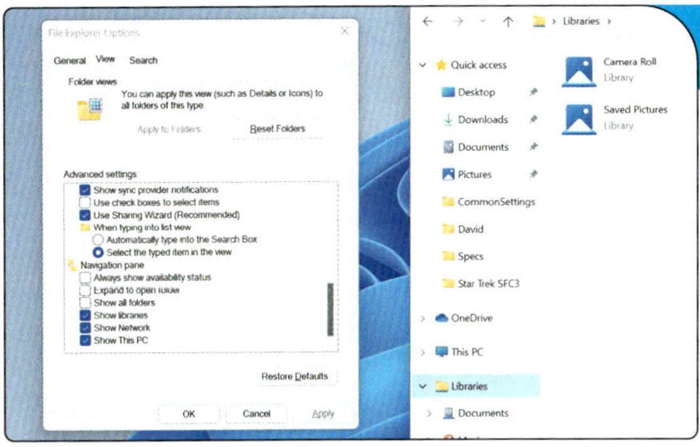


## Step 3

At the bottom of the Advanced Settings section, you'll notice a box labelled Show Libraries. Click the box to tick, and re-enable the option. When you've done that, click the Apply button to activate the change and you'll see that the Libraries are now available via File Explorer.

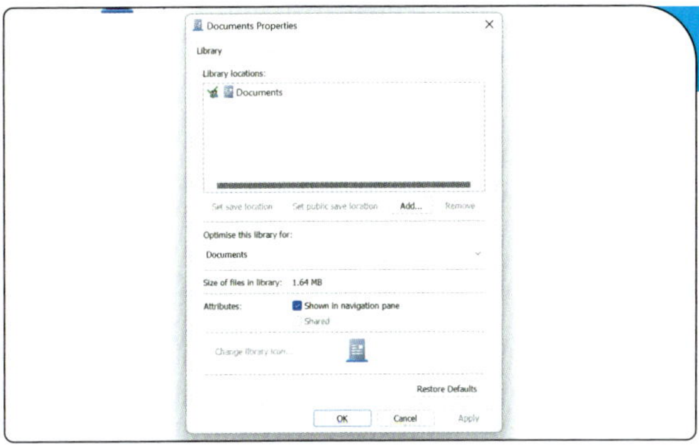


## Step 4

You can now close the File Explorer Options pop-up window. The Libraries are, by default, setup as area specific shortcuts. You can right-click each Library entry, select Properties from the menu, and create new Library locations, change the icon and much more. Restore Defaults will return the Library to its original setup.

# Get More from Your Library

**With Libraries now setup, you can use them to compile multiple areas whenever you click to view their contents. For example, if you have a network storage setup, such as a NAS unit, you can include folders on the NAS unit into one of your Libraries.**

**Right-click the library you have folders included, such as the Documents Library folder, and select Properties from the menu. Click the Add button, then enter the network address of the folder you want to include in the library. For example, depending on the name of your NAS unit, you would use:**

**\\NASDRIVE\Documents**

**Then, whenever you open the library folder, it will always display the contents of the remote folder on the NAS unit.**

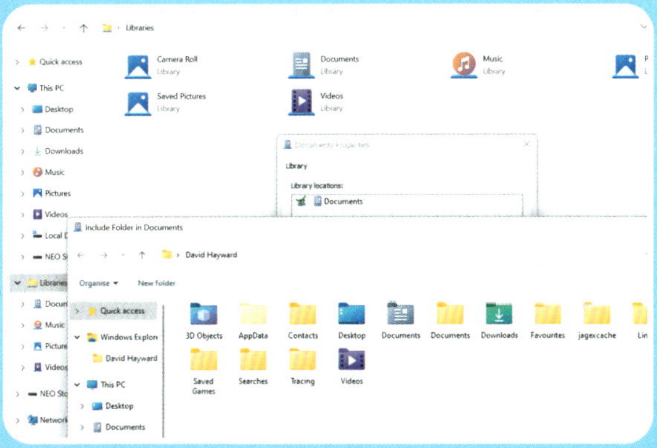

# Improving Wi-Fi Security

Most routers from an ISP have a reasonable amount of protection enabled by default, however, as with most things of a technical nature, it's possible to improve this further. Here are our top ten tips on how to improve your Wi-Fi security.

## Router Defence

### Password

The default password from the ISP to the administrative layer of the router can be quite good, depending on the ISP. Some, though, are terrible and use the likes of admin/admin as the username and password. If yours isn't up to scratch, create your own strong password using numbers, letters and special characters.

### Limit Access

Although it may be tempting, and it's difficult, you might consider saying 'no' when someone asks you for your password. Passing friends of the kids, the neighbour who needs to check something, anyone who's doing work on the house… the list goes on. Don't give out your password, and it'll remain secure.

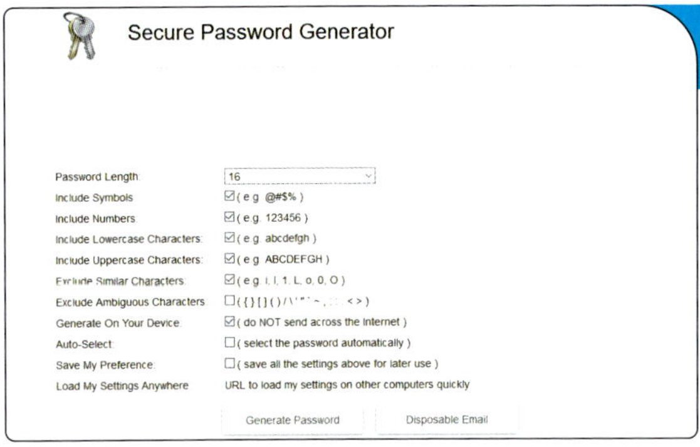


## Keep Changing

If you want to remain secure, then change your router's access password often. Perhaps keep a list of password reminders to hand, that mean nothing to anyone else, so you can easily pick a strong one to change it to.

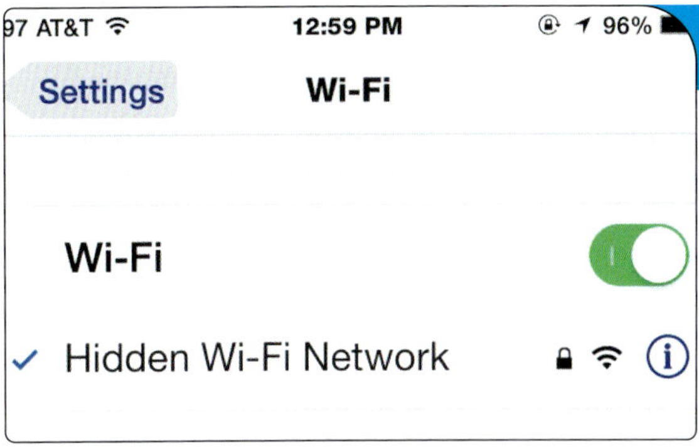


## Change SSID

The Service Set Identifier (SSID) is your router's wireless network name. It's broadcast with the router's signal so you can find it and connect to it. But if you can see it, so can others. Consider opting for the Hide SSID option in your router's configuration (if it's available), otherwise you can use a single underscore with spaces to lessen its presence (_ ).

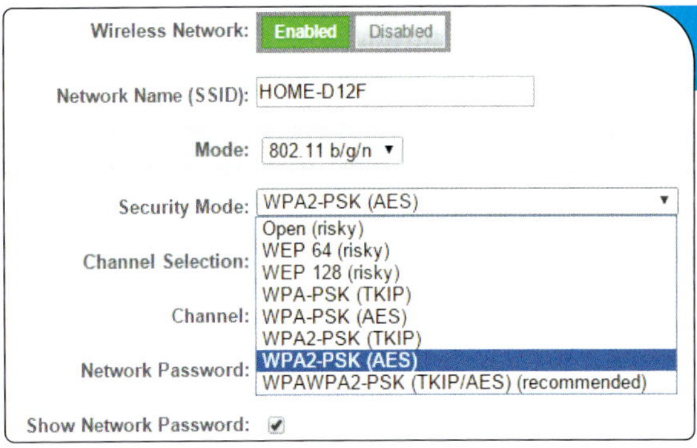


## Encryption

WEP, WPA and WPA2 are all encryption types for wireless networks. WEP is the weakest, so ensure that your router is trafficking data on its network with the strongest possible encryption, WPA2. Don't be tempted to go for less to support older hardware.

## Turn it Off

If you're not at home, or you're away for a while (on holiday), then turn off your router. If it's not needed, such as remote access to the heating controls or security cameras, turning it off is the best form of security; since no one can hack something that isn't powered on.

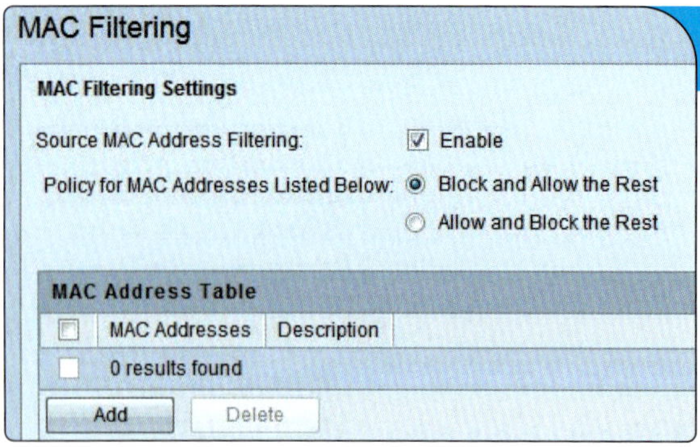


## MAC Filtering

Every network interface has a unique identifier known as a MAC (Media Access Code) address, regardless of whether it's a computer, tablet or games console. If your router supports MAC filtering, you can obtain the MAC addresses for each device and enter them into the router. Only those devices will be able to connect.

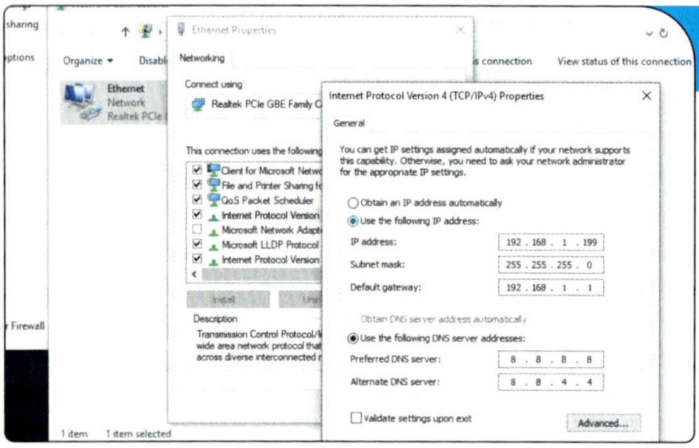


## Static IP

By default your router will allocate IP addresses to any connecting device out of an available pool. If you remove this feature, and use your own addresses, then anyone gaining access won't have an IP address to see the rest of your network.

## Router Position

Router position isn't just for the best possible signal. Limiting the router to the middle of the house will benefit not just your wireless network broadcast, but it will also limit access to the signal to others from beyond the walls of your home.

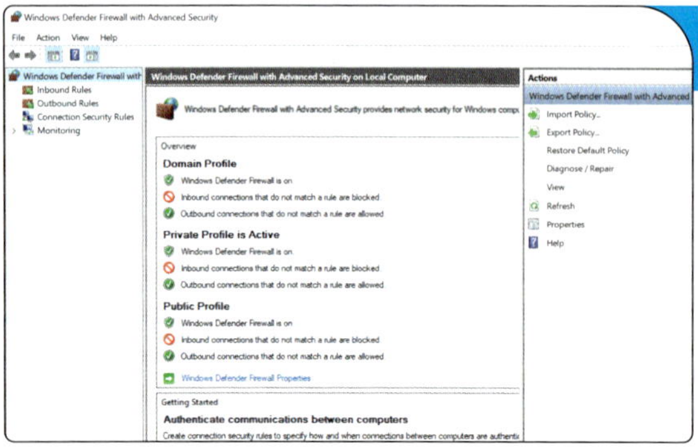


## Monitor Firewall

It's a good idea to keep tabs on what's being added to your router's and computer's firewalls. It's not easy, but also not impossible for malicious content to secretly add a route through a firewall for hackers to gain entry to a network.

# Command Cheat Sheet

**The Windows platform contains numerous built-in commands for networking. These utilities and tools will help you discover problems with your network, as well as help you improve performance and monitor what's going on in your system.**

## Useful Networking Commands

| | |
|---|---|
| **Ping** | Ping is probably the most familiar of networking command line tools. With it you're able to send an echo request to a device locally, or on the Internet, and receive a reply. |
| **Netstat** | Stands for Network Statistics, this command will display connection information, routing tables and so on. Entering the command will display what's going on while you use the network and Internet. Use netstat -e for interface stats. |
| **Arp** | Stands for Address Resolution Protocol displays and modifies entries in the ARP cache, which contains one or more tables that are used to store IP addresses and their resolved Ethernet or Token Ring physical addresses. |
| **NbtStat** | The nbtstat command is a diagnostic tool for NetBIOS over TCP/IP. Its primary design is to help troubleshoot NetBIOS name resolution problems. It'll display the human-friendly names of devices on the network along with their IP addresses. |
| **Hostname** | If you're struggling to find the name of a Windows computer you've got on your network, simply enter the hostname command and it'll display the computer's local name. |

## Tracert

Stands for Trace Route and will examine the path to a remote computer, either locally or on the Internet. For example, entering tracert google.com will display the hops taken over networking devices to get to one of the Google servers.

## Ipconfig

Probably one of the most used networking command in Windows. Ipconfig will display information on the local computer's network interfaces, such as IP addresses (both IPv4 and IPv6), Hostname, gateway and so on.

## Route

The Windows Route command allows you to view the device's routing tables. To do so, simply type Route Print. This will print the network interfaces, IPv4 and IPv6 route tables.

## Pathping

This is a handy command that combines the best elements of Ping and Tracert. It will display the latency and packet loss between one computer and another (either locally or on the Internet), and after 300 seconds display a detailed report.

## Netsh

This is a complex command that when entered will put you into a different shell, the Network Shell (netsh). It's capable of displaying and configuring information regarding a computer's networking setup.

## Getmac

Every network interface has a unique Media Access Code assigned to it. Some routers are able to limit connection to the network by only allowing user-entered MAC addresses in. You can get the MAC address of a windows computer by entering getmac.

## Nslookup

This troubleshooting tool can be used to look up and diagnose the Domain Name System (DNS), of a location on the local network or Internet, and check DNS records propagation and resolution with different servers.

## Telnet

This is a command that can be used to connect to another computer, or manage a router or switch. You can send and receive files, send commands and much more. With Telnet you're also able to connect to active Bulletin Board Systems. For example, enter: telnet bbs.balcos.net

# Command Line Actions

Ever since the early days of DOS, the command line has proved to be the ultimate playground for those who aren't afraid to delve into its murky depths. From the command line, you can do almost anything - even within Windows 11.

## Take Command

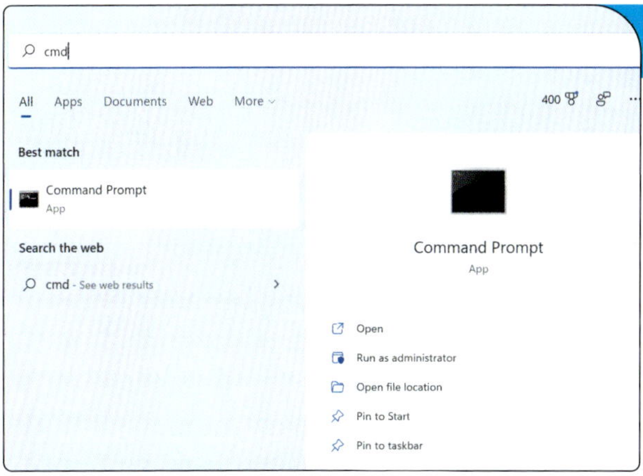


### Step 1

To open the Command Prompt, where we'll enter the lines of commands, click on the Windows Start button and type: cmd. The first entry will be the Command Prompt. Click on this to open it. You can also click on Run as administrator, which will give you elevated access within the command line – but we won't do that just yet.

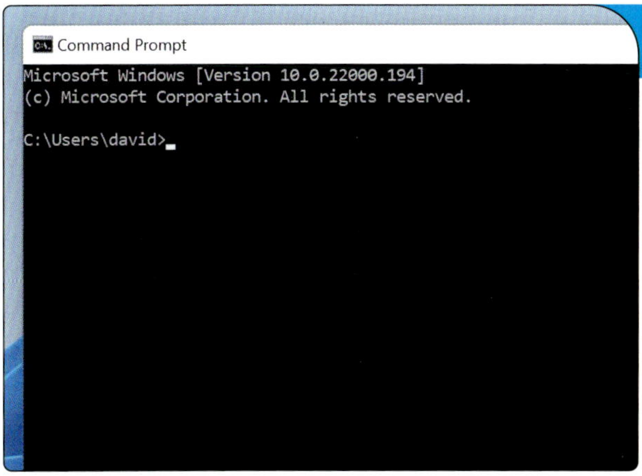


### Step 2

This is the Command Prompt (or Command Line). It may not look like much, but here be dragons, so be careful. From this simple interface you can ping network routers around the world, connect to ancient Bulletin board Services, wipe your entire hard drive, or start Global Thermonuclear War (extra points to those who can spot the movie reference).

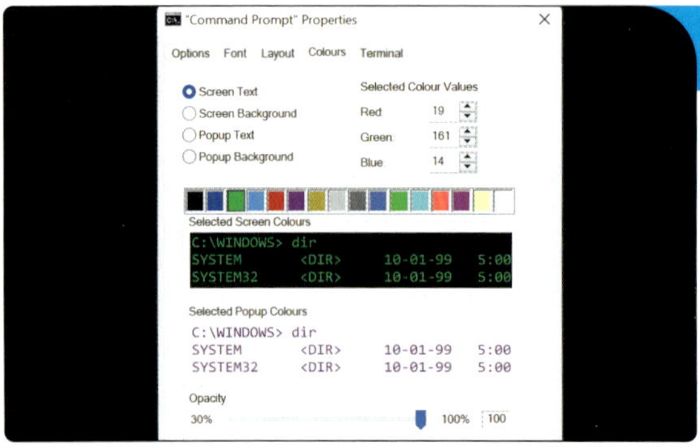


## Step 3

You can change the colours of the Command Line by right-clicking the bar at the top of the window, choosing Properties from the menu, then clicking on the Colours tab. Screen Text, Pop-up Text and Background can all be clicked and altered using the colour bar. Green text on a black background is our favourite.

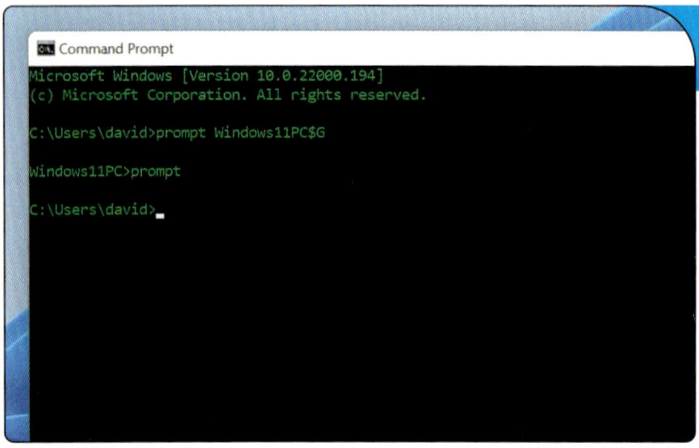


## Step 4

The current prompt is your specific user account on the computer. In our case it's: C:\Users\David, since I'm signed in under my name. However, you can change that with the following command. Enter:

**prompt Windows11PC$G**

The $G part at the end ensures there's a > at the end of the prompt. To return to normal, type **prompt**.

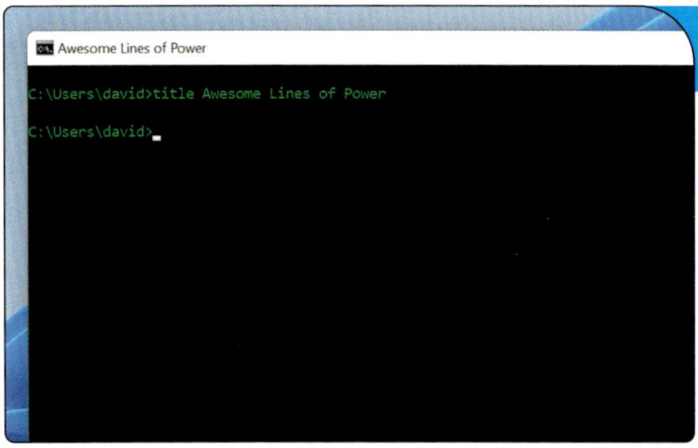


## Step 5

You can further customise the Command Prompt window by changing its title. By default it's Command Prompt, but it can be altered to anything you want, by typing:

**title Awesome Lines of Power**

When you close the Command Line window, and re-open it, the title will be gone.

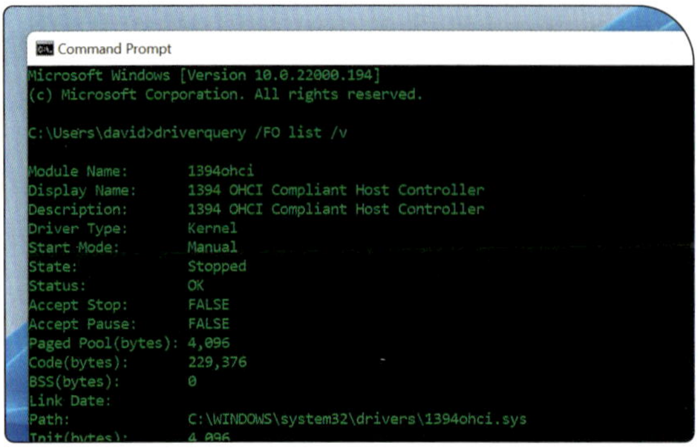


Something a little more complex now. If you're trying to resolve a driver issue on Windows 11, you can list all the currently installed drivers on the system by entering:

**driverquery /FO list /v**

With this you can see the driver module name, type, start mode, path and more.

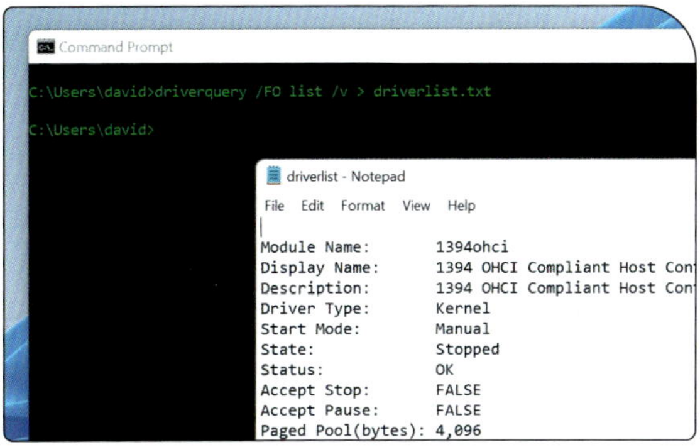


Sadly, the list from the previous action is often ridiculously long to scroll through, and you'll soon come to realise a lot of available content via the Command Line is quite expansive. If only there was a way to output the content directly into a text file…? Try this: **driverquery /FO list /v > driverlist.txt**
It makes things a little easier.

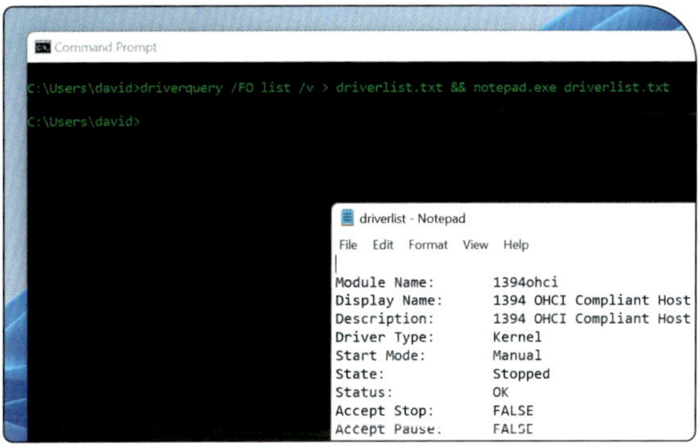


Did you know you can chain two separate commands together? And you can launch any of the apps on your system within the Command Line? Let's mix the last two entries, and auto-launch Notepad to view the contents:
**driverquery /FO list /v > driverlist.txt && notepad.exe driverlist.txt**
Providing the command after the && part is correct, the entire line will be executed.

F1: Tap or hold this key to retype your last command letter by letter.
F2: Copies the current command up to a specified character.
F3: Retypes the entire previous line
F4: Auto-deletes the current command up to a specified character.
F5: Similar to F3, but lets you cycle through previous commands.
F6: Enters the EOF indicator into CMD.
F7: Opens a list of previously entered commands.
F8: Similar to F5, but doesn't stop at the end of your command history in the session. Instead, it goes all the way to the start.
F9: Enters a previous command by entering a number associated with that line.

The Function keys are great shortcuts to learn when navigating the Windows 11 Command Line. F1 to F9 are used, with each doing a different task and making life a little easier when dealing with multiple commands, and commands that contain special characters that can be error prone when entering.

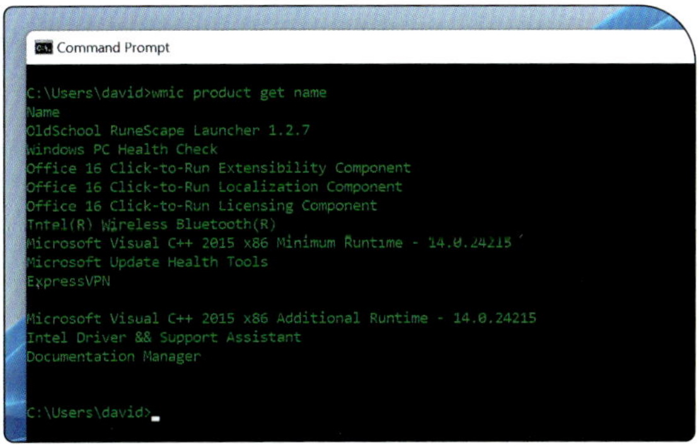


You're able to list all the currently installed apps on your Windows 11 system by entering the following command:
**wmic product get name**
Remember, if the list is getting a bit too long to look at in the command window, use:
**wmic product get name > productname.txt && notepad.exe productname.txt**

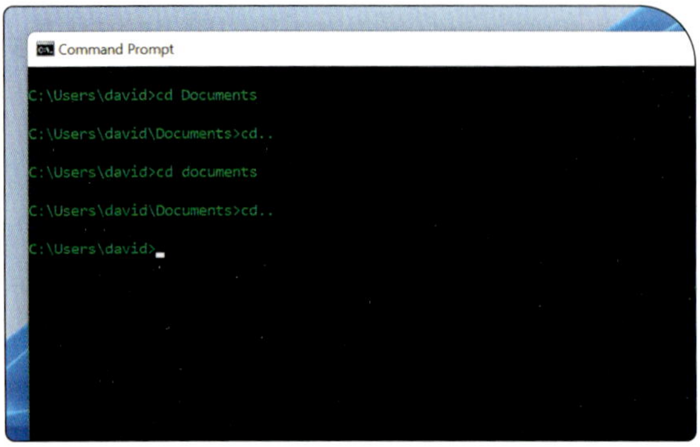


To change folders in the command window, you'll need to use the CD (Change Directory) command. So, to change into the Documents folder, you would use:
**cd Documents**
To change back a folder level, use:
**cd..**
Note: the CD command isn't case sensitive, so the following works just as well:
**cd documents**

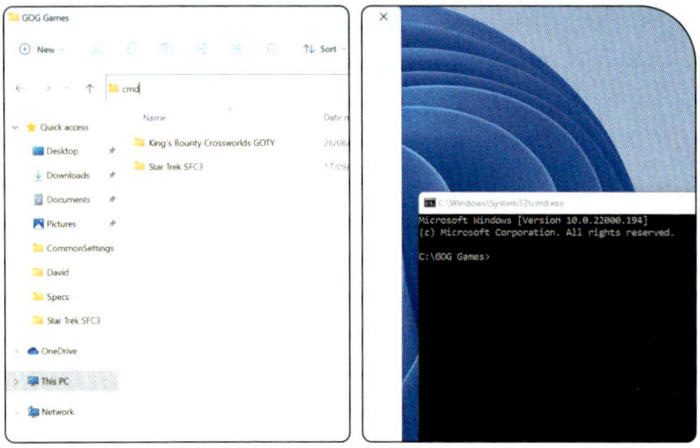


Instead of changing directories within the command window, you can instantly launch a command window from within the File Explorer. Simply open the File Explorer, go to the directory you want to open a command line window from, and enter: **cmd**, into the Address Bar. Hit Enter, and a new command line window will be displayed, in that directory.

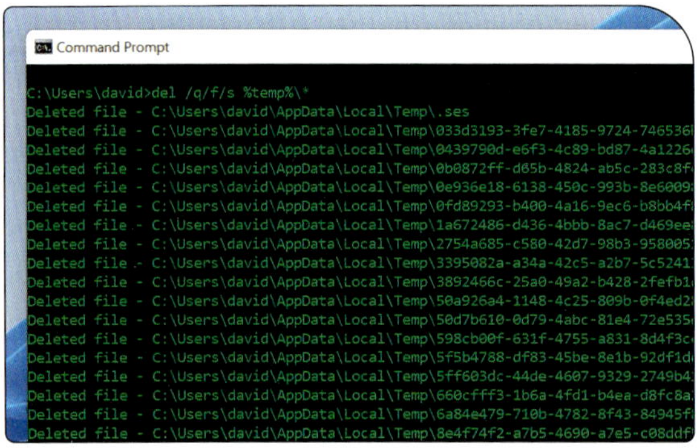


If you're running low on space, then it's recommended that you clean out the Temp area that Windows 11 uses to store stray and temporary data. You can enter this command:
**del /q/f/s %temp%***
This is your localised temp storage area. To clear out the global (Windows whole) temp storage area, you'll need administrative privileges.

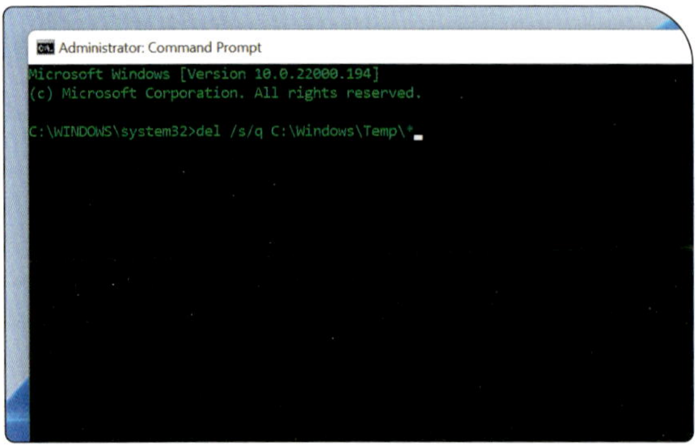


Close your current command window, then return to the Windows Start button and enter **cmd** again. This time, however, click on the Run as administrator option. You'll be warned if you want to continue, so click Yes. This is the admin-level Command Line, so be careful in here. To clear the Windows global temp area, enter the following command:
**del /s/q C:\Windows\temp***

# Wired Network Issues

Wired networks are often a lot more sturdy compared to a wireless network, but they're not bulletproof. Thankfully, problems can easily be fixed, so here are our top ten troubleshooting tips for solving wired network issues.

## Troubleshoot Wired Networks

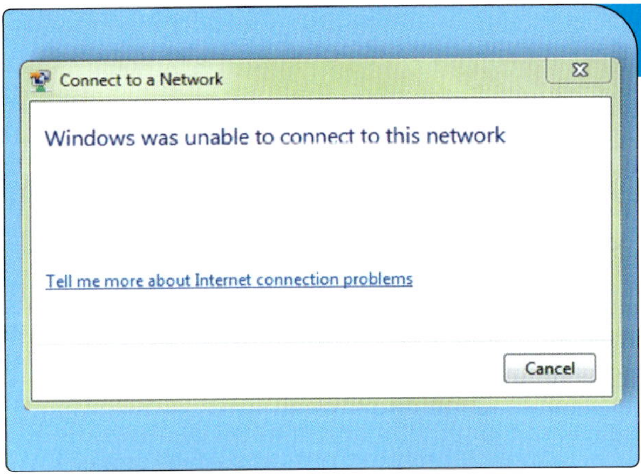


### PC Connection

If your computer is reporting no connection, it's time to get behind the machine and double-check the Ethernet port. Check that the cable is fully inserted, as they can get caught by feet and pulled slightly. Check the cable end isn't damaged. If there's still no connection, check other machines (a router reboot may be needed).

### All Connections

If all your computers and other devices aren't connecting, check any switches that they're connected to. Switch plugs, and even powerline adapters, can blow a fuse. Check your router's switch connection LED is lit up, if not try a different port. If all else fails, try direct connection to the router, as it could be faulty.

## Drop Connection

One of the main reasons as to why wired connections keep dropping is a damaged, or poorly created network cable end. Check the cable with a cable tester, check the ends by giving them a pull. If they're loose, or the cable test fails, then replace the ends or the cable itself.

## Poor Speeds

A main culprit of poor wired network speeds is the cable is too long. If the cable is over 100 metres (300 ft), then the signal will begin to drop significantly. If your cable is coiled up behind furniture, or in the loft space, try to shorten its length and check the connection speed.

## Powerline Loss

Often powerline adapters will lose their connection with each other. When this happens, power off both adapters, then power up one and after a few seconds power up the other. Wait for a few more seconds to see if the connection is okay. If it fails, try pin-hole resetting the adapters.

## Pair Powerlines

Sometimes powerline adapters won't pair with each other if there are already a set of powerline adapters already on the network. Turn off the existing powerline adapters, then power up the new pair. After a connection has been made, power up the existing pair.

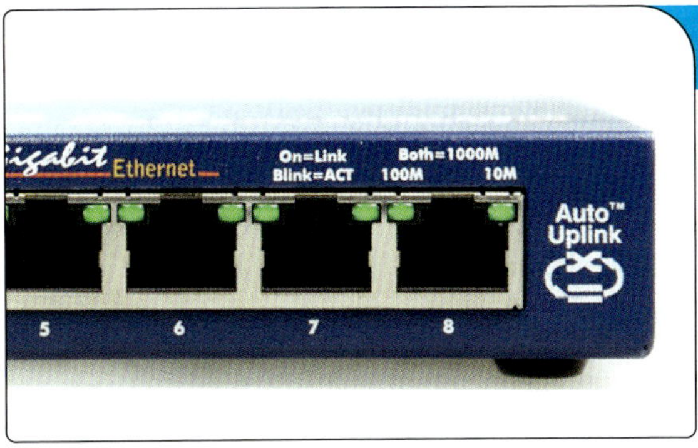


## Slow Ports

If you discover that some of the ports on your switch appear to be operating at 100Mb/s instead of 1Gb/s, then check the following. Ensure that devices connected to the port have a 1Gb/s Ethernet port (some smart TVs don't). Check that the switch has more than one 1Gb/s port – some are 100Mb/s with a 1Gb/s uplink port.

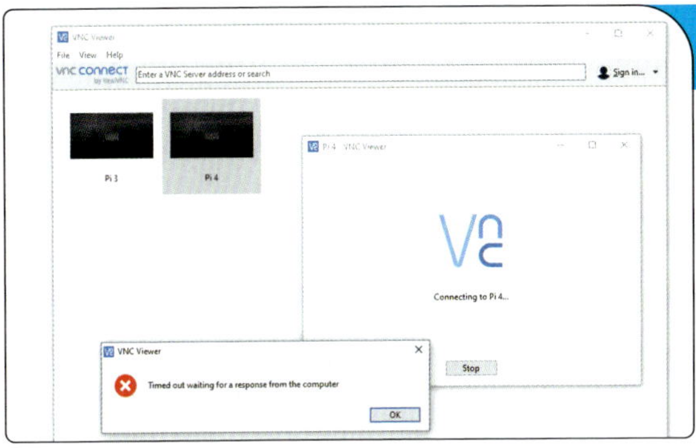


## PC to Router

If you're unable to connect to another PC on your network, check the connections to the router, on both PCs. Also, check that the PC you're connecting to isn't blocking your connection via the firewall.

## No Internet

No Internet connection usually means there's something going on with the router, so that should be your first port of call. Check the router's LEDs, if the Internet is off, try and reboot, otherwise use a phone to check the status of the ISP's services.

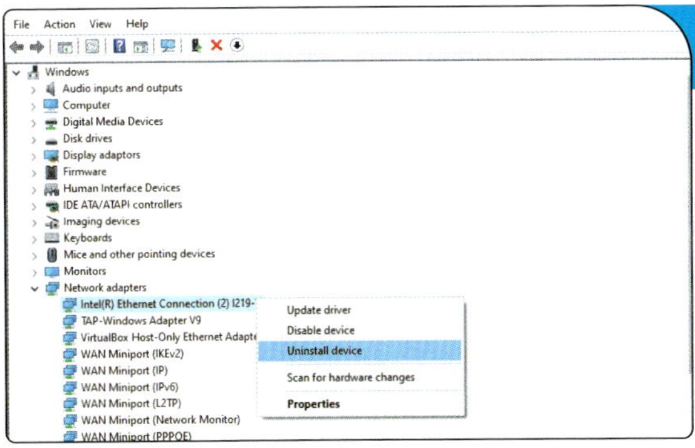


## Ethernet Issues

This could be one of several reasons. First check the cable going into the Ethernet port; use a different cable if necessary. Check the drivers by opening Device Manager and locating the network device. Right-click and select Update Driver. Also, try Uninstall Device, then Search for New Devices.

# Wi-Fi Network Issues

Wi-Fi is like electricity, you only notice it when it's not working. Thankfully, there's no need to worry, as most Wi-Fi issues can easily be fixed with a few simple tweaks here and there. Here's our top ten troubleshooting tips for your wireless network.

## Troubleshoot Wi-Fi Networks

### Slow Access

There's a good chance that the room in question has become a bit of Wi-Fi dead zone. Load up a network analyser and check the signal output in the room in question. If needs be, reboot any network extenders and the router.

### Slow Internet

This could one of two things: a problem with the router and your network, or a problem with the ISP. Test the connection by directly plugging a device into the router's Ethernet ports. If the problem persists, then call your ISP. If it's okay, then turn off all your networking equipment and one-by-one power them up and keep testing to find the culprit.

## Refuse Connection

Occasionally, there's a device that will refuse to establish a connection with your wireless network. First thing to try is a physical, Ethernet, connection (if it has one). If it works, try re-installing the Wi-Fi drivers on the device. If that's not possible, try another Wi-Fi network, it could be a problem with the device's Wi-Fi card.

## Bandwidth Loss

The first check is to establish a pattern. Does it happen when you power on something else in the house, if so, it could be causing interference with the signal. Does it happen when a certain device is connected? Check the device, as it could be downloading a huge file, or it could have some form of malware.

## Unknown Device

If you maintain good network order, and you've just spotted an unknown device on your network, then you need to act quickly. If possible, drop the connection via the router's web interface, then change your access password. Check all devices for malware, ask other family members if they know who it could be. Worst case, change all passwords.

## Wi-Fi Signal Lost

If nothing is connecting to your Wi-Fi, then the problem is likely with your router. Check the router and, if you can access its web interface, check the access logs and check for any recent updates (an update from the ISP could have damaged it). If a reboot doesn't fix it, contact your ISP.

## No Internet

Check the indicator lights on the router, if the Internet LED is off, then reboot the router and wait for a connection. If the LED is on, but still no Internet, try installing a VPN and see if you can connect; it could be an issue with the ISP's DNS entries.

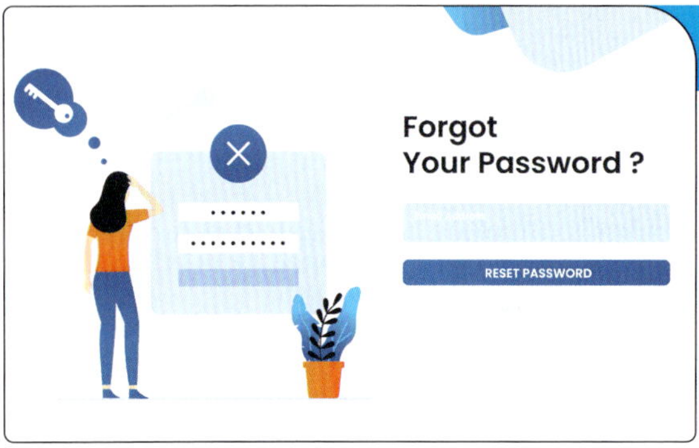


## Forgot Password

If you've forgotten your Wi-Fi password, then you may need to factory reset the router. Use a paperclip and locate the tiny pin-hole (usually marked Reset). Poke the paperclip in for 30 seconds. Reboot the router. It should be reset back to its original settings and password.

## Poor Signal

Providing your router is working well, check with a wireless device while standing next to the router. If it's okay, then the problem is likely poor signal spread. Try and reposition the router, don't put it in a cupboard, and see if that helps. If the signal is poor while next to it, there could be a problem. Try rebooting, otherwise contact your ISP.

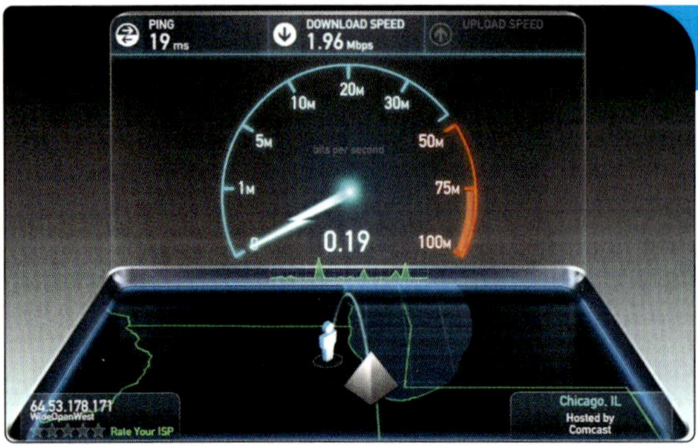


## Advertised Speeds

If your network extender or router isn't performing at the speeds it was advertised, try the following. Ensure that the router's configuration is setup for maximum signal strength. Move external antennae around to change the signal spread. Reboot the router and any Wi-Fi extenders. Reposition the router and extenders for better signal through walls etc.

# Diagnosing Windows 11

Windows 11 includes some useful tools for checking on and solving problems, but sometimes you need to look deeper. Occasionally you have to go back to basics. These tips will help you solve some common problems encountered in Windows 11.

## First Things to Check

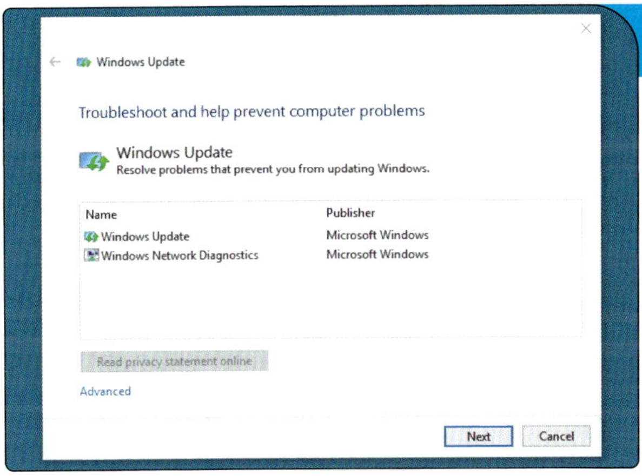


### Updates

Microsoft knows that things don't always go smoothly when updating and have provided a dedicated trouble-shooting tool for use during this key task. If you're having problems with Windows Update, the Windows Update Troubleshooter might be able to automatically fix the problem for you. Go to Microsoft.com and search for Update Troubleshooter.

### Check Updates

Keeping your copy of Windows 11 up-to-date with the latest releases can really help to avoid problems before they happen. Press the Windows logo key and click Settings. Then choose Windows Update and then select Check for updates. Install any available updates and restart your PC if required.

## System Specs

If you're having trouble installing or running an app or game, it may be that your PC hardware is not up to scratch. All commercial software will provide details of required and (sometimes) recommended specification needed to run it. You can check system spec at any time, just go to Control Panel and select System and Security, then System.

## App Updates

If an app or program isn't working with Windows 11, particularly after the Anniversary update, try looking in the Windows Store for an update and if that doesn't work, delete and reinstall it. To check for available app updates on the store, click the user icon next to the search bar and select Downloads and Updates.

## Slow Boot Fix

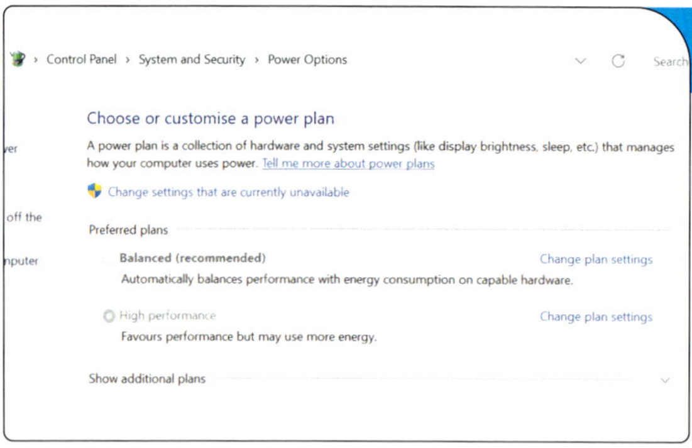


Like Windows 10 before it, Windows 11 uses a hybrid boot to enable fast boot times. It sounds great but can actually slow down boot for some users. Disable it by searching for Power Options in the Start menu and running the matching Control Panel applet, then in the settings click Choose to decide what the power buttons do.

## Non-responsive

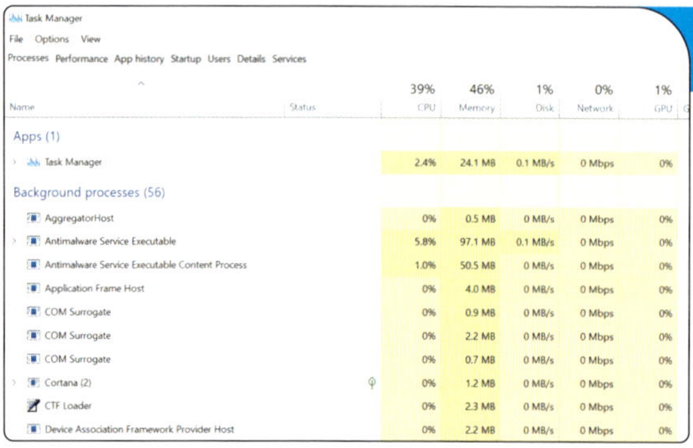


Windows 11 has a different shell than previous versions. The Explorer.exe process is still at its core but there are a few additional components too. If you click the Start button or the taskbar and they refuse to respond to an interaction, open Task Manager, find Windows Explorer in the task list and click the Restart button.

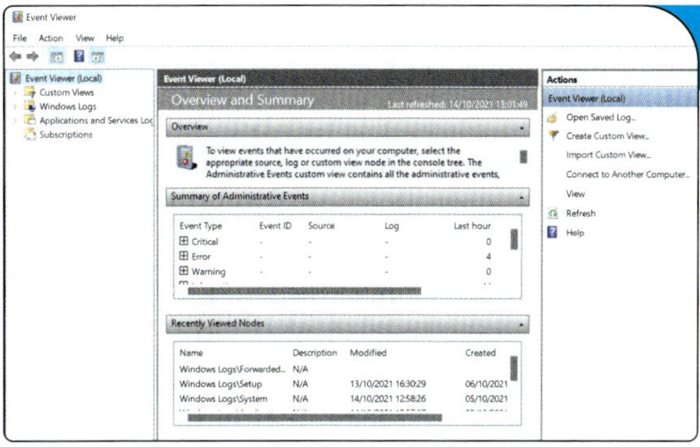


## Check Event Logs

You can scrutinise the Windows 11 event logs to see if they reveal any more information regarding the problem you're having. Right-click the Windows Start button, and select Event Viewer from the list. In here you'll find everything that's happened to your system since the day you turned it on.

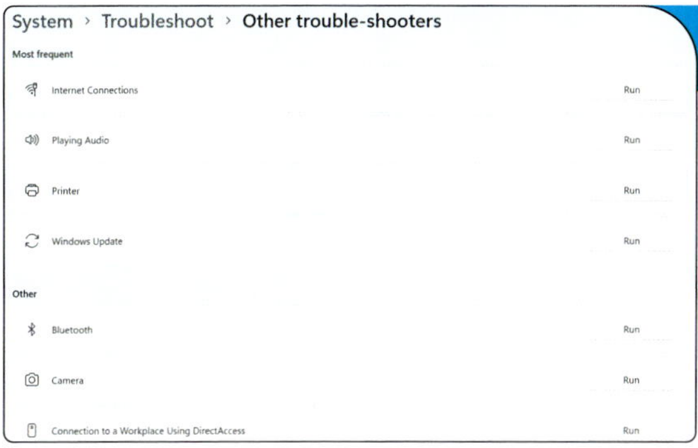


## Troubleshooters

Go to System > Troubleshoot > Other Trouble-shooters. This is where you'll find troubleshooter tests that can be carried out for a wide range of Windows 11 components and situations. Everything from Internet connectivity to keyboard issues, power and video playback can be run from here.

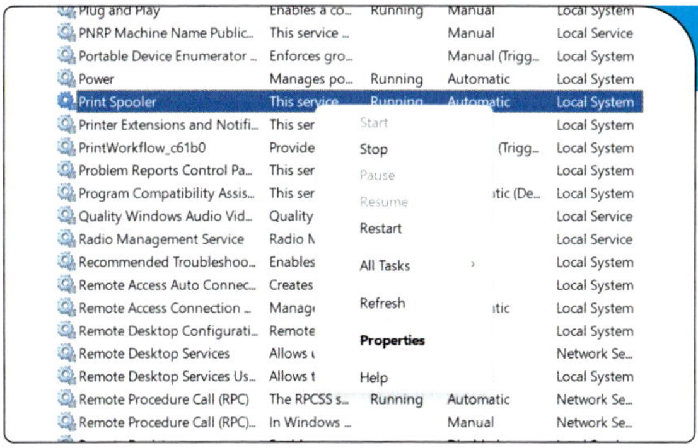


## Restart Services

Often, a problem could simply be a Windows 11 service hasn't started, or failed to start. For example, a printer not printing may not be the fault of the printer, but the Print Spooler Service. Click the Start button, type 'services' and click to open the Services App. Find the service, right-click, then click Restart or Start.

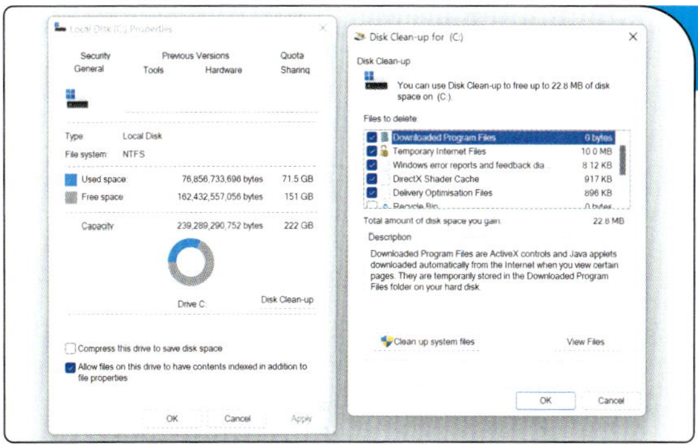


## Clean Disk Space

There are times when a lack of available disk space can lead to an unresponsive, or slow PC. System > Storage is a good place to start, then follow the Clean-up Recommendations. Also, right-click the C:\ drive in File Explorer, select Properties > Disk Clean-up. Finally, also check Clean up Systems Files in the same window.

# Laptop Care & Maintenance

## Keep Food and Drink Away

However careful you are when eating and drinking, if you do it while using your laptop it is inevitable that at some point, crumbs and splashes will hit the screen, keyboard, etc. Unlike a desktop, replacing a crumb-filled keyboard on a laptop is not just a case of buying a new one.

## Wipe the Screen Carefully

Laptop screens are generally not as clear or bright as a desktop monitor screen, so keeping them clean is important. Use a lint-free cloth regularly to gently wipe away dust and dirt. If there are more stubborn marks, buy and  use an LCD screen cleaner. These are cheap to buy online.

## Clean the Keys and Ports

Laptop keyboards are hard to replace, so keep yours clean and free from dust. You can buy small USB-keyboard vacuum cleaners fairly cheaply, and these can help keep dust from building up. You can also buy keyboard cleaner putty very cheaply online. The same rule applies to the various ports on your laptop.

## Don't Block Vents

Despite the name, few laptops are actually designed to be used on your lap (or on any soft surface). This is because the heat vents of many laptops are on the bottom, and soft surfaces will often block them. if it happens regularly, this can cause lasting heat damage to the laptop.

**Laptops are great! They are small, portable and can be easily put away when not in use. They are also becoming increasingly powerful. They are not, however, as robust as a desktop, so good care and maintenance is a must if you want your laptop to last.**

## Don't Overcharge the Battery

Try not to keep your laptop plugged into the mains all the time. Charge it, and then use the battery power until you need to charge it again. This helps to keep the battery in good condition. If you only ever use your laptop at home on a desk, keep it plugged in, but remove the battery.

## Close the Lid

When you have finished using your laptop for the day, close the lid. When you are moving your laptop, close the lid. When you leave your laptop for any length of time, close the lid. This not only protects the screen from accidental damage, but it will also help keep your laptop running between charges.

## Buy a Laptop Stand

If your laptop sits in one place and is rarely moved around, consider buying a laptop stand. These not only help to give you a better screen viewing angle, but they also give the laptop vents some extra clearance and, therefore, better airflow. You can even buy stands with built-in cooling fans.

## Buy a Good Laptop Bag

If you ever take your laptop with you out of the house, make sure you buy and use a decent laptop bag. Go for one that is at least water resistant, if not waterproof, to protect your laptop from rain. Try to buy one that is padded, or even better, has a floating laptop "sling" for better impact protection.

# Windows 11 Index

**By now you should be a Windows 11 expert, and ready to embrace any improvements to the operating system as Microsoft roll them out to us mere mortals. However, if you do get a bit stuck on some aspect in the future, you can quickly jump to it via this index.**

# Discover, learn and master your tech with Black Dog Media

Black Dog Media

Since their launch in 2004, BDM have gained a reputation of breaking with tradition and pushing the boundaries of tech publishing. BDM's All About series continues this trend. Our guidebooks are compiled not by a single author, but instead by a highly skilled team. Each expert member brings their focused skill set to a core area of editorial and design, meaning the reader gets the very best from each writer and ultimately the publication itself.

BDM's All About series of publications offer the highest quality and are fully independent, user friendly and, more importantly, have the most up-to-date content possible. That's why, our customers know that they can rely on the BDM brand to deliver not only market leading and fully updated publications, but also piece of mind. Safe in the knowledge that with our help, they are guaranteed to gain the very best foundation to build their knowledge, confidence and understanding of their new software and hardware.

For more information scan the code or visit us at:

**www.bdmpublications.com**